Ethical Business Leadership in Troubling Times

STUDIES IN TRANSATLANTIC BUSINESS ETHICS

Series Editors: Laszlo Zsolnai, *Corvinus University, Hungary* and George Brenkert, *Georgetown University, USA*

Over the past several decades the importance of ethical issues in business has become widely acknowledged. Business scandals, globalization, the Internet, outsourcing of production, environmental concerns, and a growing appreciation for business responsibilities for human rights have led to a greater appreciation of the importance of business ethics. In addition, increased concern for trust, humanity and purpose in an age of crisis leads us to ask fundamental questions about the role of business ethics and the legitimation of business. In this setting, there is an obvious need for more refined studies of business ethics as informed by an international perspective. Though American and European business ethics have developed differently, many problems are similar on both sides of the Atlantic. Based upon this insight we established the TransAtlantic Business Ethics Conferences (TABEC) in 2000 for promoting exchange and collaboration between American and European scholars and practitioners.

The first TABEC was held in Budapest in 2000 at the Budapest University of Economic Sciences. The second one was organized in Washington D.C. in 2002 at Georgetown University. Subsequent conferences have been held at such prominent locations as the ESADE Business School (Barcelona), the Wharton School (Philadelphia), the SDA Bocconi School of Management (Milan), York University in Canada, and NHH Norwegian School of Economics (Bergen). The intention in each case was to bring together a group of distinguished business ethicists from Europe and North America to address current and central problems of business ethics.

The purpose of the Studies in TransAtlantic Business Ethics series is to publish some of the best thinking on business ethics that is currently available on either side of the Atlantic. Though the main engine behind the series is TABEC, the series is not limited to papers presented at one of the TABEC conferences. Other contributions from prominent business ethicists are welcome too. It is our hope that our series can catalyze fresh and innovative thinking and practices in America, Europe and beyond.

Titles in the series include:

Business Ethics and Corporate Sustainability
Edited by Antonio Tencati and Francesco Perrini

Business and the Greater Good
Rethinking Business Ethics in an Age of Crisis
Edited by Knut J. Ims and Lars Jacob Tynes Pedersen

Ethical Innovation in Business and the Economy
Edited by Georges Enderle and Patrick E. Murphy

Ethical Business Leadership in Troubling Times
Edited by Joanne B. Ciulla and Tobey K. Scharding

Ethical Business Leadership in Troubling Times

Edited by

Joanne B. Ciulla

Professor, Department of Management and Global Business and Director, Institute for Ethical Leadership, Rutgers Business School–Newark and New Brunswick, USA

Tobey K. Scharding

Visiting Assistant Professor, Department of Management and Global Business and Research Fellow, Institute for Ethical Leadership, Rutgers Business School–Newark and New Brunswick, USA

STUDIES IN TRANSATLANTIC BUSINESS ETHICS

Edward Elgar PUBLISHING

Cheltenham, UK • Northampton, MA, USA

Cover image: René Kanters, Roman Forum, 2009.

Published by
Edward Elgar Publishing Limited
The Lypiatts
15 Lansdown Road
Cheltenham
Glos GL50 2JA
UK

Edward Elgar Publishing, Inc.
William Pratt House
9 Dewey Court
Northampton
Massachusetts 01060
USA

A catalogue record for this book
is available from the British Library

Library of Congress Control Number: 2019951602

This book is available electronically in the **Elgar**online
Business subject collection
DOI 10.4337/9781789903058

MIX
Paper from responsible sources
FSC® C013604

ISBN 978 1 78990 304 1 (cased)
ISBN 978 1 78990 305 8 (eBook)

Typeset by Servis Filmsetting Ltd, Stockport, Cheshire
Printed and bound by CPI Group (UK) Ltd, Croydon, CR0 4YY

Contents

Figures and tables

FIGURES

TABLES

Contributors

Mahmut Arslan is Professor of Business Ethics at the Ibn Haldun University of Istanbul, Turkey. He is also a visiting scholar at Rutgers University, Institute for Ethical Leadership. Arslan is the founder and the president of the European Business Ethics Network Turkish Chapter. His area of research is business ethics and religion.

Zsolt Boda is research chair and Director General of the Center for Social Sciences of the Hungarian Academy of Sciences as well as a professor at the Business Ethics Center of the Corvinus University of Budapest. He holds an MA in economics and a PhD in political science. Boda's academic work focuses on the problems of governance, public policy, business ethics and international ethics. Recent research is institutional trust, its social roots and its consequences for policy effectiveness.

Johannes Brinkmann is Professor of Business Ethics, BI Norwegian Business School, in Oslo, Norway. He obtained a PhD in sociology, after studying in Münster and Oslo. Since 2016 Brinkmann has also worked as a professor at the University of Tromsø. His academic work includes 43 academic articles (mostly in English), nine academic books (in Norwegian), numerous book chapters, conference papers, industry and professional journal papers.

Joanne B. Ciulla is Professor of Leadership Ethics and Director of the Institute for Ethical Leadership at Rutgers Business School and Professor Emerita of the Jepson School of Leadership Studies, University of Richmond, USA. A philosopher by training, Ciulla has published extensively on ethics in the context of philosophy, leadership, business and work. She is the recipient of Lifetime Achievement Awards for her scholarship from the Network of Leadership Scholars, the International Leadership Association, and the Society for Business Ethics. Ciulla served as president of the International Society of Business, Economics, and Ethics and the Society for Business Ethics.

Cynthia E. Clark directs the Harold S. Geneen Institute of Corporate Governance focused on connecting academic researchers with corporate governance professionals. She has been cited in the media on governance issues including *The Wall Street Journal*, *The Boston Globe*, *CNN*, *Forbes* and *Reuters* as well as on Bloomberg Radio. Clark is a Professor of Management at Bentley University and a Fulbright Scholar. Her research is on how firms address conflicts of interest, shareholder activism and environmental, social and governance (ESG) information, and recently on director selection and diversity. Clark is published in *Business Ethics Quarterly*, *Journal of Business Ethics*, *Harvard Business Review* and *Business Horizons*. She worked in the financial services industry for many years.

Wim Dubbink is Full Professor Ethics of Business and Organization at Tilburg University, the Netherlands. He has a special interest in (organizational) integrity and institutional design and specializes in Kantian ethics and metaphysics. Dubbink has published on corporate duty, human maliciousness and the problem of ethical cynicism. His current research involves the duty of beneficence versus the duty of rescue, the metaphysics of morality and the meaning of love. Dubbink is associate editor of the *Journal of Business Ethics*.

Georges Enderle is the John T. Ryan Jr. Professor of International Business Ethics at the Mendoza College of Business, University of Notre Dame, USA, and a former president of the International Society of Business, Economics, and Ethics. Educated in philosophy, theology, economics and business ethics, he has extensive research and teaching experience in Europe, the United States and China. Enderle has authored and edited 20 books and over 150 articles.

Daryl Koehn is the Wicklander Chair of Business Ethics and Managing Director of the Institute for Business and Professional Ethics (IBPE) at DePaul University in Chicago, USA. She has published widely in the fields of ethics, political theory and corporate governance. Koehn's monographs include *The Ground of Professional Ethics* (1994); *Rethinking Feminist Ethics* (1998); *Local Insights, Global Ethics* (2001); *The Nature of Evil* (2005); *Living with the Dragon: Thinking and Acting Ethically in a World of Unintended Consequences* (2010); and *Toward a New (Old) Theory of Responsibility: Moving beyond Accountability* (2019). Edited volumes include *Corporate Governance: Ethics across the Board*; *Ethics and Aesthetics in Business Ethics* (2013); and *Business, Corporate Governance and Civil Society* (Professor Lu Xiaohe, Shanghai Academy of Social Sciences as primary editor, 2005). In addition, she has published numerous articles in the *Harvard Business Review*, *Business Ethics Quarterly*, *Journal of Business Ethics* and other journals. She consults regularly with major corporations and has served on a major corporation's compliance committee. In addition, she has been profiled in *Time* and *Life* magazines.

Donna Ladkin is Professor of Leadership and Ethics with Antioch University's Graduate School in Leadership and Change, USA. A philosopher and musician by background, Ladkin's work conceptualizes ethics as a practice that is informed by aesthetic and embodied sensitivities. Her book, *Mastering the Ethical Dimension of Organizations* (2015) offers a mode of engaging in the ethical paradoxes inherent to organizational life that extend beyond the range of compliance-based solutions. Her current research interests include pursuing how a Foucauldian approach to ethics could inform organizational leaders as they grapple with the dilemmas of our time.

Christoph Lütge holds the Chair of Business Ethics at the Technical University of Munich (TUM), Germany. He has held visiting professorships in Taipei, Kyoto and Venice and was awarded a Heisenberg Fellowship. In 2019, Lütge was appointed Director of the new TUM Institute for Ethics in Artificial Intelligence. He has been a member of the Ethics Commission on Automated and Connected Driving of the German Federal Ministry of Transport and Digital Infrastructure, as well as of the European AI Ethics initiative AI4People. He has also done consulting work for the Singapore Economic Development Board and the Canadian Transport Commission.

Chris MacDonald teaches ethics and critical thinking at Ryerson University's Ted Rogers School of Management in Toronto, Canada, where he is Director of the Ted Rogers Leadership Centre. A philosopher by training, MacDonald is also Chair of the Department of Law & Business. He is co-editor of the *Business Ethics Journal Review*, and co-author of the *Concise Encyclopedia of Business Ethics* (2018).

Dirk Matten is Professor at the Schulich School of Business, Canada, where he holds the Hewlett-Packard Chair in Corporate Social Responsibility. He is also a visiting Professor at Copenhagen Business School, the University of London, the University of Nottingham and at Sabancı University in Istanbul. Matten has published 28 books and edited collections as well as more than 90 articles and book chapters that have won numerous prestigious awards. In 2018, he won the "Paper of the Decade Award" from the *Academy of Management Review* and was ranked among the "Top 100 Corporate Social Responsibility Influence Leaders" by Assent Compliance.

Jeremy Moon holds the Velux Chair of Corporate Sustainability, Copenhagen Business School, Denmark. Recent publications include: *Visible Hands: National Government and International CSR* (2019, co-authored with J.S. Knudsen); "New roles of governments in the governance of business conduct: implications for management and organizational research," *Organization Studies* (2019, with A. Kourula, M.-L. Salles-Djelic and C. Wickert); "Micro-processes of translation in the transfer of practices from MNE headquarters to foreign subsidiaries: the role of subsidiary translators," *Journal of International Business Studies* (2019, with G. Gutierrez Huerter O, S. Gold and W. Chapple).

Eleanor O'Higgins is Adjunct Associate Professor at the College of Business at University College Dublin, Republic of Ireland, and an Associate at the London School of Economics, UK. She specializes in business ethics, corporate responsibility and governance, and strategic management. O'Higgins is the author of numerous papers in academic and professional journals, book chapters and case studies. Recent publications include her book, *Progressive Business Models – Creating Sustainable and Pro-Social Enterprise* (2017, co-authored with Laszlo Zsolnai).

Tobey K. Scharding is a visiting Assistant Professor at Rutgers Business School, USA. She received her PhD in philosophy from Stanford University. Scharding researches topics in business ethics including managerial decision making, finance ethics, ethics of risk and ethics of new technologies. Her work has appeared in *Business Ethics Quarterly*, *Georgetown Journal of Law and Public Policy*, *Journal of Business Ethics* and *Business and Society Review*. Her book, *This is Business Ethics*, was published in 2018.

Alejo José G. Sison is Professor of Business Ethics at the School of Economics and Business of the University of Navarre, France. He is also visiting Ordinary Professor at the Busch School of Business of the Catholic University of America. Sison investigates issues at the juncture of ethics, economics and politics from the perspective of the virtues and the common good. He is the editor of *Business Ethics: A Virtue Ethics and Common Good Approach* (2018).

Laura J. Spence is Professor of Business Ethics at Royal Holloway, the University of London, UK, where she is also Associate Dean Research for the Faculty of Management, Economics and Law. Spence's research interests include critical corporate social responsibility, small business social responsibility and ethics. She has published in *Business Ethics Quarterly*, *Human Relations*, *Journal of Management Studies* and *Organization Studies*. She is consulting editor of *Journal of Business Ethics*. Recent books include *Business Ethics: Managing Corporate Citizenship and Sustainability in the Age of Globalization* (2019, co-authored with A. Crane, D. Matten and S. Glozer) and *Research Handbook of Small Business Social Responsibility: Global Perspectives* (2018, Edward Elgar Publishing, co-edited with J.G. Frynas, J.N. Muthuri and J. Navare).

Steen Vallentin is Associate Professor in the Department of Management, Society and Communication at Copenhagen Business School, Denmark. He is Academic Director of the CBS Sustainability Center. Vallentin's research interests focus on corporate social responsibility (CSR) as a social and political phenomenon in the broadest sense, including studies of the role(s) of government and the political-ideological dimension of CSR and sustainable development. He regularly contributes to international journals in his field of study.

Sandra Waddock is Galligan Chair of Strategy, Carroll School Scholar of Corporate Responsibility, and Professor of Management at Boston College's Carroll School of Management, USA. Winner of numerous awards, including a 2017 PRME Pioneer Award, Waddock has published over 150 papers and 13 books, including *Healing the World* (2017) and *Intellectual Shamans* (2014). Current research interests include transformational system change, memes and narratives in transformations, intellectual shamanism and management education, among others.

Patricia H. Werhane is the Ruffin Professor Emerita at Darden School of Business, University of Virginia and Wicklander Professor Emerita at DePaul University, USA. Before joining the Darden faculty in 1993, Werhane served as the Wirtenberger Professor of Philosophy at Loyola University Chicago. She was a Rockefeller Fellow at Dartmouth College and Senior Fellow at Cambridge University. She has authored or edited 30 books including *Moral Imagination and Management Decision-Making* (1999), *Adam Smith and His Legacy for Modern Capitalism* (1991) and *Alleviating Poverty through Profitable Partnerships* (2009). Werhane is the founder and former editor-in-chief of *Business Ethics Quarterly*. She is currently co-producer of an Emmy award-winning television series, *Big Questions* (www.bqnow.com).

Mustafa K. Yilmaz is Professor of Finance and Dean of Business School at Ibn Haldun University, Turkey. He is also Director of the Ethics Research Center in the same university. Yilmaz investigates issues on capital markets, corporate governance and sustainability from the perspective of improving long-term viability and performance of companies in emerging markets.

Laszlo Zsolnai is Professor and Director of the Business Ethics Center at the Corvinus University of Budapest, Hungary. He is Co-chair of the Future Earth Finance and Economics Knowledge-Action Network, as well as President of the European SPES Institute in Leuven, Belgium, and a Fellow of the Royal Society of the Arts in London, UK. He has been a guest professor/visiting scholar at the University of Cambridge, the University of Oxford, the University of California at Berkeley, Georgetown University, the University of Richmond, Concordia University Montreal, the University of St. Gallen, Bocconi University Milan and the Netherlands Institute for Advanced Study.

Acknowledgments

We first want to express our gratitude to the authors in this collection for generously contributing their time and insights into the role of business in troubling times. We would also like to thank our editor, Alan Sturmer, and our assistant editor, Caroline Kracunas, for their help in making this book possible. In particular, we'd like to thank Edward Elgar Publishing for its continuing commitment to publish serious books on important issues.

For Margot, Michael and René

Introduction: troubling times

Joanne B. Ciulla and Tobey K. Scharding

These are troubling times on both sides of the Atlantic. Immigration, Brexit, terrorism, the financial crisis, the election of Donald Trump, and the emergence of nationalism in the US and Europe have created ethical challenges for business leaders as well as most others. Populist political leaders have tapped into the feelings of voters who have been ignored by leaders, left behind during globalization, replaced at work by new technologies, and disheartened by social legislation in areas such as gay marriage and abortion. While some citizens in the US and Europe believed that the world was getting better, others silently watched in dismay. Meanwhile, we also see an increase in xenophobia, racism, antisemitism, and Islamophobia. The increasingly polarized political environment has made it difficult for leaders to reach a consensus about how to best tackle pressing questions about immigration, human rights, the environment, and the regulation of business and new technologies. This is a challenging environment, one where business leaders may sometimes be called upon to decide where they stand.

In a speech, Apple CEO Tim Cook said, "The reality is that government, for a long period of time, has for whatever set of reasons become less functional and isn't working at the speed that it once was. And so it does fall, I think, not just on business but on all other areas of society to step up" (Sorkin, 2017). His comment raises a cluster of foundational questions about Corporate Social Responsibility (CSR) and the role of business in turbulent times: Who should be responsible for what in a society? What are the responsibilities of businesses and business leadership to society? Moreover, do the responsibilities of businesses increase when there are social and political problems? And finally, what does it mean for a business to "step up"?

This book brings together the work of twelve CSR and business ethics scholars from the UK and Europe and eight from North America to explore various facets of these questions. They offer a variety of cultural perspectives as they write about problems in their own countries and the broader questions about the role of business in society. The first chapter challenges the very idea that businesses should "step up." Maybe businesses are the problem and not the solution because they have had undue influence on the elected officials and the policies of government that currently don't seem to work. Some of the authors in this volume consider the moral agency of businesses and what they can and cannot do, while others begin with the assumption that CSR begins at home with how organizations treat their employees and other stakeholders and govern their organizations. Several authors examine the various ways in which businesses decide what their responsibilities are to society in areas ranging from human rights and the treatment of immigrants. In the last part of the book, contributors explore the role of business in ethical problems involving technology and climate change. These are both areas where businesses have created problems and they have the ability to help solve them.

ORGANIZATION OF THE BOOK

The book is divided into four parts: "Business and Politics," "Agency and Responsibility," "Models for Decision Making," and "Applied Topics: Technology and the Environment." In the part on "Business and Politics," contributors address the extent that businesses should "step up," in Tim Cook's phrase, to address social and political challenges, such as those present in our troubling times. Donna Ladkin begins the volume with her chapter challenging what is perhaps the dominant view within theories of CSR: that when governments fail to respond adequately to social and political challenges businesses should assume responsibility for doing so in their stead. To the contrary, Ladkin argues that businesses should, ethically speaking, take a position on social and political challenges at an equal status to other democratic actors. To fulfill their ethical mission, businesses should focus on ensuring that their internal management is ethical and that employees have adequate time (and other resources) to engage in social and political activism, among other activities, in their personal lives.

Dirk Matten and Jeremy Moon, in turn, detail the ways in which expectations that business should serve the public good have been normalized over the past 40 years. The authors christened these expectations "explicit CSR" in their previously published research (Matten and Moon, 2008). They contrast explicit CSR with "implicit CSR," which captures businesses' efforts to act in socially responsible ways without an expectation that such social responsibility will contribute to their overall profit maximization (Matten and Moon, 2008). In the present chapter, Matten and Moon revisit these concepts in light of new empirical research, suggesting that explicit CSR is more closely aligned with implicit CSR than they had previously acknowledged.

In his contribution, Zsolt Boda also offers an alternative paradigm to CSR, this time focused on the limits of business ethics to effect meaningful responses to fundamental social, political, and environmental problems. Whereas business ethics has proved effective in describing how to build ethical organizations and include stakeholders in ethical decision making, it has not done enough to make the case for why businesses should be ethical in the first place. This means that few businesses actually enact business ethics prescriptions: because few are motivated to put ethical concerns over the profit motive. For this reason, Boda argues that addressing many of the social, political, and environmental challenges that we currently face will require legal, institutional, and/or political treatments beyond mere ethics.

In the final contribution to this part, Laura J. Spence and Steen Vallentin focus on internal politics within the corporation. They offer a view of CSR in which corporations become responsible only as a result of an internal, political process that acknowledges and engages conflicts brought about by power hierarchies within the organization. The authors bring Foucault's view of "governmentality" to bear on corporate organization, arguing that corporate "responsibilization" is a nuanced process that deserves to be understood in its own respect. They illustrate their ideas through BP's response to the Deepwater Horizon disaster.

Next, in the part on "Agency and Responsibility," authors address organizational issues related to ensuring that corporations behave ethically in troubling times such as "who in the organization is acting when things go wrong, ethically?" and "who is responsible?" In his contribution, Wim Dubbink advances a strategy for overcoming a common objection to the idea that corporations should act ethically. Whereas some scholars have argued that corporations lack moral agency and, as such, cannot be held to an ethical standard, Dubbink shows that no one – corporation, human being, other apparent agent – has agency by the standards the objectors require. Moreover, all that is needed to hold corporations to an ethical standard is a demonstration that corporations have the capacity to constrain their actions to serve an ethical principle. In order to achieve this capacity, Dubbink argues that corporations should encourage their members to act as though the organization possesses moral personhood. Improving corporate ethics begins, in this sense, with the understanding that the corporation is able to act ethically.

Daryl Koehn, in the next contribution, discusses the importance of apologies in assuming and maintaining responsibility. She distinguishes between personal apologies (in which the apologizer takes responsibility for a past act of the apologizer's), corporate apologies (in which the apologizer takes responsibility for a past act of the apologizer's organization), and collective apologies (in which the apologizer takes responsibility for a past act of the apologizer's nation). Keeping these categories straight will allow communities to demand only those apologies – and forms of responsibility – that are appropriate to particular forms of wrongdoing, thus avoiding confusion between corporate and political wrongdoing (and the responsibility thereafter).

In her contribution, Cynthia E. Clark investigates the role of corporate boards and corporate directors in value creation and accountability. Drawing upon synergies between stakeholder and shareholder conceptions of corporate accountability, she sets forth a view of proper roles and responsibilities within the firm. According to this view, accountability enhances value creation and value creation enhances accountability to both shareholders and stakeholders. She concludes by explaining how corporate values contribute to this process.

Finally, in this part, Georges Enderle offers an extended case study focused on the efforts of his own university, Notre Dame, to secure ethical supply chains in the production of goods bearing the university's logo. Investigating well-known problems in supply chains – forced labor, air and water pollution, environmental degradation – Enderle argues that Notre Dame's policy from 2001–15 was inadequate to the task of securing ethical supply chains. Although it highlighted the importance of freedom of association and collective bargaining rights for the workers who manufactured goods branded with the Notre Dame logo, the policy's implementation did not produce significant results for workers. A pilot program that was in effect in 2015 brought important improvements for workers' rights but neglected broader social, political, and environmental concerns. Subsequently, Notre Dame partnered with a third-party surveying and auditing organization to focus on its specific needs with respect to ethical supply chain management. The third-party organization, which included a large number of social, political, and environmental concerns in its decision making and supplemented by the United Nations Guiding Principles on Business and Human Rights, proved effective for producing the results for which Notre Dame held itself responsible.

In the part on "Models for Decision Making," five contributors offer novel models for ethical decision making in corporations. In the first chapter, Patricia H. Werhane sets forth a new model for 21st-century ethical decision making: embedded leadership. Embedded leadership is neither hierarchical nor dependent on antiquated notions of "authority" (what she calls the "Boss" or "Master" point of view). Rather, Werhane reconceives Miller and Page's (2007) notion of complex adaptive systems (CAS) as complex adaptive *social* systems (CASS) or sets of embedded systems. The systems thinking encouraged by this model offers a novel model of leadership focused on "adaptive" work whereby leaders permit employees to self-organize (or "emerge" within an organization, as she says). Werhane argues that organizations employing such embedded leadership will be more successful – in both the short and the long term – than those employing hierarchical management structures.

Next, Sandra Waddock also advocates a systems approach. She explains that what characterizes contemporary ethical challenges is their systemic nature, something that business ethics (and ethics generally) has not yet learned how to address. To do so, she argues that business leaders should adopt a holistic approach in which they prioritize systemic interests – the well-being of the whole system – over individual interests.

In his contribution, Alejo José G. Sison offers an alternative model for evaluating businesses' relationships with social and political struggles, specifically as regards the protection of human rights. Whereas most CSR programs are individualistic and focus on satisfying the preferences of various stakeholders, Sison recommends Francisco de Vitoria's teachings on *ius gentium*, which focuses on the equality of human beings and securing a common good for human communities. The *ius gentium* is particularly promising for determining businesses' appropriate responsibilities when addressing contemporary social and political struggles to the extent that it regards businesses as forces for the common good (especially insofar as they further price discovery, the free market, and entrepreneurship). Our current troubling times reflect the negligence of the *ius gentium*, generally. Although businesses cannot and should not try to single-handedly address social and political challenges, following the *ius gentium* in their business decision making is a promising way to begin addressing them.

Next, Johannes Brinkmann argues that business ethicists' distinctive skills in critical reflection, including inviting critical self-reflection in others, suggest a strategy for addressing social problems such as those that currently afflict communities worldwide. In particular, Brinkmann argues that modeling dialogues between conflicting parties can help to overcome mutual prejudice. By listening to one another's different viewpoints parties are more likely to find consensus and resolve common problems.

In the final chapter in this part, Mahmut Arslan and Mustafa K. Yilmaz study how local managers of medium-sized companies in Gaziantep (a Turkish city near the Syrian border) make ethical decisions about how to treat Syrian refugees. A series of interviews reveal some confusion in the managers' decision-making processes, especially when there are economic and social conflicts. These conflicts tended to undermine managers' abilities to reach decisions that they found acceptable. Interestingly, these decision-making problems were most acute in the initial phase of the crisis.

Finally, in the part on "Applied Topics: Technology and the Environment," three contributors explain how corporations should address technological and environmental troubles. Chris MacDonald begins this part by discussing how corporations should respond when social media users demand that they fire employees for actions that some people on social media condemn. MacDonald argues that decision makers should hesitate to accede to social media users' demands concerning actions that employees take when they are not on the job, even when those actions are egregious. Corporations should take particular caution, according to MacDonald's argument, when the corporations can easily carry out the demands and/or when it is in the corporations' self-interest to carry out social media users' demands.

In the next contribution, Christoph Lütge addresses a more general issue concerning corporate responses to technology: the lack of clear ethical rules for corporate uses of technology. He addresses topics as varied as data protection, data security, artificial intelligence (AI), internet of things, and autonomous vehicles. All of these new technologies raise pressing, unresolved ethical concerns; Lütge calls upon business ethicists to provide rules to resolve them. Devising clear ethical rules for corporate uses of technology is especially important because the parties making decisions about technology that have great ethical importance are huge corporations. As such, the principles they follow will have outsized importance.

In the final chapter in this part, Eleanor O'Higgins and Laszlo Zsolnai recommend that corporations focus on whole entities rather than mere parts of them; they emphasize, in particular, the importance of the whole *Earth*. Following Hans Jonas's account of ethics for the Anthropocene, O'Higgins and Zsolnai argue that business leaders' primary ethical concerns should be preserving life on Earth: including human, non-human, and future lives. Extending their argument via cases studies, O'Higgins and Zsolnai argue that Unilever and Patagonia offer models for this kind of ethical leadership.

REFERENCES

Matten, D. and J. Moon (2008), "'Implicit' and 'explicit' CSR: a conceptual framework for a comparative understanding of corporate social responsibility," *Academy of Management Review*, **33** (2), 404–24.

Miller, J.H. and S.E. Page (2007), *Complex Adaptive Systems*. Princeton, NJ: Princeton University Press.

Sorkin, A.R. (2017), "Apple's Tim Cook barnstorms for 'moral responsibility,'" *New York Times*, 28 August. https://www.nytimes.com/2017/08/28/business/dealbook/tim-cook-apple-moral-responsibility.html (accessed 11 February 2019).

PART I

Business and Politics

1. Stepping down rather than up: the ethical option for business in our troubling times

Donna Ladkin

In an interview with the *New York Times* in August of 2017, the Chief Executive of Apple Computers, Tim Cook was quoted to have said that because government was becoming 'less functional' and 'less able to work at the speed it once did', businesses and other areas of society needed to 'step up' to fulfil the roles that government once played (Sorkin, 2017). This chapter argues a contrary view: that the truly ethical response for business in our troubling times is to step 'down', rather than 'up'. The idea that corporations need to step up in order to fill a moral gap speaks to the assumption that they are now the prime actors within society whose operational approaches will best serve society at large. Secondly, it assumes that businesses, rather than elected government officials, are best placed to decide how to serve wider societal interests. Furthermore, it intimates that businesses themselves can choose the ways of stepping up that suit them best. This is clearly the case for Apple, who donated $10 million to hurricane relief in 2017 (Mejia, 2017) but simultaneously holds over $252 billion in offshore accounts in order not to pay tax on these profits (Drucker and Bowen, 2017).

Stepping down, that is, businesses taking a place as one voice among many rather than assuming the role of central actors in society, offers a direct challenge to the neoliberal ideology of our times. Neoliberalism places market mechanisms and the pursuit of profit as central to human endeavour. As primary players within markets businesses have become dominant actors whose interests trump all others (Klein, 2014). Cook's statement speaks of the hubris that attends principal and privileged positions. Indeed, corporations' central position is so unequivocally dominant that Cook's statement is interpreted as an indication of his intent to take a moral lead, rather than as a practice of applying band-aids to good causes (as well as a step which attracts favourable media attention).

From a practical perspective the chapter argues that stepping down would involve fulfilling the basic civic obligations of a commercial operation (such as paying tax, something that Apple assiduously avoids through holding greater offshore cash reserves than any other non-financial-based company in the world; Webb and Gurman, 2018) reducing the waste products it creates (Apple is currently under investigation by the French government for 'planned obsolescence', which drives consumer need to buy new phones; BBC, 2018) and creating an organizational culture in which work is only one aspect of employees' balanced life, leaving them free to create further value for themselves through family and community relationships (another aspect on which Apple falls down badly with employees citing experiences of working in a high stress, competitive environment; Ehrenkranz, 2016).

Rather than offering the 'band-aid' remedy of corporate social responsibility or even business ethics, the chapter proposes a radical reorientation of the relationship between businesses and governments. If Milton Friedman's assertion that the ethical responsibility of an organization is to increase shareholder wealth (Friedman, 1970) this drive needs to be balanced against other societal projects that protect and support those who are not shareholders: workers, those living in communities in which companies do their business, and most importantly, future generations of the planet.

The chapter proceeds as follows. Firstly, three key aspects of our troubling times are highlighted: the growing disparity in wealth distribution apparent throughout the USA and Europe, global climate change, and the rise of populism and with it the rise in hostile factionalism. Each of these is shown to be linked to neoliberal ideology. The growth of business ethics and corporate social responsibility as ethical responses to corporate wrongdoing is reviewed and critiqued. The argument then turns to consider the basics of corporate ethical responsibility and ends with the question of why these basics – paying an appropriate level of tax, safeguarding the environment in which the firm is situated, and placing the wellbeing of employees above the profit of the corporation – have become such radical base line requirements. The argument begins by identifying key aspects of our 'troubling times'.

1.1 CHARACTERISTICS OF OUR 'TROUBLING TIMES'

Our times are indeed troubled, and these difficulties are taking their toll on human beings in a number of ways. For instance, the incidence of suicide has risen by 25 per cent in the USA over the last two decades (Vance, 2018). The use of opiates and opiate-related death has increased five times from 1999 to 2016 (CDC, 2018) and in the USA, one out of every five people is diagnosed as suffering from anxiety or other mental health disorders (NAMI, 2018). Among the factors contributing to this worrying trend in human suffering are cited increased isolation and social fragmentation, heightened fear and the breakdown of family, and religious identification. Here I focus on three factors which go beyond the personal, yet also affect individuals' sense of security and happiness. These are: the growing disparity between the wealthy and the poor throughout the world but in the USA and UK in particular, climate change and environmental degradation, and the rise of populism which seems to be normalizing acts of racism and hostility in the USA and UK (Sidahmed, 2016; Weaver, 2018).

1.1.1 Growing Disparity between Wealthy and Poor

Writing for the National Bureau of Economic Research, Wolff (2017) notes the exponential growth of disparity in wealth distribution in the USA since the 1970s. His statistics indicate that the richest 1 per cent of Americans now hold more wealth that the combined 90 per cent below them. Hardest hit by the reduction in wealth has been the middle class, whose median household wealth in 2017 was equivalent to that in 1969. Although other developed economies are following this trend (for instance, the UK's progressive thinktank the Institute for Public Policy Research writes that in 2018, 44 per cent of the UK's wealth is held by the top 10 per cent of the population; Colebrook, 2018), Wolff asserts that 'By almost any conceivable index – household income, equivalent income, poverty, and household wealth, the US is now the most unequal country (or nearly so) among the advanced industrialised nations of the world' (p. xiv).

Ironically, such large wealth distribution is itself linked to a slowdown in the economy (Stockhammer, 2015). There is much evidence to suggest that wealth disparity is detrimental to societies in which there are such large distinctions between the rich and the poor. The social ills caused by such unequal holding of wealth include increased levels of poverty, homelessness and social unrest as well as rising levels of criminal activity. Other detrimental effects include vast differences in the health of the poor, even in wealthy countries (Coburn, 2000), depression, especially among women (Belle and Doucet, 2003), and impacts on happiness (Graham and Felton, 2006). Indeed, Wilkinson and Pickett (2009) argue in their study of the relationship between national economies and wellbeing statistics that life expectancy, levels of mental illness, violence and illiteracy are all a function not of how wealthy a country is, but of the equality of its wealth distribution.

1.1.2 Climate Change

There is now little doubt among climate scientists that global temperatures are rising due to human activities, particularly the release of CO_2 as a bi-product of the burning of fossil fuels into the environment (IPCCC, 2018). The most recent report by the Intergovernmental Panel on Climate Change suggests that if we are able to halt temperature rise at 1.5 degrees Celsius, we will avert the very worst of climate change effects. Their report stresses that doing so will require '"rapid and far-reaching" transitions in land, energy, industry, buildings, transport, and cities. Global net human-caused emissions of carbon dioxide (CO_2) would need to fall by about 45 percent from 2010 levels by 2030, reaching "net zero" around 2050' (IPCC, 2018). However, although the deadline for halting that scenario has been variously set at 2017, 2020 or 2030 – apart from a dip in fossil fuel consumption after the 2007–08 global financial crisis, emissions have continued to rise (Klein, 2014).

Climate change is probably the most troubling of all aspects of our current times, in that ultimately it threatens the viability of life on Earth. Within the northern hemisphere its effects have largely been experienced through the increase in the number and ferocity of storms. However, the southern hemisphere and on islands rising sea levels, desertification and disruption of seasonal weather patterns are already contributing to the loss of human as well as other life forms. It is estimated that should temperatures rise by 4 or even 6 degrees Celsius life as we know it will no longer be possible on the planet.

We do not have to wait to see the effects of climate change. It is already resulting in parts of the world becoming uninhabitable due to heat, desertification or rising seas. This is forcing people to move from their homelands, at a time when populist sentiment which is taking hold throughout Western Europe as well as the USA means legal immigration is increasingly difficult.

1.1.3 The Rise of Populism

The shocking result of the UK referendum in 2016 to leave the European Union, along with the election of Donald Trump as president of the USA have been cited as the result of populism expressing itself through democratic means (Cox, 2017). These occurrences are underpinned by increasing numbers of people who are feeling confident to express isolationist, anti-immigrant sentiments. After both the UK referendum and the election of Donald Trump incidences of hate crimes in the UK and the USA spiked dramatically. It has been argued (Klein, 2014; Korten, 1995) that these three issues (the results of the UK referendum and US election, the rise of populism and the increase in hate crime) are all linked, but also that they have their roots in the dominant ideology of our times: neoliberalism.

Contemporary business models, fixations and assumptions are all underpinned by this ideology which sees market mechanisms as the panacea to all society's ills. This taken-for-granted assumption informs the kind of managerialism to which public sector provisions such as healthcare, education and social services are now subject. The predominant business view that human beings can be treated as cogs in machines (which can be dispensed with in order to cut costs) has limitations when applied within institutions where care, time and genuine human contact are essential. The next section of the chapter examines neoliberalism and draws the connections between it and these worrying aspects of our contemporary context.

1.2 WHAT IS NEOLIBERALISM?

It is important to place neoliberalism within its own socio-historic context. Hamann (2009) explains that neoliberalism was a reaction to the over-involvement of government that had its most extreme expression in Stalinist Russia and Soviet-style communism, but could also be seen in elements of Roosevelt's New Deal liberalism. In its original form, neoliberalism was aligned with a sense of freedom from overly stringent government regulation. The unbiased 'invisible hand' of the market was idealized as a means of enabling maximum freedom to individuals, in which by pursuing individual interests the common good could be served (Smith, 1863). In order for this to work, human beings had to be reconceived as 'homo economicus'; creatures whose primary functions were economic, rather than aesthetic, communal or spiritual (Fleming, 2017).

Indeed, Hamann (2009, p. 38) writes that 'neoliberalism strives to ensure that individuals are compelled to assume market-based values in all of their judgements and practices in order to amass sufficient quantities of "human capital"'. In this way we are all at the mercy of this ideology – increasingly our very lives are things that we 'produce' and that accrue 'capital value'. This notion lends itself to the idea that those who do not accrue sufficient 'capital' can be considered 'waste' people (Hage, 2017) who do not have to be considered from a moral perspective.

Klein (2014, p. 9) identifies three policy pillars of the neoliberal agenda: the privatization of the public sphere, deregulation of the corporate sector and lowering of corporation taxes – the last of which results in fewer funds being available for public spending. Tim Cook's assertion that government is no longer effective fails to recognize that a contributing factor to that lack of effectiveness is the reduction in funds governments have to work with as a result of the very generous corporate tax regulations that firms have enjoyed since the 1980s. Along with a reduced requirement to pay tax Hamann (2009) asserts that there is strong evidence that government policy in the USA is increasingly influenced by lobbyists agitating for corporate interests, which in turn revolve around short-term quarterly results. This is not a sound recipe for effective government.

1.2.1 Effects of Neoliberalism

Over 20 years ago, in his text *When Corporations Rule the World*, David Korten noted a three-fold human crisis: deepening poverty, environmental degradation and social disintegration (Korten, 1995). He traced the roots of these ills to economic models that make growth the goal of development and treat people as the means by which wealth can be generated (rather than beings for whom wealth is generated). The economic model of which Korten is critical is, of course, capitalism. Whereas before the fall of the Soviet Union, capitalism was recognized as one of a number of potential economic systems, in today's context it is commonly accepted to be the dominant (and indeed only workable) economic system. Such a view is supported by the growth of neoliberal ideology.

The way in which neoliberalism has undermined government is perhaps most explicitly exemplified in the fact that Donald Trump, a rather dubious businessman, but a businessman nonetheless, was elected to be the 45th president of the USA. Qualities normally associated with the presidential role – prior experience in government, diplomacy, statesmanship or even common decency – have been eschewed in favour of a man who is perceived to be a 'successful businessman', largely because of the role he played on the reality television show *The Apprentice* (Schrodt, 2016). His promise to 'Make America Great Again' aligns with a populous who are seeking economic success in line with the American dream (Ladkin, 2017). What is not being so readily recognized is the way in which neoliberal policies tend to concentrate wealth in the hands of those who are already wealthy, rather than trickling down to those in middle and lower middle-income brackets.

Although the rhetoric of neoliberalism has a seductive element (if you work hard, you too can become a billionaire), the evidence of the last 30 years indicates that neoliberal policies result in rather different outcomes for the majority of us (Clifford, 2018). In particular, deregulation of markets and free trade agreements enable corporations to operate wherever they can employ the cheapest labour. This free movement has destroyed local communities who previously could rely on local manufacturing for employment, thus fuelling the conditions for rising populism. The fantasy of cheap goods is underwritten by huge costs to the environment in transportation costs. Interestingly, the carbon emissions that are produced through transporting goods when they are in international waters do not register on any country's carbon account sheet. Fossil fuels are subsidized by governments and the vicious circle is that fossil fuel companies donate so much money to political campaigns that politicians have to dance to their tune. These issues – wealth disparity, populism and environmental degradation – are all connected (Klein, 2014).

For instance, while enormous wealth has been created in the USA and Europe since the end of the Second World War, that wealth is not distributed evenly. One of the reasons for this is that for many organizations, their prime purpose is financial, rather than being in any way social. Reducing costs has therefore become the focus of much corporate activity, whether through moving operations to cheaper countries or increased levels of automation. This has had significant consequences for potential employees in the USA. For instance, Fort et al. (2018) note that although there has been a steady rise in the real wealth of manufacturing firms in the USA since 2000, employment has simultaneously fallen by 25 per cent. Manufacturing businesses are getting wealthier, while the human beings who were once employed by these businesses are not.

At the heart of wealth disparity is the way in which capitalist-based economics works. Businesses may be perceived to be central to generating that all important economic growth, but at what cost to human persons? Who should that growth be for, after all? Preferential tax treatment as well as limitless constraints on lobbying and supporting elected officials mean that business values, rather than human values, drive much of contemporary discourse. Businesses have indeed already 'stepped up' beyond their roles as providers of goods, services and meaningful work. The neoliberal ideology means they are no longer means for serving human purposes, but have become sumps for the top 1 per cent of the wealth-holding population.

1.3 THE BUSINESS ETHICS AND CORPORATE SOCIAL RESPONSIBILITY RESPONSE

It is interesting to note how as corporate malfeasance has been on the rise, a key response within the community of those responsible for developing managers is to promote the benefits of 'business ethics' courses and 'corporate social responsibility' (CSR). Indeed, Fleming et al. (2013, p. 339) assert that 'while companies are proclaiming [their virtues] on a scale never before seen, the "business as usual" mentality now feels completely entrenched and immovable'. Certainly, there is mixed evidence about the extent to which business ethics interventions influence corporate behaviour, with Boda and Zsolnai (2016) suggesting that as a project, business ethics has failed. A number of empirical studies have been undertaken in which MBA students or undergraduate business majors have been tested for their ethical awareness before and after being exposed to business ethics teaching (Jewe, 2008; Waples et al., 2009). These reveal mixed results (with a worrying trend in findings that those who enrol on business courses themselves start from a lower base of 'moral orientation' than humanities and science students). The relatively small amount of research that has been undertaken with actual working people (Clarke, 2011; Kirsten and Plessis, 2017) similarly reveals mixed results. It is important to note that most of these studies include self-report measures, thus offering questionable indications of what people actually do in the field.

Curiously, the key accreditors of business school programmes seem to be reluctant to champion the desirability of ethics within formal business education. Neither the Academy of Management nor the Association to Advance Collegiate School of Business require business schools they accredit to offer business ethics as part of their core curriculum (Floyd et al., 2013). A number of reasons are given for this omission, including the question about whether or not ethics can be taught.

Business schools themselves have been implicated in the growing numbers of organizations involved in cases of ethical malfeasance, including the financial crisis of 2007/08 (Giacalone and Wargo, 2009). Empirical work undertaken by Hummel et al. (2018) indicates that at the very least, business school education does not further moral development in students. They note how the emphasis placed on business models aimed at increasing profit encourages students to frame situations primarily in financial terms, rather than to adequately consider human and environmental costs, which can be difficult both to identify and measure.

What these studies fail to link up is the overarching neoliberal ideology in which business schools are embedded. I would argue that the real culprit here is the fundamental assumption that business models are the most important lens through which situations should be analysed. Ethics are often couched as standards which themselves must fit within market realities, rather than the other way around. As Clarke (2011) writes, those working in financial institutions who were selling worthless financial products and toxic loans implicated in the 2007 crash felt they were working 'within the boundaries of the free market system' (p. 2). The free market system is the frame through which ethics is considered, and more often than not the market trumps ethical considerations (Devinney, 2009).

Indeed, Korten (1995) suggests that the rhetoric of business ethics and CSR enables businesses to think they are doing all right, when in fact their problematic ways of operating remain untouched. A more fundamental question offered by Sterba (2009) drives this debate: Should businesses be accountable to the same ethical regulations that individuals would be, or is their ethical responsibility due to only their shareholders? As the main generators of economic wealth, businesses have been allowed to rise above the moral landscape to which individuals are tethered. Lamberton (2011) asserts that if businesses continue to be able to act as amoral beings within the world, they will take the planet down with them. How might this worrying scenario be avoided?

1.4 WHAT IS THE ROLE OF BUSINESS IN SUCH TIMES?

To summarize the argument thus far: the dominant ideology of neoliberalism places financial concerns at the heart of human activity. This ideology imbues contemporary consciousness to such an extent that not only do we willingly accept the injunction to make money in order to enjoy material goods and services, our very lives are now produced and measured in terms of the 'human capital' we accrue. Such a skewed focus on markets and financial growth above all else has resulted in huge disparities in wealth, life-endangering global climate change and levels of workplace stress that leave significant numbers of us suffering from mental health issues.

Within this landscape, businesses in the USA and UK have assumed a central role, evidenced by reductions in tax liabilities over the last 30 years as well as a relaxation of regulations more generally. With the cap on political donations in the USA halted in 2014 businesses can now support politicians in ways that mean that elected government officials are often indebted to them. This, along with the huge amounts of money spent on lobbying, mean that business 'calls the tune' in terms of government policy as almost never before. In these ways, businesses have already 'stepped up' significantly beyond their roles as producers of goods and services and generators of meaningful work for human beings.

Within this analysis, Tim Cook's assertion that businesses need to 'step up' to assume the role that government can no longer fulfil reveals itself as hubristic. Moreover, given Apple's record in terms of tax avoidance, creation of products with inbuilt obsolescence and the kinds of working conditions many of its employees endure, it is also startlingly hypocritical. If 'stepping up' is dismissed as an appropriate strategy for businesses to follow in order to 'do good', what might they do instead to generate social value during these troubling times?

1.4.1 Paying Taxes

A key factor in the ineffectiveness of governments in the USA and UK is the loss of funds from corporations since the 1980s. Even in an era of favourable regulations, significant numbers of multinational companies regularly find ways of avoiding tax. For instance, although GE made $14.2 billion in the tax year 2009–10 ($5.1 billion of which was earned in the USA itself), it paid a tax bill of zero (Kocieniewski, 2011). Similarly, high-profit companies such as Amazon, Google and Facebook have come under public scrutiny for their tax avoidance strategies.

After considering the question relating to the ethics of tax avoidance from principle-based and utilitarian ethics, Dowling (2014) concludes that although tax avoidance may be legal, it is indeed unethical. Noting the extent to which tax avoidance has been missing from many discussions of CSR (tax avoidance is, after all, technically legal), he argues that paying taxes is the most basic form of citizenship behaviour, and that at the very least corporations should fulfil this duty. Especially when companies such as Amazon or Apple are making such extraordinary profits, it is hard to understand why not paying a fair proportion in tax should be considered acceptable.

It is the neoliberal ideology that imbues our culture that condones such action. Instead of seeing tax avoidance as 'wrong', it is conceived of as just doing 'smart business'. If the accepted rhetoric is that 'government is wasteful and inefficient', and businesses can do it better because of the efficiency of their processes, not adhering to this basic civic duty starts to make sense. What is important here is to recognize the way it is the discourse of neoliberalism, rather than the truth of businesses' inherent superiority, which is the basis for justification of the tax avoidance argument.

1.4.2 Reduction in Waste and Care of Communities

A second fundamental duty in our troubled times is for companies to reduce the amount of waste they produce and the amount of harm they cause to the environment in which they are located. This is in line with an approach to CSR based in 'doing no harm' rather than 'doing good' (Crilly et al., 2015). Waste products, be they obsolescent goods or the waste that is generated through creating them in the first place, create huge strains on the natural environment. Levels of both industrial and consumer waste continue to rise worldwide with the World Bank estimating that global waste will triple by 2100 (Goto, 2013). The importance of organizations living within ecological constraints and taking care to produce minimal waste has been asserted by ethics scholars such as Waddock (2004) who identifies care for the environment as a key accountability of businesses in any general standard of responsible corporate behaviour.

1.4.3 Not Overworking, Stressing or Bullying Employees

At the very least, a key responsibility for organizations is not to overwork and bully employees (Fleming, 2017). Yet, firms from Sports Direct in the UK to Amazon, to Apple regularly subject employees to overwork, bullying and stress. Work practices in which employees are expected to be available through smartphones 24/7 lead to depression, anxiety and mental illness. Certainly, a basic responsibility of business is to care for those who maintain its ability to produce its goods and services.

1.5 CONCLUSION

This chapter has argued that neoliberalism plays a leading role in generating the troubled times in which we live. As Fleming et al. (2013) stress, the problem with CSR and business ethics as approaches to curbing the worst of corporatism is that they don't recognize the 'structural nature of the capitalist economic imperative' (p. 340) that fuels our fixation with the market, economic growth and profit rather than people. Neoliberalism frames what we think of as possible, and perhaps more importantly it preordains what is 'important'. Consider the fact that so often when human lives are lost due to severe weather events, the ultimate calculation is rendered in relation to financial loss: so many days of work, the cost of rebuilding, the decline in productivity.

Such a realization suggests new directions of business ethicists. Rather than trying to increase individual commitment to ethical action, perhaps our efforts might best be spent critiquing the larger neoliberal agenda and how it informs everything that we do. Perhaps we should be spending more energy exposing the ways in which the emphasis on profit and reliance on the markets is causing the problems we are having. Perhaps it is important for us to remind those with whom we engage that the way things are is not the way things have to be: businesses have worked to different rules before and they can work to different rules in the future. Perhaps most importantly, we might remind ourselves and those we teach about the things that really matter: family, community and the ecological system which supports us. The importance and value of these aspects of our lives may well become increasingly clear as capitalism shakes itself apart.

REFERENCES

BBC. (2018). Apple investigated by France for 'planned obsolescence'. Retrieved 8 October 2018 from https://www.bbc.co.uk/news/world-europe-42615378.

Belle, D. and Doucet, J. (2003). Poverty, inequality, and discrimination as sources of depression among U.S. women. *Psychology of Women Quarterly*, **27**(2), 101–13. https://doi.org/10.1111/1471-6402.00090.

Boda, Z. and Zsolnai, L. (2016). The failure of business ethics. *Society and Business Review*, **11**(1), 93–104. https://doi.org/10.1108/SBR-11-2015-0066.

CDC. (2018). Prescription opioid data. Retrieved 8 October 2018 from https://www.livescience.com/62781-why-are-suicide-rates-rising.html.

Clarke, C. (2011). A system approach to implementing business ethics in the corporate workplace. *Journal of Business Systems, Governance & Ethics*, **6**(2), 1–11. Retrieved from http://library.gcu.edu:2048/login?url=http://search.ebscohost.com/login.aspx?direct=true&db=bth&AN=76973520&site=eds-live&scope=site (accessed 30 August 2019).

Clifford, C. (2018). Warren Buffet on the US Economy: 'The tsunami of wealth didn't trickle down. It surged upwards'. Retrieved on 19 December 2018 from https://www.cnbc.com/2018/01/04/warren-buffett-on-the-failure-of-trickle-down-economics.html.

Coburn, D. (2000). Income inequality, social cohesion and the health status of populations: the role of neo-liberalism. *Social Science & Medicine*, **51**(1), 135–46.

Colebrook, C. (2018). Unfair and in need of reform: public attitudes to the UK economy. Retrieved 9 October 2018 from https://www.ippr.org/research/publications/unfair-and-in-need-of-reform.

Cox, M. (2017). The rise of populism and the crisis of globalisation: Brexit, Trump and beyond. *Irish Studies in International Affairs*, **28**, 9–17.

Crilly, D., Ni, N., and Jiang, Y. (2015). Do no harm vs do good social responsibility: attribution theory and the labeling of foreignness. *Strategic Management Journa*l, **37**(7), 1316–29.

Devinney, T.M. (2009). Is the socially responsible corporation a myth? The good, the bad, and the ugly of corporate social responsibility. *Academy of Management Perspectives*, **23**(2), 44–56. https://doi.org/10.5465/AMP.2009.39985540.

Dowling, G.R. (2014). The curious case of corporate tax avoidance: is it socially irresponsible? *Journal of Business Ethics*, **124**(1), 173–84. https://doi.org/10.1007/s10551-013-1862-4.

Drucker, J. and Bowen, S. (2017). After a tax crackdown, Apple find a new shelter for its profits. 6 November. Retrieved 4 October 2018 from https://www.nytimes.com/2017/11/06/world/apple-taxes-jersey.html.

Ehrenkranz, M. (2016). Apple employees say their mental health issues came from a hostile work environment. Retrieved 8 October 2018 from https://mic.com/articles/154788/apple-employees-say-their-mental-health-issues-came-from-alleged-hostile-work-environment#.MeEnedhDt.

Fleming, P. (2017). *The Death of Homo Economicus*. London: Pluto Press.

Fleming, P., Roberts, J., and Garsten, C. (2013). In search of corporate social responsibility: introduction to special issue. *Organization*, **20**(3), 337–48. https://doi.org/10.1177/1350508413479581.

Floyd, L.A., Xu, F., Atkins, R., and Caldwell, C. (2013). Ethical outcomes and business ethics: toward improving business ethics education. *Journal of Business Ethics*, **117**(4), 753–76. https://doi.org/10.1007/s10551-013-1717-z.

Fort, T.C., Pierce, J.R., and Schott, P.K. (2018). Manufacturing employment. *Journal of Economic Perspectives*, **32**(2), 47–72.

Friedman, M. (1970). The social responsibility of business is to increase its profit. *New York Times Magazine*, 32–9.

Giacalone, R. and Wargo, D. (2009). The roots of the Global Financial Crisis are in our business schools. *Journal of Business Ethics Education*, **6**, 147–68. Retrieved from http://www.emeraldinsight.com/doi/10.1108/SBR-11-2015-0066 (accessed 30 August 2019).

Goto, M. (2013). Global waste to triple by 2100. Retrieved 20 December 2018 from http://www.worldbank.org/en/news/feature/2013/10/30/global-waste-on-pace-to-triple.

Graham, C. and Felton, A. (2006). Inequality and happiness: insights from Latin America. *Journal of Economic Inequality*, **4**(1), 107–22. https://doi.org/10.1007/s10888-005-9009-1.

Hage, G. (2017). *Is Racism an Environmental Threat?* London: John Wiley & Sons.

Hamann, T.H. (2009). Neoliberalism, governmentality, and ethics. *Foucault Studies*, **6**, 37–59. https://doi.org/10.22439/fs.v0i0.2471.

Hummel, K., Pfaff, D., and Rost, K. (2018). Does economics and business education wash away moral judgment competence? *Journal of Business Ethics*, **150**(2), 559–77.

IPCC. (2018). Global warming of 1.5 degrees C. Retrieved 9 October 2018 from http://www.ipcc.ch/report/sr15/.

Jewe, R.D. (2008). Do business ethics courses work? The effectiveness of business ethics education: an empirical study. *Journal of Global Business Issues*, **2**(1), 1–6.

Kirsten, M. and Plessis, M. (2017). More does not always mean better: do more comprehensive ethics management programmes result in better outcomes? *African Journal of Business and Economic Research*, **12**(2/3), 149–77.

Klein, N. (2014). *This Changes Everything: Capitalism vs Climate*. London: Allen Lane.

Kocieniewski, D. (2011). GEs strategies let it avoid taxes altogether. *New York Times*, 24 March.

Korten, D. (1995). *When Corporations Rule the World*. San Francisco, CA: Berrett-Koehler.

Ladkin, D. (2017). How did that happen? Making sense of the 2016 US presidential election result through the lens of the 'leadership moment'. *Leadership*, **13**(4), 393–412. https://doi.org/10.1177/1742715017714841.

Lamberton, G.W. (2011). An ethical response to climate change. *Journal of Business Systems, Governance & Ethics*, **6**(2), 12–27.

Mejia, Z. (2017). Apple is giving $10,000 to hurricane relief. How much has Tim Cook donated to other causes? Retrieved 4 October 2018 from https://www.cnbc.com/2017/09/13/apple-gives-10-million-to-hurricane-harvey-and-hurricane-irma-relief.html.

NAMI. (2018). Mental health by the numbers. Retrieved 8 October 2018 from https://www.nami.org/Learn-More/Mental-Health-By-the-Numbers.

Schrodt, P. (2016). The Apprentice made Donald Trump's presidential campaign possible. Retrieved 19 December 2018 from https://www.businessinsider.com/the-apprentice-paved-way-for-donald-trump-presidential-campaign-2016-11?r=UK&IR=T.

Sidahmed, M. (2016). Claims of hate crimes possibly linked to Trump election reported across the US. *Guardian*. Retrieved 18 December 2018 from https://www.theguardian.com/us-news/2016/nov/10/hate-crime-spike-us-donald-trump-president.

Smith, A. (1863). *The Wealth of Nations: An Inquiry into the Nature and Causes of the Wealth of a Nation*. Edinburgh: Blacks.

Sorkin, A. (2017). Apple's Tim Cook barnstorms for 'moral responsibility'. Retrieved 4 October 4 2018 from http://www.nytimes.com/2017/08/28/business/dealbook/tim-cook-apple-moral-responsibility.html.

Sterba, J.P. (2009). Our basic human right is a right to liberty and it leads to equality. In J.P. Sterba (ed.), *Ethics: The Big Questions*, Malden, MA and Oxford: Blackwell, pp. 285–95.

Stockhammer, E. (2015). Rising inequality as a cause of the present crisis. *Cambridge Journal of Economics*, **39**(3), 935–58. https://doi.org/10.1093/cje/bet052.

Vance, E. (2018). Why are suicide rates rising? Retrieved 8 October 2018 from https://www.livescience.com/62781-why-are-suicide-rates-rising.html.

Waddock, S. (2004). Creating corporate accountability: to make foundational principles corporate citizenship real. *Journal of Business Ethics*, **50**(4), 313–27. Retrieved from http://amp.aom.org/cgi/doi/10.5465/AMP.2009.39985540 (accessed 30 August 2019).

Waples, E.P., Antes, A.L., Murphy, S.T., Connelly, S., and Mumford, M.D. (2009). A meta-analytic investigation of business ethics instruction. *Journal of Business Ethics*, **87**(1), 133–51. https://doi.org/10.1007/s10551-008-9875-0.

Weaver, M. (2018). Hate crime surge linked to Brexit and 2017 terrorist attacks. *Guardian*. Retrieved 19 December 2018 from https://www.theguardian.com/society/2018/oct/16/hate-crime-brexit-terrorist-attacks-england-wales.

Webb, A. and Gurman, M. (2018). Apple returning overseas cash and pay $38 billion tax bill. Retrieved 8 October 2018 from https://www.bloomberg.com/news/articles/2018-01-17/apple-expects-38-billion-tax-bill-on-overseas-repatriated-cash.

Wilkinson, R.G. and Pickett, K.E. (2009). Income inequality and social dysfunction. *Annual Review of Sociology*, **35**, 493–511.

Wolff, N. (2017). *A Century of Wealth in America*. Cambridge, MA: Harvard University Press.

2. The dynamics of CSR in a comparative perspective: convergence towards divergent hybrids

Dirk Matten and Jeremy Moon

2.1 INTRODUCTION

The role of business in fostering the public good has been a contentious issue from the emergence of modern capitalism onwards. From early forms of philanthropy up to contemporary corporate social responsibility (CSR) business has faced and responded to societal expectations beyond its pure economic functions (Boswell, 1983). The rise of global capitalism (often characterized as 'neo-liberal') in the last four decades has coincided with a widespread proliferation of business practices that see the responsibility for the public good as an intrinsic part of private profit maximization.

The spread of global capitalism has thus been accompanied by the proliferation of business activities in favour of the public good, driven by corporate discretion and self-interest. Matten and Moon (2008) have termed such an assumption of social responsibility by business as 'explicit CSR' – as opposed to 'implicit CSR'. The latter term refers to institutionalized, entrenched (mostly local and national) forms of assigning business responsibility for the public good, be it by law, religion, customs or traditions.

Our chapter critically examines the 'implicit/explicit' CSR dichotomy in the light of a decade of research on comparative CSR that has engaged with the proposed framework at various levels. We discuss three major research questions.

1. We question the accuracy and usefulness of the proposed 'implicit/explicit' CSR dichotomy by looking at a number of empirical studies and conceptual suggestions that posit a much less unilinear character of neo-liberal forms of capitalism and the concomitant spread of

explicit CSR. What are the institutional drivers, enablers and constraints of the spread of functionalist forms of business responsibility for the public good?
2. While Matten and Moon noted the possibility of the co-existence of implicit and explicit forms of CSR (2008, pp. 410, 418–19), the initial model evaded the question of how exactly those two forms intertwine, intersect, mutually enforce or constrain each other. We examine the vast number of empirical works that have looked at hybrid forms of implicit and explicit CSR to ask how implicit and explicit CSR are hybridized?
3. Given the dynamics of global capitalism, in particular its failures and threats (e.g., post financial crisis, Brexit, the political rise of extreme left and right criticisms, the rise of authoritarian capitalism and so on), we raise questions as to the future of specific forms of CSR. Over the last decades we have, certainly in Europe and Asia, witnessed, among other modifications, a more pronounced role of the state in orchestrating, and in some case even regulating CSR. Theorizing the ongoing research in comparative CSR we provide a framework to address the question as to what are the future trajectories for business' responsibilities for the public good?

Based on this analysis our chapter aims at making a contribution to the debate on CSR at three levels. We see those developments pan out first, at the level of the (national or regional) economic system (macro level), the level of individual companies or businesses (micro level), and at an intermediary stage (meso level), which has emerged parallel to CSR becoming an entrenched business practice over the last two or three decades.

1. *Macro level.* First, rather than focusing only on micro or meso levels of analysis that would include individual businesses or business as a societal actor, crucial dynamic changes for the wider CSR debate are a result of changes in the institutional framework. In particular, the spread of global (neo-liberal) capitalism has, seemingly irreversibly, changed many of the institutional settings that determined 'implicit CSR' and which in the initial model were treated as more or less constant and entrenched. Hence, the macro level of institutional analysis, in particular of institutional change, appears to be crucial to understanding contemporary dynamics in CSR, most notably the dominating influence of institutions of global capitalism and their global adoption and embedding.
2. *Micro level.* Looking at the last ten years of comparative research in CSR allows us to conceptualize hybrid forms of implicit and explicit

CSR within individual organizations. As such, our theoretical contribution is in dialogue with and extends rather long-standing debates in international business about the dialectics and dynamics of the global spread and local adaptation of new management practices. We theorize various types of hybrid institutionalization and the institutional conditions under which these emerge (Rasche et al., 2013).

3. *Meso level.* In some ways one of the most conspicuous outcomes of our analysis is the role of implicit CSR in shaping new, emerging forms of institutionalizing explicit forms of CSR. In particular, the spate of global standards, codes, best practices and communities of learning and practice around global, standardized and homogenized CSR practices appears to be revealing the institutional legacy of a variety of implicit CSR arrangements.

The findings of our analysis thus draw on and contribute to ongoing debates on institutional complexity, entrepreneurship and the emerging relevance of interstitial spaces in institutional theory (Furnari, 2014).

2.2 METHODOLOGY

The basis of our analysis is a literature search based on a number of search terms looking at comparative and national/regional studies of the growth, adoption and adaptation of CSR since 2008 (ten-year time frame). Our search was initially focused on some 3500 papers (in 2019) that cited Matten and Moon (2008). This was narrowed down to some 220 studies that drew on the 'implicit/explicit' dichotomy as research framework. We analysed this work further to explore three different conceptual issues. First, we looked at the core drivers of global business responsibility (mostly equivalent to explicit CSR), in particular the core actors, instruments and institutional drivers. Second, we identified the core elements of national/regional/local forms of business responsibility, most notably actors, institutional arrangements (including regulatory institutions) and coordinating mechanisms. Third – and this forms the bulk of the actual research contributions – we identified the phenomena of hybridized forms of CSR, notably new regulatory frameworks, core new institutional arrangements, and a rather heterogeneous set of locally specific instruments, tools and approaches. While our current analysis is still preliminary it is the third space where the core focus of the further work and this chapter will be located.

2.3 HISTORICAL PERSPECTIVES: CSR AND FORMS OF CAPITALISM

CSR has emerged over the last quarter of a century as a major means by which relations between corporations and society have been mediated in capitalism nationally and internationally. Two aspects are important for contextualizing this perspective. First, this is because the concept of 'implicit CSR' is premised on the idea of a multiplicity of capitalisms which are distinctive because of the way corporate–societal relations are institutionalized by relatively strongly embedded systems of regulation and organization. Matten and Moon (2005, 2008) adopted the national business systems approach on which to base their analysis (Whitley, 1999). They therefore suggest that national – and sometimes regional (Witt and Redding, 2013) – systems of CSR reflect national business systems which are composed of the 'nature of the firm', the 'organization of market processes' and the 'authoritative coordination and control systems'. These distinctive features of national business systems are in turn predicated on the ways in which they are historically institutionalized by their respective 'political', 'financial', 'education and labour' and 'cultural systems'.

Second, the 'implicit and explicit CSR' conceptualization is premised on the theory of neo-institutionalism (Matten and Moon, 2008). This points to another source of the institutionalization of organizational behaviour which arises in the globalization of management practices (DiMaggio and Powell, 1983; Meyer, 2000). The emergence of explicit CSR as a new legitimate management practice is explained with reference to three key processes identified by DiMaggio and Powell (1983) as legitimizing new organizational practices more generally: 'coercive isomorphisms', 'mimetic processes' and 'normative pressures'.

Table 2.1 summarizes the core characteristics of explicit and implicit CSR as posited in the initial 2008 paper.

Looking at the development of responsible business practices one could argue that historically explicit CSR (eCSR) and implicit CSR (iCSR) have taken on a complementary and mutually influencing role (Moon et al., 2017). As Djelic and Etchanchu (2017) have shown, early forms of paternalistic and managerial capitalist involvement in responding to demands for social responsibility of business in both Europe and the USA in the late 19th and early 20th centuries have subsequently informed welfare state provision of some of the activities of private corporations. In that sense, early forms eCSR preceded and informed later forms of iCSR. Catering to social rights, such as access to education, housing or healthcare, while initially pioneered by paternalistic and benevolent businesses were later picked up by governments and integrated in an emerging framework of

Table 2.1 Explicit and implicit CSR

Explicit CSR	Implicit CSR
Describes corporate activities to assume responsibility for the interests of society	Describes the corporations' role within the wider formal and informal institutions for society's interests and concerns
Consists of voluntary corporate policies, programmes and strategies	Consists of values, norms and rules which result in (often codified and mandatory) requirements for corporations
Incentives and opportunities are motivated by the perceived expectations of different stakeholders of the corporation	Motivated by the societal consensus on the legitimate expectations of the roles and contributions of all major groups in society, including corporations

liberal democracy with adjacent welfare state provision and concomitant institutions.

Moving on towards the early and mid-20th century one could argue that the rise of eCSR in the USA as a strategic idea was a direct reaction to a previous intensification of iCSR. As Kaplan (2014) argues, eCSR was developed and propagated by American business elites as a reaction to the New Deal in the 1930s, which saw a rise in labour protection and benefits and a host of welfare state provisions. Against the fear of a global rise of social democratic policies and the spread of communism in Eastern Europe, eCSR was seen as an attempt of business to forestall and prevent a further erosion of freedom and corporate discretion in markets for labour and capital in the USA. In conclusion, one could argue that already at its inception we see that iCSR and eCSR are closely related and mutually determining each other.

With the rise of neo-liberalism in many liberal democracies in the 1980s and onwards, we saw a significant cutback of iCSR in many countries, most notably the USA and the UK. At the same time, we see that eCSR changed from what used to be a strategic concept about the role of private business in the wider social governance of society towards a more functionalist approach of a business case-driven business practice (McWilliams and Siegel, 2001). As such, eCSR and its subsequent rise globally can be seen as a reaction of the retreat of iCSR, as it became obvious that with a retreat in social provision by governments it becomes a business self-interest to selectively address these deficits (Scherer and Palazzo, 2011). That is very obvious in places of the globe where governments so far have not provided these services, such as developing countries. But it also is very visible in developed welfare states, and maybe the UK is the most evident laboratory of such shifts (Moon, 2005).

The last decade certainly has been an interesting phase in particular in the USA, where new regulation, such as Dodd–Frank, or an invigorated welfare state approach, such as the Affordable Care Act, have boosted in some respects iCSR. It is an open question whether this trend proves sustainable under a new Republican administration, and what the impact on eCSR will be. Certainly, Trump's rhetoric on issues such as free trade and workers' protection leave space for some further expectation. It was remarkable though to witness how many private businesses in the USA reacted very strongly to some of the current administration's initiatives, most notably the retreat from the Paris Climate Change Agreement or the travel restrictions for citizens from certain countries. If anything, the trend that is currently visible is that eCSR will probably become more pronounced and an element of what has been discussed for a while as a more pronounced political role of the firm.

In (continental) Europe, the picture is rather more complex. While we witness a clear rise in eCSR practices in many European countries, it appears that CSR in terms of the 'implicit/explicit' distinction is evident as new hybrid forms of both elements, rather than the dichotomous interplay we see more pronounced in the USA (and other Anglo-Saxon economies). We will discuss this in more detail below.

2.4 THE GLOBAL RISE OF EXPLICIT CSR

One of the claims informed by the work of European institutionalists in our initial framework was that national business systems and national institutions are deeply entrenched and only change very slowly over time. Looking at regulatory developments though over the last three decades in Europe has shown that change in those fundamental institutions is rather more dynamic then hitherto anticipated. There are a number of trends which the literature, and indeed our initial conceptualization, has insufficiently taken into account. Some major ones include fincialization, deregulated labour markets and expansion of transnational political spaces.

2.4.1 Financialization

The degree to which a dominance of markets for capital and its increasing global nature and spread has progressed over the last decades has put national systems of iCSR under increasing strain. Hence, we have seen as a flipside that many corporations, in filling such governance voids, have increased their activities in eCSR. One key driver of eCSR is without doubt the rise of responsible investment practices, be it mainstream initiatives such as the Equator Principles, or the specific demands from sovereign wealth funds, pension funds or the fast growing socially responsible investment sector to push companies towards more responsible practices. Most notably the trend to self-regulation and non-market-driven forms of private governance have increased quite substantially. These forms of eCSR transcend long-standing forms of paternalistic, predominantly philanthropy-driven forms of social engagement towards stronger attempts of coordinating eCSR in industries, sectors or issue fields and factor the risk-related aspects of CSR to the bottom line into investment decisions.

2.4.2 Deregulated Labour Markets

The level to which firms now face a considerably lower degree in regulations and demands in structuring their labour relations has rapidly increased. This has led, first, to the growth of business engagement in parts of the world where these regulations were never strong or sufficiently enforced. The fact that not just global commodity users, such as the textile or food industry, are forced to address their social responsibility in terms of eCSR, but that, for instance, Apple and other high technology manufacturers now face similar demands and pressures is proof of that rapid growth. But also in parts of the globe where iCSR drove considerable amounts of business responsibility, we have seen a reduction and impoverishment of these institutional mechanisms. Not least the USA is a good example where in particular since 2008 this trend has been exacerbated. But similar trends have been visible all over Europe too.

2.4.3 Expansion of Transnational Political Spaces

There are a number of areas where we have seen an increased pressure on companies to enhance their eCSR programmes and policies. One good example is the degree to which globalization has allowed companies to reduce their tax payments (an important condition for functioning institutions of iCSR), which in turn has put them in a position to have their own 'voluntary' policies on this (e.g., Starbucks' attempt at 'voluntary' tax payments in the UK of £20 million in 2012). We have also seen a similar rise in eCSR in the corporate engagement in the various rounds of climate negotiations, resulting in the Paris Agreement. The important thing to notice here is not necessarily that corporations have always performed in a way the public would consider responsible. The core point is that the political space in which corporations are challenged to practice eCSR has arguably rapidly increased over the last decade. A particular boost for the expansion of transnational political spaces has come from the digitalization and datafication of many business practices globally. The expansion of cyber space and internet-based business practices has created yet another arena where due to lack of national or regional governmental reach eCSR has, albeit slowly, emerged as a response to new demands from wider society (Flyverbom et al., 2019).

2.5 COMPARATIVE DYNAMICS OF IMPLICIT AND EXPLICIT CSR HYBRIDIZATION

Matten and Moon (2008) deployed these two views of institutionalization in comparison of CSR in the USA and Western Europe. They note that the legacies of their respective national business systems had yielded a great emphasis on eCSR in the USA and a greater emphasis on iCSR in Europe. However, they concluded that in the light of new pressures of globalization on European business, it was witnessing a greater emphasis on eCSR. Much of the subsequent research on implicit and explicit CSR takes either a tacit or an overt comparative design.

In North America and Western Europe there is a sense that CSR as a business practice has emerged from implicit understandings of business responsibility to greater eCSR (e.g., Gond et al., 2011; Husted, 2015). Some of the research examines these processes in greater detail and finds that even in these systems the processes are, to quote Hiss (2009, p. 445), not 'radical, frictionless or uni-directional' but 'unexpected, paradoxical and dialectical'. Other research notes that the processes are iterative/stop-start/'muddling' (Berthoin Antal et al., 2009). It might be added that even the Western European trajectories from implicit to explicit CSR are not synchronized with one another as a comparison of the UK and the German trajectories reveals (Silberhorn and Warren, 2007). Most notably in continental Europe we have witnessed the emergence of eCSR not just as an element of corporate volitions and strategies but more often than not, eCSR policies and practices emerged with the involvement of governments, industry associations, chambers of commerce, non-governmental organizations and labour organizations.

While some authors have pointed to the advantages that Scandinavian companies have in conforming to new 'explicit' expectations by virtue of their strong 'implicit' CSR legacies (e.g., Gjølberg, 2009), a number of authors have also pointed to the tensions that such CSR managers face in both complying with the new – which stresses communication – and abiding with the old – in which communication was not a feature (Schmeltz, 2014; see also Kujala et al., 2013; Ursin et al., 2016). It might even be conjectured that over-zealous CSR communication would be seen as immodest in the traditional implicit model (Strand et al., 2015). This tension is exacerbated given the role of governments in driving eCSR in such countries (Carson et al., 2015; Knudsen and Moon, 2017).

Other research explores the conceptualization in very different models and developmental stages of a capitalist economic system (Jamali and Karam, 2018), ranging from those in less developed countries, through the BRICS (Brazil, Russia, India, China, South Africa), and to other more developed countries. These analyses obviously bring very different settings of national business systems predicated in turn on their distinctive systems of historic institutionalization. Moreover, they also bring very different forms of exposure to globalization, also reflecting their different political, financial, education and labour, and cultural systems, as well as more commercial considerations of their place in the emerging global value chains.

In many of these national business systems much of the recent CSR development has been 'led' by institutions encouraging eCSR, or at least there are rapid attempts to 'superimpose' eCSR systems (e.g., reporting systems and regulations; models of shared value) on extant iCSR systems. Key actors in these transitions, ironically perhaps, are state agencies and supranational governmental bodies (such as the European Union) – which Matten and Moon (2008) associate primarily with a legacy role in establishing iCSR. In particular in Asia, most notably China, India and Indonesia, we have seen a quite active role of the state in mandating CSR, while other countries, such as Singapore and Malaysia, have seen softer forms of regulation, yet nonetheless a pronounced role of the state in furthering eCSR.

A number of studies have focused on the processes by which business organizations, companies and managers alike are grappling with balancing long-standing implicit assumptions, for example, about community obligations, with new CSR systems encouraging eCSR. Kim et al. (2013) illustrate how in the case of South Korea tensions have emerged for CSR managers seeking both to conform with long-standing implicit expectations and with new regulatory demands for more eCSR conformance, and they note how the new implicit/explicit balances of CSR differ among industrial sectors. More generally, much research in this area stresses the roles of implicit institutional factors in shaping the way in which eCSR is adopted.

Other studies have explored implicit–explicit CSR transitions where implicit systems were relatively weak or fragile, particularly in sub-Saharan

Africa. Reddy and Hamann (2016) focus particularly on the disparate roles of the state in such circumstances, as well as home country environments and internal firm environments. Studies of CSR in China explore this transition predicated on different balances of state power and religious engagement (Du et al., 2016).

Conceptualizing then the dynamics of iCSR and eCSR, there are two fundamental trends visible globally.

- 'Explicitization'. Given the global trends of a general rise in eCSR discussed above, what we find in areas where companies were traditionally and historically more strongly exposed to an iCSR approach is that these companies re-define, re-brand and re-narrate their iCSR practices in terms of eCSR. There are a number of regions of the globe where this is particularly visible. If one sifts through non-financial reports, or analyses eCSR practices of many German, French, Italian or Scandinavian countries, one will find substantial amounts of social performance indicators related to environmental protection, healthcare contributions or workers' protection and participation. All these are long-standing practices of iCSR of those companies. Many of these are multinationals, or at least companies with a strong export business, and they operate in organizational fields that have made eCSR a standard mimetic practice. We also see these developments in new, or less institutionalized markets, such as newly privatized public services or new technologies. What these companies do then is define as explicit what they have traditionally done as part of the implicit expectations of their institutional environment. Another good example are Indian companies (and indeed those from other developing/emerging economies), many of which for centuries have provided welfare state emulation as part of traditional, nationalistic, often religiously motivated or tribally incentivized sets of informal institutions. Now being more exposed to global organizational fields, these companies are reframing their existing iCSR practices in terms of eCSR. Probably the most well-documented example is the TATA organization, which for close to one and a half centuries has practised iCSR, and now operates a sophisticated system of, what they call, sustainability management as a form of eCSR (Elankumaran et al., 2005).
- 'Implicitization'. In many countries and regions where iCSR has been a more long-standing form of organizing business participation and responsibility for the wider public good, we have also seen the opposite phenomenon. Governments, industry associations, labour representatives and other civil society actors have reacted to the rise

and spread of eCSR with an approach that we would conceptualize as implicitization of eCSR. There are numerous examples. Early on, the UK government created a number of initiatives to orchestrate eCSR through a CSR Academy and other coordinated incentives. Most European countries and the EU itself now have mandatory frameworks for non-financial reporting of companies – a classic eCSR practice. Trade unions and works councils – though reluctantly – have over the years become rather active in translating and importing eCSR practices into the existing frameworks of workers' participation. There are numerous industry associations that, for instance, adopted the ten principles of the United Nations (UN) Global Compact and turned them into quasi mandatory private forms of regulating their business members' social responsibility. This certainly applies to existing industrial relations systems, but also, more generally, to other neo-corporatist actors such as chambers of commerce, industry associations and non-governmental organizations. Many governments now run departments that coordinate and incentivize eCSR of companies, such as the Canadian Office of the Extractive Sector CSR Counsellor. Other governments have deployed stronger regulation to CSR, notably in China and in India, with the latter mandating large listed companies to invest 2 per cent of their pre-tax profits in eCSR. Common to all those approaches of implicitization is that businesses, governments, industry associations and civil society organizations' societal actors react to the global rise of eCSR by integrating and customizing it in a way that reflects long-standing entrenched iCSR practices and approaches.

2.6 IMPLICIT AND EXPLICIT CSR IN FORM AND CONTENT

More generally, one way of thinking about hybridization of implicit and explicit CSR is through the distinction between CSR's 'form' and 'content'. It appears that there has been an emergence of a CSR which reflects different implicit and explicit elements in the balance of its institutional form and content. At the national level there is increasing hybridization of implicit content and explicit form. This can result, for example, from the role of governmental agency in developing reporting regulations – usually relatively 'soft' – which by definition require corporations to be explicit by making reports about their CSR (i.e., an explicit form) that combine content which reflects long-standing national commitments (i.e., implicit CSR) with content which reflects global systems such as the UN Global

Compact Principles. Moreover, while the development and proliferation of explicit global systems of CSR, such as the Global Reporting Initiative and the ISO 26000, are undoubtedly proving influential, the question remains as to how these explicit forms of CSR are given content in different national business systems.

Such hybridization strategies can be identified on three basic levels.

2.6.1 Macro Level

Looking at governments, courts, industry associations and labour representatives in the 'implicit/explicit' CSR dichotomy and how these institutions shape business responsibility we see a rather complex picture. In some respects, over the last decade, it is the USA of all countries that has come up with quite substantial initiatives around enhancing iCSR. These initiatives were mostly prevalent in dealing with corporate irresponsibility. They include new regulation such as Dodd–Frank or the Bureau of Consumer Protection, but we could also point to the judicial approach taken against corporate irresponsibility by some of the banks during the financial crisis, the approach taken towards Siemens' corruption practices, or more contemporarily the approach towards Volkswagen's fraudulent practices. In a similar vein, we also saw a diplomatic approach in threatening trade sanctions against Bangladesh in 2013 in the aftermath of the Rana Plaza accident. A similar appetite of stronger state institutions in dealing with corporate irresponsibility has been visible in the European Union (EU), where the DG Competition has been rather forceful in reacting to tax evasion and monopoly concerns against many American companies (Chenou and Radu, 2019).

At the same time, as discussed above, governments are also increasingly active in regulation and coordination of eCSR and endorsing new forms of CSR, facilitating collective action and incentivizing multisector partnerships (Kourala et al., 2019). It is here where we see the most important forms of hybrid CSR, as we elaborate further below.

Ultimately, we are also continuing to see an intensive set of initiatives by business to use eCSR as a potential way of anticipating and preventing new approaches of iCSR. Maybe the recent reaction of companies to the abandoning of the Paris Climate Change Agreement by the US government is the most striking example. Certainly, large corporations with business activities at a global level have shown little interest to abandon their voluntary policies and practices, well aware that long term, and in certain jurisdictions even sooner, new regulation is very likely to emerge and to tighten corporate discretion on socially responsible practices.

2.6.2 Micro Level

If we analyse activities on the micro level, that is, level of individual business actors, we see – as above – new hybrid forms emerging in the form of explicitized iCSR practices (Brown and Knudsen, 2015). As discussed above, we can definitely also see a trend towards a continued rise of eCSR practices globally, not least reflected and evidenced in many reports on the rise of eCSR in (business) education.

With regard to iCSR there is ample evidence that there is a global trend towards continued lobbying and business initiatives against more iCSR. The current US administration is probably the most interesting example, but also the way many British (based) companies have reacted to the Brexit decision exemplifies this. And as much as Dodd–Frank or the Affordable Care Act were new pushes towards iCSR, the general criticism has also not abated that much of the initial aspirations in politics were ultimately diluted by corporate influence. Examples from Europe and other parts of the globe similarly abound, a European example being the strong lobbying efforts of energy companies to work towards exemptions from the EU emission trading system (Eberlein and Matten, 2009).

2.6.3 Meso Level

The most interesting, and probably new level of corporate engagement in CSR is what we call the meso level, where forms of iCSR and eCSR are mixed and appear as a result of complex interactions with entrenched societal institutions and global pressures towards more independent voluntary corporate engagement for the public good. The new level of CSR whose growth and spread globally we have witnessed is a so-called meso level where CSR initiatives, policies, regulation, coordinated approaches emerge in a collaborative space between entrenched societal institutions of the national business systems and individual businesses and their CSR approach. In this space we also witness new processes of explicitization and implicitization.

The most obvious examples for meso level hybrid forms of CSR are the burgeoning of codes of conducts, the proliferation of private and public standards and best practices, self-regulation, mutual regulation and civil regulation. It is here where we see new forms of business contributions to societal governance. These forms of CSR are not simply pure eCSR as they have an element of collective agreement, coordinated response and are often shaped by existing modes of implicit allocation of social responsibility for business. At the same time, they are also not pure iCSR as the very existence of those new modes of CSR is clearly based on the pressures individual businesses face from wider embeddedness in (often global) organizational fields.

It is fair to say, looking at the literature, that those new forms of structuring eCSR activities in a meso space between nationally/regionally entrenched institutions and organizational fields are not absolutely new but have been emerging over the last two decades in many places globally. Over the last decade though this space has probably shown the strongest growth and increase and is now a substantially distinct governance realm that combines to those two elements of iCSR and eCSR. There are a number of criteria by which this space can be further subdivided and structured. From our reading of the literature, the most relevant criteria include:

- *Degree of coerciveness*: most of those voluntary, self-regulatory systems have some form of monitoring compliance and, in particular, sanctioning non-compliance. While, for instance, the UN Global Compact ultimately expels non-compliant signatory companies, other regulatory frameworks such as the Forest Stewardship Council have received continuous criticism for lax enforcements of standards (Turcotte et al., 2014).
- *Role of governments*: in some cases, governments have taken on an active role in setting up such voluntary regulatory systems such as the Extractive Industries Transparency Initiative (EITI). Many of these systems, however, have thrived entirely without governmental involvement, often facing fairly antagonistic attitudes of some governments.
- *Discretion of individual corporations*: some of those regulatory systems, in particular certification systems, prescribe fairly detailed practices to companies that are pursuing the adoption of such standards. Examples are the various Fairtrade labels or sustainability indexes (e.g., FTSE4GOOD, Dow Jones Sustainability Index) which at times ask for fairly detailed measures and practices on the ground. Other systems leave more discretion to individual actors and are meant more as generally guiding principles rather than compliance-oriented standards. Examples are the Equator Principles or the UN Principles for Responsible Investment.
- *Role of trade unions and civil society*: a constant tension, especially for business, seems to be the degree to which other pivotal societal actors have an active and authoritative role in the process of designing and implementing such private regulatory systems. While some systems, such as the Mining Association of Canada's 'Towards Sustainable Mining' programme, has been criticized for being a mostly industry-driven and directed venture, other systems, such

as the ISO 26000 norms, have been part of a long and painstaking process of integrating the voices and demands of all stakeholders involved and affected by such norms.

- *Legal systems, especially litigation cultures*: there is a marked difference in adoption of those standards between regions and countries that are governed either by common law or civil law systems. The relative underrepresentation of US American companies in the UN Global Compact, for instance, can be understood by the simple reality that a potential commitment to the ten principles might expose an American company to significantly higher risks of litigation than companies from other parts of the world. A similar argument can also be made to the quite distinctly different reactions to the Rana Plaza incident in 2013 in Bangladesh, where mostly European companies engaged in a multistakeholder process ('Accord') while most of the North American companies involved engaged in different approach ('Alliance'), with fewer commitments and less involvement of non-business stakeholders (Donaghey and Reinecke, 2018).

2.7 CONCLUSION

Our short foray into understanding the relationship and interplay between implicit and explicit CSR has left us with one main conclusion: that CSR is today, more often than not, a hybrid construct which comprises both aspects of CSR. What companies do with regard to their social responsibility is shaped, on the one hand, by institutional antecedents from both the national/regional context as well as the organizational field, and, on the other hand, by their voluntary, strategic intent to use their discretion in (global) markets to react to demands and expectations of stakeholders. This leads to three aspects worth highlighting:

First, we observe that indeed the global spread of (explicit) CSR has 'won the battle of ideas' (as *The Economist* warily observed in 2005) and voluntary CSR has taken a strong foothold in most economies and large businesses in most parts of the globe. Ironically, though, in many of the new institutionalized frameworks for CSR (e.g., codes, self-regulatory systems) we see that actors from contexts with high levels of implicit CSR play a dominant role in the creation of these new forms of explicit, voluntary CSR. In many parts of the world, this reflects new ways in which governments highlight and incorporate the voluntary elements in explicit CSR into an approach which covers a continuum between orchestrated voluntarism up to mandated legalized forms of CSR (and every other form of implicitization in between).

Second, our analysis further reveals that rather than seeing a unidirectional adoption – and thus dominance – of explicit CSR we rather see what we define as 'explicitization' of implicit elements of CSR. By this we describe a process in which long-standing formal and informal arrangements around the role of business in furthering the public good are integrated into the language, tools and processes of a globally standardized set of CSR practices. This phenomenon is not only interesting as it challenges simplistic accounts of 'globalization' or 'Americanization' of global business, but also represents a 'bottom up' theorization of the global spread of local management practices which Birkinshaw (2000) and others observed and theorized in the field of international business more than two decades ago (Gutierrez Huerter et al., forthcoming).

Third, and finally, our analysis leads to one observation that might inform a future research agenda in this space. If all CSR is hybrid in nature, we could well ask whether what we initially conceptualized as explicit CSR, that is, CSR that originates and stems from liberal market economies, is just one expression of a specific institutional framework of those economies. Our initial intent in the 2008 paper was to differentiate between US-style CSR and European (and to a lesser degree Rest-of-the-World) CSR. With a ten-year distance though, and looking at the reception of the concept in the literature, it could be argued that even US-style CSR is just a reflection of companies being embedded in a particular business system, that prizes individualism, discretionary agency and isolated agency of economic actors – and hence leads to a response to demands for social responsibility that take the shape of explicit CSR. In that sense, then, what we initially conceptualized as 'explicit' CSR is hardly more than a version of 'implicit' CSR, albeit in reflection of the embeddedness in a liberal market economy such as the USA. Elements of explicit CSR then reflect an institutional embeddedness that values, just to name a few aspects, philanthropy, managerial stewardship, compliance with the law ('doing the right thing'), individualism or entrepreneurial freedom as elements of a societal consensus on the social role and responsibilities of business. It remains, therefore, a question for future research and for developments in the field in how far such a distinction will continue to be a useful and actionable concept in categorizing CSR in a comparative perspective. For further analysis of these themes, see Matten and Moon (2020).

REFERENCES

Berthoin Antal, A., Oppen, M. and Sobczak, A. (2009). (Re)discovering the social responsibility of business in Germany. *Journal of Business Ethics*, **89**(suppl. 3), 285–301.

Birkinshaw, J. (2000). *Entrepreneurship in the Global Firm*. London: Sage Publications.

Boswell, J. (1983). The informal social control of business in Britain: 1880–1939. *Business History Review*, **57**(2), 237–57.

Brown, D. and Knudsen, J.S. (2015). Domestic institutions and market pressures as drivers of corporate social responsibility: company initiatives in Denmark and the UK. *Political Studies*, **63**(1), 181–201.

Carson, S.G., Hagen, Ø. and Sethi, S.P. (2015). From implicit to explicit CSR in a Scandinavian context: the cases of HÅG and Hydro. *Journal of Business Ethics*, **127**(1), 17–31.

Chenou, J.M. and Radu, R. (2019). The 'right to be forgotten': negotiating public and private ordering in the European Union. *Business & Society*, **58**(1), 74–102.

DiMaggio, P.J. and Powell, W.W. (1983). The iron cage revisited: institutional isomorphism and collective rationality in organizational fields. *American Sociological Review*, **48**(April), 147–60.

Djelic, M.L. and Etchanchu, H. (2017). Contextualizing corporate political responsibilities: neoliberal CSR in historical perspective. *Journal of Business Ethics*, **142**(4), 641–61.

Donaghey, J. and Reinecke, J. (2018). When industrial democracy meets corporate social responsibility – a comparison of the Bangladesh accord and alliance as responses to the Rana Plaza disaster. *British Journal of Industrial Relations*, **56**(1), 14–42.

Du, X., Chang, Y., Zeng, Q., Du, Y. and Pei, H. (2016). Corporate environmental responsibility (CER) weakness, media coverage, and corporate philanthropy: evidence from China. *Asia Pacific Journal of Management*, **33**(2), 551–81.

Eberlein, B. and Matten, D. (2009). Business responses to climate change regulation in Canada and Germany: lessons for MNCs from emerging economies. *Journal of Business Ethics*, **86**(2), 241–55.

Elankumaran, S., Seal, R. and Hashmi, A. (2005). Transcending transformation: enlightening endeavours at Tata Steel. *Journal of Business Ethics*, **59**(1), 109–19.

Flyverbom, M., Deibert, R. and Matten, D. (2019). The governance of digital technology, big data, and the internet: new roles and responsibilities for business. *Business & Society*, **58**(1), 3–19.

Furnari, S. (2014). Interstitial spaces: microinteraction settings and the genesis of new practices between institutional fields. *Academy of Management Review*, **39**(4), 439–62.

Gjølberg, M. (2009). Measuring the immeasurable? Constructing an index of CSR performance in 20 countries. *Scandinavian Journal of Management*, **25**(1), 10–22.

Gond, J.-P., Kang. N. and Moon, J. (2011). The government of self-regulation: on the comparative dynamics of corporate social responsibility. *Economy and Society*, **40**(4), 640–71.

Gutierrez Huerter, G., Moon, J., Gold, S. and Chapple, W. (forthcoming). Micro-processes of translation in the transfer of practices from MNE headquarters to

foreign subsidiaries: the role of subsidiary translators. *Journal of International Business Studies*.
Hiss, S. (2009). From implicit to explicit *Corporate Social Responsibility*: institutional change as a fight for myths. *Business Ethics Quarterly*, **19**(3), 433–51.
Husted, B.W. (2015). Corporate social responsibility practice from 1800–1914: past initiatives and current debates. *Business Ethics Quarterly*, **25**(1), 125–41.
Jamali, D. and Karam, C. (2018). Corporate social responsibility in developing countries as an emerging field of study. *International Journal of Management Reviews*, **20**(1), 32–61.
Kaplan, R. (2014). Who has been regulating whom, business or society? The mid-20th-century institutionalization of 'corporate responsibility' in the USA. *Socio-Economic Review*, **13**(1), 125–55.
Kim, C.H., Amaeschi, K., Harris, A. and Shu, C. (2013). CSR and the national institutional context: the case of South Korea. *Journal of Business Research*, **66**(12), 2581–91.
Knudsen, J.S. and Moon, J. (2017). *Visible Hands: Government Regulation and International Business Responsibility*. Cambridge: Cambridge University Press.
Kourula, A., Moon, J., Salles-Djelic, M.-L. and Wickert, C. (2019). New roles of governments in the governance of business conduct: implications for management and organizational research. *Organization Studies*, **40**(8), 1101–23.
Kujala, J., Rehbein, K., Toikka, T. and Enroth, J. (2013). Researching the gap between strategic and operational levels of corporate responsibility. *Baltic Journal of Management*, **8**(2), 142–65.
Matten, D. and Moon, J. (2005). 'Implicit' and 'explicit' CSR: a conceptual framework for understanding CSR in Europe. In A. Habisch, J. Jonker, M. Wegner and R. Schmidpeter (eds), *CSR Across Europe*. Berlin: Springer-Verlag, pp. 335–56.
Matten, D. and Moon, J. (2008). 'Implicit' and 'explicit' CSR: a conceptual framework for a comparative understanding of corporate social responsibility. *Academy of Management Review*, **33**(2), 404–24.
Matten, D. and Moon, J. (2020). Reflections on the 2018 Award: the meaning and dynamics of corporate social responsibility. *Academy of Management Review*, **44**(1).
McWilliams, A. and Siegel, D. (2001). Corporate social responsibility: a theory of the firm perspective. *Academy of Management Review*, **26**(1), 117–27.
Meyer, J.W. (2000). Globalization: sources and effects on national states and societies. *International Sociology*, **15**, 233–48.
Moon, J. (2005). United Kingdom. In A. Habisch, J. Jonker, M. Wegner and R. Schmidpeter (eds), *Corporate Social Responsibility Across Europe*. Berlin: Springer-Verlag, pp. 51–65.
Moon, J., Murphy, L. and Gond, J.-P. (2017). Historical perspectives on corporate social responsibility. In A. Rasche, M. Morsing and J. Moon (eds), *Corporate Social Responsibility*. Cambridge: Cambridge University Press, pp. 31–62.
Rasche, A., De Bakker, F.G. and Moon, J. (2013). Complete and partial organizing for corporate social responsibility. *Journal of Business Ethics*, **115**(4), 651–63.
Reddy, C.D. and Hamann, R. (2016). Distance makes the (committed) heart grow colder: MNEs' responses to the state logic in African variants of CSR. *Business & Society*. doi: 0007650316629127.
Scherer, A.G. and Palazzo, G. (2011), The new political role of business in a globalized world: a review of a new perspective on CSR and its implications for

the firm, governance, and democracy. *Journal of Management Studies*, **48**(4), 899–931.

Schmeltz, L. (2014). Identical or just compatible? The utility of corporate identity values in communicating corporate social responsibility. *International Journal of Business Communication*. doi: 2329488414525439.

Silberhorn, D. and Warren, R.C. (2007). Defining corporate social responsibility: a view from big companies in Germany and the UK. *European Business Review*, **19**(5), 352–72.

Strand, R. (2013). The chief officer of corporate social responsibility: a study of its presence in top management teams. *Journal of Business Ethics*, **112**(4), 721–34.

Strand, R., Freeman, R.E. and Hockerts, K. (2015). Corporate social responsibility and sustainability in Scandinavia: an overview. *Journal of Business Ethics*, **127**(1), 1–15.

Turcotte, M.F., Reinecke, J. and den Hond, F. (2014). Explaining variation in the multiplicity of private social and environmental regulation: a multi-case integration across the coffee, forestry and textile sectors. *Business and Politics*, **16**(1), 151–89.

Ursin, L., Myskja, B.K. and Carson, S.G. (2016). Think global, buy national: CRC, cooperatives and consumer concerns in the Norwegian food value chain. *Journal of Agricultural and Environmental Ethics*, **29**(3), 387–405.

Whitley, R. (1999). *Divergent Capitalisms: The Social Structuring and Change of Business Systems*. Oxford: Oxford University Press.

Witt, M.A. and Redding, G. (2013). Asian business systems: institutional comparison, clusters and implications for varieties of capitalism and business systems theory. *Socio-Economic Review*, **11**(2), 265–300.

3. Business ethics as critical thinking: moral motivations and the limits of ethics

Zsolt Boda

3.1 INTRODUCTION: BUSINESS ETHICS AS CRITICAL THINKING

Business ethics as a field of applied ethics has been focusing on the organizational level of economizing and its social, environmental and ethical effects. However, I would argue that business ethics is much more than a special field of applied ethics: it is a discipline that contributes to our understanding of the nature of today's business by undertaking descriptive, analytical, normative, therapeutic and critical approaches.

Business ethics, like any other discipline, has a descriptive and analytical side. It describes the modern corporation as being embedded in a web of complex social interactions with its stakeholders. Business ethics portrays the company as a social institution, influenced by the norms and shared values of the broader community, and the moral commitments and beliefs of the individuals. This vision and the analytical concepts help to analyse, understand and explain some phenomena of today's business – like conflicts with stakeholders, the level of trust in different organizations and so on. Some analytical models of business ethics are appropriate to help make predictions about future events.

Business ethics obviously has a normative, or in Aristotelian term, pragmatic dimension as well. In his *Nicomachean Ethics* Aristotle made a distinction between theoretical, technical and pragmatic knowledge. For him, philosophy and metaphysics were examples of the theoretical disciplines, while technical disciplines were those which dealt with the objective, physical world. Ethics, together with politics and economics – and we may add management studies – belong to the pragmatic disciplines because they are concerned with human behavior, and make prescriptions as to how people ought to behave in certain situations: "it is a true state, reasoned, and capable of action with regard to things that are good or bad for man. We consider that this quality belongs to those who understand the management of households or states" (N.E. 1140a24–1140b12).

Of course, politics and economic studies limit themselves to their specific fields. For instance, economics defines the objective (which is welfare) of economic behavior and suggests the best means to achieve it. Managerial studies deal with a set of desirable managerial outcomes (like profitability, growing sales, efficient organization) and provide practical tools and procedures to achieve them. Ethics defines the desirable human behavior more broadly, in terms of good, right and just. Although business ethics obviously limits itself to the field of business, this self-limitation concerns only the field of inquiry, not the objectives which are still defined in ethical terms. However, it is important to stress that business ethics is not the only pragmatic (normative) discipline which deals with business – in a different conceptual framework management studies do the same.

Normative considerations are, of course, intertwined with the analytical concepts developed and used by business ethics. Even the notion of stakeholder which was initially applied in a strategic management context gets filled with value content when employed by business ethics. Other concepts, like that of corporate social responsibility (CSR) or corporate citizen, are clearly value-laden terms. But the practical character of business ethics in the Aristotelian sense is best illustrated by tools and solutions like stakeholder management models, ethical institutions and responsible decision-making algorithms.

Business ethics as an applied discipline may also have a therapeutic function. As Ian Mitroff put it in his *Smart Thinking for Crazy Times*, "the vast majority of today's organizations are deeply dysfunctional . . ." and "like alcoholics, many of today's organizations exhibit behaviors akin to those found in dysfunctional families: denial; dishonesty; faulty reasoning processes; psychological, physical and sexual abuse; and so on" (Mitroff, 1998, p. 150). According to Mitroff, ethical management can help to rediscover meaning and truth in an organization's life, and may lead to a spiritual recovery.

But I would argue that besides its descriptive, analytical, pragmatic and therapeutic dimensions, business ethics provides also ways to think critically about today's business. Critical thinking is always a systemic thinking, because it transcends the usual limits of the "problem-solving" activity of a normal discipline, it does not accept the predefined delineation of the field. Mitroff associates critical thinking to the aptitude to avoid what he calls "the error of the third kind": solving the wrong problem precisely (Mitroff, 1998). Phrasing a problem incorrectly, setting its boundaries too narrowly or failing to think systematically can lead to committing the error of the third kind, just as picking the wrong stakeholders or selecting a too narrow set of options can.

Critical thinking means that we open up new perspectives, and therefore we reinterpret the system we are studying. Critical thinking may also mean that we use normative concepts, and we provide ground for (re)evaluating the elements of the system or the concepts describing it. As Peter Ulrich put it: "Business ethics is more than just 'applied ethics' . . . The primary task of an 'integrative' business ethics is to reflect on the form of economic reasoning – it is the critique of economic reason" (Ulrich, 2002, p.9). Business ethics is, by definition, a transdisciplinary enterprise: it tries to merge the concepts of ethics with that of business; but it also relies on psychology, sociology and other studies. It is also a normative discipline. It should be, by definition, a critical enterprise which raises fundamental questions about, for instance, the business and society problematic, the ecological unsustainability of today's business, or the justice and fairness implications of economic globalization dominated by big companies.

Of course, critical thinking should not degenerate into unreflective moralizing or giving biased accounts about today's business. There are no easy ways to decide whether one deals with the wrong or the right problem. In critical thinking, just as in any other activities, we need the basic virtue of *phronesis*, practical wisdom, in order to find the right balance between the extremes. Being too critical may undermine the academic (descriptive and analytical) nature of business ethics and may lead to unfounded claims. But uncritical business ethics becomes a mere "apologetic enterprise," which suggests already by its name that business and ethics belong naturally together (see Zsolnai and Tencati, 2010). Business studies are generally "apologetic" in a sense that they accept the business game as a legitimate one, and even try to make it more efficient in its own terms. However, business ethics brings into the picture the legitimizing potential of the noble tradition of ethics. Do we believe that business could be legitimized without any problem with a reference to ethics? In other words, do we believe that today's global and incorporated business is, or can be, fundamentally ethical? These are difficult questions. I believe that business ethics should help us to better understand to what extent, when and why business is *not* ethical. Which is *also* the case. And when studying business ethics we should inquire about the core activities and systemic patterns of today's business as well, not just the accidental wrongdoings of some individuals.

In the following I illustrate the critical approach in business ethics through briefly analysing two partly interrelated problems that, I believe, business ethics should devote more attention to: the question of why be ethical and the limits of the ethical approach in addressing climate change, today's most pressing social challenge. They are interrelated in the sense that both refer to a boundary problem of business ethics: what it can and cannot achieve.

3.2 WHY BE ETHICAL?

The concepts of business ethics help to answer the question "what is to be ethical?" Answering this question has been a fundamental endeavor in modern ethics, at least since Immanuel Kant. The individual in modern society is not guided anymore by the well-defined norms of closed communities; she is bound to make choices and the traditional moral beacons either become irrelevant or seem to offer little help in the increasing social complexity. Business ethics went a step further in contextualizing the "what is to be ethical" question, applying it to organizations or, broadly speaking, business. The novelty in the approach of business ethics is bringing into the light the problem of the company as a special-purpose organization and as a node in the network of stakeholders. While the Western ethical tradition has been first and foremost concerned by the individual, business ethics has been focusing on the organizational level.

Business ethics scholarship has devoted considerable efforts to provide insights on the "how" question, closely related to the previous one: how to build ethical institutions, how to manage stakeholders, make responsible decisions and so on (see, e.g., Donaldson, 1989; Zsolnai, 2008). However, any practical tool will be only used as long as the decision maker seeks an ethical way to solve her problem at hand; if she strives for a responsible alternative. Business ethics offers concepts, ideas, as well as useful practical tools for those who are not exclusively self-interested, but take into account the moral implications of their acting.

But there is another, equally important, fundamental problem in ethics: "why be ethical?" Note that arguing that moral implications are inseparable from any action, including business decisions, does not answer this question. The CSR paradigm and mainstream business ethics have employed this argument in order to legitimize the ethics case for business (see Goodpaster and Matthews, 1982). However, even if one accepts this argument the question remains: why would a manager take into account the moral implications of her decisions instead of focusing exclusively on business objectives? It goes without saying that the "why" dilemma is a fundamental one for the prospects of ethical behavior.

However, business ethics has not devoted enough attention to address it and develop convincing arguments. Four basic approaches can be identified in the literature: the "spirituality," the "moral being," the "external factors" and the "ethical leadership" arguments.

3.2.1 Spirituality

Religion, religious teaching and religious faith have always been a powerful source of morality. For believers God or the transcendental origin give morality an ultimate justification. Judaism, Christianity, Islam and Buddhism have all developed norms and values concerning economic activities and continue to provide moral guidance to their followers (see Bouckaert and Zsolnai, 2011). However, one may point to secularization trends and the diminishing role of organized religions in modern societies. But the role of spirituality is not limited to organized religions and religious faith.

The Spirituality in Economic and Society network initiated by Luk Bouckaert and Laszlo Zsolnai, which recently founded the SPES institute, interprets spirituality in a broad sense, including the sense of connectedness to others; a search for a deep meaning of life; empathy for other living beings; a desire for being in touch with the source of life/God.

Why spirituality then? One may see some analogies between art and spirituality in their potential to help self-reflection, distantiation and ultimately creativity. Spirituality can play a role in business education, developing more conscientious leaders who make better use of their mental, emotional and spiritual resources and therefore are better equipped to make complex decisions and behave ethically in the workplace (Illés and Zsolnai, 2015).

But most importantly, spirituality may act as a "major motivational force" to behave in an ethical way (Zsolnai, 2010). In other words: spirituality is a powerful answer to the "why be ethical" question. "Ethical initiatives in business fail if they are not based on genuine ethical commitments. Serving the well-being of communities, nature and future generations requires *authentic care* (emphasis in the original), which may develop from experiential one-ness with others and with the universal source of creation" (Zsolnai, 2010, p. 89). Indeed, spirituality at the workplace was found to improve organizational performance, including ethical performance (Garcia-Zamor, 2003).

However, employing spirituality at the institutional, organizational level raises a number of issues. Many regard spirituality as a strictly personal matter and are reluctant to follow externally imposed guidance. At a deeper level, it is indeed a question of whether spirituality can be taught or whether it is supposed to emanate from inner sources (Rothman, 2009). It may be accessible for some people, but not for others. Institutionalizing spirituality in the organization may also raise problems concerning basic rights (like the freedom of conscience) and, especially in public bodies, the norm of the state-church separation. Therefore, although spirituality is present in modern, secularized societies, its role in grounding morality will remain limited.

3.2.2 The "Moral Being" Argument

It is an age-old observation that all persons naturally possess the capacity of distinguishing between right and wrong. Although both Aristotle and Kant would agree that this capacity can and should be improved, it is there in every normal person. Also, all persons possess an inner inclination to use their moral capacity. Even Kant, who founded ethics on rational grounds, admitted that an inner commitment to morality arising from the conscience is a prerequisite of the activation of moral judgement (Sullivan, 1994). Happily, we all have conscience, therefore, as Bertold Brecht put it in the *Caucasian Chalk Circle*: "Terrible is the temptation to do good!"

If people are moral beings, so are managers, business leaders, employees, investors, consumers and so on – they are all tempted to make moral choices. Research has indeed proven that there is a surprisingly high probability that people cooperate in prisoners' dilemma situations; contribute to the common good; devote considerable effort to help others against their own interest even in business-like situations when money is at stake (Etzioni, 1988; Frank, 2014; Frey and Osterloh, 2005). In this perspective the real question is not so much "why people act morally?" rather "what makes them act immorally?" Not surprisingly external temptation, especially money, was found to have the capacity of eroding or crowding out inner moral motivations (Frey and Osterloh, 2005; Marwell and Ames, 1981). As success in business is primarily measured by money, business puts people in an ethically risky situation.

However, since we are essentially moral beings, even despite strong external motivations ethically challenging choices are hard to make. Systematically violating basic norms may destroy the mental health of the perpetrator – as the story of Macbeth in Shakespeare's drama illustrates the point. That is why people need to use psychological mechanisms that help moral disengagement in those situations – Albert Bandura's social cognitive theory of moral agency can explain how otherwise pro-social managers adopt socially injurious corporate practices by distantiating themselves from the act itself, disregarding consequences, dehumanizing and blaming victims (Bandura et al., 2000). The fact that we need those supports suggests that trying to be ethical is inscribed into human nature.

Assuming that there is an external motivation to do the wrong thing, what are the factors that are in play in the struggle of moral conscience and the temptation? Some are inner factors like the moral psychological profile, or to put it simply, the moral character of the actor (Reynolds and Ceranic, 2007). Robert Frank argues that the moral psychological profile of college freshmen proved to be the most important factor in shaping their choices to find jobs as graduates. Those with stronger moral commitment were more likely to work for non-governmental organizations or in the public sector and less likely to work for business (Frank, 2014).

But we know that moral character is not immutable. Following Aristotle and Kant, the moral character and moral knowledge can be developed by practicing virtues. A similar approach points to the role of the identity of managers. James March argued that self-image and personal identity largely determine decisions: we make choices based on who we think we are (March, 2006). The strength of identity is also illustrated by the fact that managers' immoral actions are less constrained by the severity of sanctions and more by the prospect of being associated with the wrongdoing (Smith et al., 2007). Identity, just as moral character, is the result of interactions between external and internal factors.

However, moral character can also weaken. What if there are no role models to follow; the environment does not expect us to practice virtues; and our professional identity does not include strong ethical clues? Indeed, today business as a profession has a low ethical standing in the eyes of both the public and the practitioners (Frank, 2014), as a number of survey results show. Changing this for the better through responsible business education and developing the ethics of the business profession could reinforce the inner ethical source for responsible choices (Zsolnai, 2016). But in the meantime we have to admit that although our inner morality is the ultimate guardian against unethical behavior, it is an unreliable guardian in many instances – largely so because it is subject to external influences.

3.2.3 External Factors

Today's business does not necessarily provide a favorable environment for reinforcing inner moral inclinations, to say the least. Indeed, it is a source of many temptations, expectations and feedback mechanisms that push towards ethically questionable decisions. Fortunately, some external factors may, at least partly, counterbalance these tendencies. In the following. we consider the role of norms and communities, stakeholders and organizational culture as well as the possibility of the business case for ethics.

In his groundbreaking study on children's moral development, Piaget (1932) differentiated between two stages of moral thinking: heteronomous and autonomous morality. The former, typically present in children aged under ten, relies on expectations, rules and norms imposed from the outside, while the latter involves a more independent moral judgement. To what extent Piaget's theory of moral development is valid or not is not an issue here. The point is that social norms are important clues in moral thinking and action. In a similar vein, ethologist Vilmos Csányi argues that an important feature of human nature is our propensity to follow norms (Csányi, 1999).

The role of social norms and expectations in shaping behavior is particularly strong in the life-world of more or less closed, pre-modern communities. Following the norms of the community is the *sine qua non* of being and remaining a member of it (MacIntyre, 1984). But in modern, individualized societies the role of communities as either provider or guardian of morality is diminishing; people can or, as the Homo Oeconomicus model, the behavioral model of modern economics suggests, should follow their own interests, regardless of the consequences to others.

Now, communitarian thinkers, like Etzioni or Charles Taylor, argue that communities are still important in the constitution of both the self and society; that the modern person is not as desperately individualistic as her self-image portrays (Etzioni, 1988; Taylor, 1989). If empirical studies suggest that the prevalence of selfish behavior is lower than the economic theory model predicts, it is certainly partly because people take into consideration what other members of their relevant communities expect from them.

However, the question is: which are the relevant communities and what do they expect from us? In modern society, communities are numerous and their norm-systems may be conflicting with each other – one can or, better, should choose between them. If the rules of the game of the business community, organizational norms and corporate culture pressurize decision makers into choosing high profit–low ethics alternatives then it becomes difficult to act otherwise. However, other communities, like that of different stakeholders, family or society at large may uphold different norms and values than the business community. Business actors are members of those social communities which provide social support, or even pressures, towards more ethical choices. It means that social expectations can predict either ethical or irresponsible decisions.

From an individual point of view the company also acts as a kind of community which has a specific organizational culture, with specific norms prescribing certain types of behavior. The virtue ethics approach in business ethics builds on the assumption that corporate culture has an effect on the ethicality of decisions: a responsible company provides circumstances that increase the probability of morally right choices (Solomon, 2003).

However, organizational culture is not the final answer because it is not evident that a company develops a responsible way of functioning. Why would a company become ethical? The "external factor" argument points to emerging social forces and stakeholder activity that incite or even force companies to take their social responsibility seriously. Civil society organizations, using varied means ranging from cooperation to conflict, spur and assist corporations to become more sustainable (Bendell, 2000). In a number of cases both shareholders and employees have played an effective role in imposing moral, political or environmental expectations on companies. Ethical investors and ethical banks avoid bad companies, while providing funding to the responsible and sustainable ones (Soppe, 2010). Competitors, by adopting ethical standards and developing sustainable products, challenge corporations and force them to come up with new, innovative responses (Porter and van der Linde, 1995). Among stakeholders a special role was assigned to consumers. Ulrich Beck, the German sociologist, argued that while globalization and the free movement of capital undermined the power of trade unions, consumers are in a good position to influence global business (Beck, 1994). Consumers have been expected to express partly self-interested (such as in the case of bio-products which are supposed to be healthy), partly ethically motivated expectations towards corporations and use their power through conscious consumer decisions or boycotting to force companies to comply with them (see Boda and Gulyás, 2006).

These arguments lead to the "business case for ethics" approach: being ethical is also good business (Banerjee, 2008; Burke and Logsdon, 1996). Responsible and sustainable companies reach out to new markets of conscious and green consumers; have new investment opportunities; face lower financing and insurance costs due to lower risks associated with their operations; enjoy a good reputation among stakeholders; attract outstanding workforce and so on. Conversely, unethical companies are under growing pressures from their stakeholders; legal cases, media scandals and boycotts undermine their brand; are unable to employ people with high integrity; increased social and environmental risks associated with their operations imply higher insurance and investment costs as well as lower return on investment and so on.

In principle, the logic is impeccable – the question is whether it is supported by evidence. In reality, evidence on the positive ethical role of both the stakeholders and the market are sparse and contradictory; cases are hard to generalize. Responsible and relatively successful enterprises may flourish especially at the local level. It is indeed important that there are market niches for responsible, sustainable or progressive companies (see O'Higgins and Zsolnai, 2017). But, sadly, those niches are still quite small, despite the several decades-long developments on CSR and corporate sustainability – and the general picture of the corporate world is hardly convincing. Some flagships of "responsible companies" simply disappeared or were bought up by competitors, like Body Shop or Nokia; others fell into muddy waters after some time of fame – such as the example of BP and its disappointing story after announcing the "Beyond Petrol" program to the ecological disaster of the Mexican Gulf. Ethical market forces are too weak to become compelling for corporations: investors and competitors are not primarily motivated by ethical considerations. The same can be said about consumers. True, there have been some promising developments in the past years, like the rapid development of Fair Trade or organic agriculture. But overall, consumers send only weak signals to companies. People are concerned about the environment, criticize big companies and their mass products – at the same time, they enjoy the comfort and the choices of the consumer society. Consumer power is limited anyway to consumer goods and highly publicized brands (Klein, 1999). For instance, oil companies have always tried to do more in terms of environmental protection than other mining companies, simply because they are usually well-known brands, seen by people and the media. Given the rather dire account of the oil business in terms of human rights, local development and the environment, one can imagine how grim the general picture is for the totality of the mining sector.

Similar to the power of consumers, despite numerous progressive initiatives, struggles and lobbying, we must conclude that the influence of civil society on corporations has remained limited.

The social forces have ultimately failed to deliver the expected results in terms of improving ethical performance of corporations. Companies have been reluctant to make genuine ethical progress; the "business case" of CSR has remained weak; and stakeholders have been unable to pressurize companies to become socially responsible and ecologically sustainable. The structural features of the dominant business model have made it largely resistant to the challenge of CSR.

3.2.4 The Role of Ethical Leadership

Leadership is an effective way to achieve change in society, especially in complex situations characterized by conflicting interests, competing objectives and collective action problems (Burns, 1978). Leadership plays an important role in organizational change as well – and ethical leadership is able to transform a company's organizational culture (Toor and Ofori, 2009). Leadership is about the ability to motivate people and "moral leadership" motivates in the name of values and higher aims (Burns, 1978). Therefore, leadership may act as a major motivational force behind the ethical commitment of both individuals and organizations.

Now, leadership is an essentially mysterious phenomenon, as its mechanism is still not fully understood. How do some people become leaders? Why are others following them? The possible explanations abound. Leaders are sometimes assumed to possess particular individual skills or features, called charisma by Max Weber, that give them power over others and create the followership. But whether explained by charisma, a "fit" between the leader's aims and the followers' aspirations in a specific social context (Burns, 1978), a shared social identity (Haslam and Platow, 2001), some kind of collective rationality (Finkel et al., 1989) or emotions (Solomon, 2003), leadership never seems to be fully accounted for and preserves its essential mystery.

Leadership is mysterious in another sense as well: we don't know where it originates from; what makes a leader act as such and choose the particular direction she aims at. She may be led by a spiritual commitment – or a strong ambition to achieve recognition. She may respond to the call of a particular situation – or strive systematically for success. That is, the emergence of a leader is highly contingent. She may or may not show up in the critical moment, and she may change things for better – or worse.

3.2.5 The Contingency of Ethical Behavior in Business

To summarize the above: a company and its manager may choose to behave in a responsible, ethical way if spiritual inspiration suggests so; if essential, inner moral inclinations are not overshadowed by ethically dubious temptations; if external forces, like stakeholders and market opportunities, pull and push in the right direction; or if an ethical leader happens to offer guidance and motivation to do so. It is thus clear that ethical behavior in business is highly conditional and contingent.

But must this be a problem? One could argue that ethical behavior as such is always contingent: there are no ultimate guarantees against wrongdoing, just as there are no unchallengeable safeguards against law-breaking and crime.

However, there is a fundamental difference between the everyday situation and the business context. Human societies have evolved along those norms that make cooperation between people easier and, conversely, penalize uncooperative or otherwise disruptive behavior – for instance, no human society has ever developed a norm that telling lies is right (at least among the members of the relevant moral community – telling lies to strangers might be a different issue). Humans have developed a deep-rooted sensitivity to detect untrue intentions, cherish benevolence and outrage at perceived unfairness, already present in toddlers (Tomasello and Vaish, 2013). Society is conditioning us to follow those norms: we are sanctioned by our peers at very early ages if we do not abide by them; this is what we are taught by our parents and in school; this is what we are told about in church; this is upheld by public discourse and the laws and so on. In the case of a well-socialized, "normal" person the puzzle is not "why is she a moral person?" but rather the opposite: "why isn't she one?"

But this is not the case of modern, incorporated and global business, which, to use Karl Polanyi's term, has disembedded from society. As Boda and Zsolnai (2016) argue, the rules of the game, the institutional and ideational infrastructure of business largely disconnect it from the moral expectations of society.

First, at the core of the problem lies *the corporation* itself – as many have observed (see Bakan, 2005; Mayer, 2013; Stout, 2012). The corporation is a limited liability company permitting the owners to limit their liability for their business activities to the amount of capital subscribed to it. Limited liability means also limited moral liability – by nature, corporations and their owners have only limited responsibility. That there are many owners implies that individual shareholders do not necessarily have the power or simply the interest to control the corporation, influence decisions and hold the management accountable. They are interested in the dividend, that is, the return on their investment. Dispersed ownership means also a limited commitment towards the future of the company (one can sell one's shares any time) and aggravates the dangers of a hostile takeover (Mayer, 2013).

Second, today's extremely complex *financial system* makes ownership and accountability even more blurred and impersonal (see Epstein, 2005). True, if individual people are the shareholders, then there is a small chance for ethical action, as some examples of shareholder activism have demonstrated – very few examples though. However, nowadays not individuals, but institutional investors, investment funds and pension funds hold the large majority of corporate shares. Those funds – generally corporations also – are themselves managed according to the shareholder value myth and look for increasing profits at any cost. The financial system also acts as a principal evaluator of corporate performance. The core element of the shareholder value myth is the shareholder value, which is constructed by the financial market and its institutions: rating agencies, consulting firms, auditors, and finally the stock market itself (Stout, 2012). A complex institutional infrastructure that promises to evaluate corporate performance and that forces companies into an arms race for profit. Without a constant effort to increase profits and save on costs, companies are threatened with losing shareholder value and finally being discredited. Certainly, one of the most effective ways to save on costs is to externalize them, make them pay by nature, society and future generations (Daly, 2007; Princen, 1997).

Third, on top of the shareholder value myth and the operation of the financial system, corporations in addition face the consequences of *globalization* that separates corporate decisions and stakeholders, owners and workers, consumers and the places of production. This makes the externalization of costs (a polite way to say causing social and environmental problems and damages) easier. CEOs cannot be aware of what is happening down the long supply chain even if they really wanted to. However, we can safely assume that this is not the case. Shareholder value myth and competitive pressures are the guiding principles of decisions throughout the supply chain. Globalization therefore contributes to a shading of business activities and the externalization of production costs (Princen, 1997).

Externalization is made easy by the growing corporate power vis-à-vis society, especially in developing countries. Metaphorically speaking, globalization opens up new corridors of power (Jensen and Sandsröm, 2011). While corporations feel pressure from the financial markets to increase profits and are in fierce competition with other companies, they are in a comfortable power position when it comes to looking for investment opportunities, or state assistance for it. While it has been debated in the literature whether the effect of companies on softening labor and environmental regulation, that is, the "race to the bottom" thesis, could be generalized (Drezner, 2001; Vogel, 1995), there is certainly evidence to support it (Diamond, 2003).

Thus, the institutional setting of today's mainstream business helps to *dilute responsibility*, and therefore leads to an aggravation of the tragedy of the commons happening on a global scale. It is a system in which the pursuit of profits is the only ultimate goal and where the externalization of costs upon society, future generations and nature is not an unfortunate exception, but the rule. Businessmen caught by the logic of the system employ moral disengagement mechanisms on a daily basis to cope with the tension between the expectation of everyday morality and the logic of the market.

That is why the "why be ethical?" question is so relevant for business and that is why the contingency of ethics is, or should be, so disturbing in business ethics. While business ethics has studied some factors that may increase or decrease the probability of unethical corporate behavior, it has, I believe, avoided facing the reality that today's business – especially incorporated, global business – operates through rules, norms and institutions that systematically undermine the possibility of ethical choices.

Critical business ethics should be able to analyse the paradigm of today's business under this angle, identifying those ideational, normative, institutional building blocks of it that make genuinely pro-social and sustainable economizing almost impossible. Critical business ethics should contribute to the development of a new business paradigm founded in ecological sustainability and social well-being; as well as in a feasible balance between cooperation and competition, localization and globalization. Critical business ethics should develop new theories and concepts building on the work of precursors like Karl Polanyi, Ernst Schumacher and Herman Daly as well as the teaching of religions on the right way of economizing. Critical business ethics should study those institutional arrangements (like governance structures and partnerships between businesses and civil society organizations) as well as organizational solutions that may help to overcome the limitations of today's business system. Critical business ethics should devote particular attention to existing alternatives to mainstream business, like the Fair Trade movement, social entrepreneurs and the few progressive, pro-social and ecologically sustainable companies. Happily, some initiatives in business ethics point in these directions – however, mainstream business ethics has largely remained intact to these problems.

3.3 THE LIMITS OF ETHICS

In their paper on the limits of ethics in business Boda and Zsolnai (2016) argue that corporate transgressions are not exceptions, but everyday phenomena of today's business – the numerous corporate scandals of the past two decades and the growing literature of "corporate criticism" illustrate the point (see, e.g., Bakan, 2005; Klein, 1999; Korten, 1995). While these accounts are sometimes accused of presenting only occasional cases, "anecdotical evidences," academic writers have also contributed to this genre, providing thorough and critical analysis of today's business practices (see, e.g., Daly, 2007; Locke, 2013; Mayer, 2013; Milberg and Winkler, 2013; Sethi, 2011). In 1999 United Nations Secretary-General Kofi Annan called on multinational companies to embrace basic norms like respecting human rights, eliminating all forms of compulsory and forced labor, abolishing child labor. This was a recognition of the deep problems that characterize the functioning of the global economy. Kofi Annan argued that globalization was unsustainable and unfair. Unfortunately, this is still the case. Indeed, the Global Compact itself, launched by Kofi Annan, has proven to be largely ineffective in facing the problems it sought to address (Sethi, 2011; Soederberg, 2007). Our world is still environmentally unsustainable, struck by mass poverty, and full of corporate power abuses and illicit labor practices. "It is not an exaggeration to say that through their negligence, incompetence, greed, or fraud, corporations are a threat to our livelihood and the world we live in" (Mayer, 2013, p. 24).

In the previous section we overviewed some of the institutional causes of this dire state of affairs. Another issue, however, is the magnitude and urgency of the problems. Ethical solutions might be deemed ineffective not only because they collide with the rules of the game, but also because the pace of voluntary adjustments is painfully slow – certainly much slower than required.

A good example is that of climate change. In October 2018, the Intergovernmental Panel on Climate Change (IPCC) issued its latest report on global warming. The report presents evidence that the previous global warming goal to a maximum of 2°C was too high, and recommends a high of no more than 1.5°C. Given that we have already reached a 1°C rise in global temperature since pre-industrial times, meeting the new target implies that by 2030, our global CO_2 emissions should decrease to 45 percent of 2010 levels (IPCC, 2018). Needless to say, halving the global emissions in 12 years necessitates urgent and drastic measures for society and business. Patterns of both production and consumption must be fundamentally transformed across all sectors and activities including energy generation and use, housing, mining, agriculture and food, travel and transportation.

Even somebody believing in the transformational potential of ethics and voluntary compliance should admit that it is simply not enough just to execute changes at the required magnitude and pace. Unfortunately, it is increasingly doubtful that mankind is able to meet the challenge of climate change but if so, the solution will certainly include biding international treaties, major legal changes and new regulations across social domains.

I am convinced that ethics, and more particularly business ethics, cannot alone provide the solution to this immense challenge – however, it could and should contribute to the changes. First, ethical analysis can evaluate the moral weight of today's unsustainable social model and economic practices using concepts of environmental ethics and intergenerational justice theory, among others. Ethical evaluation may help in legitimizing the much-needed transformations by raising awareness about the ethical consequences of today's development model. Second, ethics should contribute to the formation of a new, sustainable business paradigm. Meeting the targets set by the IPCC requires more than a few technical, technological changes – such a comprehensive transformation needs new institutional arrangements, organizational models, systems of production and distribution, consumption styles and so on. Business ethics should have a role in developing concepts, values, norms and algorithms that provide support for the most important sustainability transformation of humanity ever. This role is similar to the one outlined previously in the chapter: contribution to the evolution of a new business paradigm.

3.4 CONCLUSIONS

Business ethics should take a critical stance towards existing business practices and a self-reflective stance towards its own transformational possibilities. Leadership in business ethics should imply acknowledging the limits of ethics in solving the most pressing problems of our times, and identify the approach that may yield a meaningful contribution to meeting the extraordinary social and environmental challenges humankind is faced with.

The chapter argues that business ethics should address two fundamental questions that have implications for its own role and possibilities.

First, why be ethical then when the business community and the rules of the game reward ruthless behavior through recognition and high monetary gains; and when we all have access to psychological mechanisms that help us to cope with the inner pain associated with unethical choices?

Second, what should be the role of ethics in contributing to the major sustainability transformation of human society and business?

Both questions refer to boundary problems of business ethics, pointing to limitations of the ethical approach as well as implying new tasks and challenges. The chapter argues that business ethics should move out of the box of the current business paradigm and contribute to the elaboration of a new one, in which the rules of the game are not in sharp contradiction with basic moral requirements and which provide support for the sustainability transformation humankind must undertake.

REFERENCES

Bakan, J. (2005), *The Corporation: The Pathological Pursuit of Profit and Power*, New York: Free Press.

Bandura, A., G.-V. Caprara, and L. Zsolnai (2000), “Corporate transgressions through moral disengagement,” *Journal of Human Values*, **6**(1), 57–64.

Banerjee, S.B. (2008), *Corporate Social Responsibility: The Good, the Bad, and the Ugly*, Cheltenham, UK and Northampton, MA, USA: Edward Elgar.

Beck, U. (1994), “The reinvention of politics: towards a theory of reflexive modernization,” in U. Beck, A. Giddens, and S. Lash (eds), *Reflexive Modernization: Politics, Tradition and Aesthetics in the Modern Social Order*, Oxford: Polity Press, pp. 1–34.

Bendell, J. (ed.) (2000), *Terms of Endearment: Business, NGOs and Sustainable Development*, Sheffield, UK: Greenleaf Publishing.

Boda, Z. and E. Gulyás (2006), “The ethical consumerism movement,” in L. Zsolnai (ed.), *Interdisciplinary Yearbook of Business Ethics*, Oxford: Peter Lang, pp. 141–53.

Boda, Z. and L. Zsolnai (2016), “The failure of business ethics,” *Society and Business Review*, **11**(1), 93–104.

Bouckaert, L. and L. Zsolnai (eds) (2011), *The Palgrave Handbook of Spirituality and Business*, London: Palgrave Macmillan.

Burke, L. and J.M. Logsdon (1996), “How corporate social responsibility pays off,” *Long Range Planning*, **29**(4), 495–502.

Burns, J.M. (1978), *Leadership*, New York: Harper and Row.
Csányi, V. (1999), *Az emberi természet. Humanetológia*, Budapest: Vince.
Daly, H. (2007), *Ecological Economics and Sustainable Development*, Cheltenham, UK and Northampton, MA, USA: Edward Elgar.
Diamond, S.F. (2003), "The 'race to the bottom' returns: China's challenge to the international labor movement," Cornell Law Faculty Working Papers, No. 10. http://scholarship.law.cornell.edu/clsops_papers/10 (accessed 16 June 2018).
Donaldson, T. (1989), *The Ethics of International Business*, New York, Oxford: Oxford University Press.
Drezner, W.D. (2001), "Globalization and Policy Convergence," *International Studies Review*, **3**(1), 53–78.
Epstein, G.A. (ed.) (2005), *Financialization and the World Economy*, Cheltenham, UK and Northampton, MA, USA: Edward Elgar.
Etzioni, A. (1988), *The Moral Dimension: Toward a New Economics*, New York: Free Press.
Finkel, S.E., E.N. Muller, and K.-D. Opp (1989), "Personal influence, collective rationality and mass political action," *American Political Science Review*, **83**(3), 885–903.
Frank, R.H. (2014), *What Price the Moral High Ground?* Princeton, NJ: Princeton University Press.
Frey, B. and M. Osterloh (2005), "Yes, managers should be paid like bureaucrats," *Journal of Management Inquiry*, **14**(1), 96–111.
Garcia-Zamor, J.C. (2003), "Workplace spirituality and organizational performance," *Public Administration Review*, **63**(3), 355–63.
Goodpaster, K.E. and J.B. Matthews (1982) "Can a corporation have a conscience?" *Harvard Business Review*, **60**(1), 132–41.
Haslam, S.A. and M.J. Platow (2001), "The link between leadership and followership: how affirming social identity translates vision into action," *Personality and Social Psychology Bulletin*, **27**(11), 1469–79.
Illés, K. and L. Zsolnai (2015), "The role of spirituality in business education," *Society and Business Review*, **10**(1), 67–75.
IPCC (2018), *Global Warming of 1.5°C*, IPCC. https://www.ipcc.ch/pdf/session48/pr_181008_P48_spm_en.pdf (accessed 8 January 2019).
Jensen, J. and J. Sandström (2011), "Stakeholder theory and globalization: the challenges of power and responsibility," *Organization Studies*, **32**(4), 473–88.
Klein, N. (1999), *No Logo*, New York: Picador.
Korten, D.C. (1995), *When Corporations Rule the World*, San Francisco, CA: Berrett-Koehler Publishers.
Locke, R.M. (2013), *The Promise and Limits of Private Power: Promoting Labor Standards in a Global Economy*, New York: Cambridge University Press.
MacIntyre, A. (1984), *After Virtue: A Study in Moral Theory*, Notre Dame, IN: Indianapolis University Press.
March, J.G. (2006), "The myth of rationality," in L. Zsolnai (ed.), *Interdisciplinary Yearbook of Business Ethics*, Oxford: Peter Lang, pp. 17–30.
Marwell, G. and R. Ames (1981), "Economists free ride, does anyone else?" *Journal of Public Economics*, **6**, 295–310.
Mayer, C. (2013), *Firm Commitment: Why the Corporation is Failing Us?* Oxford: Oxford University Press.
Milberg, W. and D. Winkler (2013), *Outsourcing Economics: Global Value Chains in Capitalist Development*, New York: Cambridge University Press.

Mitroff, I.I. (1998), *Smart Thinking for Crazy Times: The Art of Solving the Right Problem*, Oakland, CA: Berrett-Koehler Publishers.
O'Higgins, E. and L. Zsolnai (eds) (2017), *Progressive Business Models: Creating Sustainable and Pro-social Enterprise*, London: Palgrave Macmillan.
Piaget, J. (1932), *The Moral Judgment of the Child*, London: Kegan, Paul, Trench, Trubner & Co.
Porter, M.E. and C. van der Linde (1995), "Toward a new conception of the environment-competitiveness relationship," *Journal of Economic Perspectives*, **9**(4), 97–118.
Princen, T. (1997) "The shading and distancing of commerce: when internalization is not enough," *Ecological Economics*, **20**(3), 235–53.
Reynolds, S.J. and T.L. Ceranic (2007), "The effects of moral judgment and moral identity on moral behavior: an empirical examination of the moral individual," *Journal of Applied Psychology*, **92**(6), 1610–24.
Rothman, J. (2009), "Spirituality: what we can teach and how we can teach it," *Journal of Religion & Spirituality in Social Work: Social Thought*, **28**(1–2), 161–84.
Sethi, P. (ed.) (2011), *Globalization and Self-Regulation. The Crucial Role that Corporate Codes of Conduct Play in Global Business*, New York: Palgrave Macmillan.
Smith, N.C., S.S. Simpson, and C.Y. Huang (2007), "Why managers fail to do the right thing: an empirical study of unethical and illegal conduct," *Business Ethics Quarterly*, **17**(4), 633–67.
Soederberg, S. (2007), "Taming corporations or buttressing market-led development? a critical assessment of the Global Compact," *Globalizations*, **4**(4), 500–13.
Solomon, R.C. (2003), "Victims of circumstances? A defense of virtue ethics in business," *Business Ethics Quarterly*, **13**(1), 43–62.
Soppe, A. (2010), "Sustainable finance and ethics," in A. Tencati and L. Zsolnai (eds), *The Collaborative Enterprise: Creating Values for a Sustainable World*, Oxford: Peter Lang, pp. 77–96.
Stout, L. (2012), *The Shareholder Value Myth: How Putting Shareholders First Harms Investors, Corporations, and the Public*, Oakland, CA: Berrett Koehler Publishers.
Sullivan, R.J. (1994), *An Introduction to Kant's Ethics*, Cambridge: Cambridge University Press.
Taylor, C. (1989), *Sources of the Self. The Making of Modern Identity*, Cambridge, MA: Harvard University Press.
Tomasello, M. and A. Vaish (2013), "Origins of human cooperation and morality," *Annual Review of Psychology*, **64**, 231–55.
Toor, S. and G. Ofori (2009), "Ethical leadership: examining the relationships with full range leadership model, employee outcomes, and organizational culture," *Journal of Business Ethics*, **90**(4), 533–47.
Ulrich, P. (2002), "Ethics and economics," in L. Zsolnai (ed.), *Ethics in the Economy – Handbook of Business Ethics*, Oxford, Bern, Berlin, Bruxelles, Frankfurt am Main, New York, Vienna: Peter Lang, pp. 9–37.
Vogel, D. (1995), *Trading Up. Consumer and Environmental Regulation in a Global Economy*, Cambridge, MA: Harvard University Press.
Zsolnai, L. (2008), *Responsible Decision Making*, New Brunswick, NJ: Transaction Books.
Zsolnai, L (2010), "Ethics needs spirituality," in S.S. Nandram and M. Esther Borden (eds), *Spirituality and Business: Exploring Possibilities for a New*

Management Paradigm, Heidelberg, Dordrect, London, New York: Springer, pp. 87 90.

Zsolnai, L. (2016), "Ethics education of business leaders. emotional intelligence, virtues, and contemplative learning", *Journal of Management, Spirituality and Religion*, **13**(3), 266–8.

Zsolnai, L. and A. Tencati (2010), "Beyond Competitiveness," in A. Tencati and L. Zsolnai (eds), *The Collaborative Enterprise: Creating Values for a Sustainable World*, Oxford, Bern, Berlin, Brussels, Frankfurt am Main, New York, Vienna: Peter Lang, pp. 5–15.

4. Becoming responsible: understanding the organizational power dynamics of CSR and corporate ethics

Laura J. Spence and Steen Vallentin

We live in troubling times politically, socially and environmentally, and businesses have more and more to answer for. Hence, there is widespread and acute awareness of corporate (ir)responsibility in society. Awareness not only of how businesses can and should act responsibly and contribute to sustainable development, but also of how they often fail to do so in practice – even if they espouse social values and present themselves as good corporate citizens in corporate communication. One response to the problem of continued moral transgression by business is to look outside the corporate realm for answers, that is, to revisit the macro level systems/institutional frameworks in which businesses are embedded. Corporate responsibility then becomes a matter of public policy, defining the rules of the game based on democratic mandate. Given the current geopolitical turbulence and concerns regarding climate change, we anticipate renewed focus on regulations, standards and guidelines supporting responsible business behaviour. Yet we already have a vast network of serviceable hard and soft regulation in place. Often, what is lacking is proper implementation of regulations, standards and/or guidelines for responsibility. In other words, we have to look inside the organizational 'black box' to find answers to questions of why businesses manage to act responsibly or fail to act responsibly. We need better to understand the dynamics of corporate social responsibility (CSR). Indeed, we need to understand CSR as an ongoing process reflecting different levels of commitment and, in many cases, conflicts between different interests and rationalities in the organization. Instead of a view of CSR and CSR implementation that emphasizes consensus, harmony, unanimity, we believe there is value in contributing to a better understanding of the potentially conflictual – and thus political – nature of CSR as an organizational phenomenon.

In this chapter, we present a mainly conceptual analysis focusing on the micro level implementation of responsibility and ethics initiatives. We argue for the need to consider internal social responsibility implementation as a political process and use Michel Foucault's concept of governmentality as a means to problematize such processes. We do this by (a) emphasizing the contested and conflictual aspects of implementation and how social responsibility can be seen as invested with different powers; (b) showing how social responsibility can be considered as a mode of governing – a regime of practice – aiming to steer individuals and collectives in complex ways; (c) indicating how corporate responsibilization both relates to and transcends codification; (d) showing how social responsibility implementation involves processes of translation. We use the term 'responsibilization' to indicate that the becoming-more-responsible and better aligned with societal demands and expectations is not something that can be imposed effectively from the outside. It is a process that hinges on the willingness and ability of management and employees to make it happen. Although the contribution of the chapter is mainly conceptual, we use the case of the BP Deepwater Horizon incident as an illustration of our analytical points. In doing so we suggest that good rules are not the answer to mitigating troubled times in isolation.

4.1 FOCUS ON IMPLEMENTATION OF SOCIAL RESPONSIBILITY AND ETHICS

Our starting point is that prior research has largely neglected to consider the political aspects of managing and implementing CSR, which we focus on as the corporate manifestation of business ethics. Whereas issues of power are routinely addressed in the business ethics and CSR literature in the sense that corporate activity is largely considered to be a product of external – market and non-market related – social pressures and influences (Gond and Nyberg, 2017), the intricacies of the *internal* power dynamics have received less attention. CSR is most often considered as a boundary issue related to (external) stakeholders and stakeholder pressure, while the limited extant work on (internal) CSR implementation consists primarily of empirical research and case studies (see, e.g., Blair-Loy et al., 2011; Bondy, 2008; Lindgreen et al., 2009). A recent movement to look at what have been called the micro-foundations of CSR indicates a readiness to take a closer look at the internal workings of the firm, though the focus tends to be on the most senior executives (cf. Hafenbrädl and Waeger, 2017; Maak et al., 2016).

In studies of implementation, CSR tends to be viewed as an organizational strategy issue exercised by top-down managerial problem solving

(Nord and Fuller, 2009). To the extent that process issues are addressed, the purpose is often instrumental (Bolton et al., 2011), such as relating to employee engagement (e.g., Mirvis, 2012) and more intent on overcoming obstacles than understanding and reflecting upon problems and their root causes (Nord and Fuller, 2009). Hence, there has been a preference for linear or staged models both in the description of current implementation practices and in the theorization of ideal processes, structures and considerations (Bondy, 2008). It is, if only tacitly, assumed that CSR implementation, at least when it reaches higher stages of development, is a product of a concerted managerial effort to make real change happen, that it represents a moral good, is bound to be beneficial for the organization and its employees and therefore will be met with little opposition (Helin and Sandström, 2010). A special status – a sort of 'ethical exceptionalism' – is thus claimed for CSR compared to other managerial technologies which similarly face failure to implement (see Sonenshein, 2010).

Moreover, we contend that the paucity of research and theorization of CSR implementation (with some exceptions, e.g., Kourula and Delalieux, 2014; Wickert et al., 2016) is in part because of an unguarded supposition that corporate communication about CSR (via reporting and other vehicles) translates into successful operationalization of espoused values and policies (cf. Haugh and Talwar, 2010; Helin and Sandström, 2010). This is not withstanding evidence such as the observable mismatches in the actions of Volkswagen employees, and culpability of their managers, to create engineering solutions to evade accurate emissions tests and misrepresent vehicle performance (Ford, 2016). As others have found, we argue that highly visible statements and claims of CSR consistently fail to be fully implemented within the organization, and to affect the deeper inner workings of business (Wickert et al., 2016).

In other words, CSR communication is allowed to serve as a kind of shorthand for CSR practice. Either as a reflection of current practice or as performative or aspirational talk that is supposed to direct and be a precursor to future engagement (Christensen et al., 2013; Morsing and Spence, 2019). The main managerial task then becomes one of effective sense-giving (Gioia and Chittipeddi, 1991), while prospects of potential disagreements and conflicts are brushed aside. This is supported by corporate self-presentations which increasingly seek to make use of CSR as a unifying and integrating storytelling device. Examples of this are Unilever's Sustainable Living programme, IBM's Smarter Planet programme and BP's now defunct 'Beyond Petroleum' rebrand.

With this chapter we aim to contribute to a conceptual opening of the organizational 'black box' (Latour, 1987) with regard to CSR. Instead of understanding a business as an object about which we need only know the inputs (social norms and pressures) and outputs (corporate articulations and actions), we are keen to provide a vocabulary for reflecting on the complex internal workings of the organization as a system of structural cogs and wheels by which CSR may be incorporated. For this purpose, we apply the lens of *governmentality*. This allows us to view the modern business as a political arena and to stress the political nature of CSR.

Governmentality studies build on Michel Foucault's groundbreaking work on power and rule in modern society (Faubion, 1994; Foucault, 1977, 2009) and specialize in exploring the often subtle and intricate mechanisms of liberal and indirect means of governing that are widespread in CSR (due in part to its voluntary nature) and how they affect (or are supposed to affect) actions and mindsets. This perspective allows us to view CSR as a mode of governing that aims to restrict or enable human action and which is embedded in – and operates through – organizational power relations. Moreover, the governmentality perspective allows us to stress the prevalence of different rationalizations of CSR and how they represent different modes of 'truth' (Foucault, 1980a, 1980b) and thus different assumptions about what is good and valuable. Also, it enables us to address the ethical issues that pertain to corporate modes of responsibilization (Roberts, 2003; Shamir, 2008), that is, reorientating the organizational systems and structures to enable, integrate and facilitate social responsibility in particular.

In the next section we present our reading of Foucault and governmentality and how it relates to developments in (political) CSR. We then further elaborate what we consider to be four crucial themes for exploring and conceptualizing the internal politics of CSR: *power*, *government*, *codification* and *translation*. In particular, we question taken-for-granted notions of the management and implementation of CSR by fleshing out the politics of its processes, challenging its implied ethical exceptionalism and the ethics of codified responsibility. Although our contribution is mainly conceptual, in order to provide an empirical illustration for our argument we use the well-documented case of BP. We focus on the events surrounding the massive oil spill from the Macondo oil well in the Gulf of Mexico in 2010. This resulted in a fire causing 11 deaths and 17 injuries and, according to the US National Commission (2011) investigating the incident, constituted the worst environmental disaster America has ever faced. We use BP as an extreme case of failure to properly implement responsibility measures. First, however, we set the theoretical stage.

4.2 FOUCAULT, GOVERNMENTALITY AND THE POLITICS OF CSR

Michel Foucault introduced the notion of governmentality in the course of his seminal lectures at the Collège de France in the late 1970s (Foucault, 2008, 2009; Rose et al., 2006). These lectures, although general and sketchy in content, have laid the foundation for an ongoing diaspora of writings (Bröckling et al., 2011). We understand governmentality 'in the broad sense of techniques and procedures for directing human behaviour' (Foucault, 1997, p. 81). As Foucault (2009) recommends, we treat governmentality as a point of view, a method of decipherment, which can be of value in a variety of settings for management studies (McKinlay and Starkey, 1998). In the words of Miller and Rose (2008), we propose to consider the internal workings of CSR in modern business as a 'laboratory of governmentality'.

Although we are not the first to employ Foucault's work to CSR and sustainable development (Raman, 2007), only a small but growing group apply the notion of governmentality to CSR (Shamir, 2008; Siltaoja et al., 2015; Vallentin, 2015; Vallentin and Murillo, 2012). A further group of scholars has sought to use Foucault's work in the related fields of business ethics (Clegg et al., 2007; Crane et al., 2008), accounting and accountability (e.g., Spence and Rinaldi, 2014). Perhaps unsurprisingly, given the importance of the notion of governance in Foucault's work, there have also been a range of studies which make the link explicitly to corporate governance (Miller and O'Leary, 1993; Roberts, 2001).

The crux of our argument is that Foucault, particularly in his later works, introduces an element of freedom into our understanding of power and government that is vital for an understanding of CSR as a political phenomenon. As a starting point, he considers power to be omnipresent in social relations, relational, dispersed and operating from multiple centres. Hierarchy and notions of pre-ordained sovereign authority are thus rejected. Power is not something that can be possessed by a ruling body or which rests in formalized structures. Instead, it designates a mode of action. Foucault describes it as: 'A set of actions upon other actions' (Foucault, 1982, p. 341). The point being that power is different from physical force or violence. It can only be exercised over free individuals or collective subjects that have some means of escape or possible flight. Hence, Foucault presupposes that there is an acting subject at the other end of the power relation. Although some individuals (managers are obvious examples) do have formal power *over* others, 'such power is not absolute because actors have choices in an imperfect system' (Ettlinger, 2011, p. 549). This is also reflected in his definition of government as a *conduct of conduct*: a form of conduct that relates to how others conduct themselves (Foucault, 1978, 2009), and which consists not in determining how others should act but in structuring the possible fields of action of others (Foucault, 1982). According to Foucault, power cannot be reduced to a repressive force that operates in the negative form of commands or prohibiting rules, it can be a positive, productive, liberating force that can enable action and empower individuals (Foucault, 1980b). We will return to the intricacies of how this dual (controlling/liberating) form of discipline is brought to bear with regard to CSR.

The contribution of governmentality, then, is to provide us with a dynamic conception and vocabulary for reflecting on the often subtle intricacies of power and government in society and organizations. It forces us to venture beyond 'easy' shorthand or taken-for-granted notions of how power works (top-down or via formalized structures) and instead ask questions as to *how* different modes of government are actually carried out, *how* (according to which rationale and by which technical means) they work, and *how* this or that locale or agent are invested with specific powers and thus able to act as a centre of authority (Dean, 2010; Rose and Miller, 1992). It has been suggested, in regard to business ethics, that Foucault's work 'offers little more than an "abstract polemic" of "endless criticism"' (Feldman, 2002, quoted in Crane et al., 2008, p. 299). We, however, find that it has great potential for exploring and challenging practices of responsibility, and that such efforts have practical value even if they are not instrumental in nature. Indeed, the purpose of applying the lens of governmentality is to provide an alternative or corrective to instrumental approaches with their focus on effective management solutions, good governance, best practices and value creation in the realm of responsibility. What governmentality offers, among other things, is a way to subject different modes of government to closer scrutiny in order to flesh out their assumptions, blind spots and exclusions along with the inconsistencies, contradictions, conflicts and tensions they may entail (Rose, 1999). This is, however, not meant to be a negative, dystopian exercise. Our positive contribution consists in challenging the reductionism of glossy, unitary views of CSR and raising the level of knowledge and critical (self-)reflection and awareness with regard to CSR implementation – how it may work and how it may fail.

We have already argued for the value of a poststructuralist approach in spite of its inability (and disinterest) when it comes to defining and providing normative justification for the proper role of business in society. The latter part of the argument suggests that a Foucauldian approach to CSR is yoked to a certain left-leaning ideological commitment (intent on purveying a guilt-by-association – with capitalism – view of CSR). We suggest otherwise. As indicated, we are not engaging in a negative 'debunking of CSR' exercise, but in a positive effort to better understand the politics of managing CSR and address the ethical issues that pertain to corporate modes of responsibilization, including the use and limitations of ethical codes. While we touch on numerous normative issues, we strive to use the works of Foucault, and the literature that uses Foucault to reflect on management and responsibility, in an analytical (as opposed to morally or ideologically charged) fashion. Hence, we seek to define a critical and constructive middle ground allowing us to reflect on the political nature of CSR while leaving the question of its human or social value open.

We also need to point to the methodological shortcomings of governmentality. Governmentality studies have been criticized for their preoccupation with the programmatic – formal and discursive – aspects of governing and thus for studying government as it is should work rather than how it actually works (O'Malley et al., 1997). With such an approach we run the risk of reproducing corporate implementation schemes without taking proper account of the social processes they involve and their possible failures. The standard reply to the question of how to study power and government in action is to look for resistance. Before turning to this topic in a later section, we want to make the point that governmentality studies do not excel as an analytics of social practice as such. What the approach provides us with are tools to simultaneously explore and problematize the programmatic side of government by exposing it to opposition and difference and constantly challenging its claims with regard to practice, pointing, for example, to disconnects and failures. In this chapter we extend these reflections by providing a problematization of the use of ethical codes and of CSR implementation as a form of translation. This is, then, what we mean by attentiveness to the process dimension of implementing CSR.

We now proceed to unfold our four analytical themes. First, we elaborate on the theme of *power* and how it can be used to provide a more nuanced conception of CSR implementation.

4.3 REPRESSIVE AND PRODUCTIVE POWERS OF CSR

As indicated, we want to capture the positive mode of power in CSR. This means reflecting both on its repressive and productive properties, going against the dominant reading of Foucault in management studies, where the focus has mostly been on the negatives of disciplinary practice (McKinlay and Starkey, 1998). Foucauldian approaches to management and organization have made control the central concern. Based on his most influential work in the English-speaking world, *Discipline and Punish* (Foucault, 1977), the emphasis has been on 'the creation of "docile bodies" . . ., individuals constrained against their will by discipline embodied in technologies of domination' (Crane et al., 2008, p. 301). As a result, management has increasingly become a matter of 'managing the "insides" – the hopes, fears, and aspirations – of workers, rather than their behaviors directly' (Deetz, 1995, p. 87). Critical approaches have thus exposed how culture building and similar technologies can be considered as systems of management control that aim to colonize the identities of workers in order to make them more tractable and productive (Fleming and Spicer, 2003). One way of understanding this is in terms of 'engineered selves' (Kunda, 1992).

However, as Alvesson and Willmott point out, organizational members are not reducible to passive consumers of engineered employee identities (1992). We want to break with this pessimistic discourse, with its one-sided view of organizational life as a sort of disciplinary confinement and its subjugation of morality to dominating powers (Crane et al., 2008). Foucault himself was, as McKinlay et al. argue, 'indifferent to questions of who benefited [from particular strategies] or the motives of decision-makers. He was interested in the "how" of power' (2010, p. 1020). While some critical approaches tend to insist on considering power as a controlling force in the organization of CSR (see Costas and Kärreman, 2013), our point is that we cannot adequately account for the 'how' of power in CSR only with reference to the negatives of control, discipline and subjugation. We question whether businesses, apart from presenting themselves as responsible corporate citizens, are really striving to engineer 'responsible selves' and thus whether (or the extent to which) CSR can be considered a dominant rationale.

Pointing to the repressive and productive properties of power allows us to reflect on the duality of what CSR is supposed to accomplish. It is both a matter of prohibiting irresponsible behaviour and of producing responsible behaviour. To illustrate this, we will, for the sake of simplicity, distinguish between three dominant orientations in CSR: 'avoiding harm', 'doing good' and 'creating value'. These are not mutually exclusive orientations; they can be (and are most often) combined in corporate policies. We emphasize how each of these elements of CSR operates in terms of power, and how each has different effects in terms of responsibilization. While 'avoiding harm' is a repressive orientation in the sense that it translates voluntary commitment into internal codes and rule-making, 'doing good' and 'creating value' also become manifest in positive forms of power that seek to exhort and enable employees to engage and contribute on a voluntary basis.

'Avoiding harm' constitutes a realm of accountability – corporate as well as individual. The main concerns here are negative externalities, risk avoidance and compliance with external rules and norms. Individual freedom to act is considered a potential liability and thus something to be restricted. The overall aim is to limit misconduct and thus corporate irresponsibility. 'Doing good' is, in particular, related to philanthropy, that is, various forms of corporate giving in support of humanitarian or social causes or local communities. It engages employees via corporate volunteering and values ethical behaviour as a concern for others. 'Creating value' is about using CSR as a lever for (shared) value creation through business development and innovation in the value chain (Porter and Kramer, 2011). It signals a constant search for business opportunities that can be supported by a culture of self-organization (as opposed to rigid formal structures), 'treat[ing] employees as self-determining professionals who coordinate and integrate activities by self-organizing and generating new ideas' (Moss Kanter, 2011, p. 75). However, 'doing good' and 'creating value' can also be repressive orientations as they can be used for disciplinary purposes to affect subjectivities and shape mindsets in the organization. 'Doing good' is then about imposing certain (corporate) values on individuals, while 'creating value' is about ensuring that shared value creation (and not individual morality or sense of appropriateness) is the mindset that guides decisions and priorities with regard to CSR. 'Doing good' and 'creating value' may appear as innocuous invitations to engage in responsible activities – more akin to the employee benefits associated with (the benevolent side of) human resource management than deserving of a term such as subjugation. It may be equally or more relevant to speak of CSR as a weak and perhaps disappointing form of power in the sense that it is not imposing or disruptive enough with regard to the 'normal', supposedly less responsible, flow of things. To sum up, the three orientations constitute different modes of responsibilization, defining responsible behaviour in terms of obedience, virtue (altruism) and entrepreneurial spirit, respectively.

These three modes of responsible behaviour have been explicitly and implicitly aspired to, for example, by BP. First we turn to the idea of an *entrepreneurial spirit* at BP, which constitutes the most powerful orientation of responsibilization in this instance. In 2007 new CEO Tony Hayward was confronted with a relatively poorly performing company to which he responded with a desire 'to instigate a thorough management shake-up in an attempt to refocus the group' (Macalister, 2007). Already focused on commercial rather than technical advantage, Hayward instigated a drive for commercial innovation and further cost cutting resulting, some claim, in a macho culture (Bergin, 2011, p. 121). He embraced very explicitly the idea of the 'entrepreneurial spirit' in a speech to Stanford University students in the spring of 2009 (Hayward, 2009). By the publication of the sustainability report of that year, this had taken the form of a discourse around BP as a newly energized corporation; the report also points directly to the notion of responsibility, the title being: 'Operating at the energy frontiers. How a revitalized BP is driving innovative, efficient and responsible operations' (BP, 2009). The drive to be forward-looking by being 'progressive' and innovative is clearly highlighted here. Even in external media reports, the suggestion is that 'BP has long been the most swashbuckling, the most entrepreneurial, the most creative (of the biggest oil companies)' (Crooks, 2010). Indeed, the oil field associated with the now infamous Deepwater Horizon represented a major technical challenge, involving drilling deeper and in more inhospitable geological conditions than ever before. The orientation of *efficiency* is represented in the move to be performance driven, cost cutting (e.g., delaying maintenance), decentralization of control and a 'declaration of war' on BP's internal audit functions because they were deemed expensive and slowed down decision-making (Bergin, 2011, p. 125). This is a representation of the framing of the 'technologies' of CSR in the form of safety assurance as repressive and running counter to the efficiency orientation of the business.

It was in this context that the conditions for the Gulf of Mexico oil spill were created. Once the scale of the disaster became clear, the orientation to responsibility is more in line with a virtuous or altruistic one. The CEO saw 'the spill as an opportunity for a model response to a serious accident in the Gulf, demonstrating what he believed would be BP's exemplary corporate responsibility and transparency' (Crooks, 2010). At this stage, commentators noted that Hayward believed that BP would be judged not on the event itself, but on their response to it (Bergin, 2011, p. 167). This turn of events on 30 April 2010, ten days after the spill, is an example of shifting approaches to responsibilization in action. Initially, BP's leaders sought to blame Transocean for the disaster, and deny responsibility by saying 'It wasn't our accident. This was not our drilling rig, it was not our equipment, it was not our people, our systems or our processes' (Hayward, cited in Bergin, 2011, p. 162). This turnaround represents the embracing of a virtuous position, to make the repressive forms of power acting on the company at the time productive, and reorientate to the positive mode of being of power, at least as a 'responsible spiller' (Robertson, 2010). The new regime laid the foundation for social responsibility to once again be positioned as a unifying authority in BP, with the organization accepting responsibility beyond legal requirements, suggesting a shift to a virtue orientation. To summarize, while the responsibility codes remained ostensibly the same, regime shifts starting with promotion of an entrepreneurial spirit and efficiency through cost cutting and innovation gave employees the freedom to interpret responsibility codes as secondary to these orientations. After the Gulf of Mexico incident, the emphasis rapidly changed to one intended to direct employees to act in line with the idea of BP as a responsible spiller, a virtuous actor where employees could and should interpret responsibility beyond any legal or other codified minimum standards, as we shall go on to show in more detail later in the chapter.

4.4 GOVERNING CSR: FROM THE EXCEPTIONAL TO THE MUNDANE

There are several ways in which we can challenge what we have referred to as the 'exceptional' (morally superior, all-encompassing, unopposed) status of CSR, not least in terms of what it is purported to accomplish inside organizations. A first consideration in this regard is that modern, professional, systematic and thus 'explicit' CSR (Matten and Moon, 2008) almost by definition transcends conventional notions of socially embedded business (Morsing and Spence, 2019). The modern game of CSR calls for more than intuitive or spontaneous solutions. It calls for conspicuous, tangible and often standardized responses to external (market and non-market) pressures and may therefore be experienced as calculated, contrived and in some cases even narcissistic (Roberts, 2003). Regardless, there is an element of artifice and specialization to professional CSR. It produces behaviours and responses beyond the 'normal' or 'natural' (profit-driven, task-oriented) way for businesses to be in the world.

Such behaviours and responses may present themselves as 'exceptional' with reference to the usual unitary monikers 'corporate' and 'strategic'. Keeping in mind, however, governmentality's rejection of a priori distributions and divisions of power and authority, we must strive for a more differentiated understanding of its organizational functioning and impact. A first mundane observation to be made in this regard is that CSR (as a mode of governing) must be considered as a situated practice. Instead of taking a singular directive from top management for granted we need to look at how the government of CSR is often delegated to other sites of authority and/or activity and thus becomes polycentric and multidirectional. This is particularly the case when CSR is developed into a specialized effort. Regardless of whether CSR is organized in a dedicated unit or integrated into other parts of the corporate structure, it becomes relevant to speak of departmentalized or personalized change agency beyond the role of top management. This differentiated view also means that we need to consider CSR as a policy concern alongside other policy concerns that are involved in ongoing competition for resources and attention. We cannot take for granted that CSR has a higher priority than other policies and is attributed some kind of all-encompassing reverence. Thus, the government of CSR must be understood as a reflection of particular interests – as opposed to a reflection of a shared (moral) imperative. This means that we need to emphasize how CSR operates as a power regime that interacts with and affects, and is in turn affected by, other power relations in the organization. It makes a difference where in the organization the message of CSR comes from, which interests it is seen to represent and the level of authority, if any, with which it is invested. Turning to BP, we have noted above some of the shifts in dominant organizational regimes between 2007 and 2011. In terms of the particular context of the oil industry, there are also some overriding responsibility concerns. Environmental damage and safety risks are inherent in drilling for and extracting oil, and are magnified in deep sea drilling. Thus, the key goals of a socially responsible oil company are usually mitigation in terms of safety risk and environmental damage. The BP regime at the time leading up to the oil spill positioned both of these as secondary, falling some way behind promoting competitiveness, innovation and cost reduction. The company actively disinvested in their renewable energy programme, dismissing it as 'philanthropy' (Bergin, 2011, p. 122) and downgraded the resources available for safety inspections and the seniority of the global head of safety (Bergin, 2011, p. 126). Hayward (2009) stated publicly that he felt that BP was full of do-gooders, 'too many people working to save the world', and the company was restructured with substantial redundancies. Hence, apparently mundane organizational restructuring resulted in significant undermining and downgrading of social responsibility at BP, and subjugation of CSR as a regime of practice.

The second mundane observation relates to CSR as a regime of practice. The notion of 'regime' would seem to have negative connotations compared to the positive values often attributed to CSR. There is an implicit assumption (shared by many CSR proponents) that CSR is a benevolent presence, a sort of departure, or escape, not from capitalism but from a 'no holds barred' mode of morally blind capitalism characterized by indifference to anything other than economic performance and results (Ghoshal, 2005). CSR is presumed to be aligned with the interests of corporate stakeholders (indeed, it is expected to be a reflection of their demands and expectations), not least their employees (Nord and Fuller, 2009). In this sense, CSR can be seen as a liberating force that de-subjugates rather than subjugates organizational members by allowing them to act with integrity – in accordance with strong values and high moral standards. However, to speak of CSR as a regime is to challenge such idealized notions by pointing to the concrete organization of responsibility and, again, how it both enables and restricts individual action in particular and concrete ways.

Far from being considered as an embodiment of the corporate 'DNA', the government of CSR may be experienced as an impractical or irrelevant disturbance or nuisance. In BP, the quote by the CEO at the beginning of the chapter that 'assurance is killing us' is a neat indication of the rejection of CSR technologies as impeding business activity (Macalister, 2007).

The third mundane observation concerns the closely related matter of how CSR is rationalized and what difference it makes. CSR can be subjected to a variety of different logics reflecting different professional codes and disciplinary commitments, depending on what problem it is supposed to address or solve and how (or, alternatively, which opportunities it aims to pursue). Not only is CSR arguably a response to diffuse powers (what institutional theory refers to as conflicting norms), it also becomes manifest in diverse approaches that embody different rationales and tend to establish different power relations within the organization. Apart from the general orientations we have already discussed, we may, in terms of internal workings more specifically, explore how CSR can be subjected to different departmentalized interests and world views including those associated with (rational imperatives in parentheses) corporate strategy (competitive advantage), corporate communication (public appearance), sales and marketing (market differentiation), human resources (employee attraction, retention, motivation), legal affairs (risk management, compliance), environmental management (innovative and/or cost-effective solutions) or supply-chain management (labour and human rights issues) – along with, of course, specialized CSR units. To speak of CSR as a practice regime, or rather as an issue or concern that can be translated into or appropriated by a number of different practice regimes, is to focus on how the conditions are set for defining what is relevant or valuable within particular regimes and how they connect means to ends. Which features or possibilities of responsibility are illuminated and which remain obscured? How, indeed, is CSR rationalized? What types of knowledge and language – forms of reasoning, justification and so on – and which technologies (concrete devices) does it make use of (Dean, 2010; Rose and Miller, 1992)?

The oil industry is inherently complex and the multiple organizations embedded within it foster multiple rationalizations of CSR. These competing cultures were also evident within the 'black box' (Hafenbrädl and Waeger, 2017) of BP at the time of the Gulf oil spill. Safety was still part of the discourse, but its control had been decentralized under the previous regime, with individual business units being responsible themselves for managing safety and environmental risks (Bergin, 2011, p. 37). Hayward's drive to encourage entrepreneurship and performance by risk-taking noted in the previous section resulted in highly diverse, sometimes conflicting, rationalizations, with embedded polycentric, multidirectional power.

These set the conditions to enable and restrict individual behaviour, according to competing regimes of cost reduction and efficiency (National Commission, 2011), risk-taking entrepreneurship and performance outcomes (Crooks, 2010), safety and responsibility (BP, 2009), contested technological advance (Osofsky, 2011) and, arguably, a reliance on previous luck (Tinsley et al., 2011). In addition, there is a suggestion of an absent regime, that of tight legislature on standards less present in the US than, for example, in the UK (Bergin, 2011). During the time of the crisis an understanding of US politics and valuing the natural environment also seem to be missing at times from the polyphony of voices dominant within BP (Robertson, 2010). Some illustrations of the discord of these multiple rationalizations are discussed further below. As a policy concern then, CSR did not receive equal attention in comparison with the other driving regimes in BP. A rhetoric of safety as a primary goal was not matched by material evidence to support such a claim. In February 2009, Hayward told reporters: 'The mantra in BP today is "Every dollar counts"' (Crooks, 2010). While systematic evidence of conflict between regimes in BP was not formalized and has been difficult to identify, newspaper reports and legal proceedings indicated strong pressure on cost and safety working in contradiction:

> Kevin Lacy, a former official with BP's drilling operations . . . was asked whether he had been asked to choose cost over safety. After a long pause he replied: 'Not explicitly . . . I was never given a directive to cut corners or deliver something not safely but there was tremendous pressure on costs'. (Rushe, 2013)

The combination of encouraging risk-taking with a reliance on good fortune and near misses as proxy evidence of reduced risk is also a key aspect of the rationalizations at work in BP. Tinsley et al. (2011) argue that repeated near misses and previous luck in risk-taking in deep sea oil drilling for BP contributed to the series of decisions which led to the disaster, being taken as indications that safety procedures were adequate, thereby normalizing the risk. Embodying the promotion of risk, Hayward (2009) has pointed to taking risk as a personal reason for his career success. The risk-taking, entrepreneurial approach was throughout the organization's culture: 'Every week you had to have a new idea', says one BP executive. 'And the people who had the best and boldest new ideas were the ones who rose up the organization' (Crooks, 2010). The National Commission (2011, p. ix) also argued that the BP 'business culture succumbed to a false sense of security. The Deepwater Horizon disaster exhibits the costs of a culture of complacency.'

To speak of multiple rationalizations of CSR is to emphasize how responsibility is subject to the functional differentiation of modern businesses and how it is, in this sense, becoming unexceptional – as the ethical idealism that may be associated with the concept is to a large extent obscured by economic pragmatism and instrumental considerations (Spence and Rinaldi, 2014). Whether this mainstreaming constitutes a strengthening or a weakening of the responsibility agenda is another matter. On the one hand, it could be considered a strength that different core business disciplines are required to incorporate it. On the other, it may also imply that the message of responsibility is deluded as it is reduced to being – at best – a means to other ends (we return to this issue in Section 4.6 on processes of translation).

4.5 RESPONSIBILITY BEYOND CODIFICATION

This leads us to the issue of ethics and subjectivity. Government can be placed at the centre of Foucault's writings in the sense that it 'mediates between power and subjectivity, making it possible to study how techniques of rule are tied to technologies of the self' (Bröckling et al., 2011, p. 2). Arguably, the CSR discourse has had a troubled relationship with the subject in the sense that it has been more concerned with corporate action and accountability than with the particulars pertaining to responsibilization of individuals. It is often considered to be more a matter of external legitimization than internal discipline. So we need to question what CSR as a technology of rule (alongside other such technologies) is meant to accomplish and what ethical issues the government of responsibility raises. Technologies refer in this instance to the actual mechanisms through which authorities seek to shape, normalize and instrumentalize the actions, thoughts, beliefs and aspirations of others (Miller and Rose, 1990). These might be mundane processes and mechanisms as well as more sophisticated systems and structures. Tools or technologies of CSR government are well developed and may consist of particular vocabularies, training, auditing, internal procedures and guidelines (Spence and Rinaldi, 2014).

CSR is usually seen to represent a moral good. At the same time, however, it often appears, for better or worse, as a strangely de-personalized discourse and practice. As mentioned, this has to do with the element of artifice brought on by making responsibility into a specialized, technical endeavour. It also has to do with the substitutes that CSR makes use of instead of individual responsibility. Pride of place among these are to ethical codes or codes of conduct (although, as we have shown, CSR is not reducible to such rule-based modes of governing). Codes and processes of codification are morally ambivalent matters. On the one hand, codification is a prerequisite for holding corporations accountable for their actions. On the other, it may be questioned what the purpose of codification is. Is it to make organizational members more responsible – and thus minimize corporate misconduct? Is it about external signalling or about pushing responsibility downward in the organization ('passing the buck') in order to make middle managers and employees liable if things go wrong – thus leaving the C-level and the corporate body less exposed to the damages that may be incurred by costly litigation. With governmentality we can show how codification relates to issues of power and ethics.

As we have argued, CSR can operate via different forms of power. Ibarra-Colado et al. (2006, p. 48). suggest that '[t]he value of the concept of governmentality lies in the possibilities it offers for examining the connection between power and ethics, which enable a connection between a political component (the governing of others, i.e. management) and a subjective component (the governing of oneself)'. According to Jackson and Carter, governmentality means that 'people should voluntarily and willingly delegate their moral autonomy and moral responsibility to obedience to the rules, to being governed in their conduct by a "moral" force . . . which is external to the "self"' (1998, p. 51). This depiction emphasizes the repressive, rule-based view of power. It is in line with conventional uses of Foucault in management studies and the critical literature on ethical codification (Gilbert and Rasche, 2008; Jones, 2003; Roberts, 2003). What is at stake here is the relationship between codification and ethical behaviour in organizations. According to Foucault, 'freedom is the ontological condition of ethics' (1987, p. 284). The question is whether or how ethical codes leave room for ethical choice or rather constitute an installment of rules of compliance. The point being that if actions are predetermined according to some external code, the individual is denied moral agency. Freedom and moral agency are only present where there is space for reflection, consideration and therefore choice (Clegg et al., 2007, pp. 111–12). This is, in our view, not a matter of denigrating the value of codes as such. In the words of Clegg et al.:

> Ethical codes, norms and models have important implications for organizational members. While they do not determine practices, they are important because they guide the enactments of subjects who exercise some degree of freedom in governing their own conduct. They become instruments that skillful and knowledgeable members can engage and play with freely in their everyday management of their own and others' affairs. (2007, p. 112)

Instead, we should investigate 'how people adhere to, violate, ignore or creatively interpret . . . ethical precepts such as may be contained in codes' (Clegg et al., 2007, p. 113). This is to position them more correctly as frameworks which may guide action but do not dictate it, leaving room for individual freedom and autonomy, in short allowing for management of the self (Clegg et al., 2007). In line with the Foucauldian understanding of power and government, the basic assumption is that codes, in practice, offer no guarantees either in terms of moral value or determining behaviour. The key task in understanding CSR codification then becomes not the existence of the canon per se so much as the manner in which others – employees and middle managers in our case – manage themselves in response to the code. How is it resisted, followed, reinterpreted, promoted, appropriated or subjugated?

There is a great deal to consider in the manner of application of BP's safety code at the time of the Gulf oil spill. We have found no evidence of BP's code at the beginning of 2010 per se being inadequate. As we suggest above, the existence of codification is not in question. However, industry insiders and observers have found the *application* of the code to have been wanting. The US Occupational Safety & Health Administration fined BP its largest fine ever for regulatory safety violations in the Texas City refinery explosion in 2005 when 15 people died. Walden Asset Management, for example, divested of BP shares in February 2010 because of its 'serious safety management problems' (Steverman, 2010). Other fund managers felt that BP 'was not as culturally committed to safety as its rivals' (Bergin, 2011, p. 265). Nevertheless, the Deepwater Horizon rig was award winning in terms of safety, with golden plaques said to be lining the dining hall (Urbina and Gillis, 2010). So if a code was in place and safety standards were being met at some level, it is somehow in translation from code to normal practice that decoupling occurred. One aspect which seems to be important here is that it was particularly process safety (the procedures for minimizing risk) rather than occupational safety (avoidance of individual injuries) that was problematic at BP (National Commission, 2011).

The mediating space between safety codes and practice is referred to in the commentary around the Gulf of Mexico disaster as 'BP's safety culture'. Indicators of an effective culture include leadership, two-way communication, employee involvement, learning culture and attitude towards blame (HSE, 2005), all of which appear to be reflected negatively in the BP case. A survey of Transocean workers which took place a couple of months before the incident found that '46 percent of crew members surveyed felt that some of the workforce feared reprisals for reporting unsafe situations (blame), and 15 percent felt that there were not always enough people available to carry out work safely'. Importantly in terms of understanding the gap between codification and implementation, there was a 'poor distinction between what is required and how this should be achieved' (National Commission, 2011, p. 224). Perhaps more telling than each of these aspects of the safety culture at BP is the statement accredited to a BP executive that BP 'push things too far' (Bergin, 2011, p. 143).

Two site managers were charged in 2012 with manslaughter for acting negligently in their supervision of key safety tests performed on the rig prior to the explosion and failure to alert onshore engineers of problems in the drilling and stopping investigation of abnormal readings (Goldenberg and Rushe, 2012), but in the end no prison time was served by any of the protagonists involved and the manslaughter charges were dropped (Kravets, 2015).

The codification of safety at BP changed when a new CEO, Bob Dudley, was instated in the summer of 2010, countering some of its earlier failed implementation. The revised BP code of ethics published in 2011 and updated in 2014 highlights its values as follows, stressing safety as the highest value and revising the performance and reward mechanisms accordingly (Bly, 2011). The most senior person responsible for safety is thus once again on the executive management board (BP, 2019). Safety is now promoted directly as 'good business' in the revised BP Code of Conduct (BP, 2014, p.3). The code also notably emphasizes individual responsibility and states 'each of us is a role model for safety' (BP, 2014, p. 12). The previously countervailing regime of financial performance is now being positioned as an element of safety. This makes sense given that the company could realistically have gone bankrupt after the disaster (Bergin, 2011, p. 176), and the cost to the organization as of 2018 was $65 billion and counting.

Thus, responsibility, or processes of responsibilization, transcends codes in a double sense. Not only is CSR not reducible to the rule-based form; it can be an enabling and empowering form of government. Even when responsibilization operates in the form of impressive looking codes, we have to look for freedom and (ethical – or unethical) choice in how organizational members are guided in order to properly understand its modus operandi. Therefore, like Siltaoja and colleagues (2015) we fundamentally question the top-down transference of CSR standards to inhabit employee actions – and how a corporate code is sometimes understood as a proxy for practice. This leads us to our final analytical theme: translation.

4.6 BEYOND SUBJECTIVATION AND RESISTANCE: TRANSLATION

According to McKinlay et al., '[g]overnmentality is the moment, always unstable, at which the strategies of the powerful and the powerless meet, the ways in which individuals are targeted by disciplines and the ways that these techniques are accommodated, ridiculed or resisted' (2010, p. 1021). In relation to the notion of ascending analysis, the idea is to analyse power relations, and to make them visible, via the antagonism of different strategies (Foucault, 1982). The question, however, is whether resistance is the most relevant concern in this regard. We suggest that it is not.

If CSR is considered only or primarily in terms of managerial control, resistance is the obvious focal point. However, there is, as we have shown, more to the government of CSR than control, and besides, we should not overestimate the critical potential of focusing on resistance. Research on resistance has tended to focus on identity politics and acts of micro resistance within the workplace (Murtola, 2012). With this focus, there is, as Fleming and Spicer argue, 'a risk of reducing resistance to the most banal and innocuous everyday actions' (2008, p. 303). According to Mumby, 'the very movement toward the study of covert, routine forms of discursive resistance is indicative of the capitulation of critical scholars to the success of managerialism and capitalism' (2005, p. 39). The obvious critical alternative is to focus on more radical and disruptive forms of resistance (Murtola, 2012). With regard to CSR this can be accomplished by engaging a broader societal perspective and focusing on the role that civil society organizations and social activists along with purveyors of radical politics play in opposing corporate capitalism and economic globalization. However, within the confines of the organization, resistance remains a more subliminal or covert activity. Although possibilities of resistance are ubiquitous, explicitly visible resistance such as whistleblowing or withdrawal of labour, that is, striking or working-to-rule, is not inevitable and is by and large relatively scarce (Ettlinger, 2011). We would expect this to be particularly the case in regard to a politically correct phenomenon like CSR. Hence, we should not anticipate finding spectacular organizational upheavals against CSR.

What we should expect to find, however, are large and small transformations of CSR taking place through a variety of processes of translation. With its focus on processes of construction, contestation and transformation from multiple and heterogeneous elements, and its relational and performative view of power (Dean, 2010), governmentality already points towards such considerations. Therefore, it seems more pertinent to turn to the related notion of *translation* from actor-network theory (which, with regard to the relational understanding of power, has close affinities with the work of Foucault – see Latour, 1986). In the 'sociology of translation' of Callon and Latour, translation refers to 'all the negotiations, intrigues, calculations, acts of persuasion and violence, thanks to which an actor or force takes, or causes to be conferred upon itself, authority to speak on behalf of another actor or force' (1981, p. 279). In this perspective, translation does not mean the correct transferral of one will into another (as in reproduction). Translation is a mode of production that expresses 'in one's own language what others say and want [and] why they act in the way they do' (Lemke, 2007, p. 51). Hence, implementation has to be considered as a 'politics of translation' that involves a myriad of relays and transfers of command that affect the meaning and impact of social responsibility (and through which, of course, the message of CSR may also be disconnected or lose momentum).

According to Latour's 'model of translation', 'the spread in time and space of anything – claims, orders, artefacts, goods – is in the hands of people; each of these people may act in many different ways, letting the token drop, or modifying it, or deflecting it, or betraying it, or adding to it, or appropriating it' (1986, p. 267). He juxtaposes this model with 'the diffusion model', which assumes an initial powerful force with a certain inertia that is transmitted wholly and fully and then may be diminished along the way due to frictions and resistances. To apply a model of translation is to turn away from a preoccupation with initial forces to focus on processes of production and transformation and the relays and transfers of command that are involved in such processes. This allows us to look at how technologies such as performance measurement systems, key performance indicators and reporting techniques (Searcy and Buslovich, 2014) not only reproduce an initial, managerial force, but also produce and transform the meaning and impact of CSR.

In the BP case we can seek to understand processes of translation through the technologies of the remuneration and bonus system. According to Bergin (2011, pp. 125–8), while a high level safety checking team was disbanded in 2008 as part of the cost-cutting programme, the head count reduction scheme was matched with a remodelling of managers' remuneration packages which supported the cost reduction achievements by encouraging managers to operate quickly and cheaply. Targets were tied to highly variable bonuses, and were dramatically higher if targets – beyond predicted possible results, even the physically impossible – were achieved. The faster they drilled, the bigger the bonus, despite the associated risk. Bergin avers that non-compliance with written policies was common, a claim backed up by Kevin Lacy who says that BP 'was not adequately committed to improving its safety protocols in offshore drilling to the level of its industry peers' (Bergin, 2011, p. 127).

If implemented fully, BP's responsibility and safety codes would have significantly reduced the likelihood of the Gulf of Mexico disaster. But responsibility for the implementation of codes was decentralized to local managers who – through financial reward and encouragement – translated and subjugated the safety requirements below short-term performance in terms of speed and efficiency. In a company driven by financial performance, 'risk had no cost – at least not for top managers' (Bergin, 2011, p. 128). Indeed, the National Commission report quotes the BP Wells

Team Leader for the Deepwater Horizon as saying that losing returns was considered the number one risk (National Commission, 2011, p. 99). It seems most likely that employees lower down the chain, highly qualified and experienced engineers in many cases, understood the risks in their own section but were driven by management to continue to take them, and ignorant of the situation in other sections.

Thus, the technologies in place in relation to process safety in BP enabled and allowed the translation of safety risks as acceptable and less important than performance and cost. In the current regime at BP, investment in safety and CSR is substantially increased. Safety, it is fair to say, has now been appropriated as a performance consideration, creating shared value in Porter and Kramer's (2011) terms and potentially reframing the governmentality processes at play.

4.7 CONCLUSION

In this chapter we have sought to present a novel conceptualization of the politics of managing ethics and social responsibility within the organization, which we deem to be just as important in 'troubled times' as the externally facing activities. We have used Michel Foucault's analytics of governmentality to show how, through understanding social responsibility implementation as a dynamic process, there is a failure in transition from externally espoused ethics and CSR to those internally practised. Rather than identify antecedents and barriers to implementation, we have conceptualized social responsibility in terms of key governmentality parameters of power, government, practice and translation. With the support of the illustrative example of the failure of safety and responsibility implementation at BP, we have demonstrated the manner in which managers fail to attend to the need to make corporations amenable to responsibilization.

In our reading of governmentality we have argued for the value of an approach that is critical, but not in the sense of being ideologically opposed to business and capitalism from the outset. By adopting a critical-analytical vantage point we have tried to show that such an approach has positive and practical value as a means to challenge unitary and instrumental views of CSR. Governmentality provides us with a rich vocabulary for analysing and reflecting on internal processes of responsibilization in business; how they succeed and how they fail. In relation to CSR, we have argued for the need to expand this vocabulary by emphasizing the notion of translation (developed in actor-network theory) as an arguably more relevant consideration than resistance. This forms part of our overall effort to address issues of power and government without succumbing to the negatives of control, discipline and subjugation. This reflects, first, an urge to avoid being locked in a position where pessimism and a dystopian view of business is the only option. Second, it is a reflection of the insight that CSR most often does not appear as (and can certainly not be reduced to) an effective means of internal control. It also has to be understood as a positive, productive form of power that enables action on a voluntary basis. In many instances it can be considered as a weak and disappointing form of power because it fails to be imposing or disruptive enough to deliver on its promises. This is, then, a clarification of what a governmentality analysis should strive to provide detailed accounts of.

The BP case is a useful example of 'exceptional failure' to implement responsibility standards resulting in severe damage to: individuals (inside and outside the firm) up to and including death; the natural environment and ecosystem; and the company's global reputation with attendant economic and social impacts. While the acute decoupling of standards and practices provides a good illustration of some parts of our theoretical argument, the case has limitations with regard to other parts. It does not, for example, reflect the positive or productive aspects of power, which we have argued for, to any great degree, with small exceptions perhaps such as the freedom exercised by Kevin Lacy when he complained about poor safety standards and ultimately resigned on safety grounds prior to the Gulf of Mexico disaster (Rushe, 2013). In the BP case, it seems, such small-scale positive use of power by one individual was entirely and completely overwhelmed by the dominant regimes of efficiency and innovation. It may well be that there were other instances where engineers and technicians prioritized safety and refused to be driven by the efficiency regime, thus reducing accident rates in the firm. This is unfortunately difficult if not impossible to ascertain as an external commentator after the fact.

We have argued against ethical exceptionalism and for a mundane, everyday view of CSR and ethical practice. How does that sit with an extraordinary case, centred on a disaster? The short answer is that the processes often working against proper adoption of responsibility measures in BP are not exceptional as such, and that such processes need more in-depth exploration. This points to a methodological shortcoming or challenge that comes with the suggested approach: how to get access to study processes of responsibilization as they unfold and through a critical lens – in companies that are often keen to maintain, to the best of their ability, an aura of excellence with regard to their policies of responsibility? The imperfect fit of the Gulf of Mexico incident to our theoretical argument is concurrent with the nature of an illustrative case, and is perhaps unsurprising given the selective and post hoc nature of the data we were able to review, and the difficulty of obtaining balanced insider perspectives in such a highly sensitive and politically charged case. Our contribution is to contend that the governmentality lens points to the conclusion that the implementation of CSR is an ongoing political process, which can neither be controlled nor completed, but which is open to incorporating the myriad forms of power, government, practice and translation. It is our hope that this is of value to those seeking to understand social responsibility and ethics implementation in depth from the perspectives of both scholarship and practice.

There are a number of wider implications and future research directions emerging from the work presented in this chapter, but which are beyond the current chapter's scope. First, as we have outlined, our main contribution has been theoretical in nature, taking the form of a new conceptualization of CSR implementation from a political perspective. Empirical work which seeks to identify the parameters of governmentality in CSR implementation programmes directly rather than by secondary data would be of considerable value. In particular, we have argued that there is an assumption of ethical exceptionalism in CSR implementation, that CSR is an obvious and overriding social good expressed as a univocal rationality. Empirical research which seeks to delineate the elements of this claim in full would be very helpful.

Second, in proposing governmentality as a valuable lens for understanding organizational change, we would not wish to suggest that its application is a simplistic process. We have identified some key parameters which we determine to be most pertinent, but these are not definitive. Other aspects which we have touched on but which might usefully be extended include identity, freedom, civil society and regulation of the self. It is not our intention to suggest that the parameters we have discussed are mutually exclusive. We have cross-referenced quite consciously since there is a certain degree of intersection which plays naturally into the corporation as our 'laboratory of governmentality'. Studies that probe deeper into the parameters of governmentality in different circumstances and contexts would be welcome contributions.

Third, given the realignment of focus within the CSR field on globalization, the governmentalization of the role of the firm and resultant politically orientated CSR and most recently their micro-foundations (Maak et al., 2016), this work could usefully be extended to seek to understand the proposition of CSR implementation within a global supply chain. Such a programme of research would multiply the complexity of the project manifold, but since supply chains are increasingly the unit of analysis in research rather than individual organizations, more advanced conceptualization would be of value. Thus, while our context has been internal to the corporation, this research could usefully be expanded to consider inter-organizational CSR implementation, such as the supply chain, industrial clusters, cross-sector initiatives, and regional CSR and ethics programmes. Similarly, while our study has focused on the corporation, the research approach could easily be applied to other organizational forms such as small and medium-sized enterprises, hybrids, co-operatives or social enterprises. There may also be opportunities to look to other kinds of strategic implementation beyond CSR. While we have put special emphasis on the ethical authority assumed in CSR, much of the approach may also be relevant to similarly imbued environmental or quality inspired initiatives of programmatic change.

Finally, our research has led us to the following key conclusion, which we think is helpful in our troubled times. To make corporations internally sensitive to the need for ethical practices and CSR is a complex, multi-faceted task, which can be informed by a governmentality approach. The process of responsibilization can neither be fully controlled nor completed, and it requires attentiveness towards the multiple forms of power to making visible the myriad forms of power, government, practices and translation in the everyday life of the corporation.

REFERENCES

Alvesson, M. and Willmott, H. (1992). *Critical Management Studies*. London: Sage.

Bergin, T. (2011). *Spills and Spin: The Inside Story of BP*. London: Random House.

Blair-Loy, M., Wharton, A. and Goodstein, J. (2011). 'Exploring the relationship between mission statements and work-life practices in organizations'. *Organization Studies*, **32**(3), 427–50.

Bly, M. (2011). 'Safety and operational risk update'. Accessed 1 July 2018 at http // www.bp.com/content/dam/bp/pdf/ investors/Safety_Operational_Risk_update_oct_2011.pdf.

Bolton, S.C., Kim, R.C.H. and O'Gorman, K.D. (2011). 'Corporate social responsibility as a dynamic internal organizational process: a case study'. *Journal of Business Ethics*, **101**, 61–74.

Bondy, K. (2008). 'The paradox of power in CSR: a case study on implementation'. *Journal of Business Ethics*, **82**, 307–23.

BP (2009). 'Sustainability review 2009: Operating at the energy frontiers. How a revitalized BP is driving innovative, efficient and responsible operations'. Accessed 28 August 2019 at https://www.bp.com/content/dam/bp/business-sites/en/global/corporate/pdfs/sustainability/archive/archived-reports-and-translations/2009/bp_sustainability_review_2009.pdf.

BP (2014). 'Our Code: it's what we believe in'. Accessed 28 August 2019 at https://www.bp.com/content/dam/bp/business-sites/en/global/corporate/pdfs/who-we-are/our-values-and-code-of-conduct/bp-code-of-conduct-english.pdf.

BP (2019). 'Our Executive Management team, their roles and responsibilities'. Accessed 28 August 2019 at https://www.bp.com/en/global/corporate/who-we-are/board-and-executive-management/executive-team.html.

Bröckling, U., Krasmann, S. and Lemke, T. (2011). 'From Foucault's lectures

at the Collège de France to studies of governmentality: an introduction'. In U. Bröckling, S. Krasmann and T. Lemke (eds), *Governmentality: Current Issues and Future Challenges*. New York: Routledge, pp. 1–33.
Callon, M. and Latour, B. (1981). 'Unscrewing the big Leviathan: how actors macrostructure reality and how sociologists help them to do so'. In K. Knorr-Cetina and A.V. Cicourel (eds), *Advances in Social Theory and Methodology: Toward an Integration of Micro- and Macro-Sociologies*. Boston, MA: Routledge & Kegan Paul, pp. 277–303.
Christensen, L.T., Morsing, M. and Thyssen, O. (2013). 'CSR as aspirational talk'. *Organization*, **20**(3), 372–93.
Clegg, S., Kornberger, M. and Rhodes, C. (2007). 'Business ethics as practice'. *British Journal of Management*, **18**(2), 107–22.
Costas, J. and Kärreman, D. (2013). 'Conscience as control – managing employees through CSR'. *Organization*, **20**(3), 394–415.
Crane, A., Knights, D. and Starkey, K. (2008). 'The conditions of our freedom: Foucault, organization and ethics'. *Business Ethics Quarterly*, **18**(3), 299–320.
Crooks, E. (2010). 'BP: the inside story'. *Financial Times*, 2 July. Accessed 1 July 2018 at http://www.ft.com/cms/s/2/4e228e56-84ae-11df-9cbb-00144feabdc0.html#axzz2ZEd9fsun.
Dean, M. (2010). *Governmentality: Power and Rule in Modern Society*, 2nd edn. London: Sage.
Deetz, S. (1995). *Transforming Communication, Transforming Business: Building Responsive and Responsible Workplaces.* Cresskill, NJ: Hampton Press.
Ettlinger, N. (2011). 'Governmentality as epistemology'. *Annual of the Association of American Geographers*, **101**(3), 537–60.
Faubion, J.D. (ed.) (1994). *Power: Essential Works of Foucault 1954–1984*. New York: The New Press.
Feldman, S. (2002). *Memory as a Moral Decision: The Role of Ethics in Organizational Culture.* New Brunswick, NJ: Transaction Publishers.
Fleming, P. and Spicer, A. (2003). 'Working at a cynical distance: implications for power, subjectivity and resistance'. *Organization*, **10**(1), 157–79.
Fleming, P. and Spicer, A. (2008). 'Beyond power and resistance: new approaches to organizational politics'. *Management Communication Quarterly*, **21**(3), 301–9.
Ford, J. (2016). 'Car emissions scandal exposes crippling compromises behind the rules'. *Financial Times*, 24 April.
Foucault, M. (1977). *Discipline and Punish: The Birth of the Prison*. London: Penguin Books.
Foucault, M. (1978). 'Governmentality'. In J.D. Faubion (ed.) (1994), *Power: Essential Works of Foucault 1954–1984*. New York: The New Press, pp. 201–22.
Foucault, M. (1980a). *Power/Knowledge: Selected Interviews and Other Writings 1972–1977*. New York: Pantheon Books.
Foucault, M. (1980b). 'Truth and power'. In J.D. Faubion (ed.) (1994), *Power: Essential Works of Foucault 1954–1984*. New York: The New Press, pp. 111–33.
Foucault, M. (1982). 'The subject and power'. In J.D. Faubion (ed.) (1994), *Power: Essential Works of Foucault 1954–1984*. New York: The New Press, pp. 326–48.
Foucault, M. (1987). 'The ethics of the concern for self as a practice of freedom'. In J.D. Rabinow (ed.), *Ethics: Essential Works of Foucault 1954–1984*. New York: The New Press, pp. 281–301.
Foucault, M. (1991). 'Questions of method'. In J.D. Faubion (ed.) (1994), *Power: Essential Works of Foucault 1954–1984*. New York: The New Press, pp. 223–38.

Foucault, M. (1997). 'On the government of the living'. In J.D. Rabinow (ed.), *Ethics: Essential Works of Foucault 1954–1984*. New York: The New Press, pp. 81–5.
Foucault, M. (2008). *The Birth of Biopolitics: Lectures at Collège de France 1978–1979*. Basingstoke, Hampshire: Palgrave Macmillan.
Foucault, M. (2009). *Security, Territory, Population: Lectures at Collège de France 1977–1978*. Basingstoke, Hampshire: Palgrave Macmillan.
Ghoshal, S. (2005). 'Bad management theories are destroying good management practices'. *Academy of Management Learning and Education*, **4**(1), 75–91.
Gilbert, D.U. and Rasche, A. (2008). 'Opportunities and problems of standardized ethics initiatives: a stakeholder theory perspective'. *Journal of Business Ethics*, **82**, 755–83.
Gioia, D. and Chittipeddi, K. (1991). 'Sensemaking and sensegiving in strategic change initiation'. *Strategic Management Journal*, **12**(6), 433–48.
Goldenberg, S. and Rushe, D. (2012). 'BP agrees to pay largest penalty in US history in $4.5bn Gulf oil spill deal'. *Guardian*, 15 November. Accessed 1 July 2018 at http://www.theguardian.com/environment /2012/nov/15/bp-largest-penalty-history-gulf-oil-spill.
Gond, J.P. and Nyberg, D. (2017). 'Materializing power to recover corporate social responsibility'. *Organization Studies*, **38**(8), 1127–48.
Hafenbrädl, S. and Waeger, D. (2017). 'Ideology and the micro-foundations of CSR: why executives believe in the business case for CSR and how this affects their CSR engagements'. *Academy of Management Journal*, **60**(4), 1582–606.
Haugh, H.M. and Talwar, A. (2010). 'How do corporations embed sustainability across the organization?' *Academy of Management Learning and Education*, **9**(3), 384–96.
Hayward, T. (2009), 'Entrepreneurial spirit needed'. *Stanford Business*, 12 May. Accessed 1 July 2018 at http://www.youtube.com/watch?v=FwQM00clxgM.
Helin, S. and Sandström, J. (2010). 'Resisting a corporate code of ethics and the reinforcement of management control'. *Organization Studies*, **31**(5), 583–604.
HSE (Health & Safety Executive) (2005). 'A review of safety culture and safety climate literature for the development of the safety culture inspection toolkit'. Research Report 367. Accessed 1 July 2018 at http://www.hse.gov.uk/research/rrpdf/rr367.pdf.
Ibarra-Colado, E., Clegg, S.R., Rhodes, C. and Kornberger, M. (2006). 'The ethics of managerial subjectivity'. *Journal of Business Ethics*, **64**, 45–55.
Jackson, N. and Carter, P. (1998). 'Labour as dressage'. In A. McKinlay and K. Starkey (eds), *Foucault, Management and Organization Theory*. London: Sage, pp. 51–64.
Jones, C. (2003). 'As if business ethics were possible, "Within such limits" . . .'. *Organization*, **10**(2), 223–48.
Kourula, A. and Delalieux, G. (2016). 'The micro-level foundations and dynamics of political corporate social responsibility: hegemony and passive revolution through civil society'. *Journal of Business Ethics*, **135**(4), 769–85.
Kravets, D. (2015). 'Manslaughter charges dropped in BP spill case – nobody from BP will go to prison'. *ARS Technica*, 3 December. Accessed 1 July 2018 at https://arstechnica.com/tech-policy/2015/12/manslaughter-charges-dropped-in-bp-spill-case-nobody-from-bp-will-go-to-prison/.
Kunda, G. (1992). *Engineering Culture: Control and Commitment in a High-Tech Corporation*. Philadelphia, PA: Temple University Press.

Latour, B. (1986). 'The powers of association'. In J. Law (ed.), *Power, Action and Belief*. London: Routledge & Kegan Paul, pp. 264–80.
Latour, B. (1987). *Science in Action*. Cambridge, MA: Harvard University Press.
Lemke, T. (2007). 'An indigestible meal? Foucault, governmentality and state theory'. *Distinktion: Scandinavian Journal of Social Theory*, **15**, 43–64.
Lindgreen, A., Swaen, V. and Maon, F. (2009). 'Introduction: corporate social responsibility implementation'. *Journal of Business Ethics*, **85**(S2), 251–6.
Maak, T., Pless, N.M. and Voegtlin, C. (2016). 'Business statesman or shareholder advocate? CEO responsible leadership styles and the micro-foundations of political CSR'. *Journal of Management Studies*, **53**(3), 463–93.
Macalister, T. (2007). 'BP boss warns of shake-up after dreadful results. Successor to Browne plans to slash management fat. Hayward says oil company has become too cautious'. *Guardian*, 26 September.
Matten, D. and Moon, J. (2008). '"Implicit" and "explicit" CSR: a conceptual framework for a comparative understanding of corporate social responsibility'. *Academy of Management Review*, **33**(2), 404–24.
McKinlay, A. and Starkey, K. (eds) (1998). *Foucault, Management and Organization Theory*. London: Sage.
McKinlay, A., Carter, C., Pezet, E. and Clegg, S. (2010). 'Using Foucault to make strategy'. *Accounting, Auditing and Accountability Journal*, **23**(8), 1012–31.
Miller, P. and O'Leary, T. (1993). 'Accounting expertise and the politics of the product: economic citizenship and modes of corporate governance'. *Accounting, Organizations and Society*, **18**(2), 187–206.
Miller, P. and Rose, N. (1990). 'Governing economic life'. *Economy and Society*, **19**, 1–31.
Miller, P. and Rose, N. (2008). *Governing the Present: Administering Economic, Social and Personal Life*. Cambridge: Polity.
Mirvis, P. 2012. 'Employee engagement and CSR: transactional, relational and developmental approaches'. *California Management Review*, **54**(4), 93–117.
Morsing, M. and Spence, L.J. (2019) 'Corporate social responsibility (CSR) communication and small and medium sized enterprises: the governmentality dilemma of explicit and implicit CSR communication'. *Human Relations*. doi:10.1177/0018726718804306.
Moss Kanter, R. (2011). 'How great companies think differently'. *Harvard Business Review*, **89**(11), 66–78.
Mumby, D. (2005). 'Theorizing resistance in organization studies: a dialectical approach'. *Management Communication Quarterly*, **19**, 19–44.
Murtola, A. (2012). 'Materialist theology and anti-capitalist resistance, or, "What would Jesus buy?"' *Organization*, **19**(3), 325–44.
National Commission (2011). *Deep Water: The Gulf Oil Disaster and the Future of Offshore Drilling*. January. Accessed 1 July 2018 at http://www.oilspillcommission.gov/final-report.
Nord, W. and Fuller, S. (2009). 'Increasing corporate social responsibility through an employee-centered approach'. *Employee Responsibilities and Rights Journal*, **21**(4), 279–90.
O'Malley, P., Weir, L. and Shearing, C. (1997). 'Governmentality, criticism, politics'. *Economy and Society*, **26**(4), 501–17.
Osofsky, H. (2011). 'Multidimensional governance and the BP Deepwater Horizon oil spill'. *Florida Law Review*, **63**, 1077–137.

Porter, M.E. and Kramer, M.R. (2011). 'Creating shared value'. *Harvard Business Review*, **89**(January–February), 62–77.
Raman, K.R. (2007). 'Community–Coca-Cola interface: political-anthropological concerns on corporate social responsibility'. *Social Analysis*, **51**(3), 103–20.
Roberts, J. (2001). 'Trust and control in Anglo-American systems of corporate governance: the individualizing and socializing effects of processes of accountability'. *Human Relations*, **54**(12), 1547–72.
Roberts, J. (2003). 'The manufacture of corporate social responsibility: constructing corporate sensibility'. *Organization*, **10**(2), 249–65.
Robertson, C. (2010). 'White House takes a bigger role in the oil spill cleanup'. *New York Times*, 29 April.
Rose, N. (1999). *Powers of Freedom: Reframing Political Thought*. Cambridge: Cambridge University Press.
Rose, N. and Miller, P. (1992). 'Political power beyond the state: problematics of government'. *British Journal of Sociology*, **43**(2), 173–205.
Rose, N., O'Malley, P. and Valverde, M. (2006). 'Governmentality'. *Annual Review of Law and Social Science*, **2**, 83–104.
Rushe, D. (2013). 'Former BP boss Tony Hayward defends company's actions before Gulf disaster'. *Guardian*, 27 February. Accessed 1 July 2018 at http://www.guardian.co.uk/environment/2013/feb/27/bp-deepwater-oil-spill-hayward.
Searcy, C. and Buslovich, R. (2014). 'Corporate perspectives on the development and use of sustainability reports'. *Journal of Business Ethics*, **121**(2), 149–69.
Shamir, R. (2008). 'The age of responsibilization: on market-embedded morality'. *Economy and Society*, **37**(1), 1–19.
Siltaoja, M., Malin, V. and Pyykkönen, M. (2015). '"We are all responsible now": governmentality and responsibilized subjects in corporate social responsibility'. *Management Learning*, **46**(4), 444–60.
Sonenshein, S. (2010). 'We're changing – or are we? Untangling the role of progressive, regressive, and stability narratives during strategic change implementation'. *Academy of Management Journal*, **53**(3), 477–512.
Spence, L.J. and Rinaldi, L. (2014). 'Governmentality in accounting and accountability: a case study of embedding sustainability in a supply chain'. *Accounting, Organizations and Society*, **39**(6), 433–52.
Steverman, B. (2010) 'BP disaster vexes socially responsible investors'. *Business Week*, 2 June. Accessed 1 July 2018 at http://www.businessweek.com/investor/content/jun2010/pi2010062_229025.htm.
Tinsley, C., Dillon, R. and Madsen, P. (2011). 'How to avoid catastrophe'. *Harvard Business Review*, **89**(4), 90–7.
Urbina, I. and Gillis, J. (2010). 'Workers on oil rig recall a terrible night of blasts'. *New York Times*, 7 May.
Vallentin, S. (2015). 'Governmentalities of CSR: Danish government policy as a reflection of political difference'. *Journal of Business Ethics*, **127**(1), 33–47.
Vallentin, S. and Murillo, D. (2012). 'Governmentality and the politics of CSR'. *Organization*, **19**(6), 825–43.
Wickert, C., Scherer, A. and Spence, L.J. (2016). 'Walking and talking corporate social responsibility: implications of firm size and organizational costs'. *Journal of Management Studies*, **53**(7), 1169–96.

PART II

Agency and Responsibility

5. Disciplining the organization through moral personhood

Wim Dubbink

5.1 INTRODUCTION

If the organization is to retain legitimacy in a democratic society, the citizens must be assured that the actions that they attribute to organizations remain within the bounds of justice (Donaldson, 1982; Stone, 1975). Society's primary venue to secure justice has consistently been the imposition of legal prescriptions. Unfortunately, as witnessed daily in media, legality has it limits. It never succeeded in keeping the organization within the bounds of justice (Maus, 1986; Stone, 1975; Yeager, 1991) 'They have no soul to damn and no body to kick', as judge Thurlow famously said in 1845, in order to explain why it is harder to discipline an organization than a human being through legal means (see Coffee, 1981).

In the case of human beings, morality has always been another practice restricting and disciplining conduct. It seemed therefore only natural for business ethicists to consider the possibility to discipline organizations through the authority of morality, next to legality, as another safeguard to attain justice (Donaldson, 1982; French, 1979 [1991], 1992). A fierce debate ensued on the issue; a debate that still has not gone away (Arnold, 2006; Danley, 1999; De George, 1981; French, 1979 [1991], 1992, 1996; Goodpaster, 1983; Hasnas, 2012; Hess, 2013; Keeley, 1988; Ladd, 1970; Moore, 1999; Philips, 1995; Rönnegard, 2015; Sepinwall, 2016; Velasquez, 1983 [1991], 2003; Werhane, 1985; Wolf, 1985, 2015).

In this chapter we focus on business ethicists who turned to morality for instrumental reasons only: to discipline the organization and keep it from causing trouble like environmental problems, fraud, human rights violations and so forth. We refer to these business ethicists as 'functionalists' and regard French (1979 [1991], 1992) and Donaldson (1982) as primary examples of such a functionalist approach. Functionalists look at morality as applied to the organization as a mere means that must help to attain a goal that legality is not able to attain by itself: justice for all citizens. A good reason why it makes sense for functionalists to be attracted to morality is that its modus operandi differs from legality. Ultimately, legality disciplines human beings through the threat of external punishment. Morality disciplines human beings through – what we will later explain as – 'voluntarily induced restraint'. Because of this different modus operandi, using morality can be seen as a real addition to legality, at least as regards human beings. The functionalists claim that it can also work in relation to organizations – but that remains to be seen.

We agree with the functionalists that society needs an additional mechanism to discipline the organization. We also agree that discipline through voluntary induced restraint is a good addition – if it would work. At the same time, the chapter acknowledges that the project of the functionalists has failed, at least partly. Considering what the functionalists aimed at, their suggestions should have launched:

1. A discussion on society's political, legal and moral right to demand that organizations are internally constituted (i.e., designed) in certain ways (e.g., society's right to require a whistle-blower protection arrangement, its right to demand how to – and how not to – exert leadership and so forth).[1]
2. A pragmatic discussion on how to design organizations such that – given the totality of all these institutional demands – citizens have reason to feel secure that organizations will exercise voluntary induced restraint, beyond (direct) legal enforcement. For example, because there is a whistle-blower arrangement, citizens of a society have reason to feel more secure that organizations will exercise voluntary induced self-restraint.

But nothing of the sort happened. Instead, the discussion was hijacked by a 'perennial' (Solomon, 1992) metaphysical discussion on the possibility of moral agency of the organization. In hindsight, it can be concluded that the phrasing by the functionalists was unfortunate. They spoke about 'the moral corporation' or 'the moral organization' and naturally that raised the issue of whether a non-human entity can be a moral agent. So, it can be said that because of their way of speaking, the functionalists themselves provoked the argument that if the organization is to be a moral agent, it must have the properties we attribute to human beings, as preconditions for moral agency. This argument is intuitively strong because people tend to link morality to humanity. The argument has impaired the cause of the functionalists. Many have pointed out that organizations do not fulfil these conditions (e.g., Rönnegard, 2015; Velasquez, 1983 [1991]). Especially because the functionalists were only interested in morality from an instrumental point of view, they would have fared better if they had framed the issue differently, for example, in terms of disciplining the organization through 'voluntary induced restraint'.

In this chapter we aim to re-launch the cause of the functionalists exactly along these lines. We assume that society has a moral right to discipline the organization and we focus on point 2. How should the organization be designed, such that the citizens have reason to feel secure that the organization will be disciplined through voluntary induced restraint? We do not answer this question by identifying concrete institutional measures (like a whistle-blower's arrangement and so forth). We focus on the formal condition necessary for voluntary induced restraint to be effective. This formal condition precedes any concrete institutional arrangement. It boils down to the demand that the (informal and formal) institutional structures of the organization enable the representatives of the organization to develop and maintain moral autonomy as persons.

This chapter aims to contribute to various discussions.

First, the discussion on the control of organizations. We aim to show that organizations can only be thought of by human beings as entities that keep within the bounds of justice if they allow their human representatives to become morally autonomous individuals, that is, *persons*. We think that this is an important conclusion as it demonstrates that correct organizational conduct *depends upon* the personhood of the representatives of the organization. If so, stimulating the personhood of representatives becomes an important requirement within organizations.

Second, the discussion on personhood of representatives within organizations. Morally speaking, stimulating personhood within the organization is important in its own right. We demonstrate that it is also important for political reasons. If society wants to secure that organizations do not cause effects that may lead to injustice for its citizens, it must ensure that the human representatives of organizations are stimulated to become persons.

Third, this chapter may fuel the discussion on the nature of the organization. Often the organization is conceptualized as a 'mere instrument' or 'a decision-making structure'. Conceptualizations like these belong to a family of 'rational' conceptualizations. But this is just one kind (Scott, 1981 [1998]). Selznick (1992) and other organizational 'naturalists' (Scott, 1981 [1998]) have demonstrated that the idea of the organization can only be made sense of as an entity that is *inherently related* to its human representatives. If so, it cannot be conceptualized as a *mere* tool. We support the naturalist's view; not just because it is helpful to our cause to make sense of the idea of 'voluntary induced restraint' as pertaining to the organization, but also because it seems to be correct.

Fourth, eventually we also contribute to the discussion on the moral agency of the organization or 'the metaphysical issue' (Rönnegard, 2015).

We think we contribute to the latter by insisting that it is impossible to reflect on the possibility of organizational moral agency without a proper concept of what the organization *is*, that is, without having a proper idea of *how the organization exists*. In this respect, we hold the position that to a large extent, the organization *is* what the citizens *demand it to be* (in terms of requirements put on its legitimate presence in society). This implies that the discussion on moral agency in business ethics has been partially misdirected. Oftentimes people argue that the organization cannot be A, because it lacks the requirements for the possibility of being (like) an X. However, our approach makes it clear that the organization does not have a nature that is (completely) fixed. If the organization does not fulfil the conditions for being (like) an X, then its nature *can and should be changed*. In the past, organizations were established through 'charters' in which the sovereign stipulated what it would take for an organization to have a legitimate place in society. Because the organization is an artificial entity, the charter should include the definition of what it means to *be* an organization in the first place, or so we argue.[2] Another contribution relates to the substantive normative criteria that we think ought to be part of the charter that allows organizations into society. We argue that organizations can only be disciplined through voluntary restraint if they can be brought under a two-fold authority. One authority is the instrumental goal it pursues; the other is an internally induced commitment to justice, restraining the pursuit of the instrumental goal. We also argue that the organization can only be brought under the second authority if its representatives can be moral persons. Both the two-fold authority and the personhood of its representatives must thus be made part of the charter by which organizations come into existence.

Someone may object to our approach by saying that we do not really get around the issue of organizational personhood. 'Why should the organization *itself* care about this?', someone might ask. We hope to demonstrate that this objection is beside the point. Our approach does not depend upon the possibility of the organization *itself* having a *consciousness*. The real question is whether it makes sense for *the citizens of a society* to be confident that *treating* the organization as *if it were* an agent that can be voluntarily restrained will make a difference in an empirical world that has already accepted that organizations exist as legal entities. We argue that this makes sense under specific conditions; the most important one being that the representatives of the organizations are (moral) persons.

A further objection might be that we are actually not discussing the voluntary restraint of *the organization* but the voluntary restraint of the *representatives of the organization*. We think that this criticism is invalid. We are referring to the restraint of the *organization.* The institutional design of the organization has an effect on the set of actions that citizens attribute to the organization. A well-chosen design will be a positive factor in bringing about a situation in which the sum total of all actions that citizens attribute to a particular organization will contain less actions that must be qualified as 'directly or indirectly leading to effects that will happen to be causes of violations of justice'. The fact that the human representatives of the organization (indirectly) play a role in bringing about this situation – because they are responsive to the design – does not change anything about the fact that because of the design the citizens have reason to believe that a change will come about in the actions *that they attribute to the organization*. So the citizens have reason to hold that *the organization* is restrained, not just its representatives.

Our attempt to skirt the discussion on 'organizational agency' may also be considered unsuccessful because the idea of moral agency of the organization is immanent within the idea of 'voluntary induced restraint'. All the problems with the concept of agency are hidden in the concepts 'voluntary induced' and 'restraint'. We agree that this criticism must be rebutted if this chapter is to make sense. Rebutting this will be an important part of the chapter.

The chapter is structured as follows. In Section 5.2 we deal with a few preliminaries. In Section 5.3 we lay out a characteristic of the modern experience and modern thinking of morality that historians of ethics have called attention to. Inspired by the insights of these historians of ethics, we work out a conception of the idea of 'voluntariness' that does not presuppose agency in Section 5.4. In Section 5.5 we repeat the same operation with the concept 'restraint'. Until that point in the chapter our exercise has merely been a *formal* one: we have explored the conceptual possibilities of a set of ideas. We slowly move to the empirical level in Section 5.6. We establish that the citizens of a society can meaningfully interpret the organization as an entity that is able to restrain itself – *provided* it is established as an entity that is under a two-fold authority. In Section 5.7 we work out some consequences of these ideas, in particular that this implies the organization must stimulate the personhood of its representatives.

5.2 LIMITATIONS

In this chapter we take for granted that human beings have reason to attribute – at least some – actions to the organization, legally and socially speaking. The organization is conceived of as a unity of action, at least in those respects. This assumption is widely shared (Donaldson, 1982, p. 19; Rönnegard, 2015, p. 1), but we realize it is not shared by all (e.g., Velasquez,

1983 [1991]). We think that denying this assumption disconnects one from the reality of modern society. Modern society has established the organization *as a unity of action* within social reality as a matter of fact by turning the organization into a legal entity. That is to say: establishing the organization through law means that the citizens of a society have decided that – from then on – *they will and must use the distinction* between 'action to be attributed to the organization' and 'action to be attributed to the representative of the organization' whenever they interpret an act that causally originates with the representatives of an organization.[3]

We must also build in a limitation with regard to the use of the word 'organization'. The law has established a wide variety of possible entities, all of which are commonly referred to as 'organization'. Our discussion is only relevant for empirically existing organizations that have procedures, a hierarchical structure and human beings as representatives. For present purposes exemplary organizations are entities like Shell, Microsoft, Oxfam or even the local school. We exclude 'dummy corporations', one-man operations, letterbox companies and the like. Our focus on this kind of organization also leads to an extension of the domain under review, compared to the business ethics discussion. We expand the domain of inquiry from the 'corporation' to the 'organization'. We see no reason to exclude (public) hospitals, schools or organizations like Oxfam. The political need to discipline the organizations also exists for these entities. Yet, we have excluded from our investigation the massive literature that takes 'collective agency' rather than 'the organization' as topic (Bratman, 2004; Hindriks, 2018; Pettit, 2001, 2007). We believe that the organization is a special collective agent, worthy of separate treatment (see Sepinwall, 2016, p. 4).

Furthermore, in terms of the problems organizations cause, we focus on violations of justice. We think that justice is both an uncontroversial and core value of humanity (Rawls, 1971; Sen, 2009, pp. viiff.). Naturally, the concept of justice can be interpreted in many ways. An important distinction is whether we speak of legal justice or moral justice. Typically, legal justice is seen as less demanding in terms of bringing it about at a societal level. We focus on violations of *legal justice*, albeit legal justice understood in an encompassing, non-legalistic sense. It includes that agents behave in a fair way in the process of law-making (and thus lobbying within limits) as well as regards the process of implementing laws (and thus do not frustrate government by withholding information for example). The focus on legal justice may seem odd, as we are discussing 'voluntary induced restraint'. There is no contradiction: in terms of *problems* caused by organizations, we limit ourselves to violations of legal justice; in terms of the ways in which organizations can be *disciplined* to keep within the bounds of justice, we focus on 'voluntary induced restraint' as an addition to legality.

5.3 MORALITY'S COMPLEXITIES

The goal of the current section is to present a phenomenology of the meaning and the experience of morality, based on work done in the history of ethics. We aim to show that the discussion on 'organizational moral agency' may have failed to take sufficiently into account something that we refer to as 'the broken identity of morality'. In modern society, morality has various meanings; each has its own set of preconditions and this makes it impossible to talk about *the* preconditions for being a moral agent. The insights provided by the work done in the history of ethics will help us when we subsequently develop the concepts 'voluntary' and 'restraint'.

Schneewind (1998) wrote an historical analysis of ethical thinking in the post-medieval to modern ethical thinking (1500–1750). He contends that the problems and solutions people wrestled with in order to understand (the meaning of) morality were brought to a (temporary) synthesis in Kant's thinking on the meaning of ethics. The key problem philosophers and others wrestled with was constructing a unified (metaphysical) account of the meaning of morality. Morality did not seem to have a unified identity. For example, the logic of morality seemed to require that rules and principles need a standard interpretation and that this standard interpretation must simply be followed. The members of a society cannot each give their own interpretation to the principle 'do not kill' (i.e., determine its relative importance in relation to other important principles, like 'self-defence'). The logic of morality demands a standard interpretation that all agents must abide by.[4] Yet, at the same time, the logic of morality seemed to imply that each moral agent must not just obey rules and principles; they must *recognize* them as valid. Otherwise morality cannot deliver on the important idea that morality requires a true motive.

According to Schneewind, Kant – as a moral anthropologist describing his culture – had a keen eye for this core metaphysical problem of morality. He gave expression to the problem of dis-unity by distinguishing two dimensions of morality, each with its own meaning-giving discourse. As a metaphysician, Kant also united the two dimensions. In this chapter we merely need Kant as a moral *anthropologist*, who used his own terms to give expression to a general problem of Western culture. According to Kant, morality must be understood in terms of the constitution of personhood. This is the core of the first of Kant's discourses on morality. Morality's meaning is that it is meaning-giving for human beings. Through morality a human being can become at the same time free, autonomous and a person. Morality in this sense refers to the will. The chief goal is to constitute the will as a free will. A modern philosopher interpreting morality in this sense is Christine Korsgaard. She argues that morality is about the constitution of the *person* (2009).

Kant developed this dimension of morality as 'morality as Virtue' (1797 [1996, 2003]). Morality as Virtue is a praxis in the classical sense. It is a means and an end at the same time, relating to the goal, meaning and/or the worthiness of life for human beings. Morality as Virtue is grounded in the human capacity to 'will to will' (Loose, 2013). 'Willing to will' is different from merely possessing the faculty of willing (i.e., wanting). In Kant's view, human beings conceptualize (the idea of) the animal as a creature that can 'will' things. But when interpreting themselves as moral creatures, human beings think themselves differently – as creatures that can *endorse* the things they will. Through this process of endorsing, the mere willing loses its arbitrariness (Herman, 1993). Exactly because of that reason, 'willing to will' becomes constitutive for personhood (Korsgaard, 2009).

However, Kant also developed a second discourse on morality. According to Kant, morality can also be understood in terms of the constitution of *society* (Kant, 1797 [1996, 2003]). As such, morality is a functional practice. Interpreting morality in terms of its function is also quite common. For example, in his book *The Cement of Society* Elster (1989) limits the meaning of morality to its function. Kant (1797 [1996, 2003]) discusses morality in its functional dimension as morality as Right. As Right, morality is a mechanism to discipline human beings. When looking at morality from the perspective of Right, we are not investigating the personal experience of morality. We are only looking at moral commandments as devices that discipline agent X in the interest of all other human beings who need to be protected from injustice performed by agent X. Hence, in 'morality as Right' the ground of an action has no role to play. More generally speaking, 'motivation' is not relevant in making sense of – or even justifying – this dimension of morality (Kant, 1797 [1996, 2003]: AA 6, p. 219). Morality as Right concerns morality insofar as *others* need to be *secured* in their rights and freedom. In Kant's view, it does not matter whether someone shuns away from wrongdoing because of fear of punishment or because of the virtue of one's nature. What matters is that one shuns from wrongdoing. Morality as Right is thus related to disciplining agents. It has a clear content. It is focused on the attainment of justice.

Legality and social norms can also be looked upon as disciplining practices (Habermas, 1981; Sorell, 1987). One way to distinguish morality from these other practices is its modus operandi. The modus operandi of morality we define as 'voluntary induced restraint'. We discuss this concept in full later. For now, we merely claim that a voluntary induced restraint means a restraint not induced by (the threat of) punishment. Legality and morality also differ in terms of the enforceability of their duties. Legality can actually enforce its duties. Kant (1797 [1996, 2003]: AA 6, p. 231) insists that the duties of morality as Right can legitimately be enforced. Yet, this does not mean that morality *itself* can enforce its duties. If something is a duty of Right, it is legitimate to enforce it. However, when it is *actually* enforced, the moral duty is transformed into something else (i.e., a legal duty or a social norm). To the extent that force is actually being called upon, the enforced principle is no longer part of morality as Right.

The dis-unity of morality's identity – a cultural phenomenon expressed by Kant in terms of Morality of Right and Morality as Virtue created a lot of problems for modern morality, as it became loaded with paradoxes that lead to misunderstanding if one does not keep a keen eye on the fact that morality must be understood in terms of the two discourses. One of these paradoxes is that morality must simply be obeyed (because of morality as Right) and also be acknowledged (because of morality as Virtue). In some contexts, these two meanings do not add up. Herman (2007) points at another: the tension between morality always being conservative (because of morality of Right) and constantly being in need of reflection, refinement and change (because of morality as Virtue) at the same time.

What enhances the problems in understanding morality is that many concepts of modern morality get a double meaning: one more tuned to morality as Right, the other more tuned to morality as Virtue. Keeping track of the distinction between these meanings is not always easy, which leads to further misunderstandings. For example, the concept 'moral wrongdoing' can be interpreted in a very strict sense that only relates to violations of the duties of Right. In that case refusing to help others as a matter of principle is not wrong as helping others is not a duty of Right. Yet, many people talk about 'wrongdoing' when speaking of a person who never helps others. In that case they use a broader concept of wrong that has to be related to the duties of Virtue. We can also say that, for example, having a jealous character and not caring about this is 'wrong' while this is at the same time not wrong, in a stricter sense (see Hill, 2002, p. 316).

This paradoxical nature of morality in modern times was overlooked in the business ethics discussion on moral agency. Within modern thinking morality does not have a (simple) unified metaphysics. Put differently: what was ignored in the discussion is that the issue was only in part how to transfer morality to a non-human entity, that is, the organization. Understanding morality *as it applies to human beings* was in itself already a problem. Transferring moral agency to the organization did not *create* many problems. To a large extent, *existing* metaphysical problems only became more pronounced with the arrival of the new subject, the organization.

We provide two illustrations of where the discussion went wrong. In the discussion on moral agency of the organization, many (still) cling on to the assumption that the organization must (metaphysically) mirror the human being, if it is to fulfil the conditions of moral agency (e.g., Rönnegard, 2015, p.9). This assumption may make sense in relation to morality as Virtue but does not obviously make sense in relation to morality as Right. In the case of the latter, personhood is not the issue; the only function of morality is to discipline an entity. It may even be true that in relation to human beings, discipline in terms of morality as Right only works if these human beings think of themselves as free agents; but if morality *would happen to work* as a disciplinary force as regards some non-human entity without that condition, it would be odd to insist that this entity must still mirror the human being. The point of morality in terms of Right is simply to protect the freedom of others.

Another example is the weight put by many on the concept of 'blame'. Academics asked: does it make sense to 'blame' an organization? If not, can the organization be a moral agent? For example, Sepinwall (2016, p.4) strongly links the possibility that the organization can be a moral agent to the issue of whether human beings can think of this entity as a proper object of 'blame'. But this way of framing the issue is unfortunate. 'Blame' is a concept like 'moral wrong'. It has meaning in both accounts of morality but these meanings are not identical and thus easily give rise to misunderstandings. The concept blame can be linked to the kind of 'wrongdoing' relevant to the constitution of society. But the concept blame can also be linked to 'the ground of action' and thus to the constitution of the person. The complexity of the concept shows itself in the legal context. On the one hand, legality is focused on making sure that 'wrongful kills' are being punished. This is necessary to secure order in society. There is a sense in which every wrongful killing must be punished regardless of the ground of action of the killer. Insofar as blame is relevant in this context, it only is relevant as 'violating morality of Right'. On the other hand, it is hard to conceive of murder *as murder*, without involving the ground of action of the perpetrator. When referring to this aspect of a crime (e.g., when determining punishment) 'blame' as concerns the ground of action is relevant. Hence, at that moment personhood is the issue.

Some may object to our analysis of the debate as overlooking important contributions. For example, Donaldson (1982, p.30; see also French, 1979 [1991], 1992; Hess, 2013) seems aware of the two discourses on morality when he employs the distinction between the moral *person* and the moral *agent*. A 'moral person' is an autonomous creature that is valued as an end and for whom morality has meaning. A 'moral agent' is a creature that can and must comply with the commandments of morality in its function of constituting the social order. But we do not argue that the discussion on moral agency *completely* overlooked the two discourses. It overlooked the problem that because of the two discourses, giving (metaphysical) meaning to morality is itself *already a problem* in relation to human beings. That is to say, Donaldson forgot to show that his distinction, while very intuitive, is at the same time problematic: it can only be understood in terms of the dis-unity of the modern understanding of morality.

We realize that our argument in this section is sketchy and depends upon many things, including the correctness of work done in the history of ethics. Still, we hope to have established enough credit to further the cause of the functionalists by taking a different angle. Therefore, we leave aside the discussion on the moral agency of the organization and focus on 'voluntary induced restraint'. In the next two sections we will investigate whether that change is merely word play.

5.4 FROM 'VOLUNTARINESS' TO 'PROPER POSITIONING'

We would like to make a new start with the discussion on the possibility to discipline the organization by non-legal means. This implies that we only interpret morality in terms of morality of Right. In this interpretation, the core of morality – as a disciplinary force – is 'voluntary induced restraint'. The question we need to answer thus becomes: Is there a way to make sense of voluntary induced restraint when applied to organizations? This issue contains two sub-questions:

1. Is it possible to apply the concept 'voluntariness' to the organization in a meaningful way (addressed in this section)?
2. Is it possible to apply the concept 'restraint' to the organization in a meaningful way (addressed in Section 5.5).

Note that in this section and the next (Section 5.5) we undertake a metaphysical exercise. We only ask: can we make sense of the *ideas* voluntariness and restraint in relation to the *idea* organization. So, we are not (yet) claiming anything empirical.

Many in business ethics believe that the discussion on the concept 'voluntariness' is crucial to the debate on organizational agency (see, e.g., Hess, 2014). It may therefore be thought that making the changeover to 'voluntary induced restraint' will not help us in getting round the discussion on organizational moral agency. But that changes once you look upon the concept 'voluntariness' like we looked at the concept 'wrong'. It has a meaning in both discourses on morality but these meanings are distinct. What we need to do is carve out these two distinct meanings and demonstrate that one meaning, relevant to us, can be used in relation to the idea of the organization.

The basic lack of clarity in the concept 'acting voluntarily' has been noted by others (Van Hees, 2003). When people say that an agent acted 'voluntarily', they may mean to say that the agent's *will* was not impaired in the action. In this sense, to 'act voluntarily' pertains to the *ground* of the agent's action. An agent acting voluntarily – in this sense – is (potentially) in control of his or her own will, that is, his or her process of willing to will. In Kantian terms, the action must not only be interpreted as an outward action (i.e., the movement of a leg or an arm). It is also – at the same time – an inward action (Korsgaard, 2009). As such, the 'voluntariness' of the action is a reason to argue that it expresses and – at the same time – constitutes the agent, as to her nature. As inward action, the action thus relates to the constitution of personhood. It is clear that human beings cannot make sense of voluntariness in this sense, in relation to the organization.

When using the expression 'acting voluntarily' people may also mean to point *at the conditions under which the action was decided upon and executed* (see Scanlon, 1998). How was the agent *situated* when it performed an action? When used in this sense while pertaining to human beings, the concept 'voluntariness' has a role to play in *intersubjective responsibility attribution* in a given case, needed to constitute a society. As such, the concept of 'voluntariness' is thus related to morality as Right. It is related to disciplining agents.

Even in relation to human beings, voluntariness as pertaining to 'responsibility attribution' and thus discipline is not directly related to the concept of free will. It is related to something that we will refer to as 'the conditions of freedom'. The conditions of freedom spell out when it makes sense to hold an agent responsible for an action (Scanlon, 1998). In the human context, the core condition is freedom (that is why we refer to these conditions as 'the conditions of freedom'). Other conditions are, for example: 'no compulsion' and 'having the proper knowledge'. The reason why the conditions of freedom are relevant for responsibility attribution is that the idea of morality includes the idea of fairness. It is meaningless for others to hold an agent responsible for an action if that attribution is in no way linked to something that belongs to the agent. This is why the idea of responsibility attribution to human beings becomes fundamentally uprooted if others hold a person responsible, for example, a knee reflex or another purely bio-mechanical reflex that his or her leg accidentally performs. Such a movement should be considered an act, not an action (Korsgaard, 2009).

Taking stock: we are investigating whether it makes sense to think of the organization as an entity that can be disciplined by 'voluntary induced restraint'. In this section we look at the concept 'voluntariness' and find that this concept can be made sense of as 'being properly positioned' in relation to responsibility attribution. This is a promising outcome, especially since we were able to distinguish voluntariness as 'being properly positioned' relevant for responsibility attribution and voluntariness as 'free will'. This is especially promising since the two meanings of voluntariness are not necessarily linked. This is true even for human beings. Insofar as we are interested in whether a human being does not do wrong in relation to morality as Right, we are not directly interested in free will. If there were a direct and immanent relation to 'free will', we could not hold a heroin addict accountable who committed a murder to get the money needed for his or her addiction. As an addict, he or she could convincingly make the case that his or her free will was effectively impaired. In daily life we reject this argument by the addict. He or she will be held accountable for the action. It will be established that he or she acted wrongly (even if in passing judgement *on the amount of punishment*, we may take into account the addiction). This means that in daily life human beings indeed use the distinction and reject the direct and immanent relation: at least in some cases, the ground of an action does not count in relation to a judgement concerning morality of Right.[5]

We realize that we are only half-way there. Someone may object: even if it makes sense to argue that there is a difference between voluntariness as 'freedom of will' and as 'fulfilling the conditions of freedom', it must still be shown that the 'conditions of freedom' can meaningfully be applied to the organization. That does not seem obvious: do all the old problems not come back, once more? For example: does it make sense to argue that an organization can be 'compelled'?

In rebutting this criticism, we emphasize again how important the distinction between the two discourses on morality is. In morality as pertaining to the constitution of the person, the idea of voluntariness as freedom of will is crucial. In morality as pertaining to the constitution of society, we deal with the conditions of freedom. As we see it, these conditions are not core to the issue of responsibility attribution. They 'only' belong to this core insofar as *human beings* are the subjects. The core issue in the attribution of intersubjective defined responsibility is *fairness*. If human beings are to be disciplined through intersubjective responsibility attribution, the distribution of responsibility must be fair. Human beings must only be held responsible for the things they can be responsible for. The 'conditions of freedom' are crucial in this respect: they define whether the agent was well positioned to take responsibility. This implies that if the citizens of a society want to attribute responsibility to non-human entities, there is no reason why they should necessarily involve the conditions of freedom.

They merely have to consider whether there is a way in which the *concept of fairness* can meaningfully be applied to this other type of subject. This is to say: it makes sense for human beings to think of the organization as a subject that can act 'voluntarily' if it makes sense for human beings to assess the way in which the organization was *situated* in relation to actions that violated justice.

So, if the citizens of a society want to discipline the organization by non-legal means (as an addition to legal forms of discipline), they need to bring the organization into the circle of entities that are assessed in terms of voluntary responsibility attribution. In the case of human beings, we refer to this as 'morality' but in the case of organizations that concept is better evaded. For this responsibility attribution to work well, the system of attribution must operate fairly. In order to work fairly, a system of responsibility attribution needs to assess the position which the agent had in relation to the action attributed to it. The concept 'voluntariness' can be used to define the situation in which responsibility attribution makes sense, that is, is fair.

Two issues require further clarification. In the case of human beings, we evaluate actions and we use the 'conditions of freedom' to define voluntariness. What would the parallel notions be in the case of organizations? So:

(a) what criteria define voluntariness?
(b) what aspect(s) of the organization are we going to assess in terms of voluntariness, relevant for the idea of fairness, that is, what counts as a 'voluntary action' in the case of the organization?

As this exercise is a merely formal one, we will – as yet – not dwell on the specific fairness criteria relevant for responsibility attribution in the case of the organization. We will only consider the second question. When assessing a case in which an agent's responsibility must be determined, it is widely regarded as unfair to hold an agent responsible for something it has no control over. Hence, if human beings aim to discipline the organization through voluntary responsibility attribution, we must link the responsibility attribution to something that human beings have reason to think the organization has control over. Wolgast (1992; see also Section 5.5) has argued that what typifies the organization is it being an *indirect agent*. It can only perform actions that have concrete consequences in the empirical world by means of its human representatives. This would lead to an important conclusion. In terms of voluntary responsibility attribution, the organization can never be made directly responsible for an action attributed to it (from the legal or social perspective). Ultimately, this attributed action is performed by a *representative* of the organization and thus the organization cannot be said to have full control over the attributed action. Following the same logic, it does make sense to hold the organization responsible for the *formal and informal institutional conditions* that make up the framework within which the human representative must produce actions (that will be attributed to the organization). Hence, it does make sense for human beings – who have already accepted the organization as legal and social agent – to think of the organization as in control of the framework by which it is constituted, a framework that presorts the acts of the representatives that will be attributed to the organization.

This idea may strike one as odd at first sight. We put forward two arguments to overcome the oddity. First, we are not saying that the organization cannot be held directly responsible for the actions attributed to it from other points of view, for example, legality. Legally speaking, the organization *can* and is held responsible for the acts produced by a representative that society attributes to the organization. Legality has different conditions for the possibility of imputing actions. We are only speaking of the responsibility that pertains to voluntary induced restraint. Second, if discipline through voluntary induced restraint is really to be an *addition* to discipline through legal means, then finding a mechanism that assesses a different aspect of the organization may actually work well. Otherwise the same action is evaluated twice, from different angles.

In this section we have considered the question of whether the concept 'voluntariness' can be made sense of in relation to the organization. That is a requirement in order to look at the organization as if it is capable of being disciplined through voluntary induced restraint. We conclude that there is a way in which it can make sense. We need to interpret the concept as it pertains to morality as Right. In morality as Right, voluntariness relates to the conditions under which responsibility attribution can be considered fair. In the case of a human being, the conditions of freedom define these. If the organization is to be assessed in this way, the citizens must look at its formal and informal institutional make-up that presort acts of representatives; not at the actions attributed to the organization as organizations do not have full control over these (even if they are attributed to the organization).

5.5 SERVING 'TWO AUTHORITIES' AS CONDITION FOR SELF-RESTRAINT

In this section we engage with the concept 'restraint'. Is it possible to think of the organization as an entity that can be restrained? Put in this general way, the answer is obvious. Yes, it is possible for human beings to think of the organization in that way. After all, commercial organizations (i.e., companies) are considered to be oriented towards profit. This means that they are restrained by the principle of profit seeking. Hence, insofar as human beings can think of the idea of a corporation, they can think of the idea of the organization as an entity that can be restrained. What is more, organizations are constituted as agents *under the law*. If it were completely impossible for legality to restrain organizations, society would be completely mad in establishing agents to whom actions will be attributed without the possibility to restrain these agents.

The real issue is: does it make sense to pertain the concept of *self-restraint* to the organization? Voluntary induced restraint does not call for the possibility of restraint; it calls for the possibility of self-restraint. In order to understand the difference between 'restraint' and 'self-restraint' we must distinguish between:

- restraint because of an externally imposed goal or condition (like profit seeking)
- restraint of the pursuit of the goal (e.g., restraint of profit seeking).

Let us engage in a thought experiment, and merely ask what would it take to *think* of the (idea of the) organization as an entity capable of self-restraint. As yet, we are not bothered by the empirical feasibility of our conclusions.

It belongs to the essence of the idea 'organization' to think it as – at least also – restrained by an externally given goal or identity. The organization is – at least also – an *instrument*. All conceptualizations of 'organizations' include this idea (see Lammers et al., 1997; Scott, 1981 [1998]; Selznick, 1957). If we aim to include the idea of self-restraint in the idea of the organization, we must think it as an entity that is not necessarily thought of as *merely* an instrument; an entity subservient to one, externally defined goal. The possibility of self-restraint implies that there is:

(a) another goal, identity or authority
(b) the other goal or identity needs to be – somehow – internally connected to the entity
(c) in case of a direct conflict between the goals, that other goal needs to have priority.

(ad a) There needs to be another goal or identity because human beings can only think the possibility of 'restraint of the goal' if there is something that is also important to the entity that can exercise the restraining force. It is exactly because the company is thought an instrument in view of one

goal (i.e., profit) that authors like Ladd (1970) and Bakan (2005) argue that it is *relentless* in the pursuit of that goal. Therefore, if we aim to include the possibility of self-restraint of the goal in the idea of the organization, we must define it as something that has to take into account *two* goals, *two* identities or authorities; if so the one can restrain the other. Also, the other authority must be the restraining power. The functionalists are concerned about the constitution of justice in society. This means that 'preservation of justice' must be core to the other authority.

(ad b) The idea of self-restraint implies that something internal to the entity ensures the restraint. If that something were a force that came from outside the entity, it would not make sense to speak of 'self-restraint'. One way for human beings to think of the concept of 'self-restraint' is to think of it as a force inherently related to one's personally (developed and) endorsed *identity*. If a person forsakes an action because, if he or she would perform it, he or she would lose one's individually endorsed identity, we can think of that agent as restrained by something internal to the agent: it is restrained by a force that he or she considers key to his or her identity and thus key to being as such.

(*ad c*) The two goals or identities may often be in harmony. However, there is also the possibility of conflict. If we aim to include self-restraint in the idea of the organization, we must think of the internally endorsed identity as the most important one. Otherwise there would be no self-restraint of the pursuit of the goal.

The conclusion of our thought experiment, therefore, is that the organization can be conceived of as an agent, restraining itself, if it can be conceptualized as an agent bound by two identities or authorities, one of which is constituted by the instrumental goal; the other is the internally endorsed commitment to preserve justice. When conflict arises, it is this last-mentioned identity that ought to be the *primus inter pares* of the two authorities.

5.6 THE FEASIBILITY OF THE ORGANIZATION AS SELF-RESTRAINING ENTITY

Our thought experiment bracketed the empirical feasibility of our conclusions. We turn to this issue now and ask: is it possible to conceive of the organization as a phenomenon present in reality, as an entity that must submit to two authorities? It is important to take note of the level at which we are working now. We are in between thinking mere ideas and describing concrete empirical objects. We are conceptualizing an empirical concept (comparable to conceptualizing 'lion' instead of describing a concrete lion). We refer to this empirically informed process of conceptualizations as developing an 'ideal-types'.

The most common ideal-type of the organization – as least in business ethics – is the Weberian ideal-type (1921 [1972]) as understood in the post-Weberian (Anglo-Saxon) literature (see Perrow, 1972).[6] The post-Weberian ideal-type of the organization excludes the possibility of 'restraining itself' by definition. It defines the organization as a pure instrument that is relentlessly oriented towards an established goal through rational means (e.g., Ladd, 1970). In his analysis of various ideal-types of the organization, Scott (1981 [1998], pp. 33–55) speaks of the organization 'as rational system', when people conceptualize it as a rational tool, fully and completely designed to serve a certain externally defined goal. We will thus speak of the post-Weberian ideal-type as one that fits the rational form. If all possible ideal-types of the organization would fit in with the rational form, there is no (ideal-typical) way to think of the organization as an entity itself restraining the pursuit of its instrumental goal.

It may seem that we need to seek further. It seems natural to argue that it is flat-out *impossible* to conceive of an organizational ideal-type that we can picture as able to restrain itself. After all, the possibility of self-restraint implies the possibility of 'internally endorsed identity' and that possibility presupposes the idea of a creature able to *endorse* something. Organizations obviously lack that possibility. (If they can be said to have an identity, it is the identity conferred on them by the instrumental goal.)

However, the observation that *human beings* are able to have an internally endorsed identity creates a possibility. After all, human beings have a role to play as representatives in organizations, so perhaps human beings can function as guardians of the necessary commitment to justice. If that route is going to work, then two conditions must hold:

(a) The relation between the organization and human beings functioning as its representatives must be an inherent relation.
(b) The human representatives must be able to let their commitment to justice prevail above the external goal of the organization in cases of conflict.

We investigate condition (a) in this section; condition (b) in the next.

Rationalist ideal-types of the organization conceive of the relation between the organization and its human representatives as an accidental relation: the organization is primarily defined as a tool. However, there is an important alternative tradition in organization theory that disputes the correctness of this ideal-type. Scott (1981 [1998]) refers to this tradition as the 'natural tradition'. According to naturalists like Perrow (1972) and

Selznick (1992), the organizational ideal-type is best not wrapped around the idea of mere tool. Ideal-typically the organization is best conceived of as organic or natural tool.

It is important to understand the naturalist position exactly. Naturalists are not saying that rationalists are mistaken because 'in practice' all organizations have 'multiple rationalities' (i.e., marketing, production and so on). That idea is compatible with the rationalist idea as long as it is understood that these rationalities somehow work together or ought to work together. Naturalists are also not saying that in practice all organizations differ somewhat from the rationalist form, in the same way that all concretely living lions differ from the empirically based concept of a 'lion'. They are saying that rationalists are *fundamentally mistaken* in their characterization of the organizational ideal-type.

According to naturalists, organizations are *inherently related* to their human representatives. Conceptually – as to their form – the organization differs from a robot or a machine. Because of that inherent relation to its human representatives, organizations *are better not defined as* mere tools.[7] According to the naturalists, organizations will *never* become mere tools. Failing at being a mere tool, therefore, cannot be considered failing as an organization. The impossibility to be a mere tool must be part of the ideal-type, as this is an empirically informed conceptualization. The reason why naturalists think the organization cannot be a mere tool is the inherent relation with the human representatives. Because of that relation the organization is to some extent always serving interests and values that cannot be explained by the externally given goal. These other goals and values are linked to the human beings that make up the organization. Yes, they work as representatives but at the same time they are always something beyond this role as representative.

The inherent relation between the organization and the human being is explained by, for example, Wolgast (1992, p. 9; see also Sepinwall, 2016, p. 6). She follows Hobbes (1651 [1985]) in suggesting that the idea of the organization must be grasped in terms of an 'author' and a 'representative'.[8] An 'author' is a unity of action that can only act through one or more representatives (or another author). A representative is a human being who has ceased to be an (autonomous) person in his or her own right, insofar as he or she is representing an author. Hobbes emphasized that in terms of internal hierarchy all representatives are subject to the author. Organizational theorists within the naturalist tradition emphasize that the reverse is also true: in terms of the possibility of action, the author inherently depends on its representative. Without a representative acting, there is no organizational action. In that sense, the organization is mediated and constituted by human representatives. As the human being is always more and different from being a representative (own private goals, character traits, failings and so on), it is mistaken to think of the organization as a mere instrument.

We conclude this section on the feasibility of defining organizations as entities subject to two authorities that the first condition (a) holds. There is an inherent relation between the organization and its human representatives. At least this is true in the naturalist's tradition. Obviously, we lack the space to determine which ideal-typical characterization makes most sense. Just one argument for the naturalist's ideal-type: ever since its rise organization theory has shown that in practice organizations are not mere tools. Think, for example, about all the literature on 'goal-displacement' (Lammers et al., 1997; Perrow, 1972; Scott, 1981 [1998]). Economic inspired research on behaviour in organizations (e.g., on the 'principal-agent problem') has confirmed this.[9] We therefore think it is reasonable to argue that the rationalist characterization of the organization as 'mere tool' is more normative than ideal-typical; while the naturalist tradition properly defines an ideal-type.

5.7 ORGANIZATIONAL DISCIPLINE THROUGH PERSONHOOD OF THE REPRESENTATIVE

At the beginning of this chapter we embraced the functionalists' claim that society needs an additional mechanism to make sure that the actions that human beings attribute to the organization remain within the bounds of (legal) justice. We investigated whether 'voluntary induced restraint' can function as this kind of disciplinary mechanism. In the last section we concluded that this will only work if (a) the relation between the organization and its human representatives is an inherent relation and (b) that the human representatives are able to let their commitment to justice prevail over the external goal of the organization in cases of conflict. In this section we will investigate the latter condition.

In this chapter we settle for a very simple, but effective answer to the question of when the human representatives will be able to let their commitment to justice prevail: human representatives will have this capacity when they are persons, that is, mature moral agents. A person or mature moral agent is an agent who knows and values the importance of morality. Hence, he or she knows how important it is – from a moral point of view – that justice prevails in the organization and this will heavily influence all decisions that he or she makes as a representative of the organization. Naturally, this stipulation raises multiple questions. For example: is the mature moral agent a moral hero? We do not think he or she needs to be a hero; that is why we did not write 'the mature moral agent lets justice prevail' but 'knows how important that is and this will heavily influence . . .'. This formulation creates room for manoeuvre and cautious decision making of the mature moral agent, without it being possible that he or she ever becomes indifferent about his or her organization exceeding the bounds of justice.

We argue in this section that:

(i) The personhood of human representatives in the organization is not something merely good or desirable. It is a condition for an entity to be called an organization.
(ii) The citizens of a society can only take seriously that an organization is exercising voluntary restraint if it makes a serious effort to stimulate personhood (i.e., moral maturity) of its human representatives.
(iii) In empirical reality, organizations often fail to stimulate the personhood of its human representatives.

(*ad i*) The functionalists' main concern is that organizations often go beyond the bounds of (legal) justice. That is why there needs to be an additional mechanism in place. Following this line of thought, it can be argued that the situation in which the human representatives let justice prevail must be considered a *necessary requirement* for an organization to be considered a legitimate organization. After all, when this condition is not met, the citizens have reason to doubt whether the organization will remain within the bounds of justice. Therefore, the citizens will insist that the (legal) definition of an organization contains the need for any organization to nurture the moral personhood of its representatives.

(ad ii) In the exact formulation of this requirement the citizens must take into account an important principle prevalent in Western morality. This principle reads that whether human beings eventually become mature moral agents depends upon themselves. Becoming a person is and only makes sense as an individual achievement. Hence, it would be odd to hold the organization accountable for its representatives actually *being* mature moral agents. Yet, it is also considered a general truth that the environment in which people have to live affects the individual's rise to personhood. Some environments are conducive to that development while others pose an (extra) barrier. This seems to suggest that the citizens can only have confidence that an organization exercises voluntary restraint if it demonstrates through the things it controls that it is serious about implementing voluntary restraint. This is to say: an organization that is serious about implementing voluntary induced restraint is an organization whose institutional framework is conducive to the development of the moral

personhood of its representatives. Naturally, this is especially relevant if the organization is a strong 'institutional field' that affects how people act and how they develop morally. Precisely this view is strongly corroborated by empirical research (Powell and Dimaggio, 1991; Waters, 1978; see also Ariely, 2012; Hollis, 2008; Kant, 1793 [1914, 2004]; Sharp-Paine, 1994; Trevino et al., 2006; Vardi and Weitz, 2004).

(ad iii) An organization, worthy of its name, stimulates the personhood of its human representatives, or at least this follows from the argument we laid out in this chapter. It must do this because this is the way to secure that the organizational goal is restrained through self-restraint. If this is true, modern societies should worry about the ways in which many organizations operate nowadays; not only in terms of actual transgressions of the bounds of (legal) justice but also in terms of their organizational design. Organizations are often neither designed nor operated in line with the requirements that voluntary induced restraint imposes upon the organization. In fact, there is a lot of empirical evidence demonstrating that the organizational context has an adverse effect on the development of the personhood of the human representatives. Without trying to be complete, we cite a few examples. It has been documented that the organizational context may lead to a process of personality 'doubling' (Lifton, 1986). Through this process human beings de-couple from their evil actions by creating two selves, each with its own distinct morality (see also De Swaan, 2015). Next, the ways in which the organizational context may create 'moral silence' have been documented (Bowie, 2013). Many have also discussed that the rationalizing inclination of human beings only becomes stronger in the organizational context (Bandura et al., 2000; Goodpaster, 2007; McLaughlin and Rorty, 1988). 'Rationalization' is a process in which people convince themselves of the validity of the crooked justifications and excuses they have constructed to get around their own immoral conduct, for example, pointing at others, suggesting that they were mere victims following orders and so forth. Finally, many have shown how organizations can create a context in which people merely obey orders rather than decide as mature moral agents (Arendt, 1963 [2006]).

A natural question to ask would be: why? How can we understand that organizations negatively affect the moral development of their human representatives? Looking at this question from the idea of an organization as requiring a two-fold identity, the answer is obvious: the instrumental identity (defined by the external goal) often achieves dominance over the other identity: the internally endorsed commitment to preserve justice kept alive by the moral personhood of the representatives. We agree with the functionalists that this dominance is a serious problem for a (democratic) society. We hope to have demonstrated that society can – and should – tackle this problem by requiring of organizations that they stimulate the development of personhood of their human representatives. If organizations do that, they can be considered as organizations that exercise voluntary restraint. Entities that do not fulfil this requirement should not be considered 'organizations' at all. There is no place for these entities in society. That is to say: if it were possible for an organization to be a pure instrument, there would be no place for such an organization in society. People who conceptualize the organization as a pure instrument (e.g., Ladd, 1970) and argue from this that organizations cannot be moral agents are in this sense totally right. It is only when you leave the purely instrumental view on the organization and demand that it serves two masters that morality can surface inside the organization.

5.8 CONCLUSION

This chapter tried to revive the attempt by French, Donaldson and other functionalists to find an additional means to discipline the organization. We share the functionalists' worry that in reality organizations often violate the bounds of (legal) justice. We moved away from the discussion in business ethics on the 'moral agency of the organization' as it derails the central issue: how to discipline the organization.

We defined 'voluntary induced restraint' as core to the modus operandi of the internal mechanism that should discipline the organization by a means that is not externally imposed upon the organization. It was established that it makes sense to think of the organization as an entity that can be thought of by the citizens of a society as capable of 'voluntary induced restraint'. In order to make sense of this possibility the organization must be conceptualized as an entity under the reign of two identities: the externally imposed instrumental goal and an internally induced commitment to justice. In relating the idea of a reign of two authorities to empirical reality, it was established that this is only possible through a commitment of the organization's representatives to justice. It is also required that there is an inherent relation between the organization and its human representatives. The naturalist's tradition in organization theory confirms that the organization must indeed be conceptualized as an entity that is inherently related to its human representatives. Empirical research points out that today the moral personhood of representatives inside the organization is undermined and eroded instead of supported by the design of the organization and the relentless pursuit of an instrumental goal.

In a modern society in which organizations exist as artificial agents (through law) human beings attribute (some) actions to the organization.

But the organization cannot be considered fully in control of its actions, as it depends on its representative to perform the action. This would make it unfair to hold organizations responsible for its actions, morally speaking. Yet, organizations must be considered in control of *the institutional framework that (strongly) presorts the conduct of its representatives.* As the development of personhood of human representatives is crucial to the presence and viability of the commitment to justice, the degree to which organizations exercise 'voluntary induced restraint' can be measured by the way in which strengthening the moral dimension of representatives is an inherent part of the institutional make-up of the organization. Modern societies have reason to make strengthening this institutional make-up part of the charter that defines what it means to be a (legitimate) organization in society.

This chapter has deliberately moved away from the regular discussion on organizational (or corporate) moral agency in business ethics. Still, we hope that it is clear how it contributes to the real-life problems this discussion addresses, in particular the problem as identified by the functionalists. We hope to have shown that the long-standing discussion on the moral agency of the organization can at least partly be enlightened by relating it to the problem of thinking morality as a unified identity in the first place. We see a way out of this metaphysical discussion by speaking of 'voluntary induced restraint' instead of morality. Next, we hope to have shown that the discussion on organizational moral agency presupposes a particular understanding of the nature of the organization. The organization should not be understood as a 'tool'. What is more, even if organizations in real life function as tools, society need not and should not accept this as a matter of fact. If anything, it is a degeneration of what the organization is supposed to be. Yet, most importantly, we hope to have shown that the desire to make sure that organizations must remain within the bounds of justice requires that its representatives can develop as moral persons.

NOTES

1. Some people nowadays argue for the idea that organizations ought to be treated as moral subjects. In this chapter we take the common view that organizations *as such* have no immanent value. They have only instrumental value.
2. Thank you Daryl Koehn for this suggestion made at the TABEC meeting 2018, at Rutgers University Newark.
3. Naturally, this formal statement leaves open which actions must be attributed to either the organization or the representative. The choices that are made here are always a matter of interpretation and the criteria are determined by historical circumstances.
4. This does not necessarily mean rigid principles, interpreted without case sensitivity. It means that judgements on concrete cases make a universalist claim in the sense that each

moral person should be able to understand and acknowledge this particular judgement on the case.

5. Note: it may count in relation to the determination of the measure of punishment (when guilty) and a lot of other issues, but not as such in relation to a verdict of morality of Right.
6. On the significant differences between Weber's ideal-type and post-Weber interpretations, see, for example, Perrow (1972).
7. If you define the organization as a 'mere tool', then, if you encounter a manifestation in empirical reality that does not work like a tool, you have reason to think that you have encountered an entity that somehow fails at being an organization; comparable with encountering a lion in practice without a tail, say. Such a lion is a sick or handicapped lion (when the concept lion defines it as tailed animal).
8. Actually, Hobbes speaks of the 'author' and 'artificial person' instead of 'human representative'. Yet, nowadays many think of the organization as the artificial person. So Hobbes's use of concepts is confusing (for us). To stop confusion, we use the word 'representative' instead of 'artificial person'.
9. https://www.ukessays.com/essays/economics/the-principal-agent-problems-in-organizations-economics-essay.php (accessed 22 August 2019).

REFERENCES

Arendt, H. (1963). *Eichmann in Jerusalem: A Report on the Banality of Evil.* Reprinted in 2006. Penguin Group, New York.

Ariely, D. (2012). *The (Honest) Truth about Dishonesty.* Harper Collins, London.

Arnold, D.G. (2006). Corporate moral agency. *Midwest Studies in Philosophy* **30**(1), 279–91.

Bakan, J. (2005). *The Corporation: The Pathological Pursuit of Profit and Power.* Free Press, New York.

Bandura, A., Caprara, G.-V. and Zsolnai, L. (2000). Corporate transgressions through moral disengagement. *Journal of Human Values* **6**(1), 57–64.

Bowie, N. (2013). Organizational integrity and moral climates. In *Business Ethics in the 21st Century. Eminent Voices in Business Ethics* (pp. 183–205). Springer, Dordrecht.

Bratman, M. (2004). Three theories of self-governance. *Philosophical Topics* **32**(1–2), 21–46.

Coffee, J.C. (1981). 'No soul to damn, no body to kick': an unscandalized inquiry into the problem of corporate punishment. *Michigan Law Review* **74**, 386–459.

Danley, J. (1999). Corporate moral agency. In R.E. Frederick (ed.), *A Companion to Business Ethics* (pp. 243–56). Cambridge University Press, Cambridge.

De George, R.T. (1981). Ethical responsibilities of engineers in large organizations: the Pinto case. Reprinted in L. May and S. Hoffman (eds) (1991), *Five Decades of Debate in Theoretical and Applied Ethics* (pp. 151–66). Rowman and Littlefield Publishers, Lanham, MD.

De Swaan, A. (2015). *Killing Compartments: The Mentality of Mass Murder.* Yale University Press, New Haven, CT.

Donaldson, T. (1982). *Corporations and Morality.* Prentice Hall, Englewood Cliffs, NJ.

Elster, J. (1989). *The Cement of Society.* Cambridge University Press, Cambridge.

Fia, M. and Sacconi, L. (2018). Justice and corporate governance: new insights from Rawlsian social contract and Sen's capability approach. *Journal of Business Ethics*, 1–24. doi: https://doi.org/10.1007/s10551-018-3939-6.

French, P.A. (1979). The corporation as a moral person. Reprinted in L. May and S. Hoffman (eds) (1991), *Five Decades of Debate in Theoretical and Applied Ethics* (pp. 133–50). Rowman and Littlefield Publishers, Lanham, MD.

French, P.A. (1992). *Responsibility Matters*. University Press of Kansas, Lawrence, KS.

French, P.A. (1996). Integrity, intentions, and corporations. *American Business Law Journal* **34**, 141–55.

Goodpaster, K. (1983). Morality and organizations. In T. Donaldson and P. Werhane (eds), *Ethical Issues in Business* (pp. 137–45). Prentice Hall, Englewood Cliffs, NJ.

Goodpaster, K. (2007). *Conscience and Corporate Culture*. Blackwell Publishers, Malden, MA.

Habermas, J. (1981). *Theorie des kommunikativen handelns*, two vols. Suhrkamp, Frankfurt am Main.

Hasnas, J. (2012). Reflections on corporate moral responsibility and the problem solving technique of Alexander the Great. *Journal of Business Ethics* **107**(2), 183–95.

Herman, B. (1993). *The Practice of Moral Judgment*. Harvard University Press, Cambridge, MA.

Herman, B. (2007). *Moral Literacy*. Harvard University Press, Cambridge, MA.

Hess, K.M. (2013). 'If you tickle us . . .': how corporations can be moral agents without being persons. *Journal of Value Inquiry* **47**(3), 319–35.

Hess, K.A. (2014). The free will of corporations. *Philosophical Studies* **168**(1), 241–60.

Hill, T. Jr (2002). Wrongdoing, desert, and punishment. In *Human Welfare and Moral Worth. Kantian Perspectives* (pp. 310–39). Oxford University Press, Oxford.

Hindriks, F. (2018). Collective agency: moral and amoral. *Dialectica* **72**(1), 3–23.

Hobbes, T. (1651). *Leviathan*. Reprinted in 1985. Penguin Books, London.

Hollis, J. (2008). *Why Good People Do Bad Things*. Gotham Books, New York.

Kant, I. (1793). *De religie binnen de grenzen van de rede*. Reprinted in 1914. Trans. G. van Eekert, W. Van Herck and W. Lemmens (eds) (2004). Boom, Amsterdam.

Kant, I. (1797). *The Metaphysics of Morals*. Reprinted in 1996. Trans. M. Gregor (ed.) (2003). Cambridge University Press, Cambridge.

Keeley, M. (1988). *A Social Contract Theory of Organizations*. University of Notre Dame Press, Notre Dame.

Korsgaard, C.M. (2009). *Self-constitution: Agency, Identity, and Integrity*. Oxford University Press, Oxford.

Ladd, J. (1970). Morality and the ideal of rationality in formal organizations. *The Monist* **54**(4), 488–516.

Lammers, C.J., Mijs, A.A. and van Noort, W.J. (1997). *Organisaties vergelijkenderwijs* (7[e] geheel herziene druk). Het Spectrum, Utrecht.

Lifton, R. (1986). *The Nazi Doctors: A Study of the Psychology of Evil*. Basic Books, New York.

Loose, D. (2013). Kants architectuur van de vrijheid. In P. Oomen (ed.), *Vrije wil een hersenkronkel? Wetenschappers en Dilosofen over een fascinerende vraag* (pp. 173–94). Klement, Zoetermeer.

Maus, I. (1986). Verrechtlichung, Entrechtlichung und der Funktionswandel von

Institutionen. In *Rechtstheorie und politische Theorie im Industriekapitalismus* (pp. 277–331). Fink Verlag, München.
McLaughlin, B. and Rorty, A.O. (1988). *Perspectives on Self-deception*. University of California Press, Berkeley, CA.
Moore, G. (1999). Corporate moral agency: review and implications. *Journal of Business Ethics* **21**, 329–43.
Perrow, C. (1972). *Complex Organizations: A Critical Essay*. Scott, Foresman and Company, Glenview, IL.
Pettit, P. (2001). *A Theory of Freedom: From the Psychology to the Politics of Agency*. Polity, Cambridge.
Pettit, P. (2007). Responsibility incorporated. *Ethics* **117**, 171–201.
Philips, M.J. (1995). Corporate moral responsibility: when it might matter. *Business Ethics Quarterly* **5**, 555–76.
Powell, W.W. and DiMaggio, P.J. (1991). *The New Institutionalism in Organizational Analysis*. University of Chicago Press, Chicago, IL.
Rönnegard, D. (2015). *The Fallacy of Corporate Moral Agency: Issues in Business Ethics*, Vol. 44. Springer, Dordrecht.
Scanlon, T.M. (1998). *What We Owe to Each Other*. Harvard University Press, Cambridge, MA.
Schneewind, J.B. (1998). *The Invention of Autonomy*. Cambridge University Press, Cambridge.
Scott, W.R. (1981). *Organizations: Rational, Natural and Open Systems*. Reprinted in 1998 (4th edn). Prentice Hall, Upper Saddle River, NJ.
Selznick, P. (1957). *Leadership in Administration: A Sociological Interpretation*. University of California Press, Berkeley, CA.
Selznick, P. (1992). *The Moral Commonwealth: Social Theory and the Promise of Community*. University of California Press, Berkeley, CA.
Sepinwall, A.J. (2016). Corporate moral responsibility. *Philosophy Compass* **11**(1), 3–13.
Sharp Paine, L. (1994). Managing for organizational integrity. *Harvard Business Review* March–April, 106–17.
Solomon, R.C. (1992). *Ethics and Excellence: Cooperation and Integrity in Business*. Oxford University Press, Oxford.
Sorell, T. (1987). Kant's good will and our good nature. *Kant Studien* **78**(1), 87–101.
Stone, C.D. (1975). *Where the Law Ends: The Social Control of Corporate Behaviour*. Harper and Row, New York.
Trevino, L.K., Weaver, G. and Reynolds, S. (2006). Behavioral ethics in organizations: a review. *Journal of Management* **32**(6), 951–90.
Van Hees, M. (2003). Voluntariness, suffering and euthanasia. *Philosophical Explorations* **6**, 50–64.
Vardi, Y. and Weitz, E. (2004). *Misbehavior in Organizations: Theory, Research, and Management*. Laurence Erlbaum Associates, London.
Velasquez, M. (1983). Why corporations are not morally responsible for anything they do. Reprinted in L. May and S. Hoffman (eds) (1991), *Five Decades of Debate in Theoretical and Applied Ethics* (pp. 111–31). Rowman and Littlefield Publishers, Lanham, MD.
Velasquez, M. (2003). Debunking moral responsibility. *Business Ethics Quarterly* **8**, 531–62.
Waters, J.A. (1978). Catch 20.5: corporate morality as an organizational phenomenon. *Organizational Dynamics* **7**(1), 3–14.

Weber, M. (1921). *Wirtschaft und Gesellschaft: Grundriss der Verstehenden Sociologie.* Reprinted in 1972. J.C.B. Mohr/Paul Siebeck, Tübingen.
Werhane, P.H. (1985). *Persons, Rights and Corporations*. Prentice Hall, Englewood Cliffs, NJ.
Wolf, S. (1985). The legal and moral responsibility of organizations. *Nomos* **27**, 267–86.
Wolf, S. (2015) Responsibility, moral and otherwise. *Inquiry* **58**(2), 127–42.
Wolgast, E. (1992). *Ethics of an Artificial Person: Lost Responsibility in Professions and Organizations.* Stanford University Press, Stanford, CA.
Yeager, P.C. (1991). *The Limits of Law: The Public Regulation of Private Pollution.* Cambridge University Press, Cambridge.

6. Crucial differences among three types of apologies and their shared ethical grounding in integrity*

Daryl Koehn

Today the behavior of political and business leaders is often viewed with suspicion, if not dismay. The #MeToo movement and the periodic groundswell to impeach President Trump reveal a popular impulse to hold famous figures and those in power responsible for their speech and deeds. However, defining what exactly we mean by responsibility is not easy. Its precise meaning, the ways in which it differs from accountability and liability, and its deep connections to self-reflection and to various virtues are all aspects that deserve attention.[1] While intriguing, these large topics lie beyond the scope of this short chapter. Here I focus on a narrower aspect of what the public has historically taken to be involved in responsible leadership – namely, the making of ethically sound apologies. Corporate apologies are one major way used by firms seeking to manage the fallout from crises or disasters. So it is important that they get these apologies right.

A good apology is a speech act in which the apologizer seeks to rebuild trust by taking responsibility for a past deed committed either by the apologizer (personal), by the apologizer's institution (corporate), or by the apologizer's country (collective). I argue that theorists and citizens alike have failed to pay sufficient attention to differences among apologies. One of the significant dangers associated with demanding responsibility from others is the possibility that the accusers make one or more serious category mistakes, demanding a type of responsibility that is not appropriate.

The majority of those writing about apologies have tended to assume that all ethically sound apologies must exhibit the features we attribute to ethically good *personal* apologies.[2] This category mistake suggests that we should be extremely cautious when we demand that business leaders act to make politicians more responsible or when we ourselves seek to enforce responsibility norms upon others. In particular, we need to think long and hard about what exactly we want from our leaders and what exactly their roles and positions may allow them to deliver. These two may not be the same. Section 6.1 establishes a preliminary typology of apologies. I argue that the various types are considerably more different than most researchers have realized to date and that these differences should be respected. In Section 6.2, I examine whether there is a shared ethical ground of all three types of apologies and suggest that the concept of integrity can function as this ground.

6.1 RESPECTING SIMILARITIES AND DIFFERENCES AMONG PERSONAL, CORPORATE, AND COLLECTIVE APOLOGIES

An apology is an extremely complex speech act.[3] Therefore, those who wish to analyse apologies and their efficacy and ethicality are well-advised to look at many apologies of each type before making broad assertions about the essence or nature of apologies. Koehn and Goranova examined over one hundred corporate apologies offered by Chief Executive Officers (CEOs).[4] Nick Smith's published work reflects his similarly extensive analysis of specific interpersonal and collective apologies.[5] Examining only a few apologies will inevitably prove misleading because they are so varied in their form and content.

Instead of forcing all apologies into simple single schema, it is, I think, more useful to think of apologies using a Venn diagram (Figure 6.1). Although in this chapter I have more to say about differences among the types of apologies, I would be remiss if I did not acknowledge at the start that there clearly are numerous similarities among these types as well (Domains #4–7 on the diagram). In addition, even those areas depicted as regions of uniqueness or non-overlap (Domains #1, #2, and #3) are best interpreted as representing what one very often or typically sees in that particular arena or domain. However, one can certainly find occasional cases in which behaviors or attributes usually seen in connection with one type of apology are present in another type as well.[6] In this chapter, I explore and delineate possible contours of each of the seven domains depicted in Figure 6.1.

6.1.1 Domain #1: Corporate Apologies' Distinctive Characteristics

Several features of corporate apologies appear to be distinctive. When we receive interpersonal or collective apologies, we expect the apologizer to acknowledge that wrongdoing has occurred. Both the apologizer and the harmed or victimized party agree that the apologizing agent or those he or she represents has done something wrong. There is no possibility in

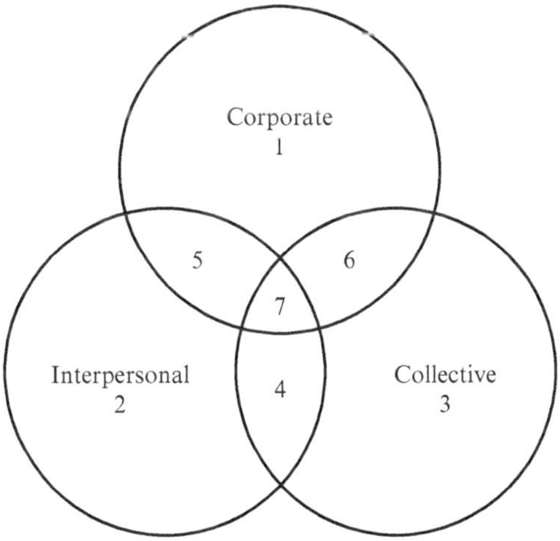

Figure 6.1 Typology of apologies

play that the "wrongdoing" might only be perceived or may not actually have occurred. Indeed, if Konrad Adenauer in his collective apology for the Holocaust had suggested that the Holocaust was only *perceived* as a monumental offense against humanity, his apology would immediately have been dismissed as unacceptable and characterized as a non-apology.[7] However, we need to remember that corporations are often accused of having acted unjustly (or even criminally) by individuals who have their own (sometimes hidden) agendas or who have based their accusations on false or incomplete information. Attempts by customers to extort firms or sellers are so widespread that vendor sites such as amazon.com have discussion boards dedicated to dealing with these attempts. "Social media blackmailing" of firms is not uncommon either.[8] Customers threaten to post unfavorable reviews if hotels or restaurants do not give them free meals and room upgrades in addition to an apology.

This problematic behavior by corporate stakeholders has two consequences. First, unlike individuals and nations, firms may face social demands that they apologize, when no apology is owed. Anything that they say in the face of such demands is then unjustly proclaimed to be a failed apology. Second, in some cases, firms want to apologize for some wrongdoing with which they are associated, but the firm's perception of the wrongdoing is not identical with the perception of stakeholders who see themselves as victimized by the firm. Toyota CEO Akio Toyoda's apology before Congress falls into this second class. The firm was accused of having manufactured cars with faulty accelerators. This accusation was found by credible investigative bodies to be unsubstantiated. On the other hand, in his Congressional testimony which was heard as an apology, Toyoda did state that the firm had failed to attend adequately to quality control issues in general. He testified that the firm had become so caught up in marketing that it had lost its focus on product quality. In his apology, Toyoda took responsibility for this loss of focus. Another case: after the Ashland Oil spill, the firm was accused by the press of having built the oil storage tank that ruptured without first obtaining the necessary permits. The firm believed (rightly as it turned out) that its employees had obtained the relevant permits, even though the firm's managers could not locate the requisite forms in the immediate aftermath of the spill. It was publicly alleged as well that the ruptured tank had not been tested prior to being deployed. That widely reported initial allegation also turned out to be unfounded. Nevertheless, despite these public misperceptions of the wrongdoing, the firm desired to reach out to those who had suffered on account of a spill that could unquestionably be traced back to an exploded Ashland Oil storage tank. So the Ashland Oil CEO offered an apology to local citizens as part of a four-hour press conference in which he did his best to answer questions from the media and from individuals who were directly affected by the spill.

So when CEOs offer apologies, sometimes the CEOs must grapple with or address a difference in perception as to what, in fact, the firm's misdeed was. In the case of collective apologies, by contrast, although the description of the wrongdoing can be contested (see my comments below on iterative apologies), the apologizer and wronged or aggrieved parties usually agree on the wrongdoing or the offense – for example, the American government's internment of Japanese-Americans during World War II or the Canadian government's head tax on Chinese. As I noted above, if we were to speak of "perceived" wrongdoing in these cases, we would be rightly accused of seriously misunderstanding the situation or perhaps even of deliberate obfuscation. Similar reasoning applies to purely personal apologies. Personal apologies beginning with "I'm sorry if you think I harmed you in some way" are quickly dismissed as failed apologies (or deemed to be non-apologies) by infuriated victims. The victim expects convergence between his or her and the apologizer's understanding of the wrongdoing or injustice.[9] Victims of one priest's sexual abuse were understandably incensed when the priest apologized not for the abuse but only for the sin of breaking his vow of chastity. Those on the receiving end of this "apology" rejected it *tout court*.

A related difference among apologies centers on causality. In interpersonal incidents calling for an apology, we know who caused the harm. If I spill coffee on you, we both know that I caused the harm (the burn, the damaged silk blouse, etc.). Incidents involving corporations frequently are not that clear-cut. Causality is very often a matter ascertained by the courts. Did Halliburton, British Petroleum, or a third party cause the Gulf of Mexico oil spill? There was much finger-pointing. Causality as well as some facts of the case have been the subject of years of litigation. In other cases, firms may suspect sabotage or terrorism caused the harm the public associates with the firm. It is thus naive to expect that an apology offered by a CEO must always feature an admission that the firm caused the offense. Many of the more ethically sound corporate apologies focus instead on rectifying the harm with which the public associates the firm, even if the firm did not cause the harm or did not do so in any simple sense of the matter.[10] The firm takes responsibility for ameliorating the harm or preventing future harm of this sort without admitting guilt.

Perhaps causality is clearer when it comes to collective apologies. The Canadian state removed more than 150,000 Aboriginal children from their families and communities and placed them in Indian Residential Schools. Yes, we can debate whether the state did so as an agent of the Canadian public.[11] And, yes, we may be unsure as to the number of victimized individuals. However, the cause of the wrongdoing is not contested in the same way in which the causes of particular corporate disasters (Gulf Oil spill; the Ashland Oil spill, etc.) are routinely disputed. In cases of alleged corporate wrongdoing, parties contend over issues of fact touching upon what exactly was done and who did or did not do it; while in the case of national or collective apologies, we may be dealing less with questions of causation and more with thorny theoretical problems inherent in the attribution of responsibility to a collective.[12]

While reparations are often an element of collective and interpersonal apologies, they are not so common in corporate apologies. As is well-known, the United States has a very litigious business environment. Settlements are generally arrived at through class action suits, not freely bestowed by firms accused of wrongdoing. Moreover, often the firms themselves can claim they, too, have been victimized. Data breach-related CEO apologies are among the most common corporate apologies. In such cases, the firms did not themselves cause the breach, although they may have been negligent in protecting customer or third party data. The hacked firms usually announce the breach, express regret for the inconvenience and worry experienced by customers whose data has been compromised, and then outline the steps they are taking to prevent future breaches. After the breathtaking hacking of the credit bureau Equifax, Equifax did eventually offer a year's worth of free identity theft protection to those who definitely were or might have been affected. Volkswagen offered owners of VW vehicles affected by the emissions cheating scandal a cash "good will" payment and several years of free roadside assistance if these owners bought a new VW.[13] After admitting to a 14-year-long price-fixing scheme, the Canadian grocery store Loblaw offered customers a $25 gift card for use in their stores.[14] Such corporate bestowing of something of economic value on apology recipients, however, is relatively rare.

By contrast, national settlements accompanying collective apologies are not rare. The US government made a cash settlement to the interned Japanese-Americans, and the Canadian government did the same in the case of children warehoused in residential schools. Even personal apologies may involve some sort of reparation possessing economic value. After spilling red wine on my sister's carpet and sofa, I not only apologized profusely but gave her money to hire a professional cleaning service to remove the stain. Parents who get home later than they had forecasted may apologize and give the babysitter extra money as compensation for any inconvenience or harm they caused by staying out too long. Such gestures can be thought of as small-scale reparations.

In general, corporate apologies aim at shoring up corporate brands. Consequently, I think that CEO apologies are best viewed as efforts to restore trustworthiness in the firm and perhaps even in the larger capitalistic system rather than as instances of confessional repentance, designed to elicit forgiveness from consumers or other stakeholders. The market system relies upon trust, and so it is not surprising that firms are frequently concerned with maintaining or repairing trust.[15] Indeed, forgiveness cannot be the main concern in a corporate context. For only those who have been harmed by an offender are in a position to extend forgiveness to the offending agent. Yet many stakeholders who have not been harmed by a specific firm nevertheless listen to, expect, and find value (or an absence thereof) in CEO apologies.[16] Volkswagen's corporate apology for manipulating pollution control data and deceiving regulators spoke not only to existing owners of VW vehicles but to potential owners and perhaps even to VW employees, shareholders, and lenders. Would-be buyers of VW automobiles do not have to *forgive* VW, but they do need to think that the firm is sufficiently trustworthy that VW can be relied upon in the future to produce safe, truly non-polluting cars.

6.1.2 Domain #2: Personal Apologies' Distinctive Characteristics

Nick Smith has analysed characteristics of personal apologies in detail.[17] I have little new to add to what he has already done a fine job of explicating. In the interest of highlighting the distinctiveness of personal apologies, I would just stress that personal apologies frequently fit into a quasi-religious narrative arc involving psychological transformation. A mean-spirited individual who has harmed her friend may apologize, promising to do better in the future. The recipient of the apology who accepts it may then reasonably watch for evidence that the speaker is involved in a serious process of self-reform.

Such psychological reform makes little sense in the collective and corporate contexts if we believe that corporations and nations do not have souls or do not qualify as persons. While some business writers speak of corporate souls, many would question the use of such terminology. We think of psychological reform as growing out of a sense of shame or guilt, yet corporations and collectives, which lack a singular physical body, cannot blush. By contrast, court and judicial officials can and do look for evidence that suspects or prisoners feel remorse.[18] In the absence of remorse, these individuals may be arrested, incarcerated, and receive much heavier prison sentences. The narrative arc in the judicial context incorporates the possibility of physical imprisonment. But we cannot imprison a corporation or an entire nation. So the personal apology at least appears to be distinctively wedded to a narrative or story about psychic transformation in a way that corporate and collective apologies are not. (In Section 6.2, I suggest that even sound personal apologies may be less a matter of inner feelings and change and more a matter of the adoption of audit-able changes in behavior.)

Another point: the individual apologizer commits to reforming herself in the future. It might be argued that in the case of collective apologies some degree of moral transformation (perhaps at the individual citizen level) has already occurred prior to the utterance of the apology. It is precisely because the state/public has moved beyond a condition of complacency, indifference, or wickedness that the state/general public feels that a collective apology is now called for and warranted.

A historical note: since the 1600s onward, interpersonal apologies have been linked to repentance and forgiveness.[19] In earlier times, the West featured apologies that were spirited, personal defenses of ways of life (e.g., Socrates' famous apology before the Athenian jurors).[20] These ancient *apologia* or defenses gave way to a Judeo-Christian view of apology that asked recipients of the apology to forgive the debt or trespass committed by the offender just as the recipients, in turn, would ask (or maybe even expect!) God to forgive them their sins or trespasses.[21] These religiously based personal apologies can be construed as attempts to heal wounds, to show respect for the victim as an individual, and to make personal relations more cordial (or, more minimally, civil) through the mechanism of repentance and forgiveness. Although some collective apologies might appear to invite restorative forgiveness, in many cases the injured parties who would possess the moral standing to choose whether to forgive the offense are no longer alive (e.g., the Jewish victims of the Holocaust) and so cannot forgive the collective. Consequently, it would seem to be a category mistake to make forgiveness an integral part of collective apologies. Forgiveness would similarly appear to be out of place in the case of many corporate apologies (see above analysis of Domain #1).[22]

6.1.3 Domain #3: Collective Apologies' Distinctive Characteristics

In the case of a collective apology, a public official utters a carefully crafted statement of regret for substantial, or even monstrous, harms committed by the state and/or the general public. It is very much an open question whether the official should be interpreted as speaking as an agent of the public.[23] Perhaps the official is more a representative of a nation-state or public that is trying to imagine a better future for its citizenry. In any case, ascertaining whether the official is apologizing for past actions of the state apparatus or for those of the general public can be tricky as well. This difficulty is not merely theoretical. A substantial number of members of the general public may not be willing to accept responsibility for deeds that they did not directly commit or intend or that they may not even today find all that objectionable. Therefore, the exact status of the apologizer and the basis for his or her authority can be obscure when it comes to this class of apologies.

This state of affairs differs considerably from what we encounter with other types of apologies. The CEO who utters a corporate apology unproblematically speaks as an employee of the firm. CEOs are the "authorized" speakers for firms in a variety of contexts – for example, at shareholder meetings and on calls with financial analysts regarding earnings reports. I know of no case where the public rejected a corporate apology on the ground that the CEO did not speak for the firm. In personal apologies as well, we almost never encounter conundrums concerning the authority or standing of the apologizer. If I injure you, you will look to me to utter an apology. I am clearly the cause of the injury. Since I typically will have been acting as an individual and not as an occupant of some role, questions concerning my role, status, or authority as the apologizer simply do not arise.

Collective apologies may also require that we carefully consider who are the licit recipients of the apology for past official wrongdoing. If some of the gay men arrested by the Toronto police were themselves charged with violent sexual predatory assaults on very young men, should a collective apology for past police actions against members of the LGBTQ community cover police actions taken with respect to these alleged predators?[24]

Collective apologies involve a powerful or sovereign agent (the state apparatus/public) expressing regret over the state/nation having harmed and/or offended marginalized groups. The power differential between the apologizer and the victims is significant. While power disparities do exist in the case of corporate apologies and even in some instances of personal apologies (think of the parent apologizing to the child and vice versa), the state is in the position of being able to control access to the documents and records necessary to establish the scale and exact contours of the collective offense. The state can lock down access to or even seal relevant records for decades. While corporations can and sometimes do try to paper over facts, the press often is able to locate sources or evidence that prevents firms from controlling a breaking story along the lines that corporate management might desire. When we are thinking about collective apologies, then, we should not lose sight of the possible effects of this ever present, substantial power difference.

Given that those injured lack power, it can take time for them to find and to gain a voice. That means that collective apologies occur within a milieu of contestation and struggle. For example, Canadians moved from thinking of the residential schools' injustice as consisting in abuse within the schools to realizing that the schools as such (which did little educating of children[25]) were unjust. This sort of evolution in how a wrong should be conceptualized means that collective apologies (e.g., Canada's residential schools' apology) may need to be iterative:

> [Collective or political] apologies that had already been given appeared later to be undermined by an expansion in public knowledge; new historical findings and new civic narratives emphasized details and dimensions of causal and political responsibility ignored in the earlier regretful admissions . . . Political apologies . . . tend to occur within longer-run processes in which state admissions of wrongdoing interact dynamically with struggles over public knowledge. Thus, apologies might better be seen as moments within iterative processes of social memory and civic learning rather than their summative ends.[26]

Iterative personal apologies, though, can come across as highly neurotic, while iterative corporate apologies are frequently disastrous, undermining consumer trust in the firm. Target apologized numerous times after hackers breached its credit card database. These multiple apologies (perhaps as many as six – I, like many other customers, lost count and interest after the third apology) suggested that the firm was so befuddled and inept that it likely was not going to be able (at least in the near future) to remedy the wrongdoing or prevent future data breaches.

Finally, collective apologies typically must name some direct and extraordinary harm done to very large numbers of individuals (e.g., the interned Japanese-Americans; the millions of Holocaust victims). The Equinox data breach compromised the identifying features of more than

100 million Americans. While this breach was serious, I suspect that most people would concede that the attendant harm was not of the magnitude of a genocide or mass imprisonment. Personal apologies may result from a serious harm – an accidental killing or severe damage to another's self-esteem or reputation. Still, personal apologies more typically involve a lesser offense. Put differently: for an offense to merit a collective apology – an apology that may evolve and be crafted and re-crafted over a period of years – the wrongdoing must be horrific.

6.1.4 Domain #4: Characteristics Shared by Collective and Interpersonal Apologies

CEO apologies, especially in the United States, are drafted with input from the firm's legal department or outside counsel. Why? Because past corporate apologies have figured in lawsuits against firms. In that respect, corporate apologies reflect legal realties. Personal apologies, by contrast, are usually not legalistic. Rather they are spur of the moment speech acts.

What about collective apologies? Although lawyers have participated in the drafting of collective apologies, it is not clear that such apologies need to be as legalistic as they sometimes have been in the past. Doug Elliott contends that there are no cases, at least in Canada, in which national apologies have created legal liability for the nation/state.[27] If so, then it is simply a legal myth that official apologies must be crafted with an eye to avoiding lawsuits:

> [T]he notion that an official apology will lead to legal liability is an urban legend with no basis in fact or law in Canada. On the contrary, a well-timed and carefully crafted apology may serve to limit or avoid legal liability. Apologies do not create liability where none exists. Accordingly, the lawyer who automatically advises a client to refrain from an apology as the "safest" course is actually engaging in professional negligence. Further, in the context of government lawyers, such advice may verge on the unethical.[28]

6.1.5 Domain #5: Characteristics Shared by Corporate and Interpersonal Apologies

Those harmed by corporate agents or private individuals usually expect to receive an apology shortly after the offense occurs. Corporate leaders may be able to buy themselves some breathing room by suggesting that they are investigating a possible data breach or are looking into the allegation that their products are in some way defective. However, when many consumers have been affected, especially in some non-trivial way, the CEO cannot wait too long before offering an apology once the firm's stakeholders have come to expect one. In this era of social media, delay is not a viable option.

So, too, with personal apologies. If I spill coffee on you and then wait for two months before expressing any regret, you will likely dismiss my words as being "too little, too late."[29] If offenders genuinely respect and empathize with their victims, then we expect that they will express remorseful regret relatively promptly after having inflicted the injury.

However, any collective apology that was given too soon would appear unseemly. If German leaders had announced in 1945 that they and their fellow citizens deeply regretted the Holocaust, few would have taken their words seriously. The problem here is not just that the intended recipients of the apology would not have believed in this apparent sudden change of heart. As I noted above, I am far from convinced that the remorse narrative applies all that well to collective apologies. The problem is rather that the victims and other relevant observers or third parties (e.g., historians) would not have had sufficient time to absorb the enormity of the harm suffered by victims. And the perpetrators/apologizers would not have had the time needed to contemplate their actions and motivations or even to think about the extent to which they might share in the responsibility for wrongdoing that they did not themselves individually commit (and for which they may not feel any guilt or remorse). The very process of identifying victims typically takes years. To the extent that the specification of the nature and magnitude of these collective offenses requires sustained self-scrutiny, access to archives, detailed historical analyses, and the possible drafting of new policies and procedures designed to curtail future abuses by the state, a "quick collective apology" is an oxymoron.

6.1.6 Domain #6: Characteristics Shared by Collective and Corporate Apologies

As I have already suggested, neither corporate nor collective apologies readily fit into a narrative arc of psychological reform. That arc presupposes that the same agent is the cause of the past misdeed and the promised future reform. In the case of corporate and collective apologies, the individuals involved in the past wrongdoing – those who formulated the relevant unjust policy or procedure or designed the harmful product, those who advocated for the policy or product, and those who executed the policy or manufactured the product – may no longer be on the scene. Some of the politicians who argued for the internment of Japanese-Americans were dead by the time the collective apology was given. With respect to corporate apologies: the CEO uttering the apology may have been brought in from the outside to replace a CEO who was fired because of his or her poor handling of the crisis or on account of his or her complicity in an attempted coverup. In such cases, we cannot locate an individual agent who is using the apology to signal that he or she is embarking upon a self-initiated reform of the self.

These two types of apologies share another subtle feature. In both cases, the apologizers occupy some role (President of the United States; CEO of Domino's Pizza). It is this role that authorizes these individuals to speak on behalf of the corporate or collective entity. If prior occupants of that role are widely thought to have been corrupt or untrustworthy, the role itself can become contaminated. In other words, the apologizer will find it difficult to make an effective apology because the audience has decided in advance that the speaker's words are not worth hearing. Even before the Fukushima nuclear meltdown, prior CEOs of Tokyo Electric Power Company (TEPCO) had been implicated in various safety scandals.[30] The CEO at the time of the Fukushima disaster faced a public disinclined to trust anything he might have to say. We can readily imagine a similar problem arising in connection with a collective apology. If prior national leaders have given collective apologies that have been dismissed as hollow, then the current president or prime minister may find it quite challenging to be taken seriously.

Individual apologies are not usually subject to role contamination, for speakers do not typically offer apologies in some capacity as role occupiers. Of course, if someone has offered many apologies in the past to, say, a friend, then this victimized friend may have grounds for doubting the value of the latest apology. But victims do not reject a personal apology on the basis of what some predecessor of the apologizer has or has not said.

6.1.7 Domain #7: Characteristics Shared by Personal, Corporate, and Collective Apologies

I will end by returning to the point that I made at the beginning of the chapter. All three types of apologies qua apologies share some common elements. In all three cases, the apologizer is addressing the victims of some harm, offense or injustice (accidental, intentional or resulting from negligence) that the apologizer has directly caused or with which he or she is associated (in the victim's and/or public's mind). In addition, all of these apologies qua apologies explicitly or implicitly aim at rebuilding the broken bond of trust between the apologizing party and the person or group receiving the apology.[31]

6.2 CONCEPTUALIZING THE ETHICAL RELATION AMONG VARIOUS TYPES OF APOLOGIES

The first point to grasp is that all of three types of apologies can be more or less ethical because all three exist within the ethical realm insofar as all represent an attempt to restore trust between apologizer and victim.[32] Virtue ethics focuses on the conditions for a fulfilled life. Given that we must trust others in order to live what we take to be a fulfilled life, trust itself is an ethical phenomenon. To paraphrase Plato: there is trust even among thieves. As speech acts that aim at rebuilding trust between perceived offenders and their victims (actual or potential), apologies of all sorts are quintessentially ethical – be they ethically good or ethically deficient.

In more Kantian terms, all three types of apologies are ethical because they reflect and recognize human autonomy. In more ethically sound apologies, apologizers acknowledge that they, their country, or their institution/organization has failed in some non-trivial way to treat others as persons. The offending party has used the wronged party as a means to an end or has failed to recognize that the victim has legitimate interests that should have been respected. Confining innocent citizens within prison camps (e.g., Japanese-Americans) simply because their families had historical ties to an enemy nation (Japan) failed to consider the free and willed actions of those interned – who were loyal citizens of the United States. Instead, this policy of internment made assumptions based on ethnicity. Such a policy treats persons as though they lack will – that is, as though they are not persons who freely perform actions. Or to take a corporate example: if privacy rights are in some sense constitutive of what it means to be a person, then failing to protect the privacy of customers by keeping their financial information secure fails to respect them as persons. Companies involved in data breaches feel compelled to apologize as an acknowledgement that they have violated their customers' personhood.

It may be tempting to view corporate apologies as somehow less genuine apologies than personal or collective apologies on the ground that these corporate speech acts are instrumental – that is, they "merely" serve to shore up the corporate brand. By contrast, personal and collective apologies – to qualify as genuinely sound, robust apologies – are expected to demonstrate that the apologizer has undergone a change of heart and is committed to being more respectful of the personhood of the victim(s) going forward. But I think that line of reasoning is mistaken for numerous reasons.

First, all three apologies qua apologies exist equally within the ethical realm for reasons already given. Second, while it is true that the apologizing CEO need not personally feel guilt or shame for the corporation's perceived wrongdoing – in some cases, the apologizing CEO will not even have been with the firm at the time of the offense and, thus, can hardly be expected to feel compunction for what his or her current firm did – this same point about instrumentality could be applied to collective apologies. An apologizing president might not even have been born at the time when her country committed the serious offense. Consequently, if we adopt the deprecatory logic used to dismiss corporate apologies as merely instrumental, we risk having to categorize collective apologies as ersatz apologies as well. For in the case of collective apologies, the apologizer might be said to apologize not out of sense of personal guilt but (at least in part) with a view to committing the country to ethically better, more respectful policies in the future. But if so, then, has not the representative (or agent) of the public instrumentalized the speech act – making it serve as a gesture to shore up the country's moral self-image?

Third, as I have already argued, in the case of both corporate and collective apologies, the apologizer speaks as the representative/agent of an offending body (e.g., Canada or British Petroleum). This body as such may or may not be capable of being sincere or of feeling guilt or of undergoing psychic reform. Indeed, much ink has been spilled on the question of whether the corporation qualifies as a moral person. Theorists have raised doubts precisely because the corporation lacks an organic natural body (and thus emotions connected with such a body), has no soul, and cannot be imprisoned and punished in the way a natural individual can be.[33] If we require that the offending party be a "person," and if we insist on construing an apologizing representative as somehow embodying a nation's or corporation's remorseful personhood, we will soon find ourselves once again mired in the morass of theoretical debates about the nature of a person.

I suggest that attending to some of the key differences among apologies points to a way to sidestep that intellectual quagmire entirely. What matters most to the ethical soundness of apologies in general is whether they are structured with a view to reestablishing trust with the relevant audience. In the case of the personal apology, the wronged party is someone whom the apologizer knows that he or she has injured. In the case of professional and collective apologies, the audience may include potentially injured parties (e.g., potential customers of VW who were considering buying a VW vehicle before the emissions scandal broke) or fellow citizens who share a common future that has been threatened by a past injustice committed against a subgroup of the community. In other words, it is the formal properties of the apology itself that matter more to the recipients of the apology than the remorseful or guilty feelings of the apologizer. What needs to be conveyed in the apology is some evidence that the apologizer wishes to restore the integrity of the body whom he or she represents – to make that body (corporation; nation) trustworthy.

As Dubbink has argued, the important issue when we evaluate the ethics of a corporation's actions and speech is not whether the corporation is a moral person but whether the corporation has developed and instituted policies, incentives, programs, and procedures that encourage its members to act in ways that respect their own personhood and that of other stakeholders.[34] By analogy, as I have argued elsewhere,[35] in the case of corporate apologies, what matters is not the sincerity or guilty feelings or remorse of apologizing CEOs but whether these corporate representatives are able to articulate the policies and procedures that the company has adopted and is enforcing to ensure that future cases of similar wrongdoing do not arise. These policies may be inward- or outward-directed. However, in either case, they should be structured so as to restore the audience's trust in the company's brand going forward. Mattel's CEO Bob Eckert's apology was favorably received by audiences because he carefully outlined the new steps the toy company was taking in order to keep lead out of its supply chains and thereby to make Mattel's toys safe for children.[36]

In other words, corporate apologies are more ethical to the extent that the speaking CEO seeks to establish that the firm he or she leads is seeking to act with more integrity going forward. Integrity here means something like developing an organizational infrastructure that helps stakeholders realize their personhood ever more fully.[37] So, while at least some recipients of personal apologies are looking for the apologizer to admit guilt and to feel remorse because these are drivers of psychic change, recipients of corporate apologies are listening for institutional changes in incentives, policies, procedures, etc. A similar point can be readily applied to collective apologies. Victims of national injustices do not want to hear national leaders metaphorically wring their hands over past wrongdoing. They want to know what their leaders are going to do to help them overcome their suffering and to ensure that similar injuries are not inflicted in the future. Thus, the president or prime minister may have to speak about reparations, changes in laws and policies, new approaches to education or punishment, etc.

It does not follow that the CEO's or national leader's personal traits, character, and commitment are entirely irrelevant when it comes to assessing the ethical soundness of their apologies. Corporate apologies have an element of pathos.[38] Pathos includes the expression of empathy – that is, a clear indication that the apologizer is aware of the nature and extent of suffering that his or her firm is seen as having caused. Such an expression helps instill confidence that the CEO and the firm have sufficient moral awareness to recognize the apology's recipients as persons with rights, legitimate interests, and concerns deserving of acknowledgement and respect. When Tony Hayward, British Petroleum CEO at the time of the Deep Horizon oil spill disaster in the Gulf of Mexico, whined on national television that he wanted his life back and hated having to deal with the disaster when he would rather be out on his yacht, various stakeholders, relatives of the dead drillers, and residents along the Gulf were understandably outraged. Hayward's callous disregard for these parties' welfare and interests called into question his commitment to making BP a company with integrity. In Kantian terms, achieving corporate integrity requires that there are employees and leaders within the firm who are struggling to act as moral persons.[39]

It should be clear, then, that corporate apologies are not merely instrumental PR ploys to shore up brands. Ethically sound corporate apologies presuppose trust and moral personhood. Analogous reasoning will apply to collective apologies. Indeed, instead of judging the ethical goodness of collective and corporate apologies in terms more appropriate to private personal apologies, we perhaps should evaluate personal apologies in light of the standard of integrity we apply when assessing these other types of apologies. If I betray you by sharing a confidence, you likely will find my apology more compelling if I do not merely say "I'm sorry" and shed a few tears of remorse but instead commit myself to some new practical "policies" going forward. For example, as part of my apology to you, I may explicitly promise to keep your confidences private in the future and commit to regularly visiting a psychologist with a view to understanding why I have felt compelled in the past to blurt out other people's secrets. You may have no way to ascertain for certain what my true feelings are. However, my practical "policy" commitments are audit-able – for example, am I, in fact, seeing a psychologist? As such, these changes in my practice arguably will do more to rebuild trust than a verbal expression of remorse.

6.3 CONCLUSION

Scholars have begun to do a wonderful job of mining the rich and thought-provoking topic of the ethics of apologies. Yet if personal, corporate, and collective apologies exhibit not only similarities but also profound differences, then all of us interested in apologies need to hear not only from academics but also from elected officials, activists, practitioners, government officials, CEOs, members of the media, and victims' advocates (to name but a few groups). What do these persons think makes for an ethically good apology? In the absence of input from these individuals, any discussion of the ethics of apologies will be sadly impoverished.

Furthermore, although key differences should be identified and factored into ethical analysis of apologies, it would be misleading to treat some of these types of apologies as more inherently ethically good than others. All three types exist within the ethical realm. When we carefully analyse these types, we discover that an integrity framework centered on policies, programs, procedures, incentives, etc. can go some way to illuminating a shared ethical ground of all three types of apologies. The framework outlined in this chapter is admittedly sketchy. More work needs to be done to flesh out its details. But I hope that my argument here can point the way forward.

NOTES

* A shorter, online version of this chapter appeared as Daryl Koehn, 2017, "Preliminary Thoughts on Types of Apologies: Interpersonal, Corporate and Collective," *c4ejournal*, 25 October, https://c4ejournal.net/2017/10/25/daryl-koehn-preliminary-thoughts-on-types-of-apologies-interpersonal-corporate-and-collective/. Portions of that paper are being reprinted here with permission of that journal.

1. Daryl Koehn, 2019, *Toward a New (Old) Theory of Responsibility: Moving Beyond Accountability*. Amsterdam: Springer.
2. See, for example, Keith M. Hearit, 2006, *Crisis Management by Apology: Corporate Response to Allegations of Wrongdoing*. Mahwah, NJ: Lawrence Erlbaum Associates; John Kador, 2009, *Effective Apology: Mending Fences, Building Bridges, Restoring Trust*. San Francisco, CA: Berrett-Koehler Publishers.
3. The same point is made by Nick Smith in his 2017 keynote speech "Apologies as Remedies, Apologies as Weapons: Considerations for the Trudeau Administration," University of Toronto, 20 October.
4. Daryl Koehn, 2013. "Why Saying 'I'm Sorry' Isn't Good Enough: The Ethics of Corporate Apologies," *Business Ethics Quarterly* **23**(2), 239–68; Daryl Koehn and Maria Goranova, 2016. "Do Investors See Value in Ethically Sound CEO Apologies? Investigating Stock Market Reaction to CEO Apologies," *Journal of Business Ethics*, **152**(2), 311–12, doi: 10.1007/s10551-016-3301-9.
5. Nick Smith, 2008, *I Was Wrong: The Meanings of Apologies*. Cambridge: Cambridge University Press; Nick Smith, 2014, *Justice Through Apologies: Remorse, Reform, and Punishment*. Cambridge: Cambridge University Press.
6. For example, Hugo Boss's corporate apology for its founding CEO Hugo Boss's support of and business ties with the Nazi Party has some of the attributes of collective apologies (e.g., the apology was issued only after years of archival work done by a professional historian hired by Hugo Boss).
7. For an argument as to why apologies that fall very short of the relevant ideal type may be perceived as not being really apologies at all, see Koehn, "Why Saying 'I'm Sorry' Isn't Good Enough."
8. Maike Steggemann, 2015. "Customer Misuse of Social Media Power in the Hospitality Sector – Threats and Strategies," unpublished paper, http://essay.utwente.nl/67291/1/Steggemann_BA_Management%20and%20Governance.pdf (accessed 16 June 2016).
9. I do not think the understanding of the offense needs to be *identical*. Those causing harm may never fully understand the nature and extent of the suffering and pain they have caused to those to whom they are apologizing but they can at least show that they have tried to comprehend such matters.
10. Koehn, "Why Saying 'I'm Sorry' Isn't Good Enough."

11. Cindy Holder, "Whose Wrong Is It Anyway? Reflecting on the Public-ness of Public Apologies," Ethics of Apologies workshop paper, University of Toronto, 21–22 October 2017.
12. I do not mean to suggest that issues of fact are never contested in the collective apology context. For eye-opening historical analyses of facts connected with past and proposed collective apologies in the Canadian context, see the superb papers by Steven Maynard, "Sorry Seems to be the Easiest Word: The Gay Pardon in Canada and the 'Rehabilitation' of Queer History," workshop paper; and Mayana Slobodian, "Finding Canada's Official Apology at the Truth & Reconciliation Commission," Ethics of Apologies workshop paper, University of Toronto, 21–22 October 2017. Causation can be a highly complex matter. For example, to the extent that social attitudes and practices (e.g., anti-Semitism; prejudice against Asian emigrants or against indigenous peoples) have led to collective wrongdoing, establishing causation quickly leads researchers and thinkers into the realm of nuanced dynamics and poses questions concerning "facts" about attitudes and practices.
13. Dante D'Orazio, 2015, "Volkswagen Apologizes for Emissions Scandal with Full-Page Ad in Dozens of Papers," *The Verge*, 15 November, https://www.theverge.com/transportation/2015/11/15/9739960/volkswagen-apologizes-with-full-page-ad-in-dozens-of-newspapers (accessed 2 January 2017).
14. Aleksandra Sagan, 2017, "Loblaw Hit with Backlash over Response to Bread Price-Fixing Scheme," *The Star*, 22 December, https://www.thestar.com/business/2017/12/22/loblaw-hit-with-backlash-over-response-to-bread-price-fixing-scheme.html (accessed 3 November 2017).
15. Nico Lacetera, "Corporate Apologies and the Ethics of Trust," Ethics of Apologies workshop paper, University of Toronto, 21–22 October 2017.
16. One might try to argue that even potential customers or shareholders who do not own a firm's products or shares are harmed by the firm's wrongdoing insofar as their potential trust in the firm has been damaged. However, I think that this kind of extension of trust in order to make forgiveness applicable to corporate apologies may strain the notion of an apology beyond its limits.
17. Smith, *I Was Wrong*.
18. Smith, *Justice Through Apologies*.
19. The modern form of the apology may have developed alongside the emergence of the bourgeoisie. The language of debtors and forgiving of debts certainly has a transactional, commercial ring to it. We do need to be careful, though, not to generalize too readily about the connection between apologies, sin, repentance, and human and divine forgiveness. In Confucian contexts, apologies may have deeper links with the Confucian notion of the rectification of speech than with forgiveness. Insofar as Confucianism does not posit a transcendent god, forgiveness cannot be modeled on divine forgiveness. In Buddhism, forgiveness may be related to detachment from suffering, not to concerns with debts, sins or trespasses.
20. Mark Kingwell, "Apologies: A Stylistic Investigation," Ethics of Apologies workshop paper, University of Toronto, 21–22 October 2017.
21. See John Ricco, "On Queer Forgiveness" for a discussion of forgiveness and its links to the concept of trespass. Ethics of Apologies workshop paper, University of Toronto, 21–22 October 2017.
22. Indeed, forgiveness may not even be relevant in some classes of personal apologies. Simon Stern, "Atonement, Closure, and Narrative" makes a strong case that court "coerced" apologies given by an offender to his or her victim may still serve the valuable function of validating the victim's claim that he or she did, in fact, suffer some harm. Ethics of Apologies workshop paper, University of Toronto, 21–22 October 2017.
23. Holder, "Whose Wrong Is It Anyway?"
24. Maynard, "Sorry Seems to be the Easiest Word."
25. Slobodian, "Finding Canada's Official Apology."
26. Matt James, Jordan Stanger-Ross, and the Landscapes of Injustice Research Collective,

"Impermanent Apologies: On the Dynamics of Timing and Public Knowledge in Political Apology," Ethics of Apologies workshop paper, University of Toronto, 21–22 October 2017, p. 1.
27. Doug Elliott, "So Sorry: The Legal Myths and Social Realities of the Official Apology," Ethics of Apologies workshop paper, University of Toronto, 21–22 October 2017.
28. Ibid., p. 2.
29. Nicholas Tavuchis, *Mea Culpa*. Stanford, CA: Stanford University Press, 1991, pp. 87–9.
30. Koehn, "Why Saying 'I'm Sorry' Isn't Good Enough."
31. Ibid.
32. Or stakeholder, given that some corporate apologies are aimed at not only those directly harmed by the firm's deed but also at stakeholders who are potential customers/employees and thus not necessarily harmed in the same way that actual customers/employees may have been by the firm's actions.
33. Wim Dubbink, "Making the Organization Ready for Voluntary Discipline. Moving from Morality to Integrity." Working paper shared with the author in January 2019.
34. Ibid.
35. Koehn, "Why Saying 'I'm Sorry' Isn't Good Enough."
36. Mediacurves, 2009, "Domino's Pizza Apology Tested," http://www.youtube.com/watch?v=uFiXWboPD5A (accessed 3 April 2013).
37. Dubbink, "Making the Organization Ready."
38. Koehn, "Why Saying 'I'm Sorry' Isn't Good Enough."
39. Dubbink, "Making the Organization Ready."

7. The board of directors' role in ensuring accountability and creating value: stakeholder and shareholder complementarity

Cynthia E. Clark

7.1 INTRODUCTION

There has been much research-driven and practice-oriented discussion over the past decade about how to fix what is broken in the corporate governance of firms. This discussion is important not only because the board of directors is a central part of the firm's leadership but also because many of these boards are in the midst of troubling times. Indeed, recent corporate governance changes, ushered in by new laws (e.g., the 2002 Sarbanes–Oxley Act),[1] new global principles (e.g., OECD, 2015), and altered listing requirements from stock exchanges around the globe, created a new set of expectations for corporate boards. Combining these changes with the public's heightened expectations of directors' responsibilities (Dah et al., 2014), boards and their directors find themselves needing to be more accountable than they have ever been before (Aguilera et al., 2015).

Nearly every aspect of the board of directors' role involves leadership. The board determines strategic direction of the firm, hires and fires top management (including the CEO), and, by law, has the responsibility for the firm's overall performance (Leblanc and Gillies, 2005). Another primary role of the board is providing access to resources such as advice, counsel, knowledge of external events and influence with external groups (Boivie et al., 2016). Ideally, too, boards strengthen the status and reputation of the firm and help it to gain access to much needed external resources (Zahra and Pearce, 1989).

In fact, some critiques of corporate governance revolve around failures of leadership, specifically those that lead to diminished value for shareholders (Dalton et al., 2007). Other critiques pit the interests of shareholders against the interests of stakeholders, positing that value creation for the former comes primarily at the expense of value creation for the latter (Jones and Fleming, 2003; Spicer et al., 2009). Even while both critiques have in common the importance of value creation and accountability, they both leave these constructs underdeveloped, which limits the explanatory power of what constitutes "good" governance.

The prime responsibility for good governance, as a matter of both ethics and prudent management, should lie within the company rather than outside of it. Put another way, good governance cannot be outsourced (Luo, 2005) nor can it be singularly associated with financial metrics (Ghoshal, 2005; Raelin and Bondy, 2013). Despite the significance of their roles, relatively scant attention has been paid to how individual board members, or the board as a whole, interact in their decision-making processes or their role in ensuring accountability (Boivie et al., 2016; Forbes and Milliken, 1999; Roberts et al., 2005). As boards of directors are increasingly perceived to be responsible for firm performance as well as for the legal and ethical actions of the firm, their individual actions and collective accountability as leaders comprise integral components of corporate governance (Luo, 2005).[2] Further, since a firm's ability to demonstrate relational responsibility and morality influences the firm's market acceptance and legitimacy (Aguilera et al., 2007), understanding how these characteristics might be substantiated among individual governance actors and within the board of directors as a whole is an important discussion (Steckler and Clark, 2019).

The role of boards in ensuring accountability and participating in the value creation processes of organizations merits more attention in ethics and corporate governance scholarship. However, accountability – or the implicit or explicit expectation that one may be called on to justify one's beliefs and actions to others (Scott and Lyman, 1968; Semin and Manstead, 1983; Tetlock, 1992) – has been little written about despite its central place in a board member's responsibilities. Further, there is scant attention to how accountability gets integrated into board roles and processes (Luo, 2005) or how boards create value for stakeholders in addition to shareholders (Huse, 2007; Talaulicar, 2010). Similarly, the concept of value creation, or the relative amount of value realized in a monetary exchange by the individual, organizational, or societal user (Lepak et al., 2007), is rarely equated with metrics other than financial profit (Harrison and Wicks, 2013, excepted).

In this chapter, I consider the board's ability to create value and why its unique role in the organization's leadership places its members in a position to refocus the processes and outcomes of how they are held accountable in their effort to better govern the organization. In this way, the processes of value creation are dependent on various accountability systems (e.g., policies, processes, outcomes) that both describe the actors who are accountable and *to whom* and *for what* they are accountable. To be sure, the firm's chief executive officer is accountable to the board of directors because she has to explain and justify her conduct to board members and because they can remove or sanction her if she does not live up to expectations. However, there exist not only additional outcomes the firm is responsible for but also additional processes.

This chapter begins by taking a step back and looking into how stakeholder and shareholder views make largely complementary theoretical assumptions while both asserting the proper roles and responsibilities of firms. Doing so calls out the recognized need to address the enduring debate about the purpose of the corporation in order to enact changes in the area of corporate governance (Dhir, 2015). A firm, and ultimately its board, is assumed to adopt practices that are consistent with either one paradigm or the other. However, these theories of the firm, each associated with different practices, represent to some scholars two contradictory theoretical assumptions (Poole and Van de Ven, 1989). Yet, to others, these differing assumptions can be managed via a process that involves developing an understanding that accepts and accommodates tensions (Sundaramurthy and Lewis, 2003). Other stakeholder theorists deny the existence of conflicts at all by suggesting that shareholder interests are stakeholder interests and vice versa (Freeman et al., 2004).

Therefore, the goal is to show how shareholder- and stakeholder-oriented views can be used to direct boards toward activities that reinforce one another by first outlining two main commonalities of both perspectives – accountability and value – and then illustrating how a board's accountability to both shareholders or stakeholders can lead to value being created in the long term for the other.[3] The focus in this analysis, then, is the firm's board of directors – specifically its overarching corporate governance procedures and outcomes – and how this entity is able to connect its value to overall value creation. Thus, one aim of this chapter is to refocus the corporate governance literature toward instilling values in organizational processes as ends in themselves while at the same time illustrating the boards' ability to create value for their organizations and stakeholders through attention to accountability (i.e., the ability to justify organizational beliefs and actions) as an outcome.

7.2 LITERATURE REVIEW

Central to corporate governance is the formation of a board of directors, comprised of a set of elected members who jointly provide executive-level oversight, the provision of resources (Boivie et al., 2016), and strategic input to management (e.g., Hillman and Dalziel, 2003). The board of directors is comprised of a unique set of individuals responsible both for providing support and oversight for upper management and, at the same time, being accountable to shareholders for the actions made by management (Roberts et al., 2005). Researchers have noted this situation may not present itself as a tension, instead, "the key to board effectiveness lies in the degree to which non-executives acting individually and collectively are able to create accountability within the board in relation to *both* strategy *and* performance" (Roberts et al., 2005, p. S6, emphases in the original). Building on this research, we suggest that board accountability leads to value creation and that both need to be part of the board's core mission with a focus on good governance principles.

Increasingly, researchers note good governance includes considerations of the practices required to evaluate and enact sensible, effective, and responsible decisions (Clark and Gabaldon, 2018; Filatotchev and Nakajima, 2014) and to overcome information barriers on the individual and group levels (Boivie et al., 2016) in order to integrate financial and societal conceptions of what constitutes good governance (Raelin and Bondy, 2013). There is growing recognition that good governance is about more than the relationships between owners and managers precisely because there are other parties with a strong interest in whether a business is run well, including employees, customers, creditors, and other companies in the supply chain (United Kingdom Green Paper, 2016). In this way, Aguilera and colleagues (2015) recently identified four elements of good governance: (1) protection of shareholder rights and enforceability; (2) management of stakeholder relationships; (3) information disclosure; and (4) strategic and ethical guidance.

This reflects a shift away from the predominant economic lens used in governance toward a behavioral perspective (Hambrick et al., 2008) that views governance as a product of both the efficiency and relational parameters of strategic leadership (Bell et al., 2014; Finkelstein et al., 2009). Because boards are not directly involved in implementation, directors must demonstrate effective governance through their input on decision-making (Forbes and Milliken, 1999). Thus, board effectiveness, or the ability of – and the degree to which – the board is able to achieve its mandate to be a responsible monitor of management and an accountable steward of the firm (Clark and Gabaldon, 2018), hinges on managing the difficulties often experienced in group interactions (Forbes and Milliken, 1999).

Accordingly, looking beyond the dominant focus on financial and structural aspects of corporate governance, toward both individual and relational factors in governance roles and processes – namely, value creation and accountability – is long overdue. Relational considerations are particularly important as the purview of the board shifts from a relatively narrow focus on fiduciary obligation to shareholders toward a more holistic emphasis on ethics and corporate responsibility (Bower and Paine, 2017; Donaldson, 2012; West, 2009) to a constellation of stakeholders with heterogeneous interests (Hambrick et al., 2008; Walls and Hoffman, 2013). However, in order to shift the governance focus in this way, researchers must address the enduring debate about the purpose of the corporation (Dhir, 2015).

Boards must be persuaded to go above and beyond traditional market-based systems to provide a governance culture that sets the moral tone for accountability across the organization. Such a culture tends to include (1) communicating anti-corruption measures, an anti-cheating culture, and corporate values; (2) establishing an integrated structure for accountability policies and procedures; (3) developing a cultural climate for expressing and sharing concerns; (4) providing ethical leadership; and (5) establishing committees to draft codes of conduct (Luo, 2005). These mechanisms are geared toward refocusing the lens through which the board itself sees corporate governance, internally, and trying to move the board away from a strictly market-based system of accountability. There is an implication that these internal mechanisms are later used to more clearly express the broader role of the board in being accountable, externally, in the form of firm policies and practices. Accountability, in this line of analysis, ensures better disclosure, transparency, and communication to those stakeholders who are necessary for enterprise sustainability, which has the concomitant effect of reducing monitoring and agency costs (Luo, 2005).

Roberts et al. (2005) found that accountability signaled the potential for later processes of learning to occur through open dialogue, which can promote reciprocal understanding and creative thought. These researchers noted that creating accountability is not well served by conceptual distinctions between the "control," "service," and "resourcing" roles of the board (p. S18). Further, skillful accountability requires a fluid process that can combine elements of both control and collaboration, instead of a crude switching between the two (Sundaramurthy and Lewis, 2003). This type of governance may also be understood in terms of the moral capacity by governance actors to make ethical decisions among conflicting individual and collective goals (Mazutis and Slawinski, 2015; Novicevic et al., 2006). In sum, whether implicit or explicit, much of what is discussed in corporate governance is fundamentally about ethics and responsibility (West, 2009) reflecting a deep sense of purpose in corporate governance (Donaldson, 2012) –perspectives which tend to be under-researched.

7.3 THEORY

7.3.1 Two Camps

Stakeholder- and shareholder-oriented theories are both normative theories of corporate responsibility – advocating for what a firm ought to be (Smith, 2003); that is, its purpose. Based on prior literature, a firm is assumed to adopt expressions and practices consistent with either one paradigm or the other (Fiss and Zajac, 2006; Smith, 2003). However, in academic discourse, there have been explicit suggestions that one paradigm *should*, or *will*, in effect, replace the other (cf. Donaldson and Preston, 1995; Evan and Freeman, 1988; Hansmann and Kraakman, 2001) or the two are contradictory and incompatible (Donaldson and Preston, 1995; Marcoux, 2003). Positioning these as distinct theoretical camps (Harris and Freeman, 2008) has resulted in a body of scholarship that has largely overlooked the possibility that shareholder and stakeholder perspectives might complement one another.

There is general consensus that a stakeholder perspective operates when management believes there is a moral obligation for a firm to work toward addressing the needs of customers, employees, suppliers, the local community as well as shareowners (cf. Clarkson, 1995), keeping these needs and interests in "balance" not simply for instrumental reasons but because it is the right thing to do (Donaldson and Preston, 1995). Noteworthy here is the general acknowledgment that managers need to engage in making trade-offs (Jones et al., 2007) but must also be accountable to multiple stakeholder groups (Freeman, 1984). However, as reflective of a growing assertion that responsible management, which balances the legitimate stakes of internal and external constituencies, can lead to higher financial return (Talaulicar, 2010), research requires a second look at the concern over any real trade-offs between shareholder objectives and social responsibility (Armitage et al., 2017). Thus, a focus on accountability and value creation together should reduce the number of trade-offs between shareholder and non-shareholder stakeholder interests.

Furthermore, while management is tasked with generating profits in order to be sustainable, its work is also governed by the stakeholder emphasis on creating value for society beyond a pure monetary benefit for shareholders. Likewise, the obligation of managers extends to consider *all* stakeholders' interests even if doing so reduces company profitability (Smith, 2003). The key questions for managers under this view are threefold (Freeman, 2008): (1) if this decision is made, for whom is value created or destroyed? (2) whose rights were enabled or not? (3) what kind of person would I be if I make this decision in a particular way?

A shareholder-oriented view of the firm's responsibilities asserts that managers should spend capital advanced by shareholders in ways that have been authorized by shareholders and act in the shareholders' interests (Friedman, 1962 [1982]; Smith, 2003). The shareholder view focuses on the firm's provision of long-term market value for shareholders (Jensen and Meckling, 1976; Williamson, 1985) regardless of the benefits or detriments to other organizational or societal constituents (Hasnas, 1998). Marcoux (2003) has argued it is the shareholders who have special moral status, imbued in the fiduciary duty of managers to work on behalf of their sole beneficiaries and that the multi-fiduciary duty implied by stakeholder theory is morally inadequate. In this vein, managers must ask themselves (Jensen, 2002): how do we measure "better" versus "worse" with regard to what we are trying to accomplish? And how do we best maximize long-term value, and who should decide that – managers or shareholders (Bratton and Wachter, 2010)?

Recently, there has been much discussion of value creation in stakeholder theory (Mitchell et al., 2015). Specifically, the inquiry related to this chapter is the assertion that more value is created when firms include in their accounting and governance risk-bearing stakeholders. If these stakeholders can help in the firm's fulfillment of value, it calls for an analysis of how corporate governance processes should change in order to generate more value creation.

7.3.2 Complementarity

Still, despite the persistence of these "camps," two key aspects underlie their complementarity: accountability and value creation.

Accountability

Certainly, "we must think through what management should be accountable for; and how and through whom its accountability can be discharged" (Drucker, 1988, p. 74). Yet, this is no easy task especially since the concept of accountability appears in the accounting, management, education, behavioral science, medical, and political science literatures. However, accountability offers a natural bridge between the individual and institutional levels (Lerner and Tetlock, 1999) that lie at the core of what boards and managers are dealing with contemporarily (Barney and Felin, 2013). A fundamental question the board must ask is *to whom* and *for what* is the firm held accountable?

Accountability refers to the implicit or explicit expectation that one may be called on to justify one's beliefs and actions to others (Scott and Lyman, 1968; Semin and Manstead, 1983; Tetlock, 1992) and can refer to an action, a process, an output, or an outcome (Patton, 1992). Thus, the requirement to "give an account" (Williams, 1987) can shape, and is shaped by, leaders' values and strategic decisions (Bansal, 2003; Bourne and Jenkins, 2013). These values – the enduring beliefs that guide organizational members in their selection or evaluation of behavior (Bourne and Jenkins, 2013) – serve as a central aspect of accountability and will be elaborated in the next section. In this way, some individuals may aggregate their accountability to "society at large" (Pallot, 1991, p. 203; see also Rasche and Esser, 2006), while others may think they are held accountable for a single goal such as shareholder value (Boatright, 2006), which has been later argued to benefit a larger whole (Jensen, 2008). Though these represent different views, they are likely to produce dynamic board interactions resulting in the ability to recognize, express, and ultimately prioritize organizational values.

To whom is the firm held accountable? Critical audiences for a firm are those that can influence the organization's future performance and so these audiences are those to whom the leaders of the firm are likely to hold themselves accountable. But, determining who are a firm's critical groups has posed a challenge to most theorists, and this question is at the heart of most stakeholder/shareholder debates (Clarkson, 1995; Hasnas, 2008; Jones and Felps, 2013; Marcoux, 2003). Typically, these debates cast either theory as a convenient straw man and overemphasize the conflicts between them. On the one hand, shareholder theories argue managers should be held accountable for a single goal such as shareholder value (Boatright, 2006; Jensen, 2002, 2008), and thus held accountable to shareholders in order that they should increase the wealth of the firm's shareholders to the extent possible (Jones and Felps, 2013).[4] Thus, by entering in to a principal-agent type contract, the principal places two responsibilities on the agent: responsibility for action and responsibility to account for those actions and thus the accountability concerns generally arise between management and shareholders (Bratton and Wachter, 2010). A firm's critical audiences are typically offered as investors, analysts, and stock exchanges (Jensen and Roy, 2008), and this shareholder-oriented perspective generally privileges outcome accountability.

On the other hand, normative stakeholder theory asserts firms should manage in accordance with the multiple and competing stakeholder interests in mind and does not privilege shareholder interests above others. Some have recently built on this idea to establish "entity theory" which describes a legal, social, and economic organism with the intention of filling the "accountability vacuum" left by agency theory because its emphasis on shareholder primacy and power offers no corresponding accountability (Bower and Paine, 2017). Entity theory focuses on the company's health rather than shareholder wealth.

In general, those adopting a stakeholder perspective would tend to argue that managers are accountable to all legitimate interests (Rasche and Esser, 2006) or to legitimate groups (Phillips, 2003). Critical groups in this view are either normative, when the firm perceives it owes a moral obligation to the group, or derivative, when the group is perceived to affect the firm's activities and/or its normative stakeholders (Phillips, 2003). Further, priority should be given to one audience over another depending on their proportionate value contribution to the firm (Phillips, 2003). Therefore, accountability can vary depending on a firm's perception of legitimacy of the audience (Lerner and Tetlock, 1999) and we know at a minimum both theories uphold the legitimacy of shareholders.

For what is the firm held accountable? Managers are accountable not only to different audiences but also for different outcomes (e.g., laws, operations, product quality, sales, and so on) and, thus, the type of information required for legal accountability would be different than the information required for customer accountability (Patton, 1992) or board accountability (Steckler and Clark, 2019). In addition to decision outcome accountability, we know that decision process accountability is also important (Lerner and Tetlock, 1999) and that stakeholder theory is concerned with procedure, or "who has input in decision-making" (Phillips et al., 2003, p. 487). When viewed in this way, it suggests the stakeholder literature has been primarily focused on process accountability.

However, boards are somewhat unique in their process accountability. Forbes and Milliken (1999, p. 492) note that "because boards are large, episodic, and interdependent, they are particularly vulnerable to process losses . . . the effectiveness of boards is likely to depend heavily on social-psychological processes, particularly those pertaining to group participation and interaction for exchange of information and critical decisions."

Process accountability, or having to account for the ways in which judgments and decisions are reached (Lerner and Tetlock, 1999), has been found to lead decision-makers to be more even-handed in their evaluations of alternatives resulting in a favorable perception of the process itself regardless of the outcome (Simonson and Staw, 1992). Whereas outcome accountability, or the having to account for the judgment and decision outcome, affects information processing because it enhances the desire to please the audience (Lerner and Tetlock, 1999; Simonson and Staw, 1992), process accountability increases systematic information processing and enhances the need to obtain rich and accurate understanding of the issue (Scholten et al., 2007). Furthermore, in their experiment, Scholten et al. (2007) found groups under process accountability experienced greater need for more information, repeated certain unshared information more often, and chose the correct alternative more often. These studies underscore the importance of process accountability especially for boards.

Based on this discussion of each theory's core lies a fundamental question asked by both shareholder and stakeholder theory: for whose primary benefit is this firm managed? If one were to say the shareholders, one could equally say that we are all shareholders given the contemporary dependence on the financial markets for anything from retirement to routine banking to college savings (Gelter, 2013) and that there are many forms of "capital" to exchange, none of which is automatically privileged over the others. Likewise, one could say the firm is managed for stakeholders and recognize that employees, consumers, and suppliers can also be shareholders. This heterogeneity and overlap within most stakeholder groups has been documented (King, 2008; Reid and Toffel, 2009; Rowley and Moldoveanu, 2003) but rarely used in the context of process or outcome accountability. Thus, these theoretical positions, in fact, are not irreconcilable (Bratton and Wachter, 2010) and what I argue here is that both process and outcome accountability are important in today's complex corporate governance environment necessitating an integration of both stakeholder and shareholder perspectives. For example, in a board's effort to select the best directors, both process and outcome accountability are important for promoting good governance. These forms of accountability might equally apply to core board functions such as strategic leadership and monitoring management.

Value and value creation

Despite the overlap within most stakeholder groups noted above, attending to the demands of one stakeholder may require denying those of another (Fiss and Zajac, 2006) especially given the often troubling and complex environment of corporate governance today. In this context, what corporate audiences value in terms of business strategy and information differs within and across groups, each with differing perspectives (Freeman et al., 2018; Wolfe and Putler, 2002). This then begs the question of what kind of information, resource, or behavior is valued? And how do our current models account for it? To address this question, we must first determine what is meant by "value." Both stakeholder and shareholder perspectives address this concept.

There has been much talk recently about creating value for stakeholders (Elms et al., 2010; Harrison et al., 2010), in addition to accounting for that value (Mitchell et al., 2015). Stakeholder theory has adopted the idea of value creation (Freeman, 2008; Harrison et al., 2010) to mean that stakeholders contribute to the value creation of the firm by having a say in how the firm distributes its various resources. In this way, stakeholder theory aims to connect the concern for moral conduct with the *process* of value creation. The term "value" is defined in numerous ways (Harrison and Wicks, 2013) – from value in terms of usefulness (e.g., information) to the value of something in an exchange (e.g., what a party is willing to pay). This perspective is borrowed from the strategy literature (Lepak et al., 2007, pp. 181–2), in which value can be defined in two ways: *use value*, defined as "the specific quality of a new job, task, product, or service as perceived by users in relation to their needs" and *exchange value*, defined as "the monetary amount realized at a certain point in time, when the exchange of the new task, good, service, or product takes place, or the amount paid by the user to the seller for the use value of the focal task, job, product, or service."

Value has also been defined by shareholder theorists (Jensen, 2002) – as the sum of the values of all financial claims on the firm – and strategists, as simply benefits relative to costs (Porter and Kramer, 2011), or as the amount of monetary value that is subjectively realized by a target user or buyer (Lepak et al., 2007). Recently, academics in this stream have moved toward using the term "maximizing total firm value" instead of "maximizing the value of the firm's equity" (Jensen, 2008). When all firms in an economy maximize the total firm value, social welfare is then maximized (Jensen, 2002). Further to the point, "total value created is the value created for all business model stakeholders (focal firm, customers, suppliers, and other exchange partners)" (Zott and Amit, 2007, p. 183).[5]

This premise is complementary to the central idea of stakeholder theory – that "focusing on stakeholders, specifically treating them well and managing for their interests, helps a firm create value along a number of dimensions and is therefore good for firm performance" (Harrison and Wicks, 2013, p. 101). It is also complementary to the principle of shared value, which involves creating economic value in a way that also creates value for society by addressing its needs and challenges (Porter and Kramer, 2011). Yet, various stakeholders have differing views on what is valuable because of the variation in their knowledge bases, goals, and contexts – thus, they evaluate it differently (Lepak et al., 2007) even in terms of what is novel and appropriate (Amabile, 1996).

Despite these similarities, organizations need to specify value for whom – stakeholders (Post et al., 2002), consumers (Priem, 2007), shareholders (Jensen, 2002) – and, again, the *process* of creating value differs depending on whether it is created by an individual, organization, or society (Lepak et al., 2007). Individuals can create value by acting creatively to make their work more useful and appropriate to the firm, which in turn helps the firm to develop or invent new ways of doing things (Lepak et al., 2007; Porter, 1985). Stakeholders co-create value for each other and the firm through their interactions and exchanges of value. Society also creates value via programs and incentives that help foster a firm's ability to provide needed products or services. In this way, value is best created when it is shared value, and the burdens of creating that value are also shared (Porter and Kramer, 2011) and when management attempts to create multi-stakeholder synergies (Tantalo and Priem, 2016).

Therefore, to some degree, both agency/shareholder prescriptions as well as stakeholder perceptions are too narrow in their conceptualizations of accountability and value creation. Shareholder theory focuses on outcome accountability at the expense of process accountability – while stakeholder theory does the opposite. Shareholder theory emphasizes value created through financial means while stakeholder theory stresses value created through human and operational means.

7.4 VALUE AND VALUE CREATION ON BOARDS

Leader and organizational values help shape perceptions of how value is created, distributed, and reported (Busco et al., 2013; Finkelstein et al., 2009). But despite the areas of overlap in stakeholder/shareholder perceptions in terms of the *value*, *value creation*, and *accountability* noted above, there remain a number of questions about how to create value more broadly across stakeholders and more deeply within the organization as a way to understand the role of how an organization's values shape value creation.

Values are defined as enduring beliefs that are personally or socially preferable to converse beliefs, which transcend specific situations, and which guide selection or evaluation of behavior (Rokeach, 1973). External stakeholders and institutional actors influence an organization's values (Freeman, 1984; Kraatz et al., 2010) as do the leaders and members internal to the organization (Gehman et al., 2013; Weaver et al., 1999). Thus, both levels have relevance to how the board integrates accountability and ultimately creates value down and up the organizational ladder as well as across the internal and external environment of the firm. Furthermore, accountability and the requirement to "give an account" (Williams, 1987) can shape, and is shaped by, managers' values and strategic decisions (Bansal, 2003; Bourne and Jenkins, 2013; Hambrick and Mason, 1984).

Values can be seen to, among other things, create connections between several core organizational elements and also create boundaries by acting as a differentiating element within those concepts. However, despite their prominence, values are rarely a research focus and are often treated as if they do not require empirical examination. Recent exceptions have focused on the dynamic nature of organizational values (Bourne and Jenkins, 2013) and the emergence of values practices (Gehman et al., 2013). Even while values have distinct forms as well as interrelations (Bourne and Jenkins, 2013), there has not been much discussion of the organizational and individual levels as a reflection of, and reflected back to, the board of directors in its effort to create value more broadly (Finkelstein et al., 2009).

Given that organizational values "have a long reach and a wide span of influence on critical processes and characteristics in organizations" (Bourne and Jenkins, 2013, p. 496), I turn to the question of how boards might go about instilling broad and deep value creation through an ability to practice process and outcome accountability.

7.4.1 Broad Value Creation

Specifically, with regard to creating value more broadly, how do boards manage value for a larger set of stakeholders beyond those who are considered primary? Or for multiple groups simultaneously? How do directors take on a more inclusive notion of value and manage non-economic value? Tantalo and Priem (2016) asserted this "how" gap for value creation has been chiefly responsible for limiting stakeholder theory as a tool for strategic management. Given that strategy formulation is a key aspect of corporate governance (Roberts et al., 2005), I suggest that managing value creation broadly is a board-level responsibility.

An initial step is to expand the definition of value and what outcome is ultimately sought. While this chapter attempts to avoid opposing shareholder and stakeholder views on corporate governance – positing that they have complementary theoretical assumptions and implications – there is one nettlesome problem with the shareholder-centric approach – its overreliance on markets as arbiters of accountability and value. While market exchanges are essential for any organization, focusing primarily on markets and their outcome measures (e.g., profits, market capitalization, stock price, return on assets, and so on), they often fail to account for the ongoing and value-creating interactions offered by stakeholder management and its tendency to focus on process accountability measures (e.g., the ways in which judgments and decisions are reached). Indeed, these more relational approaches bring with them an ability to manage relationships in just and effective ways (Aguilera et al., 2007) and are able to tap into various stakeholder synergies that create other forms of value (Tantalo and Priem, 2016). Similarly, Freeman (2016) talks about using the relationship managers have – or can create – with stakeholders as the new unit of analysis rather than profit as the core purpose.

In their influential analysis of how executives can improve their firms' value creation strategies, Tantalo and Priem (2016) argue that stakeholder utility functions contain more than simply economic utilities and different groups assign different weights for these economic utilities. A firm's board of directors can find both complementary utilities across two or more stakeholders and follow-on efficiencies for other groups when they achieve these types of stakeholder synergies. A fundamental aspect of these synergies is to recognize the tangible or intangible value driver of each main stakeholder group; doing so would connect aspects of process accountability with outcome accountability. Kivleniece and Quelin (2012) have identified value creation mechanisms, in the contemporary context where public and private lines have blurred, that also call for a deeper understanding of alternative forms of economic organization. In their model, these authors propose such mechanisms are intrinsically tied to three principle groups of value claimants: the firm, the private actor, and the external stakeholders. The value-creating potential of public-private partnerships relies heavily on resource complementarities and governance efficiencies.

Perhaps the most notable recent development is to score firms based on their environmental, social, and governance (ESG) disclosures as a way to determine outcome accountably more broadly (Burke and Clark, 2016; Busco et al., 2013). And while evaluation of ESG information can be challenging, firms such as Novo Nordisk illustrate that multiple platforms are available for firms to do this (e.g., the Global Reporting Initiative, Nasdaq's Task Force on Climate-Related Financial Disclosure and Sustainability Accounting Standards Board).

Another way to create value is to focus on process accountability through the organizational values of trust and fairness. Harrison et al. (2010) suggest that firms need to build trust with stakeholders which helps firms to understand the minimum requirements that certain stakeholders need. Fairness has also been a focus of recent research. Bridoux and Stoelhorst (2014) explain that firms pursuing a fairness-centered approach to their stakeholders will tend to attract more people who reciprocate and motivate them well, while firms pursuing an arms-length approach will tend to attract and motivate self-regarding individuals. While both approaches to stakeholders can be effective for firms (Tantalo and Priem, 2016), they illustrate that process matters while at the same time stakeholder values influence organizational values.

Given that corporate board work primarily focuses on cognitive outputs, processes are vital to effective board interactions (Forbes and Milliken, 1999). There is substantial support for the effect of process accountability on, among other things, judgment accuracy. Outcome accountability, or the having to account for the judgment and decision outcome, affects information processing because it enhances the desire to please the audience (Scholten et al., 2007). Groups held accountable for their processes, like boards are or should be, tend to engage in deep information processing, and have higher motivation to develop an accurate and multifaceted understanding of the decision problem (Scholten et al., 2007). Therefore, integrating stakeholders into decision-making and deploying values that are important to relationship building may improve both process and outcome accountability.

7.4.2 Deep Value Creation

Given that values have a long reach and a wide span of influence (Bourne and Jenkins, 2013), value creation must go deep into the organization starting from the very apex of the firm's decision system – the board of directors. Researchers have noted that organizations have been thought to reflect the values of their members (O'Reilly et al., 1991; Ostroff and Judge, 2007), especially their founders and top executives (Hambrick and Brandon, 1988) and the board of directors (Huse, 2007). Values are, and have long been, a "prime function of leadership" (Selznick, 1957, p. 27). And, even while the employing organization exerts its own unique pressure on leader values, senior executives have been found to have largely "entrenched value sets" (Finkelstein et al., 2009, p. 54) leading researchers to wonder whether shareholder-oriented views, where executives are not supposed to pursue their values but rather shareholders' values, prompt executives to succumb to these value-dampening mechanisms (Finkelstein et al., 2009).

If indeed, "values live in the systems and processes" (Freeman, 2016) of organizations, whereby the ethical culture is created and maintained through the alignment of a complex interplay of formal (e.g., leadership, codes/policies, decision structures) and informal systems (e.g., work norms, stories, rituals) (Trevino and Nelson, 2011), the board of directors is the place to instill values beyond either "self-regarding" or "other-regarding" (Agle et al., 1999) which have no significant relationship to performance.

Furthermore, most board research has emphasized objectively observed board attributes rather than a director's values and beliefs, even while certain personal values play an essential but unrecognized role in board dynamics. Recent research (Clark and Gabaldon, 2018) has suggested that boards ideally want to find directors who have an attachment to the firm and are thus motivated to act in the firm's interest – those whose value congruence with the firm is rooted in a strong moral identity (Kennedy et al., 2017) where moral identity measures the degree to which people internalize specific moral traits (Clark and Gabaldon, 2018).

Similarly, in selecting or retaining a board member, boards are being forced to ask themselves whether a specific director will create or destroy value. Not only are there calls for board matrices outlining each director's skills and areas of expertise but there are also proforma disclosures to explain why this person is on the board – both elements are part of the recent New York City Controller's Boardroom Accountability Project 2.0. As part of this project, companies where the NYC Pension system is invested were asked not only to provide director biographies, but also to explain to their investors how those who serve on their boards are individually, and in the aggregate, qualified to oversee their companies' businesses, long-term strategies, and the related risks and opportunities (NYC Controller, 2018). In this way, there is external pressure on boards in effect blurring the lines between the firm, the government, and external stakeholders in an effort to create value as theorized by Kivleniece and Quelin (2012).

Likewise, other institutional actors, namely, governments, affect organizational values. Legal scholars have begun to place more emphasis on the role of non-legal rules in governing human behavior (Ribstein, 2001). Governments rely on two overarching forms in order to enact changes in organizations which mainly differ on whether they are internally controlled (i.e., self-regulatory) or externally controlled (i.e., legal mandates). While both forms are situated within the regulatory environment and are designed to meet the same regulatory goals, they differ in that self-regulation relies on firms to periodically certify their efficacy and/or progress in reaching the goal whereas legal mandates are enforced formally and externally by the government when firms do not reach the goal. Self-regulation (i.e., normative scripts for motivating voluntary actions taken on by organizations themselves) interacts with legally induced sanctions to enable corporations to attend more effectively to their social and legal responsibilities (Toffel and Short, 2011) and create value (Freeman, 2016). Similarly, in an empirical study of the relationship between informal rules and corporate governance, Boytsun et al. (2011) found firms and communities with strong social norms offer a more fertile ground for commitment with external stakeholders. As corporate governance scholar John Coffee (2001, p. 2151) explained, "corporate behavior may be more shaped and determined by social norms than by legal rules seems to be an idea whose time has come."

The many recent attempts at corporate governance reform have taken both legally mandated and self-regulatory approaches and thus have affected the establishment of organizational values with regard to governance along with processes and outcomes emphasized by boards in their attempt to create value through greater accountability.

7.5 CONCLUSION

As I have noted here, boards of directors have been under intense scrutiny and while most of the critiques have in common the importance of value creation and accountability, they leave these constructs underdeveloped, which limits the explanatory power of what is actually meant by good governance.

Accountability-based corporate governance processes are essential for organizations to be simultaneously effective in achieving their goals and in discharging their ethical obligations. In this respect, corporate governance is both process- and outcome-based and deeply value-based. However, less attention has been paid to how boards of directors can effectively bring together values, accountability, and value creation. While corporate governance and the proper role of boards has been a significant topic in management literature, comparatively little has been written about how boards integrate accountability into their processes and outcomes, manage stakeholder relationships in ways that create value, or even conceptualize how they create value for shareholders and other stakeholders. This chapter seeks to address these issues, which have implications for strategic management, corporate governance, and business ethics.

NOTES

1. The Sarbanes–Oxley Act imposed a variety of substantive requirements to enhance the integrity of financial statements and reporting for US listed firms. The United States is the largest and most dominant stock exchange network in the world.
2. The Business Roundtable recently released its 2016 Corporate Governance Principles; among other things, this set of principles emphasized investors' responsibility and accountability for long-term value creation.
3. Given that my focus is on corporate governance and that the most dominant theory in governance is agency theory (Raelin and Bondy, 2013), I liken the assumptions of agency to those of shareholder theory.
4. It should be noted here that shareholders are almost universally referred to as a monolithic group and as such there is no difference between short-term day traders and more long-term pension fund investors, for example. Following work in value creation stakeholder theory (see Mitchell et al., 2015), I posit that here it might be useful to note there is a convergence of interests between long-term shareholders and other stakeholders, but perhaps not between the interests of short-term shareholders and other stakeholders.
5. I note there is considerable debate about value capture and value creation (see Kivleniece and Quelin, 2012; Makadok and Coff, 2002), however, this analysis focuses on value creation as it necessarily precedes value capture by firms (Nickerson et al., 2007; Priem, 2007).

REFERENCES

Agle, B.R., Mitchel R.K., and Sonnenfeld, J.A. 1999. Who matters to CEOs? An investigation of stakeholder attributes and salience, corporate performance, and CEO values. *Academy of Management Journal*, **42**, 507–25.

Aguilera, R.V., Desender, K., Bednar, M.K., and Lee, J.H. 2015. Connecting the dots: bringing external corporate governance into the corporate governance puzzle. *Academy of Management Annals*, **9**(1), 483–573.

Aguilera, R.V., Rupp, D.E., Williams, C.A., and Ganapathi, J. 2007. Putting the "S" back in corporate social responsibility: a multilevel theory of social change in organizations. *Academy of Management Review*, **32**(3), 836–63.

Amabile, T.M. 1996. *Creativity in Context*. Boulder, CO: Westview Press.

Armitage, S., Hou, W., Sarkar, S., and Talaulicar, T. 2017. Corporate governance challenges in emerging economies. *Corporate Governance: An International Review*, **25**(3), 148–54.

Bansal, P. 2003. From issues to actions: the importance of individual concerns and organizational values in responding to natural environmental issues. *Organization Science*, **14**, 510–27.

Barney, J.A.Y. and Felin, T. 2013. What are microfoundations? *Academy of Management Perspectives*, **27**(2), 138–55.

Bell, R.G., Filatotchev, I., and Aguilera, R.V. 2014. Corporate governance and investors' perceptions of foreign IPO value: an institutional perspective. *Academy of Management Journal*, **57**(1), 301–20.

Boatright, J.R. 2006. What's wrong – and what's right – with stakeholder management. *Journal of Private Enterprise*, **21**(2), 106–30.

Boivie, S., Bednar, M.K., Aguilera, R.V., and Andrus, J.L. 2016. Are boards designed to fail? The implausibility of effective board monitoring. *Academy of Management Annals*, **10**(1), 319–407.

Bourne, H. and Jenkins, M. 2013. Organizational values: a dynamic perspective. *Organization Studies*, **34**(4), 495–514.

Bower, J.L. and Paine, L.S. 2017. The error at the heart of corporate leadership. *HBR'S 10 MUST*, 165.

Boytsun, A., Deloof, M., and Matthyssens, P. 2011. Social norms, social cohesion, and corporate governance. *Corporate Governance: An International Review*, **19**(1), 41–60.

Bratton, W.W. and Wachter, M.L. 2010. The case against shareholder empowerment. *University of Pennsylvania Law Review*, **158**(3), 653–728.

Bridoux, F. and Stoelhorst J. 2014. Microfoundations for stakeholder theory: managing stakeholders with heterogeneous motives. *Strategic Management Journal*, **35**(1), 107–25.

Burke, J.J. and Clark, C.E. 2016. The business case for integrated reporting: insights from leading practitioners, regulators, and academics. *Business Horizons*, **59**(3), 273–83.

Busco, C., Frigo, M.L., Quattrone, P., and Riccaboni, A. 2013. Redefining corporate accountability through integrated reporting: what happens when values and value creation meet? *Strategic Finance*, **8**, 33–41.

Clark, C. and Gabaldon, P. 2018. Board director selection process and structure: implications for diversity and efficacy. Paper presented at the 2018 JMS Conference, Babson College, Wellesley, MA.

Clarkson, M. 1995. A stakeholder framework for analyzing and evaluating corporate social performance. *Academy of Management Review*, **20**, 92–117.

Coffee, J.C. 2001. Do norms matter? A cross-country evaluation. *University of Pennsylvania Law Review*, **149**(6), 2151–77.

Dah, M.A., Frye, M.B., and Hurst, M. 2014. Board changes and CEO turnover: the unanticipated effects of the Sarbanes–Oxley Act. *Journal of Banking & Finance*, **41**, 97–108.

Dalton, D.R., Hitt, M.A., Certo, S.T., and Dalton, C.M. 2007. The fundamental agency problem and its mitigation: independence, equity, and the market for corporate control. *Academy of Management Annals*, **1**(1), 1–64.

Dhir, A. 2015. *Challenging Boardroom Homogeneity: Corporate Law, Governance and Diversity*. New York: Cambridge University Press.

Donaldson, T. 2012. The epistemic fault line in corporate governance. *Academy of Management Review*, **37**(2), 256–71.

Donaldson, T. and Preston, L.E. 1995. The stakeholder theory of the corporation: concepts, evidence, and implications. *Academy of Management Review*, **20**(1), 65–91.

Drucker, P.F. 1988. Management and the world's work. *Harvard Business Review*, **66**(5), 65–76.

Elms, H., Brammer, S., Harris, J.D., and Phillips, R.A. 2010. New directions in strategic management and business ethics. *Business Ethics Quarterly*, **20**(3), 401–25.

Evan, W.M. and Freeman, R.E. 1988. A stakeholder theory of the modern corporation: Kantian capitalism. In T. Beauchamp and N. Bowie (eds), *Ethical Theory and Business* (pp. 75–93). Englewood Cliffs, NJ: Prentice Hall.

Filatotchev, I. and Nakajima, C. 2014. Corporate governance, responsible managerial behavior, and corporate social responsibility: organizational efficiency versus organizational legitimacy? *The Academy of Management Perspectives*, **28**(3), 289–306.

Finkelstein, S., Hambrick, D.C. and Cannella, A.A. 2009. *Strategic Leadership: Theory and Research on Executives, Top Management Teams and Boards*. New York: Oxford University Press.

Fiss, P.C. and Zajac, E.J. 2006. The symbolic management of strategic change: sensegiving via framing and decoupling. *Academy of Management Journal*, **49**(6), 1173–93.

Forbes, D.P. and Milliken, F.J. 1999. Cognition and corporate governance: understanding boards of directors as strategic decision-making groups. *Academy of Management Review*, **24**, 489–505.

Freeman, R.E. 1984. *Strategic Management: A Stakeholder Approach*. Boston, MA: Pitman.

Freeman, R.E. 2008. Ending the so-called "Friedman-Freeman" debate. *Business Ethics Quarterly*, **18**(2), 162–6.

Freeman, R.E. 2016. *Responsible Capitalism: Business for the 21st Century*. Verizon Lectureship at Bentley University. https://www.bentley.edu/centers/center-for-business-ethics/about-center/thought-leadership/verizon-lectureship (accessed 18 November 2018).

Freeman, R.E., Phillips, R., and Sisodia, R. 2018. Tensions in stakeholder theory. *Business & Society*. doi: 0007650318773750.

Freeman, R.E., Wicks, A.C., and Parmar, B. 2004. Stakeholder theory and "the corporate objective revisited." *Organization Science*, **15**(3), 364–9.

Friedman, M. 1962. *Capitalism and Freedom*. Reprinted in 1982. Chicago, IL: University of Chicago Press.

Gehman, J., Trevino, L.K., and Garud, R. 2013. Values work: a process study of the emergence and performance of organizational values practices. *Academy of Management Journal*, **56**(1), 84–112.

Gelter, M. 2013. The pension system and the rise of shareholder primacy. *Seton Hall Law Review*, **43**, 909–70.

Ghoshal, S. 2005. Bad management theories are destroying good management practices. *Academy of Management Learning & Education*, **4**(1), 75–91.

Hambrick, D.C. and Brandon, G. 1988. Executive values. In D.C. Hambrick (ed.), *The Executive Effect: Concepts and Methods for Studying Top Managers* (pp. 3–34). Greenwich, CT: JAI.

Hambrick, D.C. and Mason, P.A. 1984. Upper echelons: the organization as a reflection of its top managers. *Academy of Management Review*, **9**, 193–206.

Hambrick, D.C., Werder, A.V., and Zajac, E.J. 2008. New directions in corporate governance research. *Organization Science*, **19**(3), 381–5.

Hansmann, H. and Kraakman, R. 2001. The end of history for corporate law. *Georgetown Law Journal*, **89**, 439–68.

Harris, J.D. and Freeman, R.E. 2008. The impossibility of the separation thesis: a response to Joakim Sandberg. *Business Ethics Quarterly*, **18**(4), 541–8.

Harrison, J.S. and Wicks, A.C. 2013. Stakeholder theory, value, and firm performance. *Business Ethics Quarterly*, **23**(1), 97–124.

Harrison, J.S., Bosse, D.A., and Phillips, R.A. 2010. Managing for stakeholders, stakeholder utility functions, and competitive advantage. *Strategic Management Journal*, **31**(1), 58–74.

Hasnas, J. 1998. The normative theories of business ethics: a guide for the perplexed. *Business Ethics Quarterly*, **8**(1), 19–42.

Hasnas, J. 2008. The depoliticization of law. *Theoretical Inquiries in Law*, **9**(2), 529–52.

Hillman, A.J. and Dalziel, T. 2003. Boards of directors and firm performance: integrating agency and resource dependence perspectives. *Academy of Management Review*, **28**(3), 383–96.

Huse, M. 2007. *Boards, Governance and Value Creation: The Human Side of Corporate Governance*. Cambridge: Cambridge University Press.

Jensen, M.C. 2002. Value maximization, stakeholder theory, and the corporate objective function. *Business Ethics Quarterly*, **12**(2), 235–56.

Jensen, M.C. 2008. Non-rational behavior, value conflicts, stakeholder theory, and firm behavior. *Business Ethics Quarterly*, **18**(2), 167–71.

Jensen, M.C. and Meckling, W.H. 1976. Theory of the firm: managerial behavior, agency costs and ownership structure. *Journal of Financial Economics*, **3**(4), 305–60.

Jensen, M. and Roy, A. 2008. Staging exchange partner choices: when do status and reputation matter? *Academy of Management Journal*, **51**(3), 495–516.

Jones, M.T. and Fleming, P. 2003. Unpacking complexity through critical stakeholder analysis: the case of globalization. *Business & Society*, **42**(4), 430–54.

Jones, T.M. and Felps, W. 2013. Shareholder wealth maximization and social welfare: a utilitarian critique. *Business Ethics Quarterly*, **23**(2), 207–38.

Jones, T.M., Felps, W., and Bigley, G.A. 2007. Ethical theory and stakeholder-related decisions: the role of stakeholder culture. *Academy of Management Review*, **32**(1), 137–55.

Kennedy, J.A., Kray, L.J., and Ku, G. 2017. A social-cognitive approach to understanding gender differences in negotiator ethics: the role of moral identity. *Organizational Behavior and Human Decision Processes*, **138**, 28–44.
King, B. 2008. A social movement perspective of stakeholder collective action and influence. *Business & Society*, **48**(1), 21–49.
Kivleniece, I. and Quelin, B. 2012. Creating and capturing value in public-private ties: a private actor's perspective. *Academy of Management Review*, **37**(2), 272–99.
Kraatz, M.S., Ventresca, M.J., and Deng, L. (2010). Precarious values and mundane innovations: enrollment management in American liberal arts colleges. *Academy of Management Journal*, **53**(6), 1521–45.
Leblanc, R. and Gillies, J. 2005. *Inside the Boardroom: How Boards Really Work and the Coming Revolution in Corporate Governance*. Ontario: John Wiley & Sons.
Lepak, D.P., Smith, K.G., and Taylor, M.S. 2007. Value creation and value capture: a multilevel perspective. *Academy of Management Review*, **32**(1), 180–94.
Lerner, J.S. and Tetlock, P.E. 1999. Accounting for the effects of accountability. *Psychological Bulletin*, **125**(2), 255–75.
Luo, Y. 2005. How does globalization affect corporate governance and accountability? A perspective from MNEs. *Journal of International Management*, **11**(1), 19–41.
Makadok, R. and Coff, R. 2002. The theory of value and the value of theory: breaking new ground versus reinventing the wheel. *Academy of Management Review*, **27**(1), 10–16.
Marcoux, A.M. 2003. A fiduciary argument against stakeholder theory. *Business Ethics Quarterly*, **13**, 1–24.
Mazutis, D.D. and Slawinski, N. 2015. Reconnecting business and society: perceptions of authenticity in corporate social responsibility. *Journal of Business Ethics*, **131**(1), 137–50.
Mitchell, R.K., Van Buren, H.J., Greenwood, M., and Freeman, R.E. 2015. Stakeholder inclusion and accounting for stakeholders. *Journal of Management Studies*, **52**(7), 851–77.
Nickerson, J., Silverman, B., and Zenger, T. 2007. The "problem" of creating and capturing value. *Strategic Organization*, **5**(3), 211–25.
NYC Controller. 2018. https://comptroller.nyc.gov/wp-content/uploads/2018/08/NYC-Comptrollers-Office-Matrices-Compendium-8-2018-FINAL.pdf (accessed 25 October 2018).
OECD. 2015. *G20/OECD Principles of Corporate Governance*. Paris: OECD Publishing. http://dx.doi.org/10.1787/9789264236882-en.
O'Reilly, C.A., III, Chatman, J., and Caldwell, D.F. 1991. People and organizational culture: a profile comparison approach to assessing person-organization fit. *Academy of Management Journal*, **34**, 487–516.
Ostroff, C.L. and Judge, T. 2007. *Perspectives on Organizational Fit*. Mahwah, NJ: Erlbaum.
Pallot, J. 1991. The legitimate concern with fairness: a comment. *Accounting, Organizations and Society*, **16**(2), 201–8.
Patton, J.M. 1992. Accountability and governmental financial reporting. *Financial Accountability & Management*, **8**(3), 165–80.
Phillips, R. 2003. Stakeholder legitimacy. *Business Ethics Quarterly*, **13**(1), 25–41.
Phillips, R., Freeman, R.E., and Wicks, A.C. 2003. What stakeholder theory is not. *Business Ethics Quarterly*, **13**(4), 479–502.

Poole, M.S. and Van de Ven, A.H. 1989. Using paradox to build management and organization theories. *Academy of Management Review*, **14**(4), 562–78.
Porter, M.E. 1985. *Competitive Advantage: Creating and Sustaining Superior Performance*. New York: Free Press.
Porter, M.E. and Kramer, M.R. 2011. Creating shared value. *Harvard Business Review*, **89**(1/2), 62–77.
Post, J.E., Preston, L.E., and Sauter-Sachs, S. 2002. *Redefining the Corporation: Stakeholder Management and Organizational Wealth*. Stanford, CA: Stanford University Press.
Priem, R.L. 2007. A consumer perspective on value creation. *Academy of Management Review*, **32**(1), 219–35.
Raelin, J.D. and Bondy, K. 2013. Putting the good back in good corporate governance: the presence and problems of double-layered agency theory. *Corporate Governance: An International Review*, **21**(5), 420–35.
Rasche, A. and Esser, D.E. 2006. From stakeholder management to stakeholder accountability. *Journal of Business Ethics*, **65**(3), 251–67.
Reid, E.M. and Toffel, M.W. 2009. Responding to public and private politics: corporate disclosure of climate change strategies. *Strategic Management Journal*, **30**(11), 1157–178.
Ribstein, L.E. 2001. Law v. trust. *Boston University Law Review*, **81**, 553.
Rich, B.L., LePine, J.A., and Crawford, E.R. 2010. Job engagement: antecedents and effects on job performance. *Academy of Management Journal*, **53**, 617–35.
Roberts, J., McNulty, T., and Stiles, P. 2005. Beyond agency conceptions of the work of the nonexecutive director: creating accountability in the boardroom. *British Journal of Management*, **16**(S1), S5–S26.
Rokeach, M. 1973. *The Nature of Human Values*. New York: Free Press.
Rowley, T.I. and Moldoveanu, M. 2003. When will stakeholder groups act? An interest- and identity-based model of stakeholder group mobilization. *Academy of Management Review*, **28**(2), 204–19.
Scholten, L., Van Knippenberg, D., Nijstad, B.A., and De Dreu, C.K. 2007. Motivated information processing and group decision-making: effects of process accountability on information processing and decision quality. *Journal of Experimental Social Psychology*, **43**(4), 539–52.
Scott, M.B. and Lyman, S.M. 1968. Accounts. *American Sociological Review*, **33**(1), 46–62.
Selznick, P. 1957. *Leadership in Administration*. New York: Harper & Row.
Semin, G.R. and Manstead, A.S.R. 1983. *The Accountability of Conduct: A Social Psychology Analysis*. London: Academic Press.
Simonson, I. and Staw, B.M. 1992. Deescalation strategies: a comparison of techniques for reducing commitment to losing courses of action. *Journal of Applied Psychology*, **77**(4), 419–26.
Smith, H.J. 2003. The shareholders vs. stakeholders debate. *MIT Sloan Management Review*, **44**(4), 85–91.
Spicer, A., Alvesson, M., and Kärreman, D. 2009. Critical performativity: the unfinished business of critical management studies. *Human Relations*, **62**(4), 537–60.
Steckler, E. and Clark, C. 2019. Authenticity and corporate governance. *Journal of Business Ethics*, **155**(4), 951–63.
Sundaramurthy, C. and Lewis, M. 2003. Control and collaboration: paradoxes of governance. *Academy of Management Review*, **28**(3), 397–415.

Talaulicar, T. 2010. The concept of the balanced company and its implications for corporate governance. *Society and Business Review*, **5**, 232–44.

Tantalo, C. and Priem, R.L. 2016. Value creation through stakeholder synergy. *Strategic Management Journal*, 37(2), 314–29.

Tetlock, P.E. 1992. The impact of accountability on judgment and choice: toward a social contingency model. *Advances in Experimental Social Psychology*, **25**(3), 331–76.

Toffel, M.W. and Short, J.L. 2011. Coming clean and cleaning up: does voluntary self-reporting indicate effective self-policing? *The Journal of Law & Economics*, **54**(3), 609–49.

Trevino, L.K. and Nelson, K.A. 2011. *Managing Business Ethics: Straight Talk About How to Do It Right*. New York: Wiley.

United Kingdom Green Paper on Governance Reform. 2016. Department for Business, Energy & Industrial Strategy. http://www.gov.uk/government/consultations/corporate-governance-reform (accessed 2 November 2017).

Walls, J.L. and Hoffman, A.J. 2013. Exceptional boards: environmental experience and positive deviance from institutional norms. *Journal of Organizational Behavior*, **34**(2), 253–71.

Weaver, G.R., Trevino, L.K., and Cochran, P.L. 1999. Corporate ethics programs as control systems: influences of executive commitment and environmental factors. *Academy of Management Journal*, **42**(1), 41–57.

West, A. 2009. Corporate governance convergence and moral relativism. *Corporate Governance: An International Review*, **17**(1), 107–19.

Williams, P.F. 1987. The legitimate concern with fairness. *Accounting, Organizations and Society*, **12**(2), 169–89.

Williamson, O.E. 1985. *The Economic Institutions of Capitalism*. New York: Simon and Schuster.

Wolfe, R.A. and Putler, D.S. 2002. How tight are the ties that bind stakeholder groups? *Organization Science*, **13**(1), 64–80.

Zahra, S. and Pearce, J. 1989. Boards of directors and corporate financial performance: a review and integrative model. *Journal of Management*, **15**, 291–344.

Zott C. and Amit R. 2007. Business model design and the performance of entrepreneurial firms. *Organization Science*, **18**(2), 181–99.

8. How can universities promote corporate responsibility in their supply chains? The experience of the University of Notre Dame

Georges Enderle

8.1 INTRODUCTION: SETTING THE STAGE

Universities[1] are not only institutions of higher education; they also constitute powerful economic actors as employers of hundreds or thousands of employees, as collectors of millions of dollars of tuition fees, as investors in buildings, equipment and pension plans, as organizers of multiple sports programs, and – not the least – as buyers of products and services for their own use and for sale to their customers. A special category of the products are the clothes, sportswear, T-shirts, caps, sweaters, memorabilia and many other goods which carry – often conspicuously – the logo of the university. Not only does the logo indicate the name of the university; it also represents the brand and reputation of this institution. Customers buy and use these licensed products with pride and often with the feeling of being valuable members of the institution's "family." A sample of the brand names can illustrate the wide range of colleges and universities selling their licensed products and promoting their reputation. Depending on the size and public recognition of the institution and the success of its most famous sports teams, the gross annual retail sales of trademark licensed products can amount to over 60 million dollars.

How proud can the customers be when they learn under what conditions these licensed products actually are manufactured? What responsibility does the university bear to make sure that these goods are not produced in sweatshops, but under fair and humane conditions? This chapter looks at the supply chain of the licensed products that carry the logo of universities. It argues that these institutions have a moral obligation to promote corporate responsibility in the supply chain, and it proposes ways of how this promotion can be achieved. To illustrate the search for a responsible policy, the chapter explains the experience of the University of Notre Dame and discusses, in more general terms, the challenges and opportunities for universities when dealing with these kinds of supply chain problems. This case study of international business ethics offers a concrete and persuasive way for university faculty, students and staff to care about the workers in the supply chains. It is even more important to strengthen responsibility for ethical leadership of licensees and factories when trade wars are shaking collaboration across borders.

The question of corporate responsibility in the supply chains has been an issue since the time business organizations, relying on others' resources, have been involved in supply chains and held responsible for their conduct. However, since the 1990s globalization has increased immensely and the world has become ever more interconnected (see Enderle 2005; Radin 2018). As a result, the supply chains have stretched around the globe and become much more complex and highly challenging for their management (Kryder 2018; Quinn 2017).

Therefore, it is no surprise that multinational enterprises have been criticized for multiple irresponsibilities in their supply chains, ranging from using child and forced labor to polluting water and air. One might recall the Nike scandal in the early 1990s when the sportswear company bought their products from sweatshops in China and Indonesia (Locke 2002), the suicides of young Chinese workers in 2010 at Foxconn producing iPads for Apple (Guo et al. 2012), and the collapse of the Rana Plaza factory building in 2013 in Bangladesh that killed over 1100 workers (Labowitz and Baumann-Pauly 2014).

Early on, the intensified process of globalization was applauded by many business people, economists, policy makers and media gurus. But critical voices were also raised against the downsides of globalization, pointing to the disruption of the labor markets, violations of human rights, environmental degradation, the lack of fair and strong global institutions, the reckless power play of global corporations and so on. As for North America, the negotiations for a trade agreement between Canada, Mexico and the United States took place and resulted in NAFTA – the North American Free Trade Agreement – that came into effect in 1994. On the request of President Clinton, it included the side agreements on labor cooperation (NAALC) and environmental cooperation (NAAEC). Although these side agreements were not followed up with strong implementation policies, they signaled, at least, the awareness of the lawmakers about two sensitive areas of concern occurring along with globalization.

This also led in 1996, at the initiation of the US Department of Labor, to the Fashion Industry Forum with 300 apparel company representatives (see Schein 2018). It aimed at raising awareness of labor and human rights abuses against persons employed in manufacturing clothing. As a result, the Apparel Industry Partnership (AIP) was formed that consisted of representatives of labor unions and consumer advocacy, human rights and religious groups, with the goal to improve conditions and eliminate abuse of adults and children in the garment industry, regardless of location. In 1999, AIP formed the Fair Labor Association (FLA) as a 501(c)(3) non-profit organization in order to recruit additional companies for membership, monitor compliance, and publicize the compliance with the code of conduct (www.fairlabor.org).

Another initiative of monitoring labor rights in the supply chain is the Worker Rights Consortium (WRC), founded in April 2000 by university administrators, students and international labor rights experts in North America (see Roy 2018). It conducts investigations of working conditions in factories around the world with the goal to protect the rights of workers producing apparel and products bearing university names and logos. The independent non-profit organization began with the support of 44 universities and by 2017 had nearly 200 higher educational affiliates (www.workersrights.org).

To put these initiatives into a global context, it is worth mentioning that in 2000 the United Nations launched the UN Global Compact for companies around the world to align strategies and operations with universal principles on human rights, labor, environment and (since 2004) anti-corruption, and take actions that advance societal goals (www.unglobalcompact.org). It became the world's largest corporate sustainability initiative and was followed by several other UN initiatives such as the UN Principles for Responsible Investing in 2006 (www.unpri.org) and the UN Principles for Responsible Management Education in 2007 (www.unprme.org). Of particular importance for our discussion on corporate responsibility in the supply chains are the UN Guiding Principles on Business and Human Rights unanimously endorsed by the UN Human Rights Council in 2011 (UN 2011).

8.2 THE EXPERIENCE OF THE UNIVERSITY OF NOTRE DAME: IN SEARCH OF THE RIGHT POLICY

A concrete case study presents the experience of the University of Notre Dame in its search for the right policy regarding its supply chains of Notre Dame licensed products. The narrative is based, to a large extent, on the two reports of the University of Notre Dame's Worker Participation Committee (WPC) in 2015 and 2018 (WPC 2015, 2018). It also reflects my personal view as I have been involved in the WPC's search for an appropriate policy over the last five years and learned a great deal about the intricacy of supply chains and their ethical challenges.

8.2.1 The Enthusiastic Beginning and its Failed Outcome

As described in the previous section, due to accelerated globalization, the 1990s brought about raising awareness of ethical issues in the supply chains and aroused multiple initiatives for addressing these issues. The University of Notre Dame participated actively in this movement. As the *Review of the Freedom of Association Policy* (WPC 2015, p. 5) proudly states,

> Notre Dame has always been at the forefront of efforts to improve wages and working conditions at foreign factories that manufacture Notre Dame licensed products. In 1997, Notre Dame was the first university to adopt a labor code of conduct for licensees. It was a founding member of the Fair Labor Association and is a member of the Worker Rights Consortium.

As a Catholic university, Notre Dame wanted to live up to Catholic Social Teaching that, since Pope Leo XIII's encyclical *Rerum Novarum* in 1891, has taken a stand on "social questions" as they have arisen over the years and provided guidance to address these questions. As a consequence, in 1999, President Fr. Edward A. Malloy, C.S.C., appointed a Task Force on Anti-Sweatshop Initiatives. In its report, the task force noted that "Catholic Social Teaching . . . has long recognized the rights of workers throughout the world to form labor unions and engage in collective bargaining with their employers" and proposed a Freedom of Association (FOA) Policy that was the "most effective and efficient way to give voice to these commitments" (WPC 2015, p. 5). The Policy included three recommendations:

> 1. Products bearing the name or other trademarks of the University shall be manufactured only by workers who enjoy the legal rights to freely associate, form labor unions, and collectively bargain with their employers concerning wages, hours, working conditions or other terms and conditions of employment.
> 2. A system of limited public disclosure, which would only require disclosure of factory locations to the University and its designated monitors.
> 3. The creation of a regional pilot monitoring program. (WPC 2015, p. 5)

The FOA Policy was adopted by Notre Dame in 2001. With its clear focus on legal rights of freedom of association and collective bargaining, it states that Notre Dame licensed products cannot be manufactured in countries without these rights. In other words, the decisive criterion for choosing factories are these laws of the countries where factories are located rather than practices at individual factories. However, in reality, such practices might not live up to or might even squarely violate these national laws while in countries without these laws factory practices might be much better in terms of worker participation and collective bargaining. Thus, based on this country criterion, the FOA Policy disregards the factories of a number of countries including China and ten other countries (Afghanistan, Equatorial Guinea, Iran, Laos, Oman, Qatar, Saudi Arabia, Somalia, Turkmenistan and United Arab Emirates). Not surprisingly, this exclusion later became a critical point in the discussions about the revision of the FOA Policy and was rejected by some committee members as a kind of discrimination.

The FOA Policy was announced as a strong and consequent commitment to Catholic Social Teaching. Convinced of its trailblazer role, Notre Dame was hoping that other universities would follow suit and adopt similar policies. However, none did. Moreover, as the task force itself admitted, "lobbying by licensees [would be] unlikely to have much of an impact upon the policies of governments as large and powerful as the Chinese government" (WPC 2015, p. 6). Unfortunately, the FOA Policy generated meager results and was not supervised by a standing committee. It was unclear whether and how workers' freedom of association had been respected in factories where Notre Dame licensed products were manufactured (only one specific case of assessment could be found). And no positive impact on workers' rights could be assumed in countries in which the university did not allow manufacturing of licensed products.

Despite these sobering results, Notre Dame kept its membership with FLA and WRC. In 2013 the Executive Vice President John F. Affleck-Graves was approached by FLA with the request to review Notre Dame's FOA Policy. This was the starting point of a new search for Notre Dame's policy regarding the supply chains of its licensed products.

8.2.2 A Pilot Project on Worker Participation with Verité

The situation regarding the FOA Policy in 2013 was unsatisfactory for several reasons. First, after 12 years its impact was difficult to assess so that the policy could hardly be said to have achieved its goal. Second, Notre Dame was unable to build a coalition with other universities to advance workers' rights to free association and collective bargaining. Third, Notre Dame's attitude towards China appeared somewhat inconsistent: while the FOA Policy prohibited the manufacture of Notre Dame licensed products in China, the university had expanded relationships in China in recent years on multiple levels, including the number of Notre Dame undergraduate and graduate students who visit China, the number of Chinese students who come to study at Notre Dame, the opening of a university office in Beijing, investments held by the endowment, and the many non-licensed products that the university purchases from China annually (WPC 2015, p. 6). Fourth, in order to get a more accurate grasp of workers' involvement in factories' decision making in countries with and without national legislation on FOA and Collective Bargaining (CB), a new concept of worker participation seemed to be necessary that would allow for empirical studies in factories around the world. Fifth, the university's commitment to Catholic Social Teaching was incompatible with the unsatisfactory situation of the FOA Policy.

For these reasons, in 2013 the Executive Vice President John Affleck-Graves invited a committee to review the current policy and to determine whether any changes to the policy should be recommended, specifically with regard to production in China. Under his leadership, the WPC included two (subsequently five) student representatives, four professors, two persons of the Licensing Department and eight (subsequently ten) personnel of the university's administration.

The committee considered two approaches to address the policy issue: a factory-centric approach and a country-centric approach, and recommended that the university conduct *a pilot program in China* to determine whether workers' rights have improved to the extent that factories meet and can sustain an acceptable standard of performance. By targeting workers' rights at the factory level, the focus was placed on *worker participation defined as a process by which factory management actively involves and/or engages employees/workers in business management and decision making*. In addition to assessing factories in China, this focus allowed comparison of factories across the world, independent of national legislation on freedom of association and collective bargaining.

Because the assessment of worker participation in factories requires a great deal of expertise, the university considered several specialized organizations and eventually engaged Verité, a global, independent, non-profit organization. This non-governmental organization (NGO) provides consulting, training, research and assessment services worldwide, is based in Amherst, Massachusetts, and has offices in Shanghai. Since its inception in 1995, it has partnered with hundreds of multinational brands, suppliers and international institutions to improve working conditions and social and environmental performances (www.verite.org).

In a first step, the committee selected six factories in China nominated by five Notre Dame licensees in order to better understand the status of worker participation in China. The factories included two plants producing headwear, three producing apparel and one producing a variety of non-apparel products (for example, tailgate tents, chairs and soft sided coolers). Their sizes ranged from 80 to more than 3000 workers.

The committee worked with Verité to develop a solid and detailed assessment tool with 71 criteria (formulated in English and Chinese) against which all factories were measured as well as an agreed upon standard of acceptable performance against those criteria. The tool focused on worker participation and the ways in which line workers and management experience these rights and protections, thereby targeting three fundamental aspects: communication, consultation and participation in decision making (specified below).

Verité next administered online self-assessment of management and then conducted on-site assessments at each of the six factories, including individual interviews with managers and workers. As a result, Verité determined that two factories met the committee's standards; two required additional improvements to meet the standards; and the remaining two needed substantially more capacity building to reach an acceptable level. In addition, seven committee members visited four of the six factories in China and confirmed the results of the Verité assessments.

After a campus-wide conversation and dialogue on the proposed pilot program, university President Fr. John I. Jenkins, C.S.C., approved the recommendations of the WPC in September 2015. Based on the experience in the six Chinese factories, the pilot project was refined with an assessment tool of 80 criteria, with follow-up assessments of the Chinese factories and extended to eight factories in Bangladesh, El Salvador, Guatemala and India – all countries with the *de jure* right of freedom of association and collective bargaining, in which the university currently allows production.

As a result, three of the four Chinese factories showed sufficient improvement against their corrective action plan and, along with the first two factories, which met the standards right away, began production for 12 months. The eight factories outside China are plants producing apparel (4), infant, toddler and youth apparel (2), headwear (1) and wallets (1), and employing 42 to 2100 workers. Their assessments used the same method as in China, namely, a series of online assessments followed by a factory visit and in-depth on-site audit by Verité. Like the investigation in China, upon receipt of Verité's assessments, a subcommittee of the WPC conducted an on-site visit of four factories in El Salvador and Guatemala to evaluate the working conditions at the factories, which confirmed the WPC's confidence in Verité and the assessment tool.

Based on Verité's work, the WPC was able to compare the performance of all the pilot factories. The results revealed that some of the factories located in China performed better on the assessed criteria than many of the factories located in other countries: three Chinese factories met 85–79 percent and three met 52–62 percent of the criteria while two factories in El Salvador and one in Guatemala met 61–77 percent and the remaining five factories ranged from 47 percent to 20 percent.

Verité provided the WPC with the following conclusions about the pilot program overall (WPC 2018, p. 19):

- All factories in China demonstrated improvement from the 2014 assessments.
- Improvement was sufficient at several key suppliers to proceed with sourcing decisions, although on a pilot basis only.
- Performance of factories outside China varied, and although only audited once, some would not have met the university criteria developed for this project (including based on the presence of several zero-tolerance issues).
- Suppliers in China can achieve continuous improvement on freedom of association and worker participation at the factory level, although this requires time and management commitment.

8.2.3 Expanding the Assessment Process to a Broader Scale

The pilot program about worker participation was an important step forward in the search for Notre Dame's Policy of Freedom of Association. But it was limited in two ways: it focused only on some core workers' rights without considering a broader range of social and environmental responsibilities of the factories producing Notre Dame licensed products, and it assessed only 14 factories without regarding all or at least a majority of the factories from which Notre Dame gets its licensed products.

Given these two limitations, the WPC looked for a second assessment partner. Notre Dame's Licensing Program currently has 189 licensees and 561 licensees contracted factories. They are located in 35 countries, 55 percent within the United States and 45 percent overseas; 15 percent of the factories are owned by the licensees and 85 percent are independently owned or operated. Because Verité did not have the capacity nor interest in significantly expanding its work to cover all of the factories and, moreover, it would be very costly to conduct such detailed assessment in all factories, the WPC explored other approaches and vendors capable of implementing the assessment process on a broader scale.

After consultation with other universities, the choice fell on Sumerra, which was invited to present its approach to the WPC in spring 2017. Sumerra (a short name for "summa terra," that is, the whole earth) is a global for-profit organization that provides supply chain management, compliance management and consulting services worldwide. It is based in Portland, Oregon, with offices in Hong Kong, Bangalore and Dhaka. Sumerra has partnered with multinational brands, organizations, licensees and factories that are striving to improve working conditions and promote fair treatment of workers (www.sumerra.com).

As extensive conversations with Sumerra's CEO Jason Roberts in August 2017 showed, Sumerra offered several services crucial for the expansion of Notre Dame's pilot program. (1) It has a multi-pronged assessment platform that includes licensees by using a pre-survey and factories by employing specialized audit organizations. (2) The pre-survey and the auditing questions evaluate a wide range of human rights and environmental concerns. (3) Universities can choose to use the portions of the platform that are most appropriate for their needs. (4) Schools, which partner with Sumerra, receive access to the assessment results of any licensee and factory that uses its platform. As a result, licensees that Notre Dame have in common with other schools do not need to conduct additional assessments. (5) At the time of the WPC's initial meeting with Sumerra, 46 percent of Notre Dame's current licensees had already completed the Sumerra licensee survey at the request of another school.

Given the WPC's strong emphasis on worker participation, the WPC conducted a thorough review of Sumerra's assessment instruments in order to make sure that Notre Dame's long-standing concerns about workers' rights are fully taken into account while other social and environmental concerns are addressed as well.

As mentioned above, Verité's revised assessment tool for worker participation comprehends 80 criteria with five compliance levels: zero-tolerance, minimum, good, better and best. It distinguishes two types of worker organizations: unions and worker representation bodies. And the active involvement of these organizations and workers can take three forms:

- Worker grievance system – policies/procedures, implementation, effectiveness.
- Worker feedback system – policies/procedures, implementation, effectiveness.
- Worker participation – policies/procedures, implementation, effectiveness.

In contrast, Sumerra's assessment tool focuses on a wide range of ten topics, including a factory profile and a pre-survey (to be filled out by the licensee) and a semi-announced audit of the factory. The ten topics of the assessment data contain 409 provisions: employment relations (87 provisions), non-discrimination (14), child labor (8), forced labor (14), harassment and abuse (18), hours of work (23), compensation and benefits

(32), freedom of association (27), health and safety (94) and environment (92). The audit consists of:

- References (topics, definitions, observations, documents, interviews).
- Assessment data on ten topics and evaluated in five categories (performance, audit finding and legal/Code of Conduct violation, auditor comments (confidential), root cause analysis, recommendations/corrective action.
- Interviews (with workers).
- Scorecard: non-compliance defined using five categories: zero-tolerance, critical-high risk immediate action, critical-high risk, significant-medium risk, minor-low risk.
- Executive summary.

Moreover, Sumerra's assessment tool distinguishes – like Verité – two types of worker organizations: union and legal alternatives of worker associations (or worker organizations).

Comparing Verité's with Sumerra's assessment tool, the Criteria Subcommittee of the WPC determined that there was substantial convergence between the zero-tolerance and minimum criteria identified by Verité and Sumerra (regarding the provisions of employment relations [87] and freedom of association [27]). Both tools include a large number of criteria related to three areas of concern and based on Verité's tool:

- *Factory respects and honors workers' rights to freedom of association and collective bargaining:* 3 zero-tolerance (Z), 4 minimum (M), 3 good (G). All Z and M are met.
- *Factory refrains from any acts of interference with the operation of union or worker participation bodies (which serve the function of unions):* 3 zero-tolerance, 6 minimum, 1 good, 6 better. All Z and M are met.
- *Grievance system (confidential internal complaint system):* 8 minimum, 6 good. All M are met.

Not included in Sumerra's tool are two minimum criteria of Verité: encouraging worker feedback systems and worker participation systems; and the factory maintains complete documentation of worker grievance, feedback and participation activities and outcomes.

Given this convergence, the Criteria Subcommittee suggested adding these few missing criteria and some other changes to supplement the Sumerra tool (see the Appendix). Summera expressed a strong willingness to incorporate all of the requested suggestions in order to provide an enhanced assessment tool suitable for all factories in countries with and without *de jure* legislation on FOA and CB.

8.2.4 Drawing on the Strength of the UN Framework, the UN Guiding Principles on Business and Human Rights and its Interpretive Guide

When Notre Dame set up the Freedom of Association Policy in 2001, it was right after the promulgation of the UN Global Compact in 2000. However, it took many more years at the international level to establish the UN Framework (2008), the UN Guiding Principles (2011) and the UN Interpretive Guide (2012) on Business and Human Rights. Thanks to these developments, the WPC could benefit in its own search for an appropriate Notre Dame policy and strengthen and expand its approach to become more suitable for building up an alliance with other like-minded universities.

Although the UN Framework and UN Guiding Principles (in short UNGP) have become the most important and most widely adopted ethical standards for business around the world and are now incorporated in numerous national and international laws (for example, the Dodd–Frank Act of the United States and the Corporate Law of the European Union), many commentators have not carefully read the UNGP and are imprecise, if not confusing, in interpreting the UNGP. Therefore, it is advisable to clarify its exact meaning (see Enderle 2014).

To begin with, it is remarkable – but not surprising, given the multiple philosophical controversies about ethics and human rights – that John Ruggie (2013), the architect of the UNGP, actually avoids using ethical terms and arguments. Nevertheless, the UNGP have several crucial ethical implications: the moral status of the corporation, the notions of duty and responsibility, the distinction of different types of obligations, the criteria of assigning these obligations to different moral actors, and the concept of due diligence (see the overview in Table 8.1).

The UNGP focus on and distinguish *two subjects of obligations* for securing human rights: the states and transnational corporations (TNCs) and other business enterprises while disregarding other organs of society (such as civil society organizations, religious communities and international institutions) and individuals – all indicated but not elaborated by the Universal Declarations of Human Rights in 1948. Although the concept of the "moral actor" is not literally used, the Declaration applies it substantially to the states, whereas large-scale enterprises, at that time, were not yet understood as "moral actors." In the UNGP, however, both states and TNCs and other business enterprises are assumed to be "moral actors," which implicitly bear moral obligations, analogous but different from individuals or "moral persons"; see, for example, De George (2010).

Table 8.1 UN Framework on Business and Human Rights (2008) – concerning all human rights

	Respect		Protect	Remedy	Promote
	Direct:	Indirect (no complicity):			
States					
Transnational corporations and other business enterprises					
Other organs of society					
Individuals					

It is noteworthy that the documents do not point to or elaborate on the moral obligations of individual political and business leaders without denying them either.

The concepts of duty and responsibility are clearly distinguished, the former characterizing the obligations of the states and the latter characterizing the obligations of TNCs and other business enterprises. They are not only legal concepts, but also express moral (or ethical) content and carry different types of obligations, which depend on the ways these obligations can be fulfilled. Such a typology is crucially important in order to allocate human rights obligations in a differentiated manner. It also helps to overcome the questionable, yet widespread dichotomy between "negative" and "positive" rights by locating the difference between avoiding action (non-interference) and taking positive actions not in rights but in correlative obligations.

In line with Henry Shue's pertinent work (1996), three types of obligations of securing human rights can be distinguished (in addition to their promotion): (1) the obligation to avoid violating human rights; (2) the obligation to protect human rights by demanding recognition of the first obligation and by establishing appropriate "institutional" provisions to prevent as much as possible the violation of human rights; and (3) the obligation to provide the victims of human rights violations access to the remedy of their rights. This triple distinction coincides, by and large, with the distinction made in the UN Framework. It assigns the obligation to protect exclusively to the state, calling it "the duty of the state"; the obligation to respect relates – in addition to the state – to the TNCs and other business organizations, calling it "the responsibility of the corporation"; and the obligation to remedy pertains to both the state and the corporation.

Compared to the traditional understanding of the roles of the state and the corporation, the UN Framework offers considerable progress by significantly expanding and differentiating the responsibilities of TNCs and other business enterprises. This expansion and differentiation concerns not only the responsibility of the corporation (and the state) to respect, but also the duty of the state to protect and the remedy obligations of both.

Nevertheless, the UN Framework does not go far enough for a number of authors. Because today's powerful TNCs should be understood as quasi-governmental institutions, their responsibility should also include the protection of human rights against third parties. Moreover, TNCs should not be satisfied with a reactive attitude to avoid adverse human rights impact, but should adopt a proactive attitude to secure human rights. While the first point of criticism demonstrates a clear difference to the UNGP, the second point does not seem to recognize the very concept of due diligence, which requires a forward-looking attitude and indicates an ethical commitment to prevent adverse human rights impact. Due diligence demands (1) understanding the human rights context of the countries in which the TNC does or intends to do business; (2) assessing the TNC's own activities; and (3) analysing the TNC's relationship with business and other entities. The Interpretive Guide explains the guiding principles for human rights due diligence (UN 2012, pp. 31–62).

As becomes clear from the discussion of the subjects and the types of obligations to secure human rights, the question arises about the criteria on the basis of which the different types of obligations should be assigned to different subjects. This is a complex and far-reaching question that cannot be addressed in this chapter, but has been dealt with elsewhere (see Enderle 2014). For now, it suffices to concentrate on the three UNGP criteria of determining corporate responsibility to respect human rights. According to the Guiding Principle 13 (UN 2012, pp. 15–18), a business enterprise can be involved in an "adverse impact on human rights"[2] in three basic ways:

- It may cause the impact through its own activities.
- It may contribute to the impact through its own activities – either directly or through some outside entity (government, business or other).
- It may neither cause nor contribute to the impact, but be involved because the impact is caused by an entity with which it has a business relationship *and* is directly linked to its own operations, products or services.

Based on these three ways of involvement (causation, contribution and no contribution but direct linkage), the responsibility to respect human rights requires that business enterprises:

- Avoid causing or contributing to adverse human rights impacts through their own activities, and address such impacts when they occur.
- Seek to prevent or mitigate adverse human rights impacts that are directly linked to their operations, products or services by their business relationships, even if they have not contributed to those impacts.

Several examples may illustrate business impact on human rights:

- *Causation*: exposure of factory workers to hazardous working conditions without adequate safety equipment; being the sole or main source of pollution in a community's drinking water supply due to chemical effluents from production processes.
- *Contribution*: providing data about Internet service users to a government that uses the data to trace and prosecute political dissidents contrary to human rights; changing product requirements for suppliers at the eleventh hour without adjusting production deadlines and prices, thus pushing suppliers to breach labor standards in order to deliver.
- *No contribution, but linkage*: providing financial loans to an enterprise for business activities that, in breach of agreed standards, result in the eviction of communities; use of scans by medical institutions to screen for female fetuses, facilitating their abortion in favor of boys.

  The UNGP include all – not only economic and social – human rights expressed in the International Bill of Human Rights and the principles concerning fundamental rights set out in the International Labour Organization's Declaration on Fundamental Principles and Rights at Work (Guiding Principle 12, UN 2012, pp. 9–14). Moreover,

> the responsibility of business enterprises to respect human rights applies to all enterprises regardless of their size, sector, operational context, ownership and structure. Nevertheless, the scale and complexity of the means through which enterprises meet that responsibility may vary according to these factors and with the severity of the enterprise's adverse human rights impacts. (Principle 14, UN 2012, pp. 18–22)

To conclude this short presentation of the UNGP, it is important to emphasize the *independence* of the responsibility of business enterprises from the duty of states. The Commentary of the Guiding Principle 11 clearly states that "The responsibility to respect human rights . . . exists independently of States' ability and/or willingness to fulfill their own human rights obligations, and does not diminish those obligations. And it exists over and above compliance with national laws and regulations protecting human rights" (UN 2011, p. 13). It goes without saying that this independent attribution of responsibility to business enterprises is also relevant for Notre Dame's policy of purchasing its licensed products manufactured in Chinese factories.

8.2.5 Recommendations for Notre Dame's Policy of Promoting Corporate Responsibility in its Supply Chains of Notre Dame Licensed Products

Since Notre Dame adopted a labor code of conduct for licensees in 1997 the university has experienced many ups and downs in its search – inspired by Catholic Social Teaching – for a consistent, effective and persuasive policy for Notre Dame licensed products. It is fair to say that the search has made remarkable progress, although it has not reached its completion yet. Several key factors have contributed to this progress: the continuous engagement of the WPC over five years, the collaboration with the specialized organizations Verité and Sumerra to assess worker participation and corporate responsibility in the supply chain, and the development and worldwide expansion of the UN Framework and Guiding Principles on Business and Human Rights.

The results of Notre Dame's search process can be summarized as follows:

1. The original focus on a single issue, that is, the freedom of association, has been expanded to a *comprehensive approach to "corporate responsibility"* – understood as the policy commitment of the business organization (licensee, factory) to act ethically with regard to all economic, social and environmental aspects of corporate performance that come under the control of licensees and/or factories.
2. Corporate responsibility includes respecting *all human rights* according to the UN Framework and Guiding Principles on Business and Human Rights.
3. The University of Notre Dame is committed to its *mission* inspired by Catholic Social Teaching and *promotes* corporate responsibility in the supply chains of its licensed products.

4. Notre Dame's licensees and factories have their respective spaces of freedom and are supposed to take responsibility, *independent* of the duties of the countries' governments. This implies – among other things – that the treatment of the workers at the factory level has precedence over the country's legislation of freedom of association and collective bargaining.
5. The *enhanced assessment tool* developed in collaboration with Verité and Sumerra is a relatively comprehensive, effective and reliable instrument to evaluate the performance of corporate responsibility. Relatively reliable means that the assessment results express at least 80 percent of actual corporate performance.
6. Given the complexity and changing nature of the supply chains, a *Standing Committee* should be set up to supervise and guide the progress of Notre Dame's policy.
7. The university should help to build up an *alliance with like-minded organizations* to respect human rights and promote corporate responsibility in the supply chains in accordance with the UN Guiding Principles on Business and Human Rights.

While recognizing these important results, some limitations of this policy may be noted. First, the focus on Notre Dame licensed products does not include all the other products and services Notre Dame purchases for its operations. Second, the policy covers only Notre Dame licensed products manufactured abroad, that is, 45 percent; 55 percent are produced domestically. Third, the supply chain of Notre Dame licensed products reaches only the first tier, that is, the factories in which the final products are made, but not the second, third and other tiers that supply intermediate goods and raw materials for these final products.

In April 2018 the WPC drafted its Final Report and Recommendations, conducted a campus-wide conversation and submitted the document to President Fr. John I. Jenkins, C.S.C. In October he approved it with the following five recommendations (WPC 2018, pp. 5, 21–32):

1. A Standing Committee should be established to monitor the University's progress towards the goals outlined below and consider additional aspirational goals to advance its commitment to workers' rights, as well as other human rights and the values of Catholic Social Teaching to promote corporate responsibility.
2. The University should expand its review of licensees and factories to include a broader range of human rights issues. These assessment tools should be reviewed annually to ensure they address the broad spectrum of human rights concerns as required by the University's Licensing Code of Conduct.
3. In countries that recognize freedom of association by law, every licensee should be required to participate in the Sumerra assessment process to evaluate their organization's current corporate responsibility program and

the level of knowledge of manufacturing practices within their contracted factories. These factories would be under the ongoing oversight of the Standing Committee.

4. In countries that do not recognize freedom of association by law, the University should consider, within its discretion, a limited exemption[3] to manufacture products in those countries only after the factory has successfully completed both the Sumerra assessment and a more in-depth audit by Verité. These factories would also be under the ongoing oversight of the Standing Committee.
5. The University should cultivate partnerships with other organizations to advance respect for workers' rights, other human rights and promote corporate responsibility in the supply chain.

As the narrative of Notre Dame's experience shows, these recommendations represent a successful completion of a long search process for a policy that is solidly based and well thought-through. One can only hope that it will bear multiple fruits.

8.3 REFLECTIONS ON AND BEYOND THE NOTRE DAME EXPERIENCE

As briefly described in the Introduction, with the accelerated globalization in the 1990s the ethical challenges in the supply chains have increased enormously and become ever more complex and urgent. At the same time, these developments have provoked heated public debates, thorough and far-reaching investigations and a vast variety of practical initiatives. Compared to the early 1990s, today we are in a clearly better – though still unsatisfactory – position to understand and address the ethical challenges in the international supply chains.

Looking back to the Notre Dame experience, what can we learn about "promoting corporate responsibility in the supply chain" in more general terms that might be helpful to other like-minded universities? And what are the important research questions which remain to be investigated?

8.3.1 Suggestions to Other Universities

The Notre Dame experience of 25-plus years shows that the questions of "why," "what" and "how" to promote corporate responsibility in the supply chain are connected; but they need to be treated distinctively and, in the process, they will reinforce each other.

First, the "why" question has to be stated clearly from the beginning and answered at least in a broad and positive way. The mission statement of the university might provide the necessary guidance throughout the process of policy formation and implementation. If such guidance is not available or too general, the institution needs to set up a task force in order to determine the mission in a way that is specific enough to direct the policy search. It is crucial to clarify and embrace the mission with the full support of the leadership of the university.

Second, with regard to the "what" question, the goals and the limitations of the policy are to be clearly identified and determined, basically following the UN Framework and the UN Guiding Principles on Business and Human Rights. This approach includes four characteristics:

1. The policy is about "corporate responsibility," that is, the ethics of business enterprises.
2. The policy is factory-centered, not country-centered, which means that the factory is held responsible for what it can control, independently of the country's legislation and the "duty of the state."
3. The policy does not focus just on one or a few single issues; but it is holistic and concerns basically all economic, social and environmental aspects of the factory's performance.
4. The policy requires minimal performance standards, which consist of potentially all human rights according to the UN Guiding Principles.

An additional, fifth, characteristic of the policy – not mentioned by the UN approach – is its developmental purpose, which means enabling better factory performance in economic, social and environmental terms. Its emphasis obviously goes beyond controlling and policing factories. While this purpose concerns primarily the factories, the licensees and the universities as the buyers of the final products have to engage in this developmental task as well.

For a better understanding of this policy to promote corporate responsibility in the supply chain, three limitations should be mentioned. They are assumed and recognized here – as they are in the Notre Dame experience; but, obviously, they are not fixed forever and can be changed. First, the supply chains under consideration reach only the first tier, that is, the factories in which the final products are made, but not the second, third or other tiers that supply intermediate goods and raw materials for these final goods. Second, this policy covers only products manufactured abroad and does not include those made domestically. Third, this policy is restricted to the products that are licensed by the university, and does not relate to all the other products and services the university purchases for its operations.

With these limitations, the proposed policy is clearly focused and feasible and does not require a complete change of the university's entire supply chain policy. But it is a significant change that expresses the university's commitment to its mission. It represents a step forward that might be followed by further steps in the future; and it creates the opportunity to gather experiences of what corporate responsibility in the supply chain specifically means.

Third, not less important than the "why" and the "what" questions is the "how" question, that is, the way of implementing the policy of promoting corporate responsibility in the supply chain. An effective and efficient implementation fulfills at least five requirements:

1. The university collaborates with licensees, factories and specialized organizations in supply chain management and assessment, based on an agreed upon consensus about the policy goals.
2. To evaluate actual factory performance, the university relies on assessment tools of high quality, which are material, consistent and relatively comprehensive.
3. A Standing Committee, established by the university, monitors the progress of the policy, makes appropriate changes, and shares its experience with students, faculty and staff.
4. The university helps build an alliance of like-minded universities, based on the UN Framework and the UN Guiding Principles and using the same assessment tools.
5. While the university is committed to self-regulation within the proposed framework, it also wisely supports and uses pressures from outside (such as consumer initiatives, ethical investing and legal proposals), which help promote corporate responsibility in the supply chain.

8.3.2 Research Opportunities

To widen the reflections, several research opportunities are presented. One first set of questions concerns the *economic implications* of the policy proposal. Simply put, does "corporate responsibility" in the supply chain "pay"? What are the costs of compliance with social and environmental standards at the levels of "minimum" and "good" – for example, of labor rights such as minimal wage and grievance mechanisms or substantial energy reduction and air pollution treatment? Are there also economic benefits involved? How many? What are acceptable balances of costs and benefits? Alternatively, what results do economic cost-benefit analyses yield if the factory does *not* comply with those social and environmental standards at the "minimum" and "good" levels?

Regarding the distribution of costs and benefits of "corporate responsibility" across the supply chain, who bears the costs and who gets the benefits? How are they distributed between the factories (first, second, third and other tiers), the licensees, the sellers of the final products and the consumers? What is a "fair" distribution, based on what criteria?

To investigate these questions, one can use the *conceptual* framework of "corporate responsibility" proposed in this chapter, along with further conceptual developments. *Theoretical* explorations would gain from new approaches to understand the buyer-supplier relationship not as a principal-agent relationship, but as a relationship in which suppliers are conceived as stewards of buyers (see Assländer et al. 2016). Many research ideas about the limits of economic analysis and global labor justice and the limits of choice and the ethics of sweatshops can be found in Preiss (2014) and Kates (2015), respectively. That cultural differences do not necessarily conflict with labor rights, but can support each other is demonstrated in the stimulating article "Confucian ethics and labor rights" (Kim 2014), which reveals innovative ways of implementing human rights in different cultures.

Empirical studies may focus on particular industries (such as the apparel, toy or electronics industry) and compare the supply chains in which standards of corporate responsibility are respected with those in which they are violated. See, for example, Lin-Hi and Blumberg (2017) showing that corporations' buying behavior is decisive in order for industry self-regulation to become an appropriate means of improving labor standards in the Chinese toy industry; or Oka 2018 analysing the effectiveness of "brand advocacy" in Cambodia's garment industry. Moreover, it would be interesting to find out if, how and why these two types of supply chains differ in terms of distribution patterns of costs and benefits between the different actors. As for the management of social issues in management, see the literature review by Yawar and Seuring (2017).

Given the controversial discussion in Notre Dame's WPC on the exclusion of Chinese factories from its supply chains of Notre Dame licensed products (see pages 163 and 175), several articles help better understand critical issues of *business and human rights in China*. Whelan and Muthuri (2017) investigate human rights pressures on Chinese state-owned enterprises stemming from transnational, national and intra-organizational forces. Dawkins (2012) emphasizes the importance of collective bargaining and freedom of association while criticizing Zwolinski (2007) and Powell and Zwolinski (2012) for being "conspicuously silent" on these issues (Kates 2015, p. 207, n. 16). Still, the question remains whether Chinese factories with a decent level of worker participation should be denied from participating in supply chains. Would such denial amount to a kind of *discrimination* because those factories are located in a country whose national legislation does not allow freedom of association and collective bargaining? What are the ethical (and economic?) arguments in support of and against such denial?

Another controversial issue discussed in the WPC concerns the *reliability of the assessment tools* developed and used by special organizations for supply chain management (see Locke 2013). Critical MIT studies question Nike's long-standing audit approach (Locke and Romis 2007; Locke et al. 2006). And newer investigations have shown that even elaborated auditing schemes have been "ineffective when confronted with sophisticated deception methods that some suppliers employ" (Locke et al. 2009, quoted in Assländer et al. 2016, pp. 661–2). However, recent conversations with leaders of specialized organizations like Sumerra suggest that the quality of assessment tools has improved substantially in the last several years. It is therefore important to investigate the information content and the reliability of the assessment tools currently in use and, if necessary, to raise them to an acceptable level (see Searcy and Ahi 2014). In addition, one may analyse the structure and distribution of the *assessment costs* and develop fair schemes to charge factories, licensees, sellers and consumers.

As the UN Framework and the UN Guiding Principles on Business and Human Rights affirm the important and independent role of the (moral) responsibility of business enterprises to "respect human rights," the question arises as to what role the state (or government) should play to secure human rights. The answer – according to this framework – is that the state has "the duty to protect" its citizens against human rights violations and, along with business enterprises, to respect human rights and remedy human rights violations. While this "division of labor" is conceptually clear, although not undisputed (see, for example, Wettstein 2012, pp. 753–4), it still opens up a large number of research questions regarding the legal incentives for enterprises to respect human rights and remedy human rights violations nationally and internationally.

Three perspectives seem particularly promising. In the wake of the promulgation of the UN Guiding Principles by the UN Human Rights Council in 2011, states were invited to set up their own "National Action Plans for Human Rights," and until now more than 30 countries have followed this invitation, including the United States (2016) and China (2012, 2014 and 2016). While these plans vary a great deal, they provide a wide field of research questions about their stated and ignored objectives, their rationales, their implementation strategies, their assessments, and their proposed changes resulting from past achievements and failures.

An interesting example of incorporating the UN Guiding Principles into national legislation for global corporations was a "Petition" to the Swiss National Council in 2012, signed by 135,000 citizens. It provoked many public debates, was discussed in the national legislative body and finally defeated (https://konzern-initiative.ch). In 2015 the "Responsible Business Initiative" was launched and debated in the parliament again.

The National Council accepted a compromise in June 2018 while the Council of States was still undecided in the summer of 2019. Research questions may address the potential impact of this legislation on different constituencies: the improvement of working conditions and environmental performance in the supply chain; the competitiveness of global corporations and their willingness to stay located in Switzerland; the reputation of Switzerland and its global corporations in the world community; and the potentially pioneering role of this initiative for other countries.

With regard to international legislation about human rights, the European Union developed a range of human rights conditionality into "an autonomous instrument of foreign policy and cooperation for development" that can be included in its international agreements (Violini and Rangone 2020). A case in point are the currently ongoing negotiations on a Free Trade Agreement (FTA) between the EU and Vietnam. While the European Commission twice refused to integrate human rights in the FTA draft, the European Ombudsman – on the demand of two NGOs, the International Federation for Human Rights and the Vietnam Committee on Human Rights – found maladministration of the Commission in both cases and forwarded the issue to the complicated EU process of ratification, which at that time was not settled yet (see Carrillo and Batalli 2018; Cassel and Ramasastry 2016; Jennings 2017). On 30 June 2019 the European Union signed a landmark free trade deal with Vietnam. Vu and Phuong Nguyen (2019) write, "it still needs the approval of the European Parliament, which is not a given as some lawmakers are concerned about Vietnam's human rights record."

Research may investigate the likely impact of the agreement on promoting corporate responsibility among different types of companies in Vietnam; how the human rights requirements are perceived by business leaders of national, European and other enterprises, by worker representatives, civil society and government – as an intrusion of a foreign power, as an additional cost factor or as support of the development of the country; and how these negotiations can help develop a "National Human Rights Action Plan" for Vietnam.

8.4 CONCLUSION

As stated in the Introduction, universities are not only institutions of higher education; they also constitute powerful economic actors and sell licensed products carrying their names and their reputation. Inspired by its mission and Catholic Social Teaching, the University of Notre Dame has engaged, over many years, in the search of a policy of freedom of association and ended up with a policy of promoting corporate responsibility in its supply chains of licensed products. This experience was not only a great learning process for Notre Dame. But it also offers policy suggestions to other like-minded universities, in line with the UN Guiding Principles on Business and Human Rights, and opens up a wide range of fascinating research opportunities on corporate responsibility in the supply chains. By caring for human rights and the environment in the supply chains, the quest for consistency cannot but turn to the university itself and expect it to take them seriously at home as well. Not only business enterprises, but also other non-state actors can learn from the UN Guiding Principles on Business and Human Rights (see Kirchschläger 2017).

NOTES

1. In this chapter the term university stands for universities and colleges.
2. An adverse impact on human rights occurs when an action removes or reduces the ability of an individual to enjoy his or her human right (UN 2012, p. 6).
3. This "limited exemption" can be interpreted in two ways. It can mean that factories in countries without recognized freedom of association by law have to meet *higher* standards of worker participation than factories in countries with *de jure* freedom of association. Or it can mean that the *same* standards are applied to *all* factories across the world while the *validity* of the assessment has to be ensured by an audit of Verité in uncertain cases. The first interpretation implies a discrimination of Chinese factories and factories of other countries without *de jure* freedom of association. The second interpretation (which I support) does neither imply discrimination nor express a lack of trust in Sumerra's enhanced assessment tool; rather, it reduces the somewhat uncertain validity of the assessment results.

REFERENCES

Assländer, M.S., J. Roloff and D.Z. Nayir (2016), "Suppliers as stewards? Managing social standards in first- and second-tier suppliers," *Journal of Business Ethics*, **139**, 661–83.

Carrillo, H. and L. Batalli (2018), "European values or European profit? A case study of the EU's responsibility to protect human rights in the Free Trade Agreement with Vietnam," Research paper in the MBA Course "International Business Ethics" in the Mendoza College of Business, University of Notre Dame, April.

Cassel, D. and A. Ramasastry (2016), "White Paper: Options for a treaty on business and human rights," *University of Notre Dame Journal of International & Comparative Law*, **6**(1), 1–50.

Dawkins, C.E. (2012), "Labor relations: corporate citizenship, labor unions, and freedom of association," *Business Ethics Quarterly*, **22**(3), 473–500.

De George, R.T. (2010), *Business Ethics*, seventh edn, Upper Saddle River, NJ: Prentice Hall.

Enderle, G. (2005), "Globalization," in P.H. Werhane and R.E. Freeman (eds), *The Blackwell Encyclopedia of Management. Volume II: Business Ethics*, second edn, Oxford: Blackwell, pp. 215–18.

Enderle, G. (2014), "Some ethical explications of the UN Framework for Business and Human Rights," in O.F. Williams (ed.), *Sustainable Development: The UN Millennium Development Goals, the UN Global Compact, and the Common Good*, Notre Dame: University of Notre Dame Press, pp. 163–83.

Guo, Lei, Hsu Shih-Hsien, A. Holton and Jeong Sun Ho (2012), "A case study of the Foxconn suicides: an international perspective to framing the sweatshop issue," *International Communication Gazette*, **74**(5), 484–503. https://journals.sagepub.com/doi/full/10.1177/1748048512445155.

Jennings, R. (2017), "Vietnam's TTP backup plan, a Free Trade Agreement with Europe is facing new obstacles," *Forbes*, 2 March.

Kates, M. (2015), "The ethics of sweatshops and the limits of choice," *Business Ethics Quarterly*, **25**(2), 191–212.

Kim, T.W. (2014), "Confucian ethics and labor rights," *Business Ethics Quarterly*, **24**(4), 565–94.

Kirchschläger, P.G. (ed.) (2017), *Die Verantwortung von nichtstaatlichen Akteuren gegenüber Menschenrechten* (*The Responsibility of Non-state Actors for Human Rights*), Zürich: Theologischer Verlag, pp. 195–215.

Kryder, L.G. (2018), "Supply chain, sustainable," in R.W. Kolb (ed.), *The SAGE Encyclopedia of Business Ethics and Society*, Thousand Oaks, CA: SAGE Publications, pp. 3302–3.

Labowitz, S. and D. Baumann-Pauly (2014), "Business as usual *is* not an option: supply chains and sourcing after Rana Plaza," New York: New York Leonard N. Stern School of Business, Center of Business and Human Rights.

Lin-Hi, N. and I. Blumberg (2017), "The power(lessness) of industry self-regulation to promote responsible labor standards: insights from the Chinese toy industry," *Journal of Business Ethics*, **143**(4), 789–805.

Locke, R.M. (2002), "The promise and perils of globalization: the case of Nike," MIT Working Paper IPC-02-007, Cambridge, MA.

Locke, R. (2013), *The Promise and Limits of Private Power: Promoting Labor Standards in a Global Economy*, Cambridge: Cambridge University Press.

Locke, R.M. and M. Romis (2007), "Improving working conditions in the global supply chain," *MIT Sloan Management Review*, January.

Locke, R., M. Amengual and A. Mangla (2009), "Virtue out of necessity? Compliance, commitment, and the improvement of labour conditions in global supply chains," *Politics & Society*, **37**(3), 319–51.

Locke, R., F. Qin and A. Brause (2006), "Does monitoring improve labor standards? Lessons from Nike," Sloan School of Management, MIT, Working Paper No. 24, July.

Oka, C. (2018), "Brands as labour rights advocates? Potential and limits of brand advocacy in global supply chains," *Business Ethics: A European Review*, **27**(2), 95–107.

Powell, B. and M. Zwolinski (2012), "The ethical and economic case against sweatshop labor: a critical assessment," *Journal of Business Ethics*, **107**(4), 449–72.

Preiss, J. (2014), "Global labor justice and the limits of economic analysis," *Business Ethics Quarterly*, **24**(1), 55–83.

Quinn, F.J. (2017), "Supply chain management: past, present and future: on our 20th anniversary, SCMR asked founding editor Frank Quinn and four industry experts to weigh in on the future of supply chain management," *Supply Chain Management Review*, March–April, 10–12.

Radin, T.J. (2018), "Globalization," in R.W. Kolb (ed.), *The SAGE Encyclopedia of Business Ethics and Society*, Thousand Oaks, CA: SAGE Publications, pp. 1620–30.

Roy, A. (2018), "Worker Rights Consortium (WRC)," in R.W. Kolb (ed.), *The SAGE Encyclopedia of Business Ethics and Society*, Thousand Oaks, CA: SAGE Publications, pp. 3363–4.

Ruggie, J.G. (2013), *Just Business: Multinational Corporations and Human Rights*, New York: W.W. Norton.

Schein, D.D. (2018), "Fair Labor Association (FLA)," in R.W. Kolb (ed.), *The SAGE Encyclopedia of Business Ethics and Society*, Thousand Oaks, CA: SAGE Publications, pp. 1334–6.

Searcy, C. and P. Ahi (2014), "Reporting supply chain sustainability: a myriad of metrics," *Guardian*, 26 September.

Shue, H. (1996), *Basic Rights. Subsistence, Affluence, and U.S. Foreign Policy*, second edn, Princeton, NJ: Princeton University Press.

United Nations (UN) (2008), *Promotion of All Human Rights, Civil, Political, Economic, Social and Cultural Rights, Including the Right to Development. Protect, Respect and Remedy: A Framework for Business and Human Rights.* Report of the Special Representative of the Secretary-General on the issue of human rights and transnational corporations and other business enterprises, John Ruggie. Human Rights Council. Eighth Session, A/HRC/8/5.

United Nations (UN) (2011), *Guiding Principles on Business and Human Rights: Implementing the United Nations "Protect, Respect and Remedy" Framework*, New York and Geneva: United Nations Human Rights Council, Office of the High Commissioner.

United Nations (UN) (2012), *The Corporate Responsibility to Respect Human Rights: An Interpretative Guide*, New York and Geneva: United Nations Human Rights Council, Office of the High Commissioner.

Violini, L. and G. Rangone (2020), "Human dignity, development policies and the EU's human rights conditionality," in P. Carozza and C. Sedmak (eds), *Human Dignity and the Practice of Human Development*, Notre Dame: University of Notre Dame Press.

Vu, K. and P. Nguyen (2019), "Vietnam, EU sign landmark free trade deal." https://www.reuters.com/article/us-eu-vietnam-trade/vietnam-eu-sign-landmark-free-trade-deal-idUSKCN1TV0CJ (accessed August 2019).

Wettstein, F. (2012), "CSR and the debate on business and human rights: bridging the great divide," *Business Ethics Quarterly*, **22**(4), 739–70.

Whelan, G. and J. Muthuri (2017), "Chinese state-owned enterprises and human rights: the importance of national and intra-organizational pressures," *Business & Society*, **56**(5), 738–81.

Worker Participation Committee (WPC) (2015), *Review of the Freedom of Association Policy*, University of Notre Dame, May.

Worker Participation Committee (WPC) (2018), *Freedom of Association Policy Review. Final Report and Recommendations by the Worker Participation Committee*, University of Notre Dame, September.

Worker Participation Committee: Criteria Subcommittee (WPC CS) (2017), "Minutes from May 6, 2016 to August 9, 2017." Available from G. Enderle.

Yawar, S.A. and S. Seuring (2017), "Management of social issues in supply chains: a literature review exploring social issues, actions and performance outcomes," *Journal of Business Ethics*, **141**(3), 621–43.

Zwolinski, M. (2007), "Sweatshops, choice, and exploitation," *Business Ethics Quarterly*, **17**(4), 689–727.

APPENDIX: WORKER PARTICIPATION COMMITTEE: SUMMARY OF ASSESSMENT TOOLS (WPC CS 2017)

Factory respects and honors workers' rights to freedom of association and collective bargaining:

- Factory policies and procedures do not conflict with workers' rights to freedom of association and collective bargaining.
- Factory does not put restrictions on issues that can be addressed in collective negotiations.
- Factory has written policies and procedures that recognize and respect the rights of all workers to freedom of association and collective bargaining.
- Factory provides communication and training to management and workers on factory policies and procedures for upholding workers' rights to freedom of association and collective bargaining.
- All levels of management staff are aware of workers' legal rights to freedom of association and collective bargaining.
- Workers are aware of their basic legal rights to freedom of association and collective bargaining.
- Factory does not deny or restrict in any way union representatives' (both inside and outside of the factory) access to workers.
- No workers report any cases of workers being fired or blacklisted in any way for organizing trade unions.
- No evidence that the factory employs any form of physical or psychological violence, threats, intimidation, retaliation, harassment or abuse against workers who exercise their rights to freedom of association.
- No evidence of interference with or attempt to influence or control the formation of unions by any means (incentives or intimidation).

Factory refrains from any acts of interference with the operation of union or worker participation bodies (which serve the function of unions):

- No evidence of interference with or attempt to influence or control union or other worker representations bodies by any means (incentives or intimidation).
- No evidence of employer participation in or influence on the election of union representatives, development of union policies, strategies and programs.
- No evidence that the factory discriminates in any way against workers for union membership or worker representative activities at any

phase of their full employment cycle from recruitment, hiring to dismissal.

- There is no evidence of workers being fired or blacklisted in any way for participating in union activities.
- There is no evidence that the factory employs any form of physical or psychological violence, threats, intimidation, retaliation, harassment or abuse against union members/worker representatives.
- Factory provides necessary venues, facilities and time needed as per local law for the union's operation.
- At the time of employment, workers are informed if they are automatically enrolled in a union or a worker representative body that serves the function of a union.
- Factory does not deduct union membership fees or any other fees related to union or worker representative activities from workers' wage without obtaining their approval.
- There is a collective contract on workplace issues.
- Factory has written procedures that support collective bargaining or negotiation with worker representatives on issues related to workers' rights and welfare.
- Factory communicates to workers and management the collective contract.
- Factory keeps records of collective bargaining/labor-management negotiations.
- The union leaders/worker representatives are democratically elected directly by workers/worker representatives.
- The union leaders/worker representatives regularly organize meetings and other activities for workers on factory-related issues.
- Workers are aware of the trade union and/or the worker representation bodies; they are familiar with the functions and authority of the bodies and their representatives.
- The union/worker representative bodies engage in collective bargaining with factory management on behalf of workers, and/or systematically consult with factory management for settlement of labor disputes.
- There have been no major worker action or labor disputes caused by factory miscommunication or failure to communicate with workers.

Grievance system (confidential internal complaint system) [not: feedback, participation]:

- Factory has written statement of management commitment to solving workers' grievances.

- Factory has clear and standardized written procedures on worker grievance (#37aM).
- Responsible personnel and departments accountable for managing worker grievance processes are clearly defined and documented.
- Responsibilities are clearly defined and documented for management and supervisory staff accountable for managing worker grievance.
- Responsibilities are clearly defined and documented for workers for participating in grievance.
- Management staff involved in managing worker grievance.
- Workers are trained on grievance procedures.
- The grievance process has a mechanism for anonymous reporting of grievances and complaints.
- Factory has an established confidential communication system for workers to raise issues of concern (including treatment by their supervisors without fear of reprisal).
- Factory employs multiple channels for workers to provide grievance.
- Factory gives responses to issues raised by workers within a stipulated and reasonable timeframe.
- Factory systematically communicates to the workforce the resolution of issues or the status of issues under review or investigation.
- Factory regularly analyzes the issues and grievances raised and resolved.
- Factory communicates with workers about worker-related rules, policies, procedures, factory regulations and other important changes related to workers' rights and interests.
- Workers are asked to complete satisfaction surveys, or other surveys to evaluate the effectiveness of implementation of factory policies and procedures.

Encouraging worker feedback systems and worker participation systems:

- Management understands legal and client requirements pertaining to worker feedback and participation.

Internal audit standards:

- Factory maintains complete documentation of worker grievance, feedback and participation activities and outcomes.

PART III

Models for Decision Making

9. Embedded leadership*

Patricia H. Werhane

9.1 INTRODUCTION

The theme of this collection, "Ethical Business Leadership in Troubling Times," challenges leadership scholars to create models for leadership that address these contemporary issues. I want to set the stage by exploring a model for 21st-century leadership, what I shall call "embedded leadership," that fits well for the complex character of global economies and "troubling times." I begin with the assumption that notion(s) of leadership are socially constructed and thus can be reformulated to fit changing political and economic environments. I then argue that underlying the present global chaos (Brexit, Iran nuclear deal meltdown, ecosystem neglect, human trafficking, trade embargos and so on) is part of a larger macro complex interacting framework that demands new thinking to frame our models of leadership. Unless we change our leadership models to fit the global 21st-century knowledge-framed economy, we will not be able to adequately face these and new issues that will continue to plague our planet. One such viable model is that of embedded leadership.

In what follows I will focus on a model derived from the thinking of Uhl-Bien and colleagues (Uhl-Bien and Arena, 2017; Uhl-Bien and Ospina, 2012; Uhl-Bien et al., 2007) and Collier and Estaban (2000). This model entails framing the notion of leadership in terms of complex adaptive systems (CAS) (Miller and Page, 2007). Because the subject of these complex systems is human beings, their organizations and institutions, I shall call these complex adaptive *social* systems (CASS) or sets of embedded systems.

Systems thinking invites a different model for leadership. Ronald Heifetz calls such leadership "adaptive work" (Heifetz, 1998, p. 22). Following that lead, I will argue that what is called for and most viable, given the complex set of systems in which we live is what I shall call embedded leadership that is neither hierarchical not dependent on "authority" – the "Boss" or "Master" point of view.

I will conclude that our notion of leadership should reflect that complexity, and the network of systems in which we live and act. If we can conceive of leadership that is embedded within these complex global systems, we might be able to create a model that can address some of the challenges raised by the TransAtlantic Business Ethics Conferences (TABEC) "call for papers."

Is this a feminist model of leadership as some thinkers suggest (e.g., Borgerson, 2007; Painter-Morland, 2011; Painter-Morland and Werhane, 2011; Wentzel Wolfe and Werhane, 2017; Werhane, 2007; Werhane et al., 2006)? I shall raise that question, but not come to a precise conclusion on this contention.

9.2 SYSTEMS THINKING AND COMPLEX (SOCIAL) SYSTEMS

> In today's environment, complexity is occurring on multiple levels and across many sectors and contexts. Although many forces are driving it, the underlying factors are greater interconnectivity and redistributions of power . . . (Uhl-Bien and Arena, 2017, p. 10)

According to systems thinkers (e.g., Laszlo and Knippner, 1998; Miller and Page, 2007; Mitroff and Linstrone, 1993; Painter-Morland, 2011; Plesk, 2001; Werhane, 2000, 2002, 2008; Wolf, 1999), each of us and each of our institutions and communities is embedded in a complex historically grounded social, familial, cultural, political and even religious set of interactive social networks that affect and are affected by mutually triggered individual, institutional, community and even global decisions, choices and actions. This is what several thinkers have called "complex adaptive systems" (CAS) or complex adaptive social systems (CASS). "A complex adaptive system [CAS or CASS] is a collection of individual agents [and organizations] that [despite institutional and other social constraints to the contrary] have the freedom to act in ways that are not always predictable and whose actions are interconnected such that one agent's actions changes the context for other agents" (Plesk, 2001, pp. 311–12; see also Miller and Page, 2007, pp. 3–8). I shall address the latter part of that definition in the next section. One might think of this as a set of enormous complex interrelated and interactive four-dimensional stakeholder networks, and there is not merely one global complex system. Rather, there are layers of systems. So, for example, an individual lives within and interacts with several systems including other individuals and groups of individuals, complex organizations, messy political economies and an ever evolving global network. And most organizations themselves are complex adaptive systems as are political economies and the ecosystem with which we interact daily. And obviously, in this context complex adaptive systems refer to and are human social systems.

A basic assumption underlying this notion of CASS is that human beings are inexorably social. Going back to Adam Smith, Smith argues "[i]t is thus man, who can subsist only in society, was fitted by nature to that situation for which he is made. All the members of human society stand in need of each other's assistance and are likewise exposed to mutual injuries" (Smith, 1759 [1976], II.i.3; see also Bevan and Werhane, 2015 on this point). Thus, Smith would argue (putting his arguments in contemporary language), interacting and networking with others and other organizations is part of who we are because as social beings we are in need of each other, and indeed it could not be otherwise.

There are several provisos we should consider in this definition of a CASS. First, the term "adaptive" in this context is both descriptive and normative and these differences are not always specified. It is commonly argued that complex systems are or can be "adaptive," evolving changing systems because each of us as individual or organizational actors, although bounded by our particular situations, can act, and act with emotion, with reason or without reason, with Twitter or Facebook, and those actions and behaviors affect and change our relationships and thus the evolution of various complex adaptive social systems on each level. For example, to requote Plesk, "A complex adaptive system (CAS) is a collection of individual agents [and organizations] that [despite institutional and other social constraints to the contrary] *have the freedom to act in ways that are not always predictable and whose actions are interconnected such that one agent's actions changes the context for other agents*" (Plesk, 2001, pp. 311–12, my italics). But notice the terminology – individuals and organizations "have the freedom to act: that is, they *can* act. This statement is normative, because it implies that individuals and organizations can, but do not have to act – we have choices, albeit with many institutional restraints, and indeed there are static systems as well and individuals, organizations and institutions that do not take advantage of these possibilities. Of course, a static system affects other interacting systems. Not acting is a choice too, not to choose, but by not choosing, by not adapting to changing environmental conditions and new networks, an individual or organization is doing something that affects the system.

Corporations are complex systems "because they are the result of multiple interconnecting interrelationships so that the way they respond to their environment has the effect of creating new connections and thus increasing their complexity" (Collier and Estaban, 2000, p. 210). They are or can be adaptive because they react to, and can change, their culture, goals, direction and processes while remaining the same entity. And they are systemic because they interact with other complex systems (many of which are adaptive) both locally and globally, individually and with other organizations and communities.

We experience our lives within various complex social systems, but we can also study and separate various forms of thinking, thus accounting for the development of various empirical, experimental and normative methodologies. Moreover, while individual and institutional actions are the results of these constantly evolving networked interactions, according to CASS theorists, there is still room for choice and judgment, not always aligned with the systems in which individuals and organizations (social agents) exist, and those choices and judgments, in turn, affect the system, often in unpredictable ways. According to experts in CASS, unpredictability is a result of the complexity of the system *and* the behavior of its individual and organizational actors such that understanding the behavior of each component part will not yield full understanding of the continually evolving system (Miller and Page, 2007, p. 3). Alternately, grasping a system in its full complexity at any moment in time (although almost impossible to do in practice) will not yield perfect predictability of the future.

Indeed, according to Miller and Page, "[s]ocial agents [individuals and organizations] find themselves enmeshed in a web of connections . . . [But despite these connections] social agents are also *capable* of change via thoughtful, but not necessarily brilliant, deliberations about the worlds they inhabit" (2007, p. 10, my italics). Social agents (both individual and institutional) do not merely react or act. They can also be aware or become aware or "mindful" of their actions, and they are capable of changing their behavior and thus the systems in which they act, even alternating the course of history, albeit ordinarily very slowly and in very small ways within the restraints of the system (and its historical time/space location) in which they exist.

As Philipp Schreck reminds us when commenting on institutional theory, "even if ethics is considered a primarily institutional matter, the evaluation of an institution's ethical quality presupposes the capability of ethical judgment. This judgment remains the responsibility of individuals" (Schreck, 2016, p. 380). I would add that even if ethics is considered primarily a result of systemic interactions, the evaluation and dynamism of a complex system is ever evolving (positively or negatively) and this evolution presupposes the capability of individual and organizational ethical judgment and choice.

9.3 COMPLEX ADAPTIVE (SOCIAL) SYSTEMS AND SOCIAL CONSTRUCTIVISM

> . . . the seemingly objective social world is constructed by human action and interaction. (Berger and Luckmann, 1966, p. 1)

As I suggested in the Introduction, the term "leadership" is a socially constructed notion, defined by culture, context and the differing perspectives of various theorists in this field. That statement is part of a larger assumption that all human experience is socially constructed. That is, human beings (and thus organizations and institutions we as humans create) cannot take in all the data of their experiences. Rather, we select, order and organize this data, and we do so from what we have socially been exposed to, learned. Because they are constructed by ourselves, we can change these mindsets when exposed to new, challenging experiences, but those too are socially constructed. Because we cannot absorb all the data of our experience, just as we cannot know everything there is to know (Berger and Luckmann, 1967; Hacking, 1999; Werhane, 1999, 2012).

Herbert Simon once referred to one dimension of this phenomenon as "bounded rationality," arguing that

> decision makers (irrespective of their level of intelligence) have to work under three unavoidable constraints: (1) only limited, often unreliable, information is available regarding possible alternatives and their consequences, (2) human mind has only limited capacity to evaluate and process the information that is available, and (3) only a limited amount of time is available to make a decision. Therefore, even individuals who intend to make rational choices are bound to make satisficing (rather than maximizing or optimizing) choices in complex situations. (Simon, 1982. Requoted in *Business Dictionary*, 2018)

Because of the limitations of rationality, individuals and organizations often have blind spots (Bazerman and Tenbrunsel, 2012) or miss some important information, such as cultural differences, consumer patterns, new technologies, climate change, political movements and so on. What a CASS model takes into account is the various ways in which we can approach the data of human experience, its normative intent and its unpredictability. Each of our mindsets separates out certain components for focus, but in fact all that we experience is interconnected with other phenomena.

Within the bounded rationality of any system, however, there is leeway for decision-making or simply randomly unpredictable behaviors that cannot be fully predicted because of the mindfulness and plasticity of social agents themselves. To think of it another way, systems thinking, and the concept of complex systems appears to create a deterministic universe, but one has to account for unpredictability as well. This unpredictability or chaos generated in any complex system or subsystem can only be accounted for by the volatility of the human capacity for action. Thus, the CASS model is an explanatory framework for explaining human and organizational (social agent) choice, independence, and thus human judgment and responsibility, and, I shall argue, contemporary leadership as well.

9.4 CASS AND STAKEHOLDER THEORY

Stakeholder theory in its original formulation defended the notion that in any organization such as a corporation there are reciprocal relationships between the organization and its primary stakeholders, relationships that entail obligations of the organization to its stakeholders and reciprocal (but not identical) obligations of the various stakeholders to the organization. This is often depicted as a wheel-and-spoke graphic (Figure 9.1). But as Freeman acknowledges, "organizations are complex phenomena and to analyze them as 'black boxes' . . . with the organization in the middle of a complex world of external forces and pressures, does not do justice to the subtlety of the flavors or organizational life" (Freeman, 1984 [2010], p. 216). So, for example, the not-for-profit pharmaceutical Nova Nordisk redraws the stakeholder map to place patients with diabetes in the center. This is to emphasize that Novo Nordisk is in the business of developing drugs to ameliorate disease, and their most successful drug is for diabetes (Figure 9.2). Pfizer Europe has developed an even more complex model that abandons the wheel-and-spoke graphic altogether (Figure 9.3; Sachs, 2011). Elsewhere I have argued that in a global economy an even more complex model that is not organization-centric might better depict the very complex relationships that exist in global relationships (Figure 9.4) (see Werhane et al., 2011; see also Freeman, 1984 [2010], pp. 36–8 on

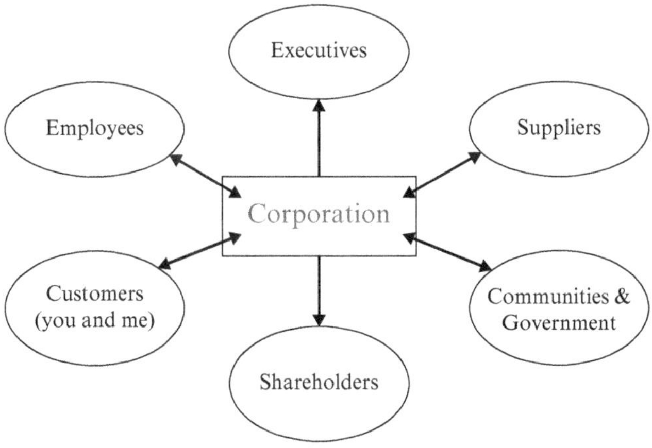

Figure 9.1 "Standard" stakeholder map

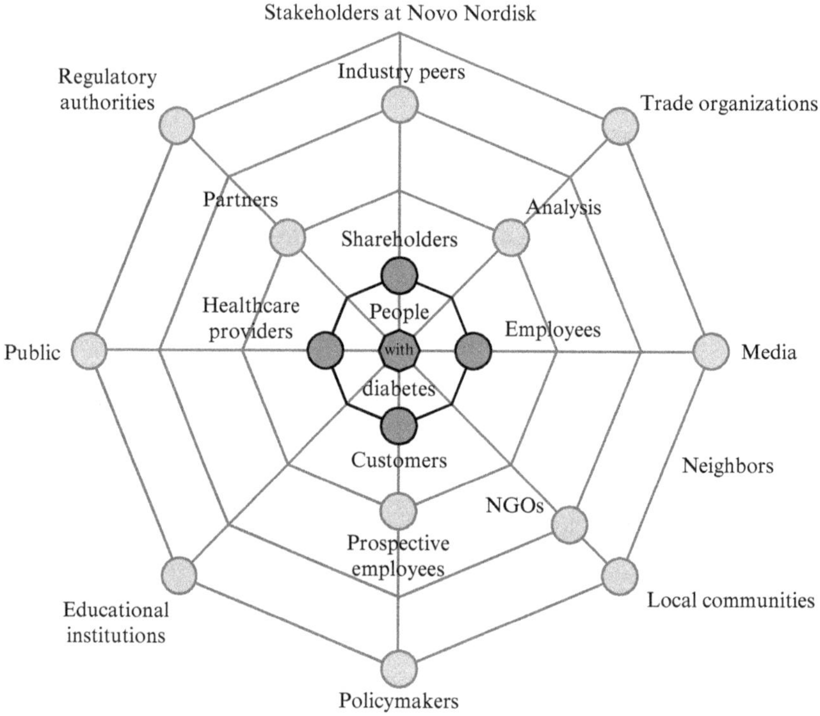

Figure 9.2 Repositioned stakeholder map

systems thinking). Leadership under Figure 9.4 is embedded within all those arrows.

9.5 CASS, STAKEHOLDER THEORY, ADAPTIVE WORK AND EMBEDDED LEADERSHIP

If, as I have argued, we are embedded and live in a complex global world, we are part of an interlocking interacting series of complex systems that require a systemic approach to leadership. According to Painter-Morland (2011), "Systems thinking allows us to acknowledge the multidirectional, tacit influences that play a role in the ways people 'lead' in organizations. Under certain [global] organizational conditions a relational, systemic model of leadership emerges, which allows individuals who don't necessarily occupy positions of authority to lead in their own unique ways" (p. 142). This model of leadership is neither hierarchical nor bureaucratic but

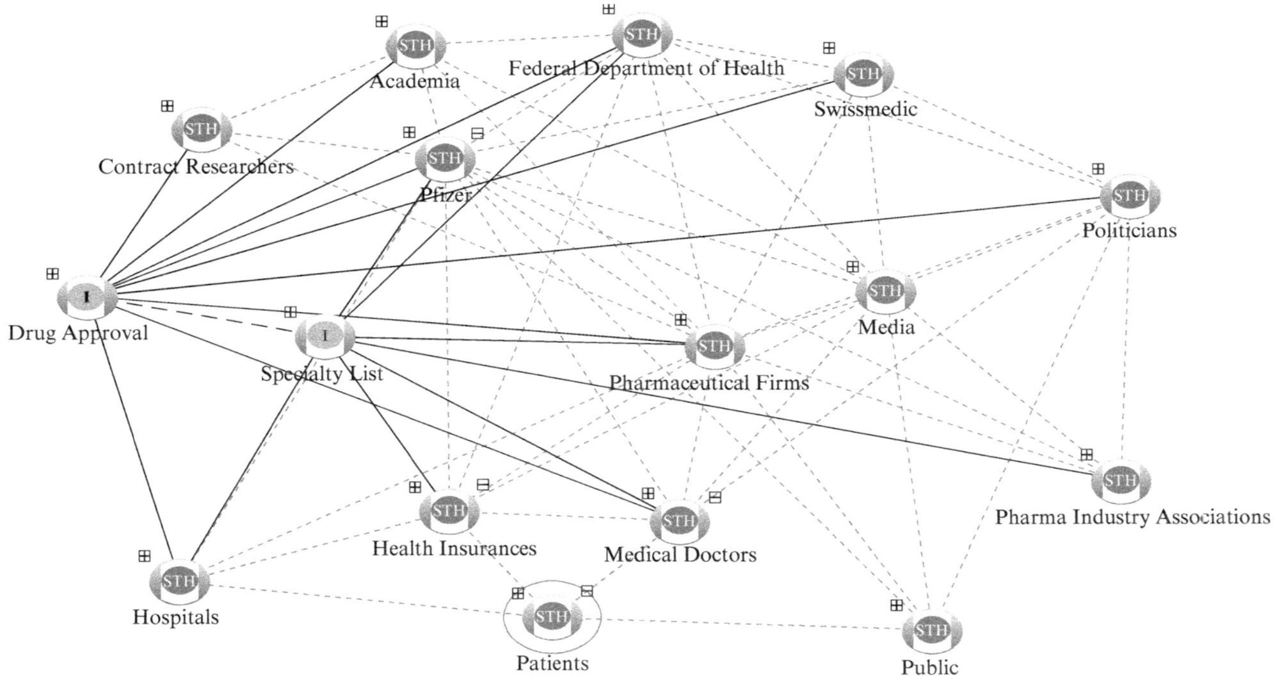

Figure 9.3 *Sachs, 2011*

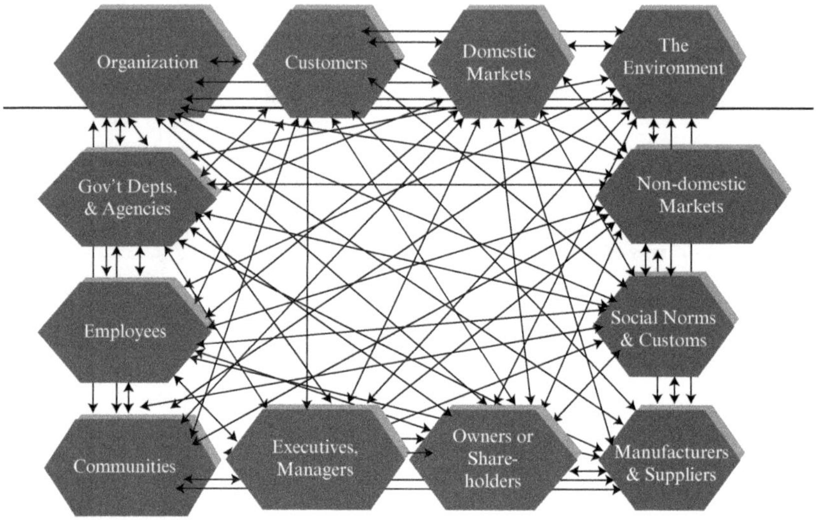

Figure 9.4 Complex systems networks

reflects that embeddedness and complexity while nevertheless allowing for adaptability and change.

Some time ago Ronald Heifetz (1998) introduced the idea of leadership as "adaptive work." Heifetz takes a normative view of leadership. He rejects the generic "values-free" definition and argues that leadership is a normative values-driven term that implies that the person we designate as "leader" is identified by a set of values that he or she has or will operationalize. Moreover, according to Heifetz's notion of leadership, leaders are not merely people who are visionaries or who try to convince others to accept her vision and values. Rather, leaders are those who "mobilize people to face problems, and . . . [to] make progress on these problems" (1998, p. 23). Twenty-first century leaders, then, are embedded in organizations and/or communities. It is the situation and its problems that enable such leaders to become active, working within this context, adjusting their vision to the particulars of the situation and the expectations of members of the community or organization in which they act. There are, then, reciprocal influences between the vision of the leader and members of her community or organization. Adaptive work "consists of the learning required to address conflicts in the values people hold, or to diminish the gap between the values people stand for and the reality they face" (Heifetz, 1998, p. 22). Leadership "means engaging people to make progress on the adaptive problems they face" (Heifetz, 1998, p. 187). As Heifetz acknowledges, much of this kind of leadership entails "Educative Strategy." The leader learns what issues and values are at stake, where there are conflicts and other difficulties, and then strategizes (adapts) her program to fit these elements, often without formal authority (Heifetzm, 1998, p. 187). This is a form of what I call embedded leadership or what others have termed "leading from the middle" (e.g., Isabella, 2010; Weick, 1996) because to achieve such goals entails being engaged with the nitty-gritty of one's situation, its values and conflicts and the networks of communities and systems in which the situation or organization is embedded. Heifetz does not mean to imply that this form of leadership is always successful. It is not. But he argues that in a complex global set of economies it is the only viable leadership style that will be successful in the long term.

I would argue that Heifetz's definition of leadership as adaptive work implies that leaders are embedded in their communities or organizations. I call this "embedded leadership." I propose that the graphic of Figure 9.4 best depicts the complex adaptive systems in which global relationships and thus leadership take place. An embedded idea of leadership is most appropriate in this era of globalization; it is also appropriate for a Figure 9.4 description of companies as embedded in sets of global political economies, and for political economies themselves. This mindset, the mindset of CASS, challenges us to think of leadership differently and it challenges any hierarchical model of leadership. More importantly, it takes business firms and even particular political economies such as the United States out of the center of things, even in today's climate of political chaos. The chaos itself illustrates how even bad leadership is no longer (if it ever was) hierarchical, because in executing a hierarchical (even dictatorial) model the designated leader runs into complex issues (e.g., trade, immigration) that cannot be predicted, much less handled (either fairly or unfairly) with this hierarchy. There are always new events and complexities in every context that are both unpredictable and messy and have to be taken into account, one by one.

In this model, "leadership is an *emergent* phenomenon within complex systems . . . involving dynamic of interaction [in an organization]" (Hazy et al., 2007, p. 2, emphasis in the original) rather than a leader-follower model. This explains how leadership can be "from the middle" of an organization and entails collaborative interrelationships between so-called designated or appointed leaders and their constituents (see Isabella, 2010). Leaders are embedded within complex systems in which they cannot avoid interacting. In a complex global world of interconnected systems, a so-called hierarchical leader is constantly challenged by events she did not predict and from other points of view she did not imagine. For example, in the United States, judges' challenges to Trumpian thinking on immigration; his now-dismissed attorney general's refusal to fire the chief investigator on Russian interventions; the governor of California's refusal to weaken environmental restrictions; German objections to Angela Merkel's immigration policy were all unpredicted and unwanted by these leaders. And the mass immigration we are witnessing from Africa, Syria and elsewhere is an unpredicted global systemic issue, not merely a "problem" for Europe.

As Collier and Estaban (2000) and Kelly and Allison (1999) argue, in a systemic complex dynamic world, leaders emerge and disappear, depending on the context. This might or might not be a result of collective thinking in various organizations, or this leadership phenomenon might simply arise from a propitious context. Hitler's rise to power in the 1930s leadership vacuum is an example of that. Still, the idea of embedded leadership does not eliminate designated-by-election leaders such as Merkel and Trump, nor appointed leaders, such as CEOs. Rather, it is to argue that these people, despite their election or appointment as "chiefs," are embedded in a global complex set of systems and networks, some of which are unpredictable (because of human actions). So embedded leadership is inescapable and descriptive of leadership relationships in the globalized world of today. This concept of embedded leadership is also normative in intent. In order to be a 21st-century successful global leader, I propose, emerging, appointed or elected leaders must acknowledge and deal directly with this complexity and unpredictability. But to do that adaptive work requires adapting the mindset of systems thinking and engage with others in embedded leadership.

9.6 IS THIS A FEMINIST MODEL OF LEADERSHIP?

Some time ago several of us argued that this model best exemplifies feminist styles of leadership. In two studies – the first on some American women leaders (Werhane et al., 2007) and a second on non-North American women leaders (Wentzel Wolfe and Werhane, 2017; Werhane et al., 2007) – we have discovered some common characteristics that fit well with the idea of embedded leadership. We studied women from diverse cultures and backgrounds including women from India, Japan, Jordan, the United Kingdom as well as the United States. We found that across these diverse sets of women are shared some leadership characteristics. Most seem to eschew hierarchies – abhorring being The Bosses of their organization, although most were, in fact, in charge of business or non-profit enterprises. They each found that to be effective they had to be self-assured of their knowledge base and their vision. At the same time, they had to be collaborative, to encourage innovation and dissent, to see themselves as part of a team transforming an organization rather than being in charge. All thought of themselves as interactive leaders engaged in empowering others. None was afraid of being superseded, and indeed, many encouraged new leadership in their organizations.

As a result, some of us argued that this notion of systems thinking and embedded leadership personified women in executive positions (e.g., Borgerson, 2007; Painter-Morland, 2011; Painter-Morland and Werhane, 2011; Wentzel Wolfe and Werhane, 2017; Werhane, 2007; Werhane et al., 2007). However, thinking again about these studies and our conclusion, these conclusions were probably exaggerations. We find many male global business leaders who exhibit many of these same characteristics we attributed to women leaders, and I would suggest that it is the global context in which organizations operate, not necessarily gender, that accounts for this kind of leadership thinking.[1] But that, too, is a tentative conclusion that needs to be supported with more data on leadership styles.

9.7 COMPLEXITY THEORY, EMBEDDED LEADERSHIP AND MATRIX MANAGEMENT

The foregoing analysis of systems thinking, CASS and embedded leadership may seem to be looking at leadership from 40,000 feet. However, in the management literature there is some relatively new thinking in two areas that links complexity theory and systems thinking to management practice: what Kelly and Allison call "The Complexity Advantage" (1999) and new work on matrix management (Global Integration, 2018), both of which are at least implicitly based on complexity theory and systems thinking.

Tracing the practical roots of their idea to projects at Citicorp, Susanne Kelly and Mary Ann Allison have used complexity theory to argue how self-organizing systems, an idea borrowed from complexity theory, can create a work environment in which "efficiency and creativity . . . emerge naturally within organizations much like nature creates order from chaos" (*The Complexity Advantage*, 1999, inside left flap of book cover). A self-organizing system is an open system that arises from the complex interrelationships in which individuals and organizations exist where there is openness and even a bit of instability (what they call "bounded instability") that forces emerging processes that adapt or react to the complex set of environments in which the organization (or individual) interacts (Kelly and Allison, 1999, pp. 1–20). Their argument is that this idea, adapted from complexity theory, is an invaluable practical guide to organizational thinking with the aim to create improved efficiencies and performance.

Moreover, leaders who recognize the artificiality of power hierarchies and allow and encourage employees and managers to self-organize (and in my terms, "emerge" within an organization) will be more successful in both the short term and longer term than those operating in a hierarchical management structure. Thus, the idea of embedded leadership where leadership emerges from a self-organizing open organization such as a corporation or small business will be best able to deal with the challenges of a 21st-century global and somewhat chaotic set of political economies.

Matrix management describes "horizontal working – structures and teams that cut across the traditional vertical silos of function, geography and business units" (Global Integration, 2018) in organizations. According to this source, 90 percent of all FTSE top 50 global companies operate with matrix management. One of the advantages of matrix management, despite its lack of clarity as to who is in charge, is that it is a more efficient way to accomplish organizational goals in complex global settings. It is useful in managing change and ambiguity, ever present in global markets. Because one works more horizontally rather than vertically across and outside the organization, managers find themselves in a complex but interconnected set of relationships. Such a format encourages flexibility and develops broadly based management skills in order to adjust to constantly evolving global commerce. Building on the literature on "leading from the middle" (see Isabella, 2010; Weick, 1996), such a format also allows for leaders to emerge from any part of an organization, Obviously, more work needs to be done on matrix management and its long-term effectiveness in a variety of organizations. I would tentatively conclude that it is an in-practice form of embedded leadership.

9.8 CONCLUSION

> We're in a knowledge economy, but our managerial models and governance systems [including leadership models] are stuck in the Industrial Era. It's time for a whole new model. (Uhl-Bien et al., 2007, p. 298)

If the globalization of political economies has created complex, interdependent networked systems, leaders are necessarily embedded within such systems. Hierarchical models defined by the leadership scholar Gardner as "individuals who significantly influence the thoughts, behaviors, and/or feelings of others . . ." (Gardner, 1995, p. 6) are not viable. Even if someone usurps a leader and becomes a dictator, or is appointed or elected as president, CEO, prime minister or principal, and tries to be a hierarchical chief with followers, such a focus obfuscates their effectiveness as leaders. The interconnected networks in which so-called leaders, alleged followers and organizations must operate, even to survive, is a reality. To become mindful of that and recognize how any leader is embedded in a set of complex systems is essential (if not sufficient) for leadership. This may or may not be a feminist model, but it is surely a 21st-century model. Successful institutions that are organized around a model of matrix management attest to that.

One critique, CASS, systems relationships, and a resulting embedded leadership is a mindset or a clustered set of mindsets – a way of looking at the world, particularly the globalized world in which we inhabit today. But it is only a mindset – one way of thinking about globalization and leadership. In defense of that idea, however, other forms of leadership have not been successful, at least in this century, in addressing "troubling times." But if one defines globalization as "a process by which [diverse groups of] people are empowered to work together synergistically toward a common vision and common goals" (Astin and Leland, 1991, p. 8), then that working together in such global contexts must entail people and groups of people who, within organizations and nation states, lead those organizations and systems from *within*. As embedded leaders, to be successful they must create trust across various populations and project a vision and sets of organizational goals that are adaptable and compelling across cultures and communities (see Adler, 1997). Embedded leaders, that is, successful embedded leaders, must be flexible, inclusive, non-authoritarian, open-minded and not afraid of new ideas or of other potential leaders.

The ubiquitous nature of mindsets is commonly acknowledged. But the idea that leadership is embedded in sets of complex adaptive social systems is not always acknowledged in the management literature nor in political writings, despite the thinkers I have cited in this chapter to the contrary. But the weakness of that acknowledgement has led to hierarchical, almost dictatorial leadership in the United States and in other so-called democratic regimes that blocks progress in international trade, the continuing mistreatment of immigrants and low-wage employees, weak development of ecosystem protections and the paucity of development investments in emerging economies. The lack of systems thinking and the resulting scarcity of strong embedded leaders has caused many of today's crises and little in the way of progress in ameliorating many global issues, many of which could have been avoided or sidetracked. If we can change our mindsets regarding leadership, abandon the hierarchical "boss" or authority-dependence thinking, and recognize the value of adaptive work and embedded leadership, we could all be participants in global progress. Redefining leadership is the first step.

NOTES

* Some of the thinking on complex systems derives from an unpublished paper I presented in 2017 in Wittenberg, Germany. Much of the ideas are not mine, but are derived from work by Collier and Estaban (2000), Miller and Page (2007), Uhl-Bien and her colleagues (e.g., 2007) and from a terrific collection, *Complex Systems and Leadership Theory* (Hazy et al., 2007). I am also indebted to Ronald Heifetz's book, *Leadership Without Easy Answers* (1998) and to Joanne Ciulla for bringing that book to my attention.

1. Or, alternately, perhaps the alleged feminist mindsets about leadership have penetrated all of leadership scholarship.

REFERENCES

Adler, Nancy. 1997. "Global Leadership: Women Leaders." *Management International Review*, **37**, 171–96.

Astin, H. and Leland, C. 1991. *Women of Influence, Women of Vision: A Cross-Generational Study of Leaders and Social Change.* San Francisco, CA: Jossey-Bass.

Bazerman, M. and Tenbrunsel, A. 2011. *Blind Spots.* Princeton, NJ: Princeton University Press.

Berger, P. and Luckmann, T. 1967. *The Social Construction of Reality.* New York: Doubleday.

Bevan, David and Werhane, Patricia. 2015. "The Inexorable Sociality of Commerce: The Individual and Others in Adam Smith." *Journal of Business Ethic*, **127**, 327–35.

Borgerson, Janet. 2007. "On the Harmony of Feminist Ethics and Business Ethics." *Business and Society Review*, **112**, 477–504.

Collier, Jane and Estaban, Rafael. 2000. "Systemic Leadership: Ethical and Effective." *Leadership & Organization Development Journal*, **21**(4), 207–15.

Freeman, R.E. 1984. *Strategic Management.* Reprinted in 2010. Cambridge: Cambridge University Press.

Gardner, H. 1995. *Leading Minds.* New York: Basic Books.

Global Integration. 2018. http://www.global-integration.com/matrix-management/?gclid=Cj0KCQjwre_XBRDVARIsAPf7zZgr27zEWTp_T1eicgCvqfItRZ9zQtnfuFk9tTbbttDDuzx2dgIxoyQaAt3gEALw_wcB (accessed 15 September 2018).

Hacking, Ian. 1999. *The Social Construction of What?* Cambridge, MA: Harvard University Press.

Hazy, J.K., Goldstein, J.A., and Lichtenstein, B.B. (eds). 2007. *Complex Systems Leadership Theory*. Mansfield, MA: ISCE Publishing.

Heifetz, Ronald. 1998. *Leadership Without Easy Answers.* Cambridge, MA: Harvard University Press.

Isabella, L.A. 2010. "Leading Change from the Middle." In Eades, K.M., Laseter, T.M., Skurnik, I., Rodriguez, P.L., Isabella, L.A., and Simko, P.J., *The Portable MBA*, 5th edn. New York: Wiley, pp. 301–13.

Kelly, S. and Allison, M.A. 1999. *The Complexity Advantage.* New York: McGraw-Hill.

Laszlo, A. and Krippner, S. 1998. "Systems Theories: Their Origins, Foundations and Development." In J. Scott (ed.), *Systems Theories and a Priori Aspects of Perception.* Amsterdam: Elsevier, pp. 47–74.

Miller, J.H. and Page, Scott E. 2007. *Complex Adaptive Systems*. Princeton, NJ: Princeton University Press.
Mitroff, H. and Linstone, H. 1991. *The Unbounded Mind*. New York: Oxford University Press.
Painter-Morland, Mollie. 2011. "Systemic Leadership, Gender, Organization." In Patricia Werhane and Mollie Painter-Morland (eds), *Leadership, Gender and Organization*. Dordrecht: Springer Nature, pp. 139–67.
Painter-Morland, Mollie and Werhane, Patricia. 2011. "Leadership, Gender and Organizations: Chapter One," in Patricia Werhane and Mollie Painter-Morland (eds), *Leadership, Gender and Organization*. Dordrecht: Springer Nature, pp. 1–10.
Plesk, P. 2001. "Redesigning Health Care with Insights from the Science of Complex Adaptive Systems." In *Crossing the Quality Chasm*, Washington, DC: National Academy Press, pp. 309–17.
Sachs, Sybille. 2011. *Stakeholders Matter*. Cambridge: Cambridge University Press.
Schreck, Philipp. 2016. "Experimental Economics and Normative Business Ethics." *University of St. Thomas Law Journal*, **12**, 360–80.
Simon, Herbert. 1982. *Models of Bounded Rationality. Volume 1: Economic Analysis and Public Policy*. Cambridge, MA: MIT Press. Requoted in 2018 in *Business Dictionary*. http://www.businessdictionary.com/definition/bounded-rationality.html (accessed 8 December 2018).
Smith, Adam. 1759. *The Theory of Moral Sentiments*. Reprinted in 1976. Oxford: Oxford University Press.
Uhl-Bien, Mary and Arena, Michael. 2017. "Complexity Leadership: Enabling People and Organizations for Adaptability." *Organizational Dynamics*, **46**, 9–20.
Uhl-Bien, Mary and Ospina, Sonia. 2012. *Advancing Relationship Leadership Approaches*. New York: Information Age Publishing.
Uhl-Bien, Mary, Marion, Russ, and McKelvey, Bill. 2007. "Complexity Leadership Theory: Shifting Leadership from the Industrial Age to the Knowledge Era." *The Leadership Quarterly*, **18**, 298–318.
Weick, Karl. 1996. "Drop Your Tools: An Allegory for Organizational Studies." *Administrative Science Quarterly*, **41**(2), 301–13.
Wentzel Wolfe, Regina and Werhane, Patricia. 2017. *Global Women Leaders*. Cheltenham, UK and Northampton, MA, USA: Edward Elgar.
Werhane, Patricia H. 1999. *Moral Imagination and Management Decision-Making*. New York: Oxford University Press.
Werhane, Patricia H. 2000. "Sustaining Alliances for Integrity." *Journal of the American College of Dentists*, **67**, 9–16.
Werhane, Patricia H. 2002. "Moral Imagination and Systems Thinking." *Journal of Business Ethics*, **38**, 33–42.
Werhane, Patricia H. 2007. "Women Leaders in a Globalized World." *Journal of Business Ethics*, **74**, 425–35.
Werhane, Patricia H. 2008. "Mental Models, Moral Imagination and Systems Thinking in the Age of Globalization." *Journal of Business Ethics*, **78**, 463–74.
Werhane, Patricia. 2011. "Globalization, Mental Models and Decentering Stakeholder Models." In Robert Phillips (ed.), *Stakeholder Theory: Its Impact and Prospects*. Cheltenham, UK and Northampton, MA, USA: Edward Elgar, pp. 111–29.
Werhane, Patricia H. 2012. "Globalization, and Its Challenges for Business and Business Ethics in the 21st Century." *Business and Society Review*, **117**, 383–405.

Werhane, Patricia H. and Painter-Morland, Mollie (eds). 2011. *Leadership, Gender and Organization.* Dordrecht: Springer Nature.

Werhane, Patricia, Gundry, Lisa, Posig, Margaret, Ofstein, Laurel, and Powell, Elizabeth. 2007. *Women in Business: The Changing Face of Leadership.* Westport, CT: Praeger Press.

Werhane, Patricia, Posig, Margaret, Gundry, Lisa, Powell, Elizabeth, Carlson, Jane, and Ofstein, Laurel. 2006. "Women Leaders in Corporate America." In Margaret F. Karsten (ed.), *Gender, Race, and Ethnicity in the Workplace*, 3 vols. New York: Greenwood-Praeger, Vol. 1, pp. 1–30.

Wolf, Susan. 1999. "Toward a Systemic Theory of Informed Consent in Managed Care." *Houston Law Review*, **35**, 1631–81.

10. Leadership ethics for a troubled world: responsibility for the whole

Sandra Waddock

Corporate (social) responsibility and business ethics are pretty much always in the news – not necessarily for positive reasons. Massive frauds like Wells Fargo's creation of millions of fake accounts, Volkswagen's intentional use of a 'defeat device' that deliberately improved diesel emission test results and United Airlines' mistreatment and severe injuring of a passenger only scratch the surface of palpable lapses of ethics – and of leadership. The biggest ethical issues facing the world today, however, are not necessarily the ones we typically think of. Ethics might be associated with business value chains (Schrempf-Stirling et al., 2016), supply chain abuses and worker mistreatment, environmental abuses or fraudulent selling practices, for example. All of these are important ethical issues, as are the challenges of ensuring individual ethical practices and responsibility, adherence to codes of conduct or even avoiding breaking the law (e.g., the Volkswagen and Wells Fargo scandals). Although all of these aspects of ethical conduct remain vitally important, I want to argue there are much bigger issues that need ethical consideration.

There is a simple reason for this claim (which does not make dealing with it simple). There are much bigger, more systemic issues that all leaders – whether in business, government, civil society, educational institutions, non-governmental organizations (NGOs) or within the family – need to become aware of and do their part to resolve. They need to do so individually as well as through the strategies and practices, that is, the business models, of their various enterprises and by participating in broader transformation initiatives that work at the policy, industry and societal levels. Business as usual in this context will no longer suffice (e.g., Gilding, 2011; Jackson, 2011; Klein, 2014; McKibben, 2011; Schor, 2010).

10.1 A RATIONALE FOR RESPONSIBILITY FOR THE WHOLE

We live in a world where humanity is facing existential threats from climate change and exploitation and overuse of ecological resources (Brown and Caldeira, 2017; Ehrenfeld and Hoffman, 2013; IPCC, 2014; Jackson, 2011; Wallace-Wells, 2017). Climate change threatens the future of humanity (IPCC, 2014) and lack of ecological sustainability is a major cause of civilizational collapse (Diamond, 2005). Further, social stability is threatened by political and social divisiveness resulting at least in part from growing inequality (Collins and Ehrenreich, 2012; Moellendorf, 2009), which is a second cause of civilizational collapse (Diamond, 2005). Along with these risk factors, humanity faces multiple other huge problems, as articulated in the United Nations's (UN) 17 Sustainable Development Goals (SDGs, 2018) that need addressing if greater equity, along with dignity and wellbeing for all are to be achieved long term.

Often called grand challenges, among the major issues noted in the 17 SDGs are providing safe drinking water, healthful agricultural practices and eliminating hunger and extreme poverty. Such issues affect how humans live on the planet, as well as how they relate to each other and to other living beings in nature. Perhaps the biggest issue facing humanity is climate change, which numerous reports and studies suggest could be an existential threat if significant steps are not taken in the near term to mitigate the impact of greenhouse gases (e.g., Ehrenfeld and Hoffman, 2013; IPCC, 2014; Jackson, 2011; Wallace-Wells, 2017).

The systemic problems facing the world, for instance, climate change, sustainability crises, growing inequality, political divisiveness, and the impacts of today's hypercompetitive yet often oligopolistic business models mean that leaders now need to learn how to think and act in the best interests of the whole system, not just for their own enterprises. They need to turn their enterprises towards what Donaldson and Walsh (2017) call collective value, not just maximizing results for shareholders (see below for more discussion of this point). Somehow, the 'me first' attitude engendered by the growth-at-all-costs, cutthroat competitive environment fostered by neoliberal economics (Monbiot, 2016a) needs to shift as leaders begin to accept the reality that as human beings operating within human enterprises, we are intimately and integrally connected to and part of nature and with each other. As quantum physics now tells us, we are truly one planet in which all is connected in a vast web of life (Capra, 1995; Capra and Luisi, 2014).

The grand challenges posed by the SDGs and climate change are daunting enough when considered as political, organizational and management challenges. They are also enormous ethical challenges because the fate and wellbeing of humanity, not to mention other living beings and Earth's ecosystems, rest on their resolution (or not). Such issues, however, are not the typical ones to which most ethical analyses pay attention, yet they are so fundamental to the long-term survival – never mind thriving – of human beings and nature's creatures and ecosystems – that it is difficult to conceive of a greater or more important set of ethical challenges. That said, it is probably true that many leaders (and human beings in many other types of positions as well) will resist the implicit call to action – systemically transformative actions – that is inherent in this recognition.

Given these challenges, the task of leading large and powerful enterprises of all sorts grows even more complicated than it has always been. For example, add to climate change problems with various ecosystems, such as overuse of fisheries, harmful industrial farming and agricultural practices. Topsoil erosion, soil depletion and increasing desertification reducing arable land, poor nutritional value in food production, technological waste, deforestation and burning of rainforests, among many other business (and sometimes governmental) practices, have created increased risks of fires, droughts, extreme rain, intensive hurricanes and cyclones. Facing such consequences of human (particularly business) activities, tomorrow's leaders need to be able to think systemically about how their decisions today impact the whole system both today and tomorrow. They need to make the link between the actions of their enterprises and the wellbeing of the system as a whole with all of its stakeholders, including non-human ones, even though doing so is difficult in the prisoner's dilemma[1] context many leaders face.

Many of the challenges facing humanity are articulated in the Sustainable Development Goals (SDGs, 2018). Two issues in particular are associated with civilizational collapse: pushing ecological resources beyond their limits and growing inequality (Diamond, 2005). Both characterize much of the current situation. Further, today's political divisiveness calls for all leaders to stand up *for* responsible and ethical practices and *for* ethical operations of their companies even when they might be able to 'get away with' acting otherwise. The foundation of ethical practice means that standards, norms, connections and consequences exist even when no one is looking. That foundational perspective applies especially to leaders whose enterprises make significant social or ecological impacts, not through their corporate social responsibility activities, but as a consequence of their business models, strategies and operating practices (Waddock and Rasche, 2012).

In the context of growing awareness about the realities of the connectedness of today's threats to human actions, no longer can the ethics and responsibilities of leaders focus solely on individual or even organizational behaviors and responsibilities. As recognition grows of how interconnected human and natural systems are, leaders now need to take into consideration the impacts of their decisions and actions on the whole, where the whole includes the industry, stakeholders and, indeed, the Earth itself (e.g., Costanza et al., 2016; Liu et al., 2015; Rockström, 2015).

Why a whole system approach? Consider the huge fires in 2017 in California, caused by years of drought conditions, which were followed in early 2018 by intensive rains that created destructive mudslides, as just one example. What kind of management – and ethical – practices are needed to cope with such exigencies when they happen – or indeed enable decision makers to think systemically in advance to prevent such human-caused disasters? Understanding the systemic implications of decisions, for example, in this case, the fragility of the land, its vulnerability to fires and risks posed by building in drought-prone areas that then become vulnerable to fires and ultimately mudslides, seems to be a foundational 'ask' of today's leaders.

Leaders need to understand, for example, how forest management practices, overbuilding in drought-prone areas on hills that are prone to mudslides during periodic (and increasingly intense because of climate change) rainstorms and other human systems interact. They need to take into consideration the risks posed by overuse of natural resources, such as overfishing or agricultural practices that erode topsoil or use chemical fertilizers and pest controls that poison rivers, streams and lakes. Although such risks do not necessarily fall within the realm of traditional managerial ethics and responsibilities, the fragile state of the Earth's ability to support much more human 'development' suggests increased need to pay attention to these systemic issues.

Further, tomorrow's leaders need to be able to consider how enterprises working in and with these systems develop their business models in ways that forestall such disastrous consequences. Are not such considerations core ethical problems that leaders, facing the big picture of increased recognition of the systemic impacts of decisions of all sorts, need to take into account? Perhaps more important, what kinds of ethical and systemic understandings of the impacts of human systems on the natural environment – and communities and whole societies – are needed for leaders to be able to make decisions that prevent – or at least reduce – these types of risks?

Many such considerations are long term in nature and most are based on an understanding of the broader systemic consequences of individual (company) actions. How do we move from today's individualistic ethic, with personal (or company) responsibility for immediate impacts, towards an ethic in which the good of the whole, for all stakeholders and Earth itself, is a priority of equal weight to the ethic of maximization of wealth/profits for shareholders?

10.2 RETHINKING ECONOMIES AS EMBEDDED SYSTEMS

The ethical crises facing humanity and its systems mean that business as usual no longer suffices. Increasingly, leaders in enterprises of all sorts are being called upon to do their part to bring about needed large systems change (Waddell et al., 2014), Earth stewardship (Chapin et al., 2011) or the 'necessary transition' towards sustainable enterprise (McIntosh, 2013). All of these ideas are compatible with the notion of ethical responsibility for the whole. The idea of continuing business as usual in a system that risks collapse for ecological, social and perhaps political reasons (Ehrenfeld and Hoffman, 2013) seems unwise at best and unethical on its face.

The Humanistic Management Network,[2] among others, has articulated a wellbeing and dignity for all approach to economics that shifts assumptions away from neoliberalism's assumptions of self-interest, 'free' trade and markets, individual responsibility, strong defense and limited government towards radically different assumptions (Pirson, 2017; Pirson and Lawrence, 2010; Waddock, 2016). New assumptions about human beings, more biologically based than traditional economic assumptions (e.g., Brosnan and de Waal, 2012; de Waal, 1996), suggest that humans are social creatures, oriented to competition, yet also and perhaps more importantly oriented towards caring and connection (e.g., Eisler, 2008), fairness and even altruism (de Waal, 1996, 2008). Humans, while they can certainly exhibit traits associated with selfishness and self-interest as neoclassical economics suggests, *also* exhibit caring, altruism, a sense of fairness and a desire to do good in the world.

Further, far from being 'free,' as neoliberalism would have it, today's markets are composed of many oligopolies (and even some monopolistic enterprises) that so dominate their industries that they hardly compete in a market free-for-all with many sellers and buyers as neoclassical economic theory posits. Also, markets do not arise magically from nature and exist without human intervention. Instead, they are constructed from human policies and practices that attempt to ensure not just their 'freedom,' but also their fairness and trustworthiness (Monbiot, 2016a; Waddock, 2016; Waddock and Rasche, 2012). That means that governments need to bear some responsibility for the construction of markets that are fair, have integrity and build trust among relevant stakeholders. Despite neoliberal rhetoric, government is not irrelevant, always incompetent or always needing to be as small as possible (Monbiot, 2016a). Some form of local/national/regional government (Albareda and Waddock, 2018) is needed to ensure that relevant policies protect citizens. Increasingly, it is clear that some form of global governance (not necessarily government), for example, Earth System Governance (Biermann et al., 2010; Biermann et al., 2012) or different ways of accomplishing stewardship of planetary resources, may well be needed to ensure global sustainability for human beings long term. That is, leaders of all stripes need to ensure the long-run ability of the 'whole' to support the human project – as well as other living beings in nature that themselves support human existence and are valuable in and of themselves.

Importantly, from the perspective responsibility for the whole, responsibilities for leaders in business are not monolithic and directed only at shareholders. As the long-standing argument for stakeholder theory suggests, leaders have responsibilities to be fair to and take into consideration the interests of all important primary stakeholders and some secondary ones as well (Freeman, 1984; Freeman et al., 2007; Parmar et al., 2010). New assumptions, or a new narrative around what economics is and what it is for, one that frames assumptions about the good of the whole is increasingly important and much needed in these tenuous times (Pirson, 2017; Waddock, 2016).

A new economics argues for a reformulation of economics better suited for the 21st century and major transformations of how businesses and other enterprises operate. It needs to incorporate an associated new sense of ethical responsibility for the whole in accord with that thinking. Towards that end, consider the Stockholm Resilience Center's work on (physical) planetary boundaries[3] that cannot be breached (and some of which have already been breached) without significant harm to humans and other living beings (Rockström et al., 2009; Steffen et al., 2015). These scientists have determined that there are nine crucial 'planetary boundaries,' physical boundaries that need to be respected, for example, by businesses, governments and other human institutions. Otherwise, they posit, irreversible ecological changes will impair the ability of humans to thrive or possibly even survive in the future. Importantly, the Stockholm Resilience Center's 2015 study (Steffen et al., 2015) demonstrates that four of the nine boundaries (climate change, loss of biosphere integrity, land-system change and altered biogeochemical cycles of phosphorus and nitrogen) have already been transgressed.

The fear, as the Stockholm Resilience Center states, is that the Earth will be driven to a 'new state.' Indeed, that 'new state,' may already be here. The Anthropocene, which is what today's geological era is being called, is a geologic age in which human activities are considered to be a dominant influence on climate and environment (think population growth, agricultural practices, production and resource consumption) (Crutzen, 2006). Leaders, whether in business, government or other types of institutions, can choose, of course, to turn a blind eye to these physical realities. They do so, in my view, at the risk of massive ethical irresponsibility.

True, motivated blindness, bounded awareness and ethical breakdowns (Bazerman and Sezer, 2016; Bazerman and Tenbrunsel, 2011; Gino et al., 2008) make it difficult for leaders to *want* to see the longer-term implications of some of their businesses/institution's practices. The existence of motivated blindness, however, does not mean that leaders' ethical responsibilities for the impacts of their enterprise's practices on people, social systems, nature and the ultimate fate of humanity go away, especially when the fate of the human enterprise as a whole is at stake (Rockström, 2015). True also that the realities of competition create a sort of prisoner's dilemma or commons problem (Hardin, 1968) that increases difficulties. The core issue is that if leaders of today's major institutions – and businesses are certainly among those institutions – do not collectively and independently take action, the risks to humanity (and other creatures) are overwhelming – and negative.

Things get even more complicated. The Stockholm Resilience Center's work only considers the physical planetary boundaries. Kate Raworth (2017) with her 'doughnut economics' and the nations of the world in the development of the SDGs have essentially articulated a set of human system boundaries that also *should not* be breached, drawing a clear ethical line for leaders and policy makers. In line with rethinking economics, Raworth focuses on the true big – planetary – picture.

Raworth has created a conceptual economic framework that integrates the planetary boundaries' physical limits on the outside of a torus shape that she labels her 'doughnut.' On the inside boundary of the 'doughnut' are 12 foundational social dimensions (which are aligned with the SDGs in her recent thinking) as an 'inside' boundary below which human suffering increases. The resulting framework, the 'doughnut' itself, creates what Raworth calls a 'safe and just operating space' for humanity (Raworth, 2012, 2017; see also Dearing et al., 2014). So in addition to physical limitations, Raworth (2017) adds the much more obvious ethically oriented dimension of social justice to thinking about appropriate boundaries and limits for human behaviors and practices, including the reframing of economics to meet the 21st century's exigencies.

In 'doughnut economics,' economists and leaders of all sorts need to pay attention to the impacts that their enterprises have on ensuring that people – everywhere and of all statuses – have sufficient access to and supply of 12 important resources. These resources include food, water, energy, health, education, income and work, peace and justice, political voice, social equity, gender equality, housing and networks (Raworth, 2017). Of course, not all leaders have the capacity to pay attention to all of these. Indeed, probably no one does. But awareness of the bigger picture can make decisions about where to make investments, what business model to engage and where emphasis might be placed in innovation more focused on each actor (company and leaders) doing its part for the good of the whole. Donaldson and Walsh (2015) in developing a theory of business have called this emphasis on wellbeing and dignity of all 'collective value.'

Taken together, thinking about planetary boundaries and a safe operating space for humanity joins a plethora of emerging initiatives aimed at rethinking economics (e.g., New Economics Foundation, WE-All (Wellbeing Economics Alliance), the Next System Project, New Economy Coalition, among numerous others). Collectively, such initiatives argue for a massive reboot of economic theory to bring it more into alignment with the situation that humanity is facing today. Of course, the forces of neoliberalism and its dominant economic narrative make this shift difficult at best. However, not to engage with this 'necessary transition' (McIntosh, 2013) is to risk the future of humanity in the views of many ecologists and climate scientists.

10.3 TAKING THE SYSTEM INTO ACCOUNT

System transformation means that the system itself needs to shift. There is a core problem here, which is both practical and ethical. Individual companies and their leaders, try as they might to become sustainable, face a systems level challenge not entirely of their making. It is a problem of the commons (Hardin, 1968), viewing the world as the relevant commons. In trying to make change, individual efforts that are costly in the short term have the very real potential to put individual companies at a competitive disadvantage in the context of the current system, thereby putting their leaders at risk. What that reality means is that real system change can only come about when the dynamics shift incentives and actual core values for all companies and other institutions to level the playing field for all players. Otherwise, leaders are placed into untenable ethical dilemmas, choosing all of humankind's best interests on the one side in the interests of the whole versus the interests of their shareholders – to whom most company leaders believe they owe fealty.

System transformation for both economies and for the enterprises in them requires a major mindset shift among leaders and probably many other people. Only then can a fair policy framework for all be developed so that business and other institutional purposes and other systemic changes that reframe institutions to be more in harmony with nature's constraints and possibilities can be made.

Einstein famously said that 'We cannot solve a problem from the same level of thinking that created it,' and that is the problem humanity is facing. A massive shift in understanding humans' place in the world, as well as how human enterprises of all sort operate is needed to bring these institutions into harmony with natural systems, resources and constraints, instead of pretending that we can exist without such considerations. This shift demands a major mindset change, which Meadows (1999) pointed out, along with the capability of transcending mindsets, is the most powerful lever for system change. Mindset shifts enable new narratives/stories to be developed and new supporting memes (e.g., values, norms, goals) to support that shift (Waddock, 2016). Shifting mindsets to recognize the need for such new purposes, reducing competitiveness in favor of sometimes collaborative enterprises that work towards ecological and societal resilience, diversity and otherwise encourage 'life' rather than simply what Frederick (1995) called economizing.

Economizing values include efficiency, growth and systemic integrity, that is, keeping the system whole (Frederick, 1995). These values are complemented by a set of political/business values around power aggrandizing that include hierarchical organizing and maintenance, managerial decision-making power and keeping the system stable or in some degree of equilibrium while continuing to enhance power (Frederick, 1995). Business values are supported by a set of technological values that include instrumental pragmatics, cooperative-coordinative relationships, technical expertise, public openness and public leveling (Frederick, 1995). These economizing, power aggrandizing and technological values are deeply embedded in managerial psyches (Frederick, 1995) and the economistic (Pirson, 2017) thinking that dominates today's economic narrative. These values have resulted in the growth-at-all-costs mentality and emphasis on profitability and shareholder wealth that characterize neoliberalism (Monbiot, 2016b; Waddock, 2016) and put the planet's ability to support life as we know it at risk. Indeed, Monbiot (2016c) has called neoliberalism a 'zombie doctrine' for its deadening impacts on people and planet (see also Quiggin, 2012).

Arguably, for leaders to be ethical in the future demands a significant mindset change away from today's over-emphasis on financial profits and growth that is putting planetary health at risk, which is in essence a death sentence for civilization as we know it. Building on a positive ethic, leaders could help shift company practices and policies, as well as public policy towards what gives flourishing, wellbeing and dignity to all (Pirson, 2017), that is, what gives life (Waddock and Kuenkel, 2019), if they assume that even a small part of their responsibility has to do with the good of the whole.

The idea of 'economizing' as put forward by Frederick (1995) is built entirely around gaining efficiencies to maximize (financial) wealth. It therefore fosters efficient use of resources and maintenance of the status quo arrangements that serve wealth and the wealthy well, as evidenced by the growing gaps between rich and poor globally and particularly in the US. But the business-as-usual model of economizing fails to take what economists call externalities into account. These externalities are things like the social costs of inequality (e.g., social unrest, people struggling to make ends meet on two and sometimes three part-time, minimum wage jobs and so on). They can be the ecological/sustainability costs of using non-renewable resources as if they were endless or taking renewable resources at so fast a rate that the Earth cannot replenish them before more are needed (e.g., overfishing, erosion of topsoil and so on). A radical transformation of the economy to create what ecologist L. Hunter Lovins calls an 'economy in service to life'[4] could dramatically shift the destructive dynamics the world is now facing and simultaneously clarify the ethical leader's tasks.

What gives life value are purposes that are generative (creative and forward looking), wholeness (not fragmentation), reasonable boundaries that provide identity yet allow for the release of toxins and new energetic inputs. Life also is characterized by adaptiveness or novelty, that is, the ability to change and evolve as needed. It is characterized by connectedness, that is, recognizing as quantum physics now does the unity of the world and how we are all connected to each other and other aspects of our world. It is further characterized by enough diversity to create resilience in the system so that it can face upheavals and still maintain health (for elaboration of these ideas, see Waddock and Kuenkel, 2019).

The key for ethical leaders is to recognize that employing business (and public) policies that foster life is what is needed to provide equity, dignified lives and wellbeing for all and not just for the already well-off in the world. Indeed, that orientation falls neatly into what I have elsewhere called shamanic leadership – leadership that recognizes that the health of the whole system is a fundamental imperative, leadership that sees the connections among all people and of all people with the rest of the natural world and that recognizes that the integrity of the whole is what matters long term. Although it seems difficult – almost impossible – in today's contentious political climate to believe that business and public policies can be developed, nationally and globally, that foster life rather than financial wealth creation, that goal is nonetheless what ethical leaders need to strive for now and, as population continues to grow, into the foreseeable future.

Such mindset shift is particularly relevant for leaders, who must be able to think sufficiently broadly about the system to actively bring about and support this transition – for the good of humanity as a whole and for other living beings in our world. It also presents a huge ethical challenge for leaders who have up to this point been largely able to view their responsibilities quite narrowly, as 'simply' managing their companies well with profitability and wealth enhancement aimed at shareholders.

10.4 ETHICAL LEADERS TODAY AND TOMORROW

To date, leaders – whether from business, government, civil society or indeed academia – seem to have been incapable of developing the vision necessary to deal adequately with these planetary issues or to take on needed responsibility for the whole. Corporate social responsibility (CSR), defined as the voluntary efforts of companies to help with societal problems (Matten and Moon, 2008), is simply insufficient as a vehicle for change, since it doesn't really deal with the business model, which is where most company impacts on societies and nature occur (Waddock, 2002; Waddock and Rasche, 2012). Many progressive and leading companies are trying mightily to become more sustainable – yet none of them actually are so today, because as Ehrenfeld and Hoffman (2013) note, becoming less unsustainable does not make an enterprise actually sustainable.

Still, many companies have joined initiatives like the World Business Council for Sustainable Development (WBCSD) to 'accelerate sustainable development,'[5] the UN Global Compact (UNGC) to 'align strategies and operations with universal principles,'[6] and the UN Principles for Responsible Investment (PRI) to develop an 'economically efficient, sustainable global financial system . . . for long-term value creation.'[7] Lucky executives attend the World Economic Forum (WEF),'[8] where they work with other high level executives to embrace the idea of working with the 'foremost political, business and other leaders' on 'improving the state of the world' and 'shap[ing] global, regional and industry agendas.'[9] Whatever CSR and even corporate responsibility efforts, which deal with the way the business model is enacted (Waddock, 2002; Waddock and Rasche, 2012), to the extent that they leave the system intact – and the tenets of neoliberalism in place – they will continue to be inadequate.

Other companies have engaged deeply with the corporate responsibility infrastructure that emerged during the late 1990s and early 2000s (Waddock, 2008). Such companies use monitoring and certification approaches to guide their internal management systems and decision making (e.g., ISO 9000, ISO 14000, in the future ISO 26000, SA 8000, AA 1000) and some report on their sustainability efforts using the Global Reporting Initiative (GRI). A (very) few (at this point) have moved towards Integrated Reporting (IR), in which they report on their ESG (ecological, social and governance) efforts integrated with their financial reports.

In contrast to simply joining initiatives, responsibility for the whole means deeply engaging with the system – and using systems thinking/understanding to make a good faith effort to understand how an organization's operations and activities affect the surrounding stakeholders, natural environment and system as a whole. Ethical and responsible leaders in the future need to deeply engage with the political realities – and advocate for incorporating societal and ecological issues and impacts explicitly into business policies, strategies and practices – across the board. Leadership in this context takes considerable courage, not to mention long-term vision that incorporates systemic realities. It means working with others in different types of institutions – political, governmental, civil society, NGOs – as the SDGs argue is needed for dealing with the global goals effectively.

It is not easy to undertake systemic approaches in today's hypercompetitive context. Yet responsibility for the whole means doing so in ways that result not in unintended harms, but in benefits for all. It means employing a kind of win/win strategy rather than the win/lose strategies so common today.

Systems thinking means acting with understanding of complexity, for organizations, societies and the natural environment are all complex adaptive systems. It means understanding processes of emergence and co-evolution, not individual or singular actions taken without regard for their unintended consequences. It means working with purpose, collaboratively with a range of diverse 'others,' whose actions cannot be controlled or 'managed' because they are coequal collaborators in the co-evolutionary processes of managing their own activities and enterprises. It means articulating purposes that are shared and agreeing to sets of values and principles that support life, wellbeing and dignity for all – and changing business models in all sorts of enterprises to meet those goals – not simply the much simpler but flawed goal of maximizing profitability or wealth for shareholders. It means doing so publicly, consistently and over long periods of time, so that the overall narrative – and its operationalizations – can shift towards dignity, wellbeing and flourishing for all of humanity and life's creations.

Thus, critical challenges are posed by the need to deal considerably more effectively with the sustainability crises, the need for true innovation – not just in products and services that foster more growth, which indeed is part of the problem. Changes are needed in the ways we relate to each other and in how we think about the role of the economy and businesses in society. Ideas about 'responsible leadership' take a similar stance, which ensures that leaders pay attention not just to companies or other institutions, but actually act holistically as 'citizens of the world' (Maak and Pless, 2009), in effect, responsible for the whole. The notion of responsible leadership (Maak and Pless, 2006, 2009; Pless and Maak, 2011) implies a broadened definition, which argues that responsible leadership involves building and maintaining a morally and ethically strong relationship with all relevant stakeholders. Here that definition also encompasses the natural environment and all of its creatures, acting 'as if' the Earth were a stakeholder (Starik, 1995) and recognizing that inherently all of us, in fact, are stakeholders to the living Earth known as Gaia (Waddock, 2011).

In short, future leaders will need *wisdom*, defined as the integration of moral imagination, systems understanding and aesthetic sensibility towards decisions and actions in the service of the common good (Waddock, 2010, 2014). This wisdom brings an ethical stance with it, because the goal becomes not individual or even company self-interest, but the good of the whole. It requires a collaborative orientation and a setting of new goals that engage wellbeing for all and what Donaldson and Walsh (2015) call collective value, not just shareholder value. 'Value' here incorporates *values* other than financial – wellbeing, dignity, flourishing for all of life's creatures would be my choices. In short, we need ethical leaders, responsible leaders, systems-thinking leaders to take responsibility for the good of the whole. In doing so, they can potentially find ways to bring other leaders along in that process so that whole economic, social and political systems shift in that direction. Such leaders would embrace the inherent diversity in systems, work towards systemic resilience, which requires diversity of all sorts, foregoes linear processes in favor of circularity and seeks strategies that benefit all, not just a lucky few.

NOTES

1. A prisoner's dilemma is a situation in which the good of the whole is often subverted because individual actors pursue their own self-interest rather than actions that would benefit the whole.
2. Humanistic Management Network, http://www.humanetwork.org/, accessed August 6, 2019.
3. Stockholm Resilience Center, https://www.stockholmresilience.org/research/planetary-boundaries/planetary-boundaries/about-the-research/the-nine-planetary-boundaries.html, accessed August 6, 2019.
4. Natural Capitalism Solutions, L. Hunter Lovins, An economy in service to life, https://natcapsolutions.org/an-economy-in-service-to-life/, accessed August 6, 2019.

5. World Business Council for Sustainable Development, About us, http://www.wbcsd.org/Overview/About-us, accessed August 6, 2019.
6. UN Global Compact, https://www.unglobalcompact.org/what-is-gc, accessed August 6, 2019.
7. UN Principles for Responsible Investment, https://www.unpri.org/about, accessed August 6, 2019.
8. World Economic Forum, Our mission, https://www.weforum.org/about/world-economic-forum, accessed August 6, 2019.
9. UN Global Compact, Who we are, https://www.unglobalcompact.org/what-is-gc, accessed August 6, 2019.

REFERENCES

Albareda, L. and Waddock, S. (2018). Networked CSR governance: a whole network approach to meta-governance. *Business & Society*, **57**(4), 636–75.

Bazerman, M.H. and Sezer, O. (2016). Bounded awareness: implications for ethical decision making. *Organizational Behavior and Human Decision Processes*, **136**, 95–105.

Bazerman, M.H. and Tenbrunsel, A.E. (2011). Ethical breakdowns. *Harvard Business Review*, **89**(4), 58–65.

Biermann, F., Abbott, K., Andresen, S. et al. (2012). Transforming governance and institutions for global sustainability: key insights from the Earth System Governance Project. *Current Opinion in Environmental Sustainability*, **4**(1), 51–60.

Biermann, F., Betsill, M.M., Gupta, J. et al. (2010). Earth system governance: a research framework. *International Environmental Agreements: Politics, Law and Economics*, **10**(4), 277–98.

Brosnan, S.F. and de Waal, F.B. (2012). Fairness in animals: where to from here? *Social Justice Research*, **25**(3), 336–51.

Brown, P.T. and Caldeira, K. 2017. Greater future global warming inferred from Earth's recent energy budget. *Nature*, **552**, 7 December, 45–50.

Capra, F. (1995). *The Web of Life*. New York: Anchor Doubleday.

Capra, F. and Luisi, P.L. (2014). *The Systems View of Life: A Unifying Vision*. New York: Cambridge University Press.

Chapin III, F.S., Pickett, S.T., Power, M.E., Jackson, R.B., Carter, D.M., and Duke, C. (2011). Earth stewardship: a strategy for social–ecological transformation to reverse planetary degradation. *Journal of Environmental Studies and Sciences*, **1**(1), 44–53.

Collins, Chuck and Ehrenreich, B. (2012). *99 to 1: How Wealth Inequality is Wrecking the World and What We Can Do about It*. San Francisco, CA: Berrett-Koehler.

Costanza, R., Fioramonti, L., and Kubiszewski, I. (2016). The UN Sustainable Development Goals and the dynamics of well-being. *Frontiers in Ecology and the Environment*, **14**(2), 20–2.

Crutzen, P.J. (2006). The 'Anthropocene.' In *Earth System Science in the Anthropocene*. Berlin and Heidelberg: Springer, pp. 13–18.

de Waal, F.B. (1996). *Good Natured* (No. 87). Cambridge, MA: Harvard University Press.

de Waal, F.B. (2008). Putting the altruism back into altruism: the evolution of empathy. *Annual Review of Psychology*, **59**, 279–300.

Dearing, J.A., Wang, R., Zhang, K. et al. (2014). Safe and just operating spaces for regional social-ecological systems. *Global Environmental Change*, **28**, 227–38.

Diamond, J. (2005). *Collapse: How Societies Choose to Fail or Succeed*. New York: Penguin.

Donaldson, T. and Walsh, J.P. (2015). Toward a theory of business. *Research in Organizational Behavior*, **35**, 181–207. doi: http://dx.doi.org/10.1016/j.riob.2015.10.002.

Ehrenfeld, J. and Hoffman, A. (2013). *Flourishing: A Frank Conversation about Sustainability*. Palo Alto, CA: Stanford University Press.

Eisler, R. (2008). *The Real Wealth of Nations: Creating a Caring Economics*. San Francisco, CA: Berrett-Koehler.

Frederick, W.C. (1995). *Values, Nature, and Culture in the American Corporation*. New York: Oxford University Press.

Freeman, R.E. (1984). *Strategic Management: A Stakeholder Approach*. Boston, MA: Pitman.

Freeman, R.E., Harrison, J.S., and Wicks, A.C. (2007). *Managing for Stakeholders: Survival, Reputation, and Success*. New Haven, CT: Yale University Press.

Gilding, P. (2011). *The Great Disruption: How the Climate Crisis will Transform the Global Economy*. London: Bloomsbury Press.

Gino, F., Moore, D.A., and Bazerman, M.H. (2008). See no evil: when we overlook other people's unethical behavior. In R.M. Kramer, A.E. Tenbrunsel, and M. Bazerman (eds), *Social Decision Making: Social Dilemmas, Social Values and Ethical Judgments*. New York: Routledge, pp. 241–57.

Hardin, G. (1968). The tragedy of the commons. *Science*, **162**(3859), 1243–8.

IPCC. (2014). Summary for policymakers. In *Climate Change 2014: Impacts, Adaptation, and Vulnerability. Part A: Global and Sectoral Aspects. Contribution of Working Group II to the Fifth Assessment Report of the Intergovernmental Panel on Climate Change*. Ed. C.B. Field, V.R. Barros, D.J. Dokken, K.J. Mach, M.D. Mastrandrea, T.E. Bilir, M. Chatterjee, K.L. Ebi, Y.O. Estrada, R.C. Genova, B. Girma, E.S. Kissel, A.N. Levy, S. MacCracken, P.R. Mastrandrea, and L.L. White. Cambridge and New York: Cambridge University Press, pp. 1–32.

Jackson, T. (2011). *Prosperity without Growth: Economics for a Finite Planet*. Abingdon, UK: Routledge.

Klein, N. (2014). *This Changes Everything: Capitalism vs. the Climate*. San Francisco, CA: Berrett-Koehler.

Liu, J., Mooney, H., Hull, V. et al. (2015). Systems integration for global sustainability. *Science*, **347**(6225), 1258832.

Maak, T. and Pless, N.M. (2006). Responsible leadership in a stakeholder society – a relational perspective. *Journal of Business Ethics*, **66**(1), 99–115.

Maak, T. and Pless, N.M. (2009). Business leaders as citizens of the world. Advancing humanism on a global scale. *Journal of Business Ethics*, **88**(3), 537–50.

Matten, D. and Moon, J. (2008). 'Implicit' and 'explicit' CSR: a conceptual framework for a comparative understanding of corporate social responsibility. *Academy of Management Review*, **33**(2), 404–24.

McIntosh, M. (ed.) (2013). *The Necessary Transition: The Journey Towards the Sustainable Enterprise Economy*. Sheffield, UK: Greenleaf.

McKibben, B. (2011). *Earth: Making a Life on a Tough New Planet*. New York: Random House Digital, Inc.

Meadows, D. (1999). Leverage points: places to intervene in a system. The Sustainability Institute, Harland, VT. http://donellameadows.org/archives/leverage-points-places-to-intervene-in-a-system/, accessed 6 August 2019.

Moellendorf, D. (2009). Global inequality and injustice. *Journal of International Development*, **21**(8), 1125–136.

Monbiot, G. (2016a). Neoliberalism – the ideology at the root of all of our problems. *Guardian*, 15 April. https://www.theguardian.com/books/2016/apr/15/neoliberalism-ideology-problem-george-monbiot, accessed 6 August 2019.

Monbiot, G. (2016b). *How Did We Get into this Mess? Politics, Equality, Nature.* New York: Penguin Random House.

Monbiot. G. (2016c). The Zombie doctrine. *Guardian*, 16 April. http://www.monbiot.com/2016/04/15/the-zombie-doctrine/, accessed 6 August 2019.

Parmar, B.L., Freeman, R.E., Harrison, J.S., Wicks, A.C., Purnell, L., and De Colle, S. (2010). Stakeholder theory: the state of the art. *The Academy of Management Annals*, **4**(1), 403–45.

Pirson, M. (2017). *Humanistic Management: Protecting Dignity and Promoting Well-being*. Cambridge: Cambridge University Press.

Pirson, M. and Lawrence, P.R. (2010). Humanism in business – towards a paradigm shift? *Journal of Business Ethics*, **93**(4), 553–65.

Pless, N.M. and Maak, T. (2011). Responsible leadership: pathways to the future. *Journal of Business Ethics*, **98**, 3–13.

Quiggin, J. (2012). *Zombie Economics: How Dead Ideas Still Walk Among Us.* Princeton, NJ: Princeton University Press.

Raworth, K. (2012). A safe and just space for humanity: can we live within the doughnut. *Oxfam Policy and Practice: Climate Change and Resilience*, **8**(1), 1–26.

Raworth, K. (2017). *Doughnut Economics: Seven Ways to Think Like a 21st-Century Economist*. White River Junction, VT: Chelsea Green Publishing.

Rockström, J. (2015). Bounding the planetary future: why we need a great transition. *Great Transition Initiative*, **9**, 1–13.

Rockström, J., Steffen, W.L., Noone, K. et al. (2009). Planetary boundaries: exploring the safe operating space for humanity. *Ecology & Society*, **14**(2), 32. http://www.ecologyandsociety.org/vol14/iss2/art32/, accessed 6 August 2019.

Schor, J. (2010). *Plenitude: The New Economics of Real Wealth*. New York: Penguin.

Schrempf-Stirling, J., Palazzo, G., and Phillips, R.A. (2016). Historic corporate social responsibility. *Academy of Management Review*, **41**(4), 700–19.

SDGs (Sustainable Development Goals). (2018). https://sustainabledevelopment.un.org/sdgs. http://www.un.org/sustainabledevelopment/sustainable-development-goals/, accessed 6 August 2019.

Starik, M. (1995). Should trees have managerial standing? Toward stakeholder status for non-human nature. *Journal of Business Ethics*, **14**(3), 207–17.

Steffen, W., Richardson, K., Rockström, J. et al. (2015). Planetary boundaries: guiding human development on a changing planet. *Science*, **347**(6223), 1259855.

Waddell, S., Waddock, S., Cornell, S., Dentoni, D., McLachlan, M., and Meszoely, G. (2014). Large systems change. *Journal of Corporate Citizenship*, **53**, 5–30.

Waddock, S. (2002). *Leading Corporate Citizens: Vision, Values, Value-Added*. New York: McGraw-Hill.

Waddock, S. (2008). Building a new institutional infrastructure for corporate responsibility. *The Academy of Management Perspectives*, **22**(3), 87–108.

Waddock, S. (2010). Finding wisdom within – the role of seeing and reflective

practice in developing moral imagination, aesthetic sensibility, and systems understanding. *Journal of Business Ethics Education*, **7**, 177–96.
Waddock, S. (2011). We are all stakeholders of Gaia: a normative perspective on stakeholder thinking. *Organization & Environment*, **24**(2), 192–212.
Waddock, S. (2014). Wisdom and responsible leadership: aesthetic sensibility, moral imagination, and systems thinking. In D. Koehn and D. Elm (eds), *Aesthetics and Business Ethics, Issues in Business Ethics*, Vol. 41. Netherlands: Springer, pp. 129–47.
Waddock, S. (2016). Foundational memes for a new narrative about the role of business in society. *Humanistic Management Journal*. 1: 91–105, doi: 10.1007/s41463-016-0012-4.
Waddock, S. and Kuenkel, P. (2019). What gives life to large system change? *Organization & Environment*, https://doi.org/10.1177/1086026619842482.
Waddock, S. and Rasche, A. (2012). *Building Responsible Enterprise: Where Vision and Values Add Value*. Palo Alto, CA: Stanford University Press.
Wallace-Wells, D. (2017). The uninhabitable earth, annotated edition. *New York Magazine*, 14 July. http://nymag.com/daily/intelligencer/2017/07/climate-change-earth-too-hot-for-humans-annotated.html, accessed 6 August 2019.

11. Francisco de Vitoria's *ius gentium*: how to engage human rights in business from the Catholic Social Teaching (CST) tradition

Alejo José G. Sison

11.1 INTRODUCTION

The problem of searching for ethical business leadership in an era of Brexit, mass immigration, populism, nationalism, and so forth has already been adequately described. What we need are solutions. But for this we first need to engage in a deep and accurate diagnosis of the current situation.

At the level of philosophical anthropology, I would propose that the difficulty lies in two closely related fronts: first, in the individualistic understanding of human beings; and second, in a notion of what human beings ultimately seek (their "final end" in Aristotelian parlance) as something exclusively material that satisfies their preferences, whatever these may be. By virtue of the first, "individualism," people are largely incapable of thinking of what lies beyond their own skin; and if they do, only insofar as it affects them almost sensorially. There is nothing "common" except what gets divided up and distributed among individuals. Nothing is shared. None is greater than the "Self," than "Myself," in truth. The individual is, by default, the unchallenged unit of thought, analysis, and action.

By virtue of the second, we take for granted that no agreement is possible regarding preferences, except perhaps their (for the most part) material nature. Nonetheless, it is imperative that they be satisfied, often without even counting the costs. These preferences become the bases of "rights" or non-negotiable claims we make as individuals on States and society. We may call this the "material preference-satisfaction imperative."

Individualism and the "material preference-satisfaction imperative" taken together yield a vision of human life as an unrelenting pursuit of gratification for which everything and everyone else is a means or instrument. It is fairly easy to see how this rule is fulfilled in each of the problems alluded to above.

If my assessment is right, Catholic Social Teaching (CST), insofar as it combines the Aristotelian-Thomistic virtue ethics with the Natural Law tradition has much to offer by way of solutions. This potential is further increased with CST's engagement with human rights discourse, albeit based on Francisco de Vitoria's *ius gentium* ("law of the nations" or, better still, "law of the peoples"), different from the one advocated by Enlightenment authors.

Why is this the case?

First, Aristotelian-Thomistic virtue ethics is premised on "personalism," the view that human beings are individual and relational or social on equal counts and at all times (contra individualism) (Sison et al. 2016). Second, it identifies non-material or spiritual faculties, such as reason and free will, as characteristics which define human beings and set them apart from others in nature. Because of their superior spiritual nature, humans are able to access immaterial realities such as knowledge, for instance, over and above the different forms of wealth and pleasures. Unlike individual, material preferences, knowledge and the like can fulfill the conditions of a "common good" (contra the "material preference-satisfaction imperative") (Sison and Fontrodona 2012). Not only are they reasonable objects of preferences or desires, but they also perfect or "make whole" their possessors. Moreover, they represent a type of goods that can, in fact, be shared and not only divided and distributed among many. For instance, it is always better for people to know traffic rules and regulations, especially drivers, than the contrary. And one person's knowledge of these rules does not in any way detract from another's. An ideal and perfect traffic situation is one wherein all drivers know the rules of the road and abide by them. This can only be achieved by all drivers working in concert and each of them would equally benefit from such a situation. Besides understanding human beings as "persons," that is, individual and relational or social, CST also acknowledges that their "final end" or ultimate aim is a common good.

Nowadays, largely because of Vatican presence in international fora like the United Nations (UN) as the official representative of the Catholic Church, CST has had to engage with human rights language (Sison 2018). The dominant human rights discourse originating from Enlightenment authors such as Locke down to more recent thinkers such as Rawls, however, is not only foreign, but also contrary, due to its individualism and rejection of the common good, to the Catholic tradition. Even the post World War II UN Universal Declaration of Human Rights garners consensus only in the letter, not the underlying basis or foundation of such rights (Maritain 1951). Hence, the tendency to use them in a positivistic or legalistic manner, that is, avoiding all reference to why those rights must be observed in the first place. Fortunately, an alternative in keeping with the Catholic tradition exists in the *ius gentium* or "law of the peoples" elaborated mainly in *De Indis* by Francisco de Vitoria (1991), a 16th-century Dominican friar who taught at the University of Salamanca.

In the succeeding I shall elaborate more on the *ius gentium*, explaining its historical context as well as the distinctive features that make it an especially potent force in responding to today's business leadership challenges. For example, it provides a basis for International Law that acknowledges as bearers of rights and responsibilities not only States and other political communities, but also individuals, both rulers and ordinary citizens. Moreover, *ius gentium* draws obligatoriness or normative force not from any particular State, Empire, or Religion, but from a universal human nature equally possessed by all individual persons. Likewise, it relies on consensus understood as shared deliberation and decision-making rather than on impositions by the powerful. And particularly salient for business, *ius gentium* recognizes a *ius communicationis* ("right to communicate") as a basic human right that derives from sociability and serves as the foundation for other economic rights whose responsible exercise is indispensable for the achievement of a universal common good, that of the *orbs* ("world") or the *communitas communitatum* ("community of communities").

11.2 *IUS GENTIUM*: THE SPANISH DISCOVERY OF AMERICA AND THE NEED FOR A LEGAL BASIS TO PROTECT THE RIGHTS OF NATIVES

Spain was the only country in Europe that questioned the legitimacy of its American conquests, and within Spain, Francisco de Vitoria was perhaps the most outspoken critic of the traditional "titles (or 'rights') of conquest." Often cited were, on the one hand, the Papal Bulls of Donation from Alexander VI (1493), by which the kings of Spain and Portugal, as well as their successors, were granted the right to any discovered land which did not already belong to a Christian ruler. On the other hand, there was also the Holy Roman Emperor Charles V's claim to "universal primacy" over the world. For Vitoria, despite being subject to both the Pope and the Emperor, neither "title" was legitimate and other reasons had to be sought. The Pope could have, at most, a spiritual, not a temporal authority over the Native Americans who, furthermore, should not be obliged to convert to Christianity. The Alexandrine Bulls were therefore invalid. Neither was Charles V's claim to be honored because, for Vitoria, all peoples equally have the right to self-government, and the Native Americans already had their own rulers. These teachings were based on a clear understanding of the distinction and autonomy of the spiritual, religious, or supernatural realm, on the one hand, from the temporal, secular, or natural realm, on the other. They also implied a rejection of the so-called "divine rights of kings," widely held during the medieval age.

However, through careful study and reasoning, Vitoria (1991) was able to devise up to eight different titles justifying the Spanish colonization of America (Fernández 2017). First and foremost was the *ius communicationis* or "right of communication" which derives directly from the social or relational nature of human beings manifested in an inclination to constitute a "universal society." This consists not so much of the freedom of speech, but the right to communicate meaningfully with others toward mutual human enrichment. No ruler can legitimately go against this natural tendency and if he did, other rulers would have the right to defend and, if violated, re-establish it. Second was the *ius peregrinandi et degendi* ("right to travel and engage in commerce") anywhere in the world, regardless of the ruler or the religion in a territory, again for mutual benefit. If the Native Americans failed to honor this right, the aggrieved Spaniards could wage a just war and retain whatever territories they gained. Third was the right to preach the Faith, closely related to the *ius communicationis*. In relation to this, although Native Americans were not obliged to convert to Christianity, if any of them freely did, and their rulers forced them to revert, other Christians could defend the converts even if it meant going to war. This was the fourth title, the defense of Christian converts. Fifth was the fact that there would already be sufficient Christian converts, who would then have the right to a Christian ruler sanctioned by the Pope. This was a version of the right to self-rule and to choose who governed. Sixth was the case of tyranny or serious harm to the innocent, such as the practice of human sacrifices. Other nations (such as Spain) had a right to stop this to restore justice and order. This meant the sovereignty of political communities over its own citizens was not absolute. A seventh title came by way of alliances between the Spaniards and the Tlaxaltecs, for instance, who were attacked by the Aztecs; the Spaniards had a right to defend their allies. And perhaps least convincing, even for Vitoria himself, was the eighth title borne of Christian charity. Spaniards had a right to teach Native Americans about just laws and institutions, as well as more advanced agricultural techniques and so forth, for their own benefit. This, too, would have justified the Spanish conquest and colonization.

One may disagree with some, even all of these titles Vitoria enumerated. However, Vitoria clearly understood that Native Americans also had rights which had to be respected, just like the Spaniards and Europeans. In many of these rights, Europeans and Native Americans were on equal footing, such as the *ius communicationis*, *ius peregrinandi et degendi*, and the right to defend allies. Although in the rights to preach the Faith, to defend Christian converts, to have a Christian ruler, and to exercise Christian charity (through teaching technological and moral advancements, for instance) there is deference toward Christian religion and culture, reciprocity with other religions and cultures is not ruled out. People of other religions and cultures such as the Native Americans equally possess the right to preach, to make converts, to have their own rulers, and to spread their cultural achievements, in principle. This means that such rights are not based on religion, race, culture, membership in a particular political community, and so forth, but on something more fundamental, such as a shared human nature. From the perspective of human nature, all individuals are equal and free.

Ius gentium or the "law of the peoples" refers to powers or faculties that accrue exclusively to all human beings as free and rational creatures. The Stoics were perhaps the first to speak of a universal human race characterized by reason, to which Christianity added the belief that all human beings are made in the "image and likeness of God" (*imago Dei*) (Sison et al. 2016). Vitoria later explains that these rights are not diminished by sin, heresy, or even unfaithfulness. That is, Native Americans, prior to European conquest and colonization, already possessed these rights afforded by the "law of the peoples" fully as well.

Part of the freedom, rationality, and sociability (in a word, "personhood") of individual human beings is the right to constitute independent political communities for their own defense, conservation, and flourishing. In this respect, we find a significant departure from feudalism dominant in the age. Similarly, these political communities are vested with power and authority (*potestas publica*, *maiestas*, sovereignty) to govern and promote the common good. Both the constitution of political communities and the power that preserves and guides them are attributes of Natural Law.

Ius gentium goes beyond Natural Law in affirming the right of all peoples to political freedom, sovereignty, and independence. Again, this was not dependent on any religious title, as the Faith or grace; moreover, *Papa non est dominus orbis* (The Pope is not the lord of the world). Yet, what is the *orbs* (world)? For Vitoria, it is the universal community of all human beings and of all peoples (*communitas communitatum* or "community of communities") united by bonds of a common human nature (Fernández Ruiz-Gálvez 2017). The *totus orbs* ("whole world"), juridically organized according to the *ius gentium*, is not a super-State like the Holy Roman Empire or a Stoic *civitas maxima* ("great city"). Rather, it represents a "family of peoples" where each constitutive *gens* (people) represents the most rudimentary form of political community.

Each *gens* constituting the *orbs* is sovereign, that is, independent from Papal and imperial authority (external interferences) and capable of self-government. The ruler of each *gens*, therefore, in the exercise of his own authority, is not subject to other States, Emperors, or Popes, but only to Divine Law, Natural Law (which is a participation in the former), *ius gentium*, and the positive laws of his own political community. Such is the understanding of the "rule of law" within the context of *ius gentium*. Each *gens* is also juridically equal to any other, that is, possessing the same rights and responsibilities within the *orbs*.

Furthermore, the *orbs* is not a hierarchical community of masters and subordinates, nor is it merely an instrument of coordination through contracts or pacts between equal subjects, States, or individuals. The subjects of the *orbs* are not just independent and separate individuals who each pursue their own interests and preferences through the *ius gentium*, as occurs with laws in liberal societies. Rather, subjects in the *orbs* constitute an authentic community wherein lies their human perfection. The bonds of the common human nature in the *orbs* are meant to integrate all subjects, by virtue of the *ius communicationis*, in universal solidarity or friendship as part of the temporal common good.

In summary, the *ius gentium* signals the transition from the hierarchical-medieval to the egalitarian-modern worldview occasioned by the Spanish or European discovery of America. Political authority and the legitimate use of power no longer derived from the Pope (religious ties) or the Emperor (imperial ties) but from a common human nature, marked by individual, personal reason and freedom. (Catholic theology sees in human nature present in each person nothing less than the *imago Dei* or "image of God.") There is a clear distinction between the spiritual and the temporal realms, despite the overlaps. By virtue of their natural sociability or relationality established by Natural Law, human beings possess a *ius communicationis* in accordance with the *ius gentium*. This "right to communicate" is the legal cornerstone of the European entry and settlement of America, and Europeans are entitled to defend it despite resistance from the Natives, even through war. The exercise of the *ius communicationis* is vital to the attainment of the universal common good.

Because of their common human nature – and not an artificial social contract – all human beings, by themselves or as citizens of their respective States or political communities, constitute the *orbs* or worldwide community of communities. Based on human nature, the *orbs* is universal in scope and excludes no one. *Ius gentium* is the law that encompasses the *orbs*, with individuals and States as subjects. According to the *ius gentium*, all political communities constituting the *orbs* are sovereign and equal in their attributions.

In the following section I shall consider the *ius gentium* in relation, on the one hand, to Natural Law and Positive Law, and on the other, to modern, conventional International Law. This will allow me to further discuss the contents of *ius gentium* as well as their logical derivation from Natural Law as source of authority. Only then will I be able to explore later their potential for responding to current business ethics challenges.

11.3 *IUS GENTIUM* BETWEEN NATURAL LAW AND POSITIVE LAW, *IUS GENTIUM* AND INTERNATIONAL LAW

It is beyond the scope of this work to explain the origin, justification, and history of Natural Law (Tierney 1997). What is important for this project is to show the continuity among Natural Law, *ius gentium*, and Positive Law (Salas 2012). Following tradition as synthesized by Aquinas (2006), by law we understand "an ordinance of reason promulgated by competent authority for the sake of common good" (*S Th I-II, q. 90. a. 4*). Law is a rational imperative (command or prohibition), the end or purpose of which is the common good. It is not simply the expression of "private interest," despite agreement or consensus on the matter. It also has to be enacted by legitimate authorities responsible over the community.

It is fairly easy to distinguish Natural Law from Positive Law. While Positive Law is explicit, derived, contingent, and "posited," Natural Law is implicit, original, permanent, and "given." The difference between *ius gentium* and Natural Law, on the one hand, and *ius gentium* and Positive Law, on the other, however, is an old chestnut. For Vitoria, Natural Law contains what is just by nature and necessary by itself, without depending on the human will, while *ius gentium* refers to what is just not by itself but in reference to another. Peace and concord are demands of Natural Law, while the distribution of property, insofar as it leads to peace and concord, is a requirement of *ius gentium*, for example. Similarly, respecting the inviolability of ambassadors is a precept of *ius gentium* inasmuch as it enables the achievement and maintenance of peace between States, an exigency of Natural Law. Vitoria considers elements of *ius gentium* those dispositions which do not necessarily, absolutely, immediately, and clearly derive from Natural Law, needing instead (near) universal consensus. Unlike Natural Law, therefore, *ius gentium* depends on universal agreement or consensus. At the same time, however, Natural Law cannot be properly observed without *ius gentium*, thus creating some mutual dependence between them.

Vitoria leaves room for some nuance regarding the universal consensus condition for *ius gentium*. For example, in matters that directly and immediately affect the common good of the *orbs*, such as rights over the sea, the enslavement of prisoners of war (instead of execution), or the non-expulsion of foreigners, Vitoria states that a majority consensus would be enough. He also recognizes that, resulting from the exercise of practical reason, *ius gentium* may fail in deriving principles from Natural Law. This allows *ius gentium* to evolve, hopefully for the better. A case in point would be the treatment of prisoners of war, who went from being executed to becoming slaves, until an almost total agreement is reached even on the abolition of slavery. *Ius gentium* is binding insofar as it derives from Natural Law and it is established by the authority of the *orbs* with a view to a worldwide or universal common good. Because of this, it is practically impossible to derogate *ius gentium* in the sense of changing its course, since this would require a near universal consensus.

Against this background, other principles of *ius gentium* besides those already mentioned include the *ius commercii* (the right to engage in business, including making contracts, acquiring, holding, and transferring property), *ius occupationis* ("finders keepers" or the right to original acquisition of property, such as uninhabited territory, through occupation), *ius migrandi* (freedom to move or migrate), and religious freedom. Indeed, Vitoria (1991) produces a host of "sentences" within the context of *ius gentium* which could be considered a forerunner of modern human rights: "Men are not born slaves but free." "By Natural Law no one is superior to others." "The child does not exist by reason of others, but by reason of itself." "It is better to renounce one's own right than to violate that of another." "It is licit for man to have private property, but there is no owner who, at times, will have to share his things . . . in extreme necessity, all things are held in common." "The perpetually demented, who neither have, nor hope to have use of reason, can be owners . . . and possess rights." "If a judge, failing to observe lawful order, obtains by force the confession of a prisoner, he could not condemn him, because by doing so he does not act as a judge should." "One cannot take the life of a person who has not been judged and condemned." "Every nation has a right to govern itself and it can accept whatever form of government it likes, even though this may not be the best." "All the king's powers come from the nation because the nation is free from the very beginning." "The whole world, which in a sense constitutes a republic, has the power to make just and convenient laws for humanity." "No war is just, if it brings more harm than good to the nation, regardless its titles for a just war." "If a subject knew that a war were unjust, he could not participate in it, despite the command of the prince." "Man is not a wolf to man, but man."

Another striking feature of Vitoria's teachings is its positive view of commerce or business and economic activity as a whole (Castillo and Zorroza

2015; Cendejas Bueno 2018). The market institution, which facilitates the free circulation of people, ideas, and goods, results from the reasonable and responsible exercise of the *ius communicationis* ("right to communicate"). It can increase the sense of brotherhood and equality among human beings and thus promote the common good. To be an entrepreneur or businessperson, therefore, to make a living from profitable exchanges, is not necessarily wrong or shameful. It can be a legitimate and even excellent activity so long as it fulfills certain conditions. Such conditions can be summarized in the theory of a "just price." Absent ignorance, force, or fraud, the "just price" is the agreed price between buyer and seller in the free market. One-sided agreements among buyers or sellers, monopsonies, monopolies, and hoarding prevent the determination of the "just price." It's not only the cost of production of goods, but should also take into account demand and supply, their value or desirability to parties, the risks they entail, and so forth (Vitoria 2006, pp. 83–5). A merchant who buys goods in a place where they are abundant and sells them at a higher price in another place where they are scarce, for example, renders a service to society and is entitled to the profit he makes (Vitoria 2006, p. 86). The expertise or virtue of a merchant lies in knowing how to buy and sell goods at a profit, absent force or fraud.

At this stage it is fairly clear that *ius gentium* may be considered a precedent of International Law. There are essential differences, nonetheless, between *ius gentium* and modern International Law as we know it. The main one refers to the statist character of modern International Law which only recognizes a specific kind of political community, States, as subjects. International Law does not acknowledge non-State communities or individual persons as subjects of rights and responsibilities. The latter, individual persons, are only recognized insofar as citizens of particular States, a very limited aspect of their identities. They have no rights in International Law as individual human persons, therefore. Once more, these characteristics of International Law can be traced to the individualism and the material preference-satisfaction imperative dominant in modern liberal societies already alluded to above.

11.4 THE NORMATIVE POTENTIAL OF *IUS GENTIUM* FOR CURRENT BUSINESS ETHICS CHALLENGES

In this final section I will distill the normative potential of Vitoria's *ius gentium* for the problems business leadership currently faces. I will end with a brief discussion of how *ius gentium* principles can help frame some issues and orient us toward morally acceptable solutions.

Ius gentium displays four particular strengths useful in dealing with today's business ethics problems. First, it draws on a personalist understanding of human nature as individual and relational or social, rational and free on equal counts. Human nature and its dignity or "intrinsic worth" is not premised on religion, citizenship, race, sex, age, socioeconomic status, culture, and so forth. It is truly universal, the same for each individual of the species, regardless of time and place. There is no room for unjust discrimination. Further, because it recognizes that humans are individual and relational at the same time, it implies that their final end or purpose is a common good, since it is the only way to satisfy that dual dimension of their being. What excludes others as a matter of fact cannot be the supreme end for us to pursue. We are never indifferent to other people's fate or destiny; this is something we share and to which we are bound by nature. Therefore, rights in *ius gentium* are not seen as absolute powers or entitlements for individuals to exercise regardless of their impact on the good of the community. Neither are States and other political communities absolutely independent of each other; their sovereignty is not absolute, as the doctrine of Westphalia would like us to believe. By virtue of the *ius communicationis* States are bound to each other at the service of the common good of the *orbs*. This establishes limits to what rulers of political communities can do with regard to their own subjects (for instance, the offering of human sacrifices in some Native American communities) and may also justify intervention by third parties in the same political communities (conversely, the attempt of Spaniards to stop such rituals).

Second, *ius gentium* acknowledges that all human beings are born equal, that is, possessing equal rights and freedoms. Consequently, the different political communities they form are also equal in this sense. Basic human rights and freedoms originate in nature, not in the power of political communities, such as States or Empires. Neither do they come from belonging to a certain religion or Church. The temporal and the supernatural or religious orders are distinct and autonomous, each within its own realm. Temporal rulers are not meant to legislate for religious communities as in the National Churches of the Reform, nor are religious rulers supposed to govern political communities as in the case of theocratic States. Individuals ought to reciprocally acknowledge equal rights among themselves and so, too, should political communities of whatever form. Might does not make right in relations among persons and their communities. Equality in rights demands reciprocity between the subjects of those rights.

In third place, *ius gentium*, insofar as it derives from the free exercise of reason by human beings reflecting upon their own nature, requires participation, consensus, or agreement. This is a consequence of taking equality among human beings and their political communities seriously.

It is not sufficient for a few enlightened to have brilliant ideas and impose them on others for their mechanical or slavish execution. Rather, everyone affected should have a say, either by themselves or through their legitimate representatives. The good pursued is not a theoretical, abstract ideal but a good in action, given the circumstances. Thus, it requires shared deliberation and concerted action. Vitoria is realistic enough to admit that complete agreement among all parties may not be possible; hence, in most cases, decisions by a qualified majority may suffice. What is important is for everyone to have an opportunity guaranteed by law to contribute to the common good. Free markets seem a peculiarly appropriate institution to promote this sort of participation.

Fourth, *ius gentium* is almost unique in tradition for advocating a positive view of business as a force for the common good. Vitoria's teachings above regarding the just price, free markets, and the role of the merchant, businessperson or entrepreneur support this perspective. Business is understood as a kind of chrematistic, concerned with the production or provision of material resources human beings need to achieve the common good of flourishing within the political community (Sison and Fontrodona 2012). Engaging in business involves freedom and reason, and is thus open to the development of knowledge, skills, meanings, proper attitudes, and even moral virtues in the businessperson. All this is possible thanks to the voluntary, mutually beneficial exchange of goods, services, and ideas taking place in markets, another expression of the *ius communicationis*. Profits are neither good nor bad in themselves. They are legitimate if produced free from force or fraud and put to good use, such as the support of oneself, one's family, or to help the poor. The same reasoning applies to interests on loans, which could also be legitimate given certain conditions.

How relevant are these characteristics of Vitoria's *ius gentium* to problems such as Brexit and the European Union (EU), Islamic immigration in Europe, the building of the wall between the US and Mexico, and the rise of Nationalism and Populism, for instance? What guidance can they offer business leaders and political rulers?

Leaders would do well to think in terms of the common good instead of merely seeking the satisfaction of their individual material preferences in terms of wealth or power. They would have to stop conceiving rights in liberal-democratic fashion as non-negotiable claims made by individuals or groups of individuals on States and other political entities by virtue of a mythical social contract. The struggle for rights must not turn into a zero-sum game, but in a situation in which all parties benefit. Rather, social leaders should acknowledge that rights originate and draw normative strength from a human nature which is universal and equal in all persons. Moreover, political leaders in particular ought to disabuse themselves of the idea of absolute sovereignty of Westphalian States. Political communities may be autonomous, but are never fully independent of each other, as they all form part of the *orbs* and contribute to the universal common good safeguarded by the *ius gentium*.

Neither the UK nor the EU should design policies based on economic considerations exclusively, but also take into account their communal moral obligations, ultimately toward the global common good. Examples of such obligations would be the preservation of peace in both the Republic of Ireland and Northern Ireland, or the welfare of Gibraltar residents, closely related to the surrounding region in the Spanish mainland. Besides respectfully acknowledging the right to self-government of constituent States like the UK, the EU should look for ways to remedy the democratic deficit in its institutions and promote greater participation at all levels of governance. In correspondence, politicians from the UK and other EU States should not instrumentalize democratic processes to further their own personal ambitions, even to the point of lying about the true state of affairs or making promises impossible to fulfill to the electorate.

The question of serious impediments to a number of *ius gentium* principles such as the *ius communicationis*, the right to engage in commerce, the right to travel and migrate (for instance, of UK pensioners to the Continent or of workers from the Continent to the UK), or the rights of minorities (such as the losing side of an almost evenly split referendum in the UK) ought to be diligently addressed.

Regarding Muslim refugees and migrants to Europe and the rise of Nationalist or Populist parties, or the building of the wall between the US and Mexico, *ius gentium* similarly has a lot to contribute. First, the right of refuge, especially when one's life is in danger, is sacred. It's also best to tackle problems at the source. This means primarily that Muslim-majority countries should respect and honor the religious and conscience rights of citizens and residents in their territories. Persecution on these grounds should stop. For this reason, it is impossible to justify the establishment of a theocracy such as that purported by ISIS or Al-Qaeda. Conversely, once religious and conscience rights are guaranteed in one's own territory, it would be much easier to demand reciprocity from other political communities. Likewise, political sovereignty should not be turned into a cover to commit atrocities against one's own people, as Saddam Hussein or Bashir Al-Assad are said to have perpetrated in Iraq and Syria, respectively.

As insinuated above, the right to save one's life, especially from unjust persecution trumps the security of State borders. As a nation of immigrants, US history has been based on this principle, and until recently, the country has been the living proof of the success of such a policy. This is what made America great. Why renege now? Politicians should not exaggerate the challenges of immigration for their own purposes, as most Nationalists and Populists do. Countries much poorer than the US or those of the EU, such as Kenya, Jordan, and Lebanon, have for decades accepted huge refugee and immigrant populations. On balance, they have been tremendously enriched, not only culturally, but also economically by taking these people in. One only has to look at the number of ethnic restaurants in American cities adding variety and flavor to palates. All it takes is mutual respect among cultures and the disposition to learn from each other. The key lies in social integration mainly by respecting the newcomers' freedom to work and create their own small businesses. Understandably, this does not imply eliminating borders, but taking the effort to accept in an orderly fashion those who need to come in because they fear for their lives, instead of simply slamming the door in their faces. At the same time, access to the benefits of the Welfare State for these incoming groups could be made gradual and conditional on their work contributions.

A few thoughts on the difficulty of an international regime based on *ius gentium* and why the UN is not the solution. Although UN documents may speak profusely of peoples, in fact, its interlocutors are States and it does nothing without them. According to *ius gentium*, the bonds of a common human nature create rights and obligations beyond citizenship in a particular State. In addition, the fact that a handful of States exercise veto-power over UN decisions demonstrates that it does not uphold the equality of peoples, as *ius gentium* requires. Lastly, as is often the case in liberal and individualistic societies, UN resolutions mainly focus on procedural issues, having given up on substantive agreements. Although necessary, this condition is not sufficient for a common good perspective as *ius gentium* suggests. The good in cooperative action sought is more than just accord in the mechanics, but also in the purpose and meaning.

What can businesses do to be more aligned with the *ius gentium*?

In all their decision-making processes, they may strive to adopt the personalist and common good perspectives instead of the individualist and material preference-satisfaction outlook. For instance, when marketing consumer goods, bear in mind that all individuals form part of families, so it would be worth considering the impact of products on other family members as well. Similarly, taking a long-term view of the environment, for example, could help refocus on the common good instead of immediate, individual satisfactions. A certain mode of production may be cheaper and translate into greater short-term profits, but cause more harm to the environment and eventually to consumers and society as a whole. Another way would be to prioritize win-win scenarios and partnerships in place of zero-sum attainments and positional goods. Businesses may likewise try to conceive rights in the manner of *ius gentium*, rather than the Enlightenment. They are not absolute individual powers guaranteed by the State, but capacities or abilities to be exercised in accordance with Natural Law, the virtues, and the common good. There is a human ecology to be protected, no less than the environment of which we all form part. In deriving normative force from free and rational human nature itself, we would then be able to defend ourselves better in the exercise of our rights from the arbitrary impositions of force.

REFERENCES

Aquinas, Thomas (2006). *Summa Theologiae* (ed. English Province of the Order of Preachers), Cambridge: Cambridge University Press.

Castillo, G. and Zorroza, I. (2015). "Actividad económica y acción moral. Una revisión del supuesto antropológico moderno en la descripción del mercado de Francisco de Vitoria," *Revista Empresa y Humanismo*, **XIX**(1), 65–92.

Cendejas Bueno, J.L. (2018). "Justicia, mercado, y precio en Francisco de Vitoria," *Revista Empresa y Humanismo*, **XXI**(1), 9–38.

Fernández Ruiz-Gálvez, E. (2017). "El *totus orbis* y el *ius gentium* en Francisco de Vitoria: el equilibrio entre tradición e innovación," *Cuadernos Electrónicos de Filosofía del Derecho*, **35**. doi: 10.7203/CEFD.35.9671.

Maritain, J. (1951). *Man and the State*, Chicago, IL: University of Chicago Press.

Salas, V.M. (2012). "Francisco de Vitoria on the *ius gentium* and the American *indios*," *Ave Maria Law Review*, **10**(2), 331–41.

Sison, A.J.G. (2018). "Virtue ethics and natural law responses to human rights quandaries in business," *Business and Human Rights Journal*, **3**(2), 1–22. doi: 10.1017/bhj.2018.5.

Sison, A.J.G. and Fontrodona, J. (2012). "The common good of the firm in the Aristotelian-Thomistic tradition," *Business Ethics Quarterly*, **22**(2), 211–46. doi: 10.5840/beq.201222218.

Sison, A.J.G., Ferrero, I. and Guitián, G. (2016). "Human dignity and the dignity of work. Insights from Catholic Social Teaching," *Business Ethics Quarterly*, **26**(4), 503–28. doi: 10.1017/beq.2016.18.

Tierney, B. (1997). *The Idea of Natural Rights. Studies on Natural Rights, Natural Law, and Church Law*, Atlanta, GA: Scholars Press for Emory University.

Vitoria, Francisco de (1991). *Vitoria: Political Writings* (ed. A. Pagden and J. Lawrence), Cambridge: Cambridge University Press.

Vitoria, Francisco de (2006). *Contratos y usura: In Summum Theologiae, II-II, qq. 77–78* (introduction, translation, and notes by Maria Idoya Zorroza), Pamplona: EUNSA.

12. "Troubling times" on the agenda of business ethics: drafting a dialogue approach, aiming at a consensus*

Johannes Brinkmann

Business ethicists, along with many others, find themselves in "troubling times" in the latter half of the 2010s: government right-wing populism, resurgent nationalism, fear in the heartland, loathing at the borders. In this chapter, I propose that business ethicists' distinctive skills in critical reflection and in inviting critical self-reflection in others can be translated into a promising strategy for addressing these troubles and effecting societal climate improvement. Risk and uncertainty are key ingredients of these troubles, and our responses to them must not promise false certainties – or we would become as dishonest as the ideologues we condemn. Rather, we must take on these risks and uncertainties, with a humble attitude of critical self-reflection.

After briefly setting forth my understanding of risk and uncertainty and explaining how risk and uncertainty underlie the troubling times in which we find ourselves, I show how a dialogue approach could address these risks and uncertainties (and, thereby, the troubling times). In such a dialogue approach, community members share different viewpoints to a social problem, similar to the stakeholder role-playing exercises that business ethicists often use in their classes. In discussing the social problem, dialogue participants aim for consensus (as we do in our business ethics classes). Even if consensus is not always possible, keeping this as our ideal allows participants to understand the difficulties inherent in their own standpoints and to see the promise in others' standpoints. Such mutual understanding is the basis of societal climate improvement.

12.1 RISK AND UNCERTAINTY

When it comes to "troubling times," a fruitful academic frame of reference, as I see it, is "risk society" or "world risk society," as developed by late sociologist Ulrich Beck (1992, 1995, 1998, 2009). Risks are possibilities of loss or harm, which are more or less measurable, manageable, insurable, attributable, voluntary, and/or justifiable (see, for a further elaboration of this frequently used but complex term, Brinkmann 2013; Brinkmann et al. 2014). A meaningful common denominator across our current troubles (specifically focused on growing right-wing populism) is risk, which seems to call for risk management or risk governance (Renn 2008), for risk and responsibility sharing (Brinkmann 2013). I discuss the problem of growing right-wing populism, and its basis in risk and uncertainty, in turn.

Populism has been defined as a "a thin-centered ideology that considers society to be ultimately separated into two homogeneous and antagonistic camps, 'the pure people' versus 'the corrupt elite' and which argues that politics should be an expression of the 'volonté générale of the people'" (Mudde and Kaltwasser 2017, p. 6). Populism is the opposite of elitism, which believes that "the people" are potentially dangerous, dishonest, and vulgar, and pluralism, which sees diversity rather as a strength than a weakness (Mudde and Kaltwasser 2017, p. 7). Certain types of political parties (and even more so political leaders) are good at discovering, seeing, and mobilizing voter segments who feel threatened by societal developments they neither understand nor like. Some of these societal developments include globalization, financialization, digitization, and multiculturalism.

In uncertain times, with complex and interdependent uncertainties and risks, there is a potential demand for simple messages, and such a demand is more or less successfully met by right-wing populist parties and their more or less charismatic leaders. Defining ingredients of such right-wing politics and their messages are: a populist rhetoric, anti-elitism, anti-system, not least a claim of speaking for the "common people" (see Mudde and Kaltwasser 2017 for further elaboration; or with a focus on an empirical mapping of its causes, see Inglehart and Norris 2016, investigating an economic insecurity versus a cultural backlash "thesis" when it comes to the roots of right-wing populism on its demand side).

12.2 BUSINESS ETHICS

Business ethics emphasizes critical reflection, using ethical frameworks to evaluate our society, including its troubling times, and not least exploiting our potential to make a difference (especially in troubling times). Such critical reflection invites, in turn, self-critical reflection among business practitioners and business scholars, including criticism of ideologies, of the economic system, of the contexts and consequences of doing business nationally and globally.

With such a critical understanding of the purpose and objectives of business, a strong focus on practicing, teaching, and learning via dialogue makes sense (cf. Brinkmann 2015; Brinkmann et al. 2016). More concretely, a potential contribution of business ethics teaching and research when critically addressing right-wing populism and its roots could begin in discourses about the economy and the public sector, about marketing and consumer ethics, about income inequality and poverty.

The remainder of the chapter will focus on four different strategies for triggering reflection, each associated with business ethics teaching and research, each apparently fruitful for addressing the troubling times in which we find ourselves.

12.3 THE USE OF SCENARIOS FOR TRIGGERING REFLECTION

Many business ethicists use, for example, stakeholder role-play scenarios to address and explore ethical controversies in business in their courses. In such scenarios, students consider an ethical controversy in business from various perspectives, such as: shareholder, employee, competitor, customer, and community member (or others, as they are relevant to a particular case). Each student takes up the part of a particular stakeholder and the students discuss the decision with one another, focusing on how the decision affects each stakeholder represented. The exercise builds empathy for the divergent perspectives on a single decision as well as problem-solving skills as students search for consensus among the various viewpoints. In seeking consensus, students realize that all perspectives are fallible and gain humility about the relative importance of their own interests (cf. Kvalnes and Brinkmann 2019).

12.4 THE USE OF LITERATURE FOR TRIGGERING REFLECTION

Exploring literature-based narratives (see, e.g., Brinkmann 2009, 2011a, 2011b, 2017) is also helpful in such discourses. The goal is to improve the students' critical thinking, their moral imagination and to develop their abilities to empathize with others. In addition to offering literature-based narratives which are self-contained as works of art and food for thought, business ethicists strive in their classes to support students' individual reflections by asking fruitful follow-up questions. With or without offering literature pieces as a point of departure[1] and then trying to build a bridge to the students' own experience with comparable situations, for example, instructors might ask:

- Is there a risk of becoming morally complicit by looking another way?
- Is it naïve to plan to make all human beings good, with improving them as a back-up plan, only?
- Is there a moral obligation to stay alive, not to give up against the evil ones in power, rather than feeling offended and withdrawing?

12.5 THE USE OF "SOCRATIC" DIALOGUES FOR TRIGGERING REFLECTION

Another option is to address a particular dialogue question using a "Socratic" dialogue design. Usually, for shortening dialogue time and for better facilitator preparation, a dialogue starts with a given dialogue question. For example, the German *Philosophisch-politische Akademie* (PPA) in its invitation for the February 2018 seminar announced the following dialogue group alternatives, by topic (http://www.philosophisch-politische-akademie.de/sggrund.html, see also http://www.socraticdialogue.org/):

- Should we strive for a "dominant" culture?
- What does it mean to be responsible for what I say?
- Under what circumstances is it justified to break certain rules?

Or, given the focus of our seminar on "troubling times," we could consider dialogue questions such as:

- Are we as business ethics persons co-responsible for the ethical climate in business and society (or is it ok to leave such responsibility to others)?
- What is a good way of voicing one's moral concerns (or frustrations) towards individuals with different convictions?
- What is the difference between an enlightening and a misleading simplification?
- Is it possible to understand without necessarily agreeing?
- Should one tolerate intolerance?
- Is it naïve to counter "troubling times" ethically rather than strategically?
- What is *Fremdschämen*, or: What does it mean if I feel ashamed to be American (or Turkish, or Hungarian, or West German)?

In the normal case where one departs from a dialogue question, a typical dialogue might proceed as follows:

- presentation of the dialogue question (such as those broached above) to be addressed
- participants share relevant experiences (as stories) to generate a narrative to be discussed
- participants select a story to focus on
- story elaboration
- participants developing core statements, rules, and principles to address the dialogue question
- regressive abstraction, perhaps leading to consensus
- a brief answer to the dialogue question.

An example story (related to the co-responsibility question above) might be a colleague sharing an experience of writing a traditional or social media contribution, building a bridge between one's teaching and research and one's concern about the contagiousness of decreasing interpersonal decency, as a consequence of political leaders serving as assumed bad role models. After choosing such a story among other participant stories and then elaborating it further until one felt a sufficient understanding of the story, a kind of joint ownership, one would try to develop a joint understanding of presuppositions, concepts, and other important abstractions in the story (continuously going back and forth between the abstract and the concrete), and eventually aim at a consensual answer of the dialogue question, perhaps modified or extended by additional questions.

If time and circumstances permit, one can start the dialogue one stage earlier, by developing the dialogue question, or even concentrate on dialogue question development, as a "preparatory dialogue" (see Kessels et al. 2009, pp. 47–51), for developing promising dialogue topics, either for ourselves or for various target groups (such as business leaders or even potential right-wing populism supporters or opponents).

12.6 A MODIFICATION: THE USE OF SOCRATIC *RISK* DIALOGUES FOR TRIGGERING REFLECTION

One of the strengths (but also the limitations) of the Socratic dialogue design is its focus on personal past experience, in its rule to focus on investigating, understanding, and evaluating something that happened in the past, as consensually as possible. In order to find usable solutions to questions about new risks, such as those associated with contemporary right-wing populism, by contrast, one needs so-called "risk dialogues" (https://www.risiko-dialog.ch/overview-in-english; according to this Swiss-German initiative, risk dialogues involve public debate about matters of great consequence with the aim of addressing the risks in a socially tolerable way). On the one hand, such risk dialogues represent an extension of stakeholder dialogues emulated in business ethics classes (mentioned above), a well-known key approach in business ethics, which business ethicists share mainly with business school colleagues in, for example, strategy, corporate communication, and corporate governance. In the context of our seminar, a hybrid of Socratic dialogue design which includes risk-related topics looks promising:

- What can be risks and opportunities in a dialogue with potential supporters of right-wing populism?
- Which societal or global risks and uncertainties are you most worried about, and whom would you trust to mitigate to manage them successfully?
- Can one justify political brinkmanship, that is, gambling for moral luck?

12.7 A FINAL REMARK

Leonard Nelson, the re-inventor of Socratic dialogue, was a colleague, a German professor of philosophy at Göttingen University, who wanted his students to learn philosophizing, to think critically themselves rather than more or less uncritically referring to thoughts and formulations of philosophers. This could also be a message for those of us who teach business ethics, do business ethics research, and attend conferences. We owe our students and one another as colleagues to trigger independent thinking, to develop new and personal ideas, instead of hiding behind impressive bodies of literature, and reproducing mainstream paradigms rather than questioning them. Or why not consider Socratic dialogue design as a "slow" investigation alternative to "fast" presentations and interactions at conventional academic conferences?

NOTES

* The author wishes to thank Tobey Scharding for good editing work. Any remaining imperfections are the author's responsibility, not hers.

1. When addressing right-wing populism and a possible co-responsibility of business for it one could offer B. Brecht's poem "To those who follow in our wake" or E. Kästner's poem "Mind the automatic firing device."

REFERENCES

Beck, U. (1992). *Risk Society: Towards a New Modernity*. London: Sage.

Beck, U. (1995). *Ecological Politics in an Age of Risk*. Cambridge: Polity Press.

Beck, U. (1998). *World Risk Society*. Cambridge: Polity Press.

Beck, U. (2009). *World at Risk*. Cambridge: Polity Press.

Brinkmann, J. (1995). Ethics of consumer boycotts. In *Proceedings of the ERP Conference*, Leeds University, 2–22 September.

Brinkmann, J. (2009). Using Ibsen in business ethics, *Journal of Business Ethics*, **84**, 11–24.

Brinkmann, J. (2011a). Putting career morality on the agenda of business students. How one could use a play and survey results for triggering moral reflection. In R.R. Sims and W.I. Sauser, Jr (eds), *Experiences in Teaching Business Ethics*. Charlotte, NC: Information Age Press, pp. 83–96.

Brinkmann, J. (2011b). Ethics as a challenge to well-established morality? In O. Jakobsen and L.J.T. Pedersen (eds), *Responsibility, Deep Ecology & the Self*, festschrift in honor of Knut J. Ims. Oslo: Forlag 1, pp. 189–98.

Brinkmann, J. (2013). Combining risk and responsibility perspectives: first steps, *Journal of Business Ethics*, **112**, 567–83.

Brinkmann, J. (2015). Socratic dialogue – designed in the Nelson–Heckmann tradition: a tool for reducing the theory–practice divide in business ethics. In K.J. Ims and L.J.T. Pedersen (eds), *Business and the Greater Good: Rethinking Business Ethics in an Age of Crisis*. Cheltenham, UK and Northampton, MA, USA: Edward Elgar, pp. 240–61.

Brinkmann, J. (2017). Nathan the Wise. Addressing enlightenment, wisdom, and tolerance, *Journal of Business Ethics Education*, **14**, 179–98.

Brinkmann, J., M. Hoffman and M. Aarset (2014). Risk. In *Wiley Encyclopedia of Management*, Vol. 2, pp. 414–17 (online version 2015, doi: 10.1002/9781118785317).

Brinkmann, J., B. Lindemann and R. Sims (2016). Voicing moral concerns: yes, but how? The use of Socratic dialogue methodology, *Journal of Business Ethics*, **139**, 619–31.

Inglehart, R.F. and P. Norris (2016). Trump, Brexit, and the rise of populism . . ., Faculty research working paper series, Harvard Kennedy School, available at: https://papers.ssrn.com/sol3/papers.cfm?abstract_id=2818659 (accessed 6 August 2019).

Kessels, J., E. Boers and P. Mostert (2009). *Free Space: Field Guide to Conversations*. Amsterdam: Boom.

Kvalnes, Ø. and J. Brinkmann (2019). Role-play in a Norwegian business ethics education context, Paper in review.

Mudde, C. and C.R. Kaltwasser (2017). *Populism: A Very Short Introduction*. Oxford: Oxford University Press.

Renn, O. (2008). *Risk Governance*. London: Earthscan.

13. An ethical problem in troubled times: ethical decision making by local managers employing an immigrant workforce in Gaziantep, Turkey

Mahmut Arslan and Mustafa K. Yilmaz

13.1 INTRODUCTION

The aim of this chapter is to reveal the understanding of managers on ethical decision making in hiring Syrian immigrant workers in Gaziantep province, Turkey. The Syrian civil war was a big crisis that created huge refugee waves and related humanitarian problems in the region. As a neighboring country, Turkey was faced with millions of war refugees. In this troubled time, Turkish managers had new challenges in making ethical decisions. Gaziantep province is the most troubled province in the South East of Turkey.

Gaziantep is a highly industrialized metropolis on the Syrian border with a population of over two million. After the Syrian civil war, the city has accommodated most of the Syrian refugees. By 2017, it is estimated that about four million refugees from Syria live in Turkey and Gaziantep hosts approximately 400,000 refugees being the second biggest industrial city with Syrian refugees after Istanbul. Although an estimated 600,000 Syrians live in Istanbul, their percentage is only 4 percent of the population, whereas it is almost 20 percent in Gaziantep.

Research question: How do Syrian immigrant refugees affect the ethical decision-making process of managers and company owners in Gaziantep province in Turkey? To what extent are they using utilitarian or Kantian approaches in their decision-making process? And how did their decision-making process change after the arrival of Syrian immigrants?

We adopted a phenomenological research philosophy. The intention was not to generate results applicable to all managers in Turkey but to try to understand the feelings of business managers in Gaziantep toward the

Syrian immigrant workforce. For this purpose, semi-structured interviews were conducted to gather data for a qualitative analysis. A total of 24 top managers from industrial companies in Gaziantep, including the chairman of the Gaziantep Chamber of Industry, were interviewed for the field work of this research.

We conducted 24 in-depth interviews in the field study. Polkinghorne (1989) noted that in phenomenological research, in-depth interviews with 5 to 25 participants who have experienced the same phenomena are sufficient for a sample size. In-depth interviews provide an intimate and secure environment that is ideal for establishing rapport and facilitating the discussion of potentially sensitive topics such as attitudes about migrant workers. When sufficiently reassured, in-depth interviews allow respondents to talk about their experiences, whether they are positive or negative, uninhibited by the presence of others. Paired in-depth interviews were also used in this study. Interviewing two persons together can be a revealing process, giving insights into different priorities, attitudes, and the role each person plays in decision making. Such interviews are also necessary for some larger firms where employment and training are separate responsibilities held by two different persons. This method allows the research to cover both employment and training issues in a single interview.

All managers in this study have at least ten years' experience in their industry. A semi-structured interview questionnaire was used and conducted in-person during the research process. Participants were asked to comment on statements. While some statements endorse Kantian ethics based on duty, others endorse utilitarian ethics. We asked the managers to tell their stories based on each statement. Their answers are not simple endorsements, but short narratives that describe the facts and their feelings about them. As a result of this type of data/information gathering process, we used narrative analysis as a methodology. It should also be noted that people tell stories in different situations and in different ways. Stories are not created in a social vacuum but are shaped by social context and interactions between the story-teller and audiences. Furthermore, in this research we focused on how stories are presented and why they are told. We believe that a story is merely a selective reconstruction or version of events. This approach may help us to identify issues or events that are significant to the individual telling the story.

13.2 IMMIGRANT WORKFORCE IN TURKEY AND RELATED LITERATURE

The immigrant workforce is an essential topic in the applied ethics literature. People escaping from war zones have no choices but to immigrate to neighboring countries. The civil war in Syria created waves of immigrants to Turkey and Europe. Turkey welcomed about four million asylum seekers and provided the basic needs for survival. The civil war in Syria started in 2011 involving numerous actors in a short time, leading to one of the worst humanitarian crises in the world. Erdoğan explains the situation in Turkey until 2017:

> As of the end of 2017, the crisis continues and is unlikely to come to an end in the short term. Even after the war is over, its impact will be felt deeply across the country. Unfortunately, everything has changed for the Syrians who lost their lives, homelands as well as their future, to the extent that it cannot be reverted back to 2011. (Erdoğan, 2017)

As a result of this tragedy, a reasonably young workforce appeared in the Turkish labor market.

Their arrival resulted in some ethical problems for local managers and company owners. A recent field study report conducted by the Business and Human Rights Resource Center (BHRRC, 2016) revealed that undeclared subcontracting is a persistent issue for textile brands that source from Turkey, which threatens their ability to identify potentially vulnerable workers. Some leading textile brands are building open and supportive relationships with first-tier suppliers that go beyond compliance so that they could understand where vulnerable workers in their supply chain are. The report argued that if accompanied by a meaningful dialogue with workers, this can be effective in tackling abuse. Low wages, child labor, and sexual abuse are reported to be the reality for some Syrian refugees working without a permit in Turkey, posing a significant challenge for the garment brands that source from the country to supply European markets. This report summarizes the responses of 28 of Europe's largest clothes brands who were asked to explain how they are protecting Syrian refugees in their supply chain. It seems that a few of them are taking some decisive actions, but many are doing too little (Goethals et al., 2017).

Turkey currently hosts a considerable number of the refugee population in the world amounting to 3.5 million. Refugees can find jobs, but almost all of them work in the informal job sector and face temporary employment for long hours, under difficult working conditions, with low wages, often paid late, if they receive payment at all (Leghtas and Hollingsworth, 2017).

In early 2016, Turkey introduced a system for issuing work permits to Syrian refugees. Turkey's decision was a significant step forward, but nearly two years later, the reality is that these work permits remain inaccessible for the vast majority of refugees in Turkey. Both Syrian business owners and employees need to have work permits. While there are now at least 6000 Syrian-owned businesses in Turkey, for those who are not able or not interested in opening their own businesses, work permits are rare. Employers must apply for the work permit on behalf of the refugees they seek to employ. They have to pay a fee for it and prove that they cannot find a Turkish citizen to fulfill that job. As pockets of hostility toward Syrian refugees appear to be increasing, the need arises for strong incentives from the Turkish government and international community, including the private sector, to encourage employers to hire more refugees (Leghtas and Hollingsworth, 2017).

Although the work permit for Syrian refugees under temporary protection in Turkey was regulated in January 2016, it is not sufficient. Since the regulation only around 10,000 Syrians have joined the workforce by getting their work permits. Syrians living in urban areas do not have many other options except working to sustain their lives. Though it is assumed that 800,000 to one million Syrians are part of the workforce, they work in unregistered status. Syrians do not really compete with local people for jobs because of their low wages, low-level jobs, and difficult working conditions. It has become an accepted fact that Syrians participate in the Turkish economy, even if informally. However, it is clear that such a large informal workforce is not sustainable. Interestingly enough, the real tensions within the Turkish society pertain not to the Syrian workforce but rather to the new businesses they establish (Erdoğan, 2017).

An AIDA (Asylum Information Database) report (2018) indicated that the number of work permits issued to temporary protection beneficiaries in Turkey has increased following the adoption of the regulation on 15 January 2016. During 2017, Syrians represented 24.5 percent of work permits granted to foreigners in Turkey. By the end of 2017, between 6000 and 8000 businesses were owned by Syrian nationals. Civil society organizations are important employers for Syrians under temporary protection. Despite the legal framework introduced in 2016 to regulate the access of temporary protection beneficiaries to the labor market, substantial gaps persist concerning access to employment in practice. Beneficiaries receive little or no information on the work permit system, as the number of community centers providing information about such opportunities remains limited. There are seven such centers in Istanbul, where a large population of Syrian refugees resides. Syrians in Turkey are affected by the widespread practice of undeclared employment under substandard working conditions and low wages. Undeclared employment flourishes, especially in the agricultural sector. In other provinces such as Muğla, unreported employment frequently occurs in the construction sector. The wages of 46 percent of Syrians and 20 percent of Turkish workers are below the minimum wage level in Istanbul, in the textile industry. According to the report, it seems that the minimum wage is not applicable in unregistered textile workshops. In terms of stratification of wages in the labor market, Turkish men are at the top, followed by Turkish women, while Syrian men are close to the bottom and Syrian women are at the bottom. About 99.6 percent of Syrian men and all Syrian women working in this industry are informally employed without social security. Unacceptable working conditions in urban centers often lead to large-scale movements such as the November 2017 strike of shoemakers in major cities including Istanbul, İzmir, Adana, Gaziantep, Konya, and Manisa, demanding lawful employment and better working conditions. Poor health and safety conditions are also a matter of concern. Women, in particular, face significant challenges in obtaining adequate access to the labor market. This situation is both due to obstacles such as lack of childcare, lack of information, and training opportunities and traditional gender roles assigned to women as caretakers, especially in Southern Turkey regions.

Additionally, when women get jobs outside their homes in the textile industry, they often face discrimination and ill-treatment. This is especially true for unregistered workshops in Istanbul. The Turkish labor market also presents particular risks for children, given the widespread phenomenon of child labor in textile factories as well as in restaurants in big cities. That is why the Ministry of Employment and Social Security announced a six-year National Action Plan to Fight against Child Labor in 2017, and 2018 is declared as the year of the fight against child labor in Turkey.

A BHRRC report (2016) pointed out that the decision of the Turkish government to allow Syrian refugees to apply for work permits is a welcome move. Giving refugees legal status would mean that they will emerge from the informal workforce to a formal one with new legal rights and protections. However, it would be unrealistic to think of work permits for Syrian refugees as a magic wand that will solve all problems. The legislation does not ensure a work permit for every Syrian refugee in Turkey in all circumstances. First, a refugee will have to wait six months after registering in Turkey under "temporary protection status" and the work permit will be restricted to the city in which they first registered – which will not necessarily be where the Syrian refugees wish to reside or seek to work, particularly if many register in border towns where job opportunities are limited. These restrictions mean it is highly likely that there will still be desperate Syrian refugees who are willing to work in exploitative conditions. Second, Syrians will only be able to make up to 10 percent of an employer's staff (although there is some flexibility in certain cases). So, there will be a significant number of refugees still in the informal workforce. There may also be some additional problems about how the permits will function in real life. The regulation states that Syrians may work in cities where they are allowed to reside and are registered. However, in practice, the local authorities in certain cities such as Antalya, a well-known tourist destination, decided that Syrians cannot reside there. It is difficult to know how this will play out. It is also not clear whether the work permits will overcome the problem of Syrian child labor. Also, there will naturally be tensions with the local population, particularly given the high domestic unemployment rate during the economic crisis in 2016. Brands must consider all these issues and fight against abuse, exploitation, and wage depression. Collaboration both within the industry and with civil society and trade unions will be the key to ensure proper working conditions (BHRRC, 2016).

The immigrant workforce is generally seen as a remedy for lack of local labor by business organizations in developed economies. Business ethics is not the main issue in hiring them. Nguyen (2008) stated that US corporations are facing dual crises with an aging workforce and a shrinking pool of younger talent. The current workforce consists primarily of baby boomers who are beginning to reach retirement age, and prospects for replacing the existing workers do not look promising. Some corporations are turning to immigrants to alleviate these problems. While there are benefits of having immigrants in the workforce, issues related to cultural and value differences also exist. Nguyen (2008) suggested that corporations must develop strategies to utilize and retain immigrants to remain competitive effectively. This suggestion is of course ethically questionable. Forde and MacKenzie (2010) investigated the role of employment agencies toward the refugee workforce in the UK. They argued that these agencies could focus on more than just the first transition of migrants into the labor market; they can formalize transitions within the labor market and link people to jobs that are more appropriate to their skills and experience as a means of preventing the perpetuation of skill underutilization.

Lundborg and Skedinger (2016) reported that they found a favorable attitude toward refugees on the part of Swedish employers, although social desirability may have biased their responses. Employers believe that refugees have generally lived up to their expectations in terms of productivity and language skills. However, such satisfaction with the job performance of refugees seems not to have been achieved by those employers who spent more resources on screening these workers than other staff. They stated that while they found little indication of generally negative employer attitudes toward refugees, this should not be interpreted as evidence of the absence of discrimination against these workers. An important finding of their survey is perhaps the heterogeneity of employer responses across different types of firms. This heterogeneity manifests itself in a variety of ways: differences in attitudes toward the anticipated employment effect of a hypothesized wage cut, differences in attitudes regarding the job performance of refugees, and differences across industries. In line with much of previous research, they find that most firms in the survey would be reluctant to lower wages for low-skilled workers. These firms tend to agree with at least one of the statements that wage reductions would be detrimental to worker cohesion, work effort, or the quality of job applicants. Accordingly, most firms do not regard minimum wages as a critical obstacle to the hiring of refugees. However, firms with many refugees on the payroll report that cutting minimum wage rates would contribute considerably to increasing employment (Lundborg and Skedinger, 2016).

Icduygu and Diker (2017) pointed out that the mass influx of Syrian refugees into Turkey has accelerated the ongoing legislative initiatives on the issue of migration. Adoption of the work permit regulation for temporary protection status holders in early 2016 is indicative of a shift toward long-term planning concerning three million Syrians. Many remain informally employed under poor working conditions. They suggested that policymakers should focus on the regulations that prevent refugees' engagement in the informal market without harming them and encourage employers to hire Syrians by providing incentives. Further, they argued that designing skills building programs that recognize refugees' skills and match them with the needs of the market will both improve refugees' quality of life and contribute to the economy.

Korkmaz (2016) stated that a large informal sector, child labor, long working hours, and problems over freedom of association are endemic within Turkey's garment industry. The movement of the Syrian refugees and their participation in the labor market has made these problems much worse and much more complicated. In the garment-textile-leather sectors, in addition to one million formal workers, it is estimated that almost one million more workers are employed informally. They do not have the legal right to receive the minimum wage, and their employers do not pay taxes and other social security contributions.

As the Turkish garment industry relies on quickly providing low-cost quality products, there has been a long-standing relationship between formal and informal economies. As formal workplaces are generally suppliers to international brands, they usually comply with the requirements of the Turkish law, international standards, and the codes of conduct of global brands. However, there are no such binding rules in the informal sector and authorities are not willing to take concrete and effective steps to eliminate such forms of business. To produce low-cost, quality products rapidly, formal companies have been mobilizing large networks of other workplaces, many of them being informal, to meet deadlines. With the movement of Syrian refugees into Turkey, the character of informality began to be transformed. Before, informal and formal workers were

Turkish citizens. Now, since the informal sector began to employ Syrian refugees, this situation has become more complicated and has caused an ethnic concentration in the industry (Korkmaz, 2016).

Similarly, Cihan Kızıl (2016) in his book chapter titled as "Turkey's Policy on Employment of Syrian Refugees and its Impact on the Turkish Labor Market" pointed out that Turkey put into force the regulation granting work permits to those under temporary protection five years after the outbreak of the Syrian crisis. Syrians are treated as a cheap labor force by small firms in Turkey. Syrians, especially with lack of the Turkish language, will continue to be exploited. However, there are a lot of medium- and large-sized companies searching for qualified workers in Turkey and now they can hire Syrian workers legally with the help of this regulation.

On the other hand, following the regulation, the labor supply in the formal labor market gradually increases; as a consequence, a decrease in wages and an increase in the unemployment rate for natives is anticipated. However, these effects might be smaller than expected because the regulation brings a 10 percent quota for the Syrian workforce. We expect that informal employment of Syrians will continue, and low-skilled Turkish workers in particular might lose their jobs or be forced to accept low wages. There will be competition in the labor market for more qualified Turkish workers as well. However, high-skilled natives might face weaker competition since the highly skilled Syrian workforce has already left the country.

A European Parliament report (2016a) indicates that for the majority of refugees, labor market integration is the most relevant durable solution. There is a widely shared consensus among experts that labor market participation is the most critical step to successful integration into host societies as presumably high numbers of asylum seekers and refugees will stay in the European Union (EU) for years. The EU Common Basic Principles of Immigrant Integration (2016) also state that

> employment is a vital part of the integration process and is central to the participation of immigrants, to the contributions immigrants make to the host society. Over the medium to long term, a positive economic impact can only be achieved if the refugees are well integrated into the labor market. Of course, this requires high investments into human capital, especially in countries where the recent inflow of refugees is seen as an opportunity to address skill shortages in an aging society. Full integration of refugees may help to close demographic and labor supply gaps in the context of an aging society. (European Parliament, 2016a)

The integration barriers identified are:

- language (including literacy), especially vocational (major priority)
- lack of work experience in the host country

- lack of host country references
- lack of appropriate training or unrecognized educational and professional qualifications
- lack of access to networks which would strengthen employment prospects and knowledge of recruitment methods (MPC, 2016).

Another European Parliament Report (2016b) is about Turkey, and it depicts that Turkey has taken significant steps on the regulations which aim to create an attractive economic environment and to facilitate the application process of work permits for foreigners as part of the integration policies. Furthermore, social integration policies are described as rather weak but have started to develop since the recent immigration flow from Syria. It is suggested that even though there have been improvements in the integration policies, policymakers should focus on the implementation of more stable and long-term policies and practices.

Companies interested in employing refugees may have numerous motivations, ranging from corporate social responsibility (CSR) to a desire to benefit from the new pool of cheap labor. While many companies are motivated to employ refugees, practical obstacles such as language skills, cultural differences, and issues related to the experience of forced displacement often stand in the way of employing them. These barriers seem to frequently override the benefits of having an enlarged workforce, as perceived by companies. Although legal frameworks differ across countries, employers referred to similar obstacles during the consultations: uncertainty regarding rights and length of stay, the need for information on skills and matching, training and hiring costs and lack of business incentives, and problems with attitudes and expectations. Even when legal access to the labor market is granted, some factors may stand in the way of employing refugees and asylum seekers (OECD/UNHCR, 2016).

Ruhs and Chang (2004) examined the critical ethical questions in the design of labor immigration programs. Their theoretical framework inspired us to construct our field study using deontological and utilitarian dimensions. They propose a two-dimensional matrix of ethical space that isolates many different ethical structures on the basis of the degree of consequentialism they allow and the moral standing they accord to non-citizens.

They argue for the rejection of extreme consequentialism and propose criteria that should guide national policymakers in their choice and application of a frame within the ethical subspace of moderate consequentialism and moderate moral standing for non-citizens. To translate these "ethical guidelines" for the design of labor immigration programs into policy practice, they advocated new types of temporary foreign worker programs. In contrast to many existing and past guest worker policies, the programs that they propose would more actively promote the interests of migrant workers and sending countries by more clearly defining, and more effectively enforcing, certain core rights of migrant workers.

13.3 DATA AND METHODOLOGY

Deontology is also known as ethics of duties and was developed by German philosopher Immanuel Kant. According to Kantian ethics, morality consists of our will to act on duties. He argued that some actions are right or wrong regardless of their consequences (Stackhouse et al., 1995). Right or wrong cannot be changed by time and place. Kant believed that happiness and benefits could not be reference points for morality since happiness is a subjective reality of each person. For Kant, the ethical imperative has to be based on something stable, unchangeable, and everlasting that is a natural ethical law. It is not a hypothetical imperative, but a categorical imperative. One should act according to the maxim that you would wish all other rational people to follow as if it were a universal law (Goodin, 1994).

From a Kantian point of view, business ethics should follow universal ethical principles. Benefits and costs should not be reference points to determine what is good or bad in the workplace. Some values can be different in different cultures, but the business world needs universal ethical principles in business organizations (Stenberg, 1994).

Utilitarianism is also a part of a broader concept of consequentialism or teleology. According to the classical utilitarian approach, the aim of human life is to pursue happiness and pleasure. Utilitarianism advocates that actions initially are not good or bad (Shaw and Barry, 1992). Consequences of actions make them good or bad, and they can be measured by the amount of utility gained (Pettit, 1994). According to the utility approach, less evil can be tolerated to avoid a bigger evil. Hobbes, Mill, Hume, and Bentham were utilitarian philosophers (Bentham, 1998).

After classical or act utilitarianism, some philosophers developed rule utilitarianism in the light of criticism to act utilitarianism. Brandt (1996) developed rule utilitarianism which advocates that utilitarian standards should be applied to whole ethical rules. Utilitarianism encourages business companies to reconsider their business policies in terms of the consequences they produced. It should be noted that some unethical business practices can easily be justified using utility as an ethical reference point. The utilitarian decision-making process is also questionable by virtue ethics and theory of justice (Smith, 1976).

Seven utilitarian and seven deontological statements were used in the research. Utilitarian statements explain a situation from a utilitarian perspective, and deontological statements explain the situation based on the ethics of duties. Although some statements are not about immigrants, these statements were used to understand the general ethical inclination of the 24 participants. For this reason, we added a statement about waste management. Gaziantep city has a high-tech sustainable waste management system. We used this statement as a control question so that we could gauge the ethical tendencies of participants. We wanted to know whether they took a utilitarian or deontological approach to ethical questions on other topics.

- Utilitarian statements: (U1) A business firm should only serve society through an increasing level of employment and GNP.
- (U2) Society should accept some social costs of business firms, including environmental pollution simply because business firms create jobs and employ people.
- (U3) Illegal employment of foreign immigrants will provide economic benefits to society. It will reduce labor costs; make business firms more profitable and productive. As a result of this, national income will increase.
- (U4) Illegal employment of foreign immigrants will help to keep them away from hunger, poverty, and crime.
- (U5) Illegal employment of refugees serves society through preventing crime.
- (U6) The existence of a refugee workforce helps different industries in Turkey to find employees for unwanted jobs which do not attract the attention of local people.
- (U7) Regarding waste management, it is more than enough for business organizations to follow up local regulations.

Deontological statements:

- (D1) Waste management needs precautions beyond local regulations.
- (D2) When we make a decision in the organization, the first question we ask should be whether that decision is right or wrong, rather than if it is beneficial or harmful.
- (D3) It is wrong to hire immigrants illegally, no matter how useful they are.
- (D4) Obeying rules and regulations is much more important than providing benefits to organizations or society.

- (D5) Integrating immigrants into society and providing them with job opportunities is a duty of the government rather than the duty of business firms.
- (D6) It is not fair to give responsibility to society to pay the costs of pollution created by business companies.
- (D7) It is simply against human rights to employ an immigrant worker illegally for dirty or inconvenient jobs that generally do not attract local people.

13.4 SUMMARY OF FINDINGS

Table 13.1 shows the endorsements of the statements.

13.5 DISCUSSION OF FINDINGS

We choose some critical phrases from the stories of participants. When we directed questions to them, we also encouraged them to tell their stories informally. This approach helped them to express their feelings wholeheartedly. Some critical quotations from the participants showed us how they had changed their ethical reasoning over time.

(U1) A business firm should only serve society through an increasing level of employment and GNP. This statement does not recognize any social or ethical responsibility of business, it only covers economic responsibilities. If a firm provides useful economic benefits to society, there should be no other ethical expectation. From a deontic point of view, this understanding limits the duties of business organizations to economic and legal responsibilities, and the ethical reasoning behind this statement is the utility provided by the companies. We observed that 20 of 24 participants endorsed this statement. They mentioned a high unemployment rate and low-income level in Turkey and stated that the most important responsibility of business companies should be to create new jobs for educated unemployed youth in Turkey. Only 4 participants acknowledged that business firms should serve society not only by producing economic outcomes but also by fulfilling some social responsibilities. For instance, Participant 23 stressed that:

> Serving society by increasing level of employment is fine, but we should ask first how?

Table 13.1 Endorsements of the statements

Statements	Endorsements n = 24
(U1) A business firm should only serve society through an increasing level of employment and GNP.	20/24
(U2) Society should accept some social costs of business firms including environmental pollution simply because business firms create jobs and employ people.	5/24
(U3) Illegal employment of foreign immigrants will provide economic benefits to society. It will reduce labor costs, make business firms more profitable and productive. As a result of this, national income will increase.	3/24
(U4) Illegal employment of foreign immigrants will help to keep them away from hunger, poverty, and crime.	6/24
(U5) Illegal employment of refugees serves society through preventing crime.	3/24
(U6) The existence of a refugee workforce helps different industries in Turkey to find employees for unwanted jobs which do not attract the attention of local people.	4/24
(U7) Regarding waste management, it is more than enough for business organizations to follow up local regulations.	5/24
(D1) Waste management needs precautions beyond local regulations.	20/24
(D2) When we make a decision in the organization, the first question we ask should be whether this decision is right or wrong, rather than if it is beneficial or harmful.	22/24
(D3) It is wrong to hire immigrants illegally, no matter how useful they are.	19/24
(D4) Obeying rules and regulations is much more important than providing benefits to organizations or society.	20/24
(D5) Integrating immigrants into society and providing them with job opportunities is a duty of the government rather than the duty of business firms.	19/24
(D6) It is not fair to give responsibility to society to pay the costs of pollution created by business companies.	24/24
(D7) It is simply against human rights to employ an immigrant worker illegally for dirty or inconvenient jobs that generally do not attract local people.	20/17

(U2) Society should accept some social costs of business firms including environmental pollution simply because business firms create jobs and employ people. We observed few endorsements, that is, only 5 participants, for this statement. They said that pollution is unavoidable in most industrial

activities and a reasonable amount of pollution may be tolerated for the sake of employment.

(U3) Illegal employment of foreign immigrants will provide economic benefits to society. It will reduce labor costs, make business firms more profitable and productive. As a result of this, national income will increase. While nearly half of the participants were in favor of this statement to some extent, only 3 of them showed strong support. These reactions reveal that Turkish managers in Gaziantep acknowledge that using cheap immigrant labor will increase the income level of the province. However, they also stated that the social costs of such economic benefits would also be higher. One of the participants reacted to the statement this way:

> If we are speaking about economic benefits to society by illegal activities I can give you other examples such as growing cannabis or using child labor, they are all very economically beneficial. (Participant 19 (U3))

(U4) Illegal employment of foreign immigrants will help to keep them away from hunger, poverty, and crime. Only 6 participants endorsed this statement. Other participants highlighted that illegal employment is not the only solution to prevent hunger, poverty, and crime. They also added that illegal employment might produce some temporary relief for immigrants, but it may at the same time result in more serious problems after that. One of the participants highlighted the criminal side of illegal employment:

> If you say illegal employment of foreign immigrants will help to keep them away from hunger, poverty, and crime, I can say prostitution and slavery can also provide such benefits too. (Participant 21 (U4))

(U5) Illegal employment of immigrants serves society through preventing crime. This statement is a continuation of (U4) putting more stress on crime rates. Only a few participants stated that it might be a short-term solution. However, they also underlined that illegal employment is also a crime by itself. For instance, a participant said:

> I don't believe that illegal employment can be a remedy. It is also a crime and how can you stop crimes through committing another crime. (Participant 16 (U5))

(U6) The existence of a refugee workforce helps different industries in Turkey to find employees for unwanted jobs which do not attract the attention of local people. There is also minimal support for this statement among participants. Although they accept that many Syrian immigrants work in

undesirable jobs in Gaziantep, they claimed that this work was executed by Kurdish citizens before the arrival of Syrian refugees.

(U7) Regarding waste management, it is more than enough for business organizations to obey local regulations. At first glance, this statement looks as if it reflects a deontological point, but it limits the duties of a business organization into a legal framework. In fact, from a deontological point of view, the duty of a business organization must be "not to pollute." This statement allows business firms to pollute the natural environment with their waste if local regulations are weak. Most of the participants did not endorse this statement. They stated that local regulations could be very flexible or avoidable in some cases. Waste management is taken very seriously by Gaziantep Municipality, and the city has a high-tech sustainable waste management system. We also observed that all participants were environmentally conscious people and this influenced their reactions to this statement. One of the participants complained about water pollution on the beaches of Turkey:

> Last summer, I took my family to a lovely Mediterranean coastal town for a holiday. The resort hotel we were staying in was very luxurious. But we were told by locals that we should not spend much time in the sea because it is polluted by hotels and boats. So we used the pool instead of the beach. I got furious and disappointed. If local regulations are not satisfactory or law enforcement is weak, do you think you are free to pollute seaside and poison innocent people? (Participant 9 (U7))

(D1) Waste management needs precautions beyond local regulations. This statement reflects a strong positive attitude toward duty based on Kantian ethics since it does not limit the environmental duties of a business organization with local regulations. In some cases, local regulations can be unsatisfactory in providing real protection of the environment. From this point of view, a business firm should focus on the real protection of the environment. Most of the participants (20 of them) showed strong endorsement for this statement.

(D2) When we make a decision in the organization, the first question we ask should be whether this decision is right or wrong, rather than if it is beneficial or harmful. Utilitarian approaches give importance to the results of the decisions, while duty ethic focuses on ultimate moral duties. Except 2 of them, all participants strongly agree with this statement. A participant explained how they were confused at the beginning of the crisis:

> At the beginning of the crisis, we were thinking about how we could help the refugees. We did not ask questions such as "am I doing the right thing?" (Participant 3 (D2))

(D3) It is wrong to hire immigrants illegally, no matter how useful they are. Most of the participants (19 of them) agree that illegal employment is wrong. Their common point is that unlawful employment generally involves the exploitation of workers and child labor. However, some of them stated that it could be a temporary solution for refugees when they urgently need a job for survival. We understood from in-depth interviews that interviewees were more tolerant toward illegal employment at the beginning of the refugee crisis; however, they concluded that it is not a real solution for immigrant employment. This is perhaps the most important finding of the study showing their shift from utilitarian reasoning to a more deontological one. One of the participants explains his feelings about the situation:

> I really believe that it is wrong to hire immigrants illegally in any case or unregistered employment whatever the name is. We all know that some small business firms employ unregistered workers and this is their way of producing cheap products with cheap labor. We started our business as a legal organization and obeyed all the rules of the government. At the beginning of the Syrian immigration, we did not have a legal framework to hire them. Some of them insisted on working in our factory as a gardener, cleaning lady or unqualified worker and at that time we thought we are helping them by providing them a temporary low wage simple job. But then we realized that we created trouble with our hands. Since there was no official contract among us, some of them left the job without telling us anything. Some of them left the job when they have better offers and complained to local authorities that we are employing them illegally. Some of them insisted on bringing their relatives to work, and when we said we had no space for them, we confronted with some troubles. After 2015, we took a decision that we will never hire a Syrian immigrant unless he or she had a legal work permit. Now, we have Syrian workers here, thanks to the employment regulation implemented after 2016. This regulation gives us an opportunity in hiring Syrians that get a work permit. We can choose qualified workers among them. (Participant 5 (D3))

(D4) Obeying rules and regulations is much more critical than providing benefits to organizations or society. This statement focuses on the importance of our legal duties. Most of the participants (20 of them) supported this statement. We understand from their comments that they are aware of the fact that sometimes legal duties are not beneficial to the company and even can be financially harmful. One of the participants stressed the difficulty of determining benefits:

> You can know clearly what the rule is, but how can you know correctly what will be the benefit? (Participant 1 (D4))

(D5) Integrating immigrants into society and providing them with job opportunities is a duty of the government rather than the duty of business firms.

This statement clarifies the duties of the government and companies. Most of the participants (19 of them) endorsed this statement. It is an essential reflection of duty ethic or deontology. Most of the participants do not deny the responsibility of businesses to create job opportunities. However, they believed that creating jobs for immigrants is a different subject and needs to be addressed by the government through proper regulations and public expenditure. An explanation by one of the participants about the issue provides a good example:

> Everyone should know his duties. I know my duties, and I work hard to do them. So, I have the right to expect from the authorities to execute their own duties. (Participant 8 (D5))

(D6) It is not fair to give responsibility to society to pay the costs of pollution created by business companies. All participants strongly endorsed this statement. They all pointed out that all companies should be environment-friendly and should protect the environment beyond legal regulations and obligations. Thus, there is a strong consensus among participants about the responsibility of companies in environmental matters.

(D7) It is simply against human rights to employ an immigrant worker illegally for dirty or inconvenient jobs that generally do not attract local people. Most of the participants (20 of them) strongly endorsed this statement. They reported that some people might work in some unwanted jobs and it is not an ethical problem as long as they are well paid. However, offering unwanted jobs to refugee workers with low wages is treated by many participants as an abuse of human rights. A few participants, on the other hand, stated that if refugees voluntarily accept the offer, this can be treated ethically within the market mechanism. One of the participants finds the situation against humanitarian and Islamic values:

> You can't make an excuse if you offer a dirty job to an immigrant with an illegally low wage. This is against Islamic values that we believe and also to all humanitarian values. This is exploitation. Of course, you can offer any dirty job to anybody if you are ready to pay fair compensation to the workers. (Participant 12 (D7))

13.6 CONCLUSION

The estimated four million Syrian refugees are a critical issue in Turkish society. Both the government and businesses must take actions to integrate these people into the labor market so that they can have a better and sustainable life in Turkey. In this respect, the views and attitudes of employers play a vital role in realizing this goal. That is why we designed a questionnaire and conducted interviews with company managers in Gaziantep, the most populated province of Turkey with Syrian refugees, to observe their approaches.

The results revealed that most of the participants to some extent were in favor of a deontological decision-making process rather than a utilitarian method. Our findings are consistent with previous studies. For instance, Mengüç (1998) found that when making ethical decisions, Turkish business people use a deontological ethical approach more than they use teleological evaluations. Similarly, the participants in our case mostly endorsed deontological statements. We found that they were also aware of their duties and what the state should do. Some of the interviewees admitted that they used illegal cheap immigrant labor when immigrants were desperately searching for jobs during the first wave of the refugee crisis. They reported that many Syrians are still working under inappropriate conditions in small companies. For example, one of the participants interestingly accepted the illegal employment of the Syrian workforce with low wages. He believed that it was inevitable in the beginning of the crisis but added that there must be a local regulation for Gaziantep and other Syrian border provinces regarding low-wage work permits. Of course, while producing that statement, he was not aware of the fact that he was using a "categorical imperative principle" of Kant. From a utilitarian point of view, legalizing work permits with a low wage for the refugee workforce looks like a practical solution. However, such legal wage discrimination serves only to foster racism and hostility of local workers against immigrants.

To sum up, many business managers admitted that they had difficulties in decision making at the beginning of the Syrian refugee crisis. They also questioned the morality of their decisions at the time. Most of them said economic and social conflicts misled them when they made some ethical decisions. During the height of the refugee crisis, they had more ethical problems to manage than in normal conditions. All these challenges and troubles led the managers to change the way that they thought about ethical problems.

We also observed that managers of large businesses were more inclined to use deontological reasoning than managers of small companies. They were aware of the long-term harmful effects of opportunist decisions. Although our findings cannot be applied on the national scale, they show us how a group of managers changed the way that they thought about ethics during a crisis. At the beginning of the field research, we were expecting more utilitarian endorsements from the participants. However, we realized that they tended to give priority to economic stability and predictability in their region. They missed the old days when they mainly worked with other Syrian companies.

REFERENCES

AIDA, 2018, Access to the Labor Market Turkey, Asylum Information Database, https://www.asylumineurope.org/reports/country/turkey (accessed 2 November 2018).

Bentham, J., 1998, *Legislator of the World: Writings on Codification, Law, and Education*, ed. Philip Schofield and Jonathan Harris, Oxford: Clarendon Press.

BHRRC Briefing Note, 2016, Syrian Refugees in Turkish Garment Supply Chains: An Analysis of Company Action to Address Reports of Serious Exploitation and Abuse Briefing Note, Danielle McMullan, Senior Researcher, Business and Human Rights Research Center, https://www.business-humanrights.org/ (accessed 22 October 2018).

Brandt, R., 1996, *Facts, Values, and Morality*, Cambridge and New York: Cambridge University Press.

Erdoğan, M.M., 2017, Syrians Barometer 2017 (Draft) Executive Summary, https://mmuraterdogan.com/ (accessed 21 October 2018).

European Parliament, 2016a, *Labour Market Integration of Refugees: Strategies and Good Practices*, IP/A/EMPL/2016-08, March, PE 578.956.

European Parliament, 2016b, *Turkey: Labour Market Integration and Social Inclusion of Refugees*, IP/A/EMPL/2016-13, December, PE 595.328.

Forde, C. and MacKenzie, R., 2010, The Ethical Agendas of Employment Agencies Towards Migrant Workers in the UK: Deciphering the Codes, *Journal of Business Ethics*, **97**, 31–41.

Goethals, S., Bardwell, J., Bhacker, M., and Ezzelarab, B., 2017, Business Human Rights Responsibility for Refugees and Migrant Workers: Turning Policies into Practice in the Middle East, *Business and Human Rights Journal*, **2**, 2.

Goodin, R.E., 1994, Utility and the Good. In P. Singer (ed.). *A Companion to Ethics*, London: Blackwell.

Icduygu, A. and Diker, E., 2017, Labor Market Integration of Syrian Refugees in Turkey: From Refugees to Settlers, *Journal of Migration Studies*, **3**(1), January–June, 12–35.

Kızıl, C., 2016, Turkey's Policy on Employment of Syrian Refugees and its Impact on the Turkish Labour Market. In Deniz Eroğlu, Jeffrey H. Cohen and Ibrahim Sirkeci (eds), *Turkish Migration 2016: Selected Papers*, London: Transnational Press, pp.164–70.

Korkmaz, E.E., 2016, BBC Panorama's Investigation and the Syrian Refugee Workers in the Turkish Garment Industry, International Migration Institute, https://www.imi.ox.ac.uk/blog/bbc-panorama2019s-investigation-and-the-syrian-refugee-workers-in-the-turkish-garment-industry (accessed 2 November 2018).

Leghtas, I. and Hollingsworth, A., 2017, "I am Only Looking for My Rights" Legal Employment Still Inaccessible for Refugees in Turkey, Field Report, https://www.refugeesinternational.org/ (accessed 4 November 2018).

Lundborg, P. and Skedinger, P., 2016, Employer Attitudes Towards Refugee Immigrants: Findings from a Swedish Survey, *International Labour Review*, **155**(2), 315–37.

Mengüç, B., 1998, Organizational Consequences, Marketing Ethics and Salesforce Supervision: Further Empirical Evidence, *Journal of Business Ethics*, **17**(4), 333–52.

MPC (Migration Policy Center), 2016, From Refugees to Workers Mapping Labour – Market Integration Support Measures for Asylum Seekers and Refugees in the EU Member States, http://www.migrationpolicycentre.eu/ (accessed 5 October 2018).

Nguyen, B., 2008, Tomorrow's Workforce: The Needs for Immigrant Workers and Strategies to Retain Them, *Public Personnel Management*, **37**(2), 175–84.

OECD/UNHCR, 2016, Hiring Refugees: What are the Opportunities and Challenges for Employers? *Migration Policy Debates*, No. 10, September.

Pettit, P., 1994, Consequentialism. In P. Singer (ed.), *A Companion to Ethics*, London: Blackwell, pp. 230–40.

Polkinghorne, D.E., 1989, Phenomenological Research Methods. In R.S. Valle and S. Halling (eds), *Existential-Phenomenological Perspectives in Psychology: Exploring the Breadth of Human Experience*, New York: Plenum Press, pp. 41–60.

Ruhs, M. and Chang, H.J., 2004, The Ethics of Labor Immigration Policy, *International Organization*, **58**, Winter, 69–102.

Shaw, W.H. and Barry, V., 1992, *Moral Issues in Business*, London: Woodworth Publishing.

Smith, A., 1976, *An Inquiry into the Nature and Causes of the Wealth of Nations*, ed. R.H. Campbell and A.S. Skinner; textual editor W.B. Todd, Oxford: Clarendon Press.

Stackhouse, M.L., McCann, D.P., Roels, S.J., and Williams, P.N., 1995, *On Moral Business*, Grand Rapids, MI: William B. Eerdmans Publishing.

Stenberg, E., 1994, *Just Business*, London: Warner Books.

PART IV

Applied Topics: Technology and the Environment

14. Corporate leadership versus the Twitter mob*

Chris MacDonald

PROLOGUE

The opening sequence of the first episode of the HBO television series *Deadwood* takes place in May of 1876, in (what was then) Montana Territory. US Marshal Seth Bullock (portrayed by Timothy Olyphant) is keeping guard over the convicted horse-thief Clell Watson, who has been sentenced to death, and who is to be hanged from the gallows across the street in the morning. A drunken mob of would-be vigilantes arrives at the jail, heavily armed, and demands that Bullock turn Watson over to them. They want Watson to receive the punishment that *they* feel he deserves. And *they* want to be the ones to inflict it. The vigilantes have no regard for Bullock's badge, and have him badly outnumbered. In desperation, the marshal brings Watson to the front porch of the jailhouse, throws a rope over a beam, and asks Watson if he has any last words. Clell Watson will die this night, one way or the other. But Bullock's last act as Marshal – he is about to retire from the job, and seek his fortune as a private citizen – is to see that Watson receives the punishment determined by the court to be appropriate, rather than that sought by a band of armed and drunken thugs.

14.1 INTRODUCTION AND EXAMPLES

What are a corporate leader's responsibilities when an employee is subject to vigilante justice at the (virtual) hands of a Twitter[1] mob? In particular, when an employee stands accused of having done wrong off-the-job, and is being vilified for it online, what should an employer's stance be? This question sits at the intersection of two broader questions, namely, what an employer's response should be to off-the-job wrongdoing, and how corporations should respond to public opinion as expressed in social media. When a wrongful act has been committed (or more specifically perhaps when an employer has good grounds to *believe* that a wrong act has been committed), the individual's employer has a choice to make about whether to take action – notwithstanding the fact that the wrongful act in question has, per hypothesis, little direct bearing on the individual's value as an employee. Such situations are rendered more complex, and more pressing, in contexts in which the employee in question has been subjected to the special form of vigilante justice meted out by the Twitter mob.

Should corporations take action against employees in such situations? Is such action permissible, or even admirable? The present chapter attempts to sketch an answer to this question. It begins by outlining a series of relatively recent, high-profile examples. Section 14.2 proceeds to examine the justification companies might have for taking action against employees who have been vilified online for off-duty wrongs. Section 14.3 moves to examine public reaction, and the reasons the public might have for *encouraging* companies to take action against employees. Section 14.4 provides a brief conceptual and ethical analysis of vigilantism. Section 14.5 considers whether corporate leaders should ever accede to the demands of Twitter vigilantes.

14.1.1 The Problem

In spite of the ostensive symmetry of commercial transactions, it goes without saying that employers often have considerable power over their employees. One way in which employers may be tempted to use that power is by taking action against employees who have committed wrongs. And in some cases, the wrongs in question will be ones that occurred while the employee was off-duty, and that have little or no bearing on the individual's organizational role, or their status as an employee. The fundamental question with which the present chapter is concerned is whether punitive action by employers in such cases is justified.

Employment law in all North American jurisdictions gives employers wide latitude in terminating employees. Labour relations in the United States (US) are generally governed by the doctrine of *employment at will.* Employment at will effectively means that an employer doesn't need a reason to fire an employee. Wanting to fire them is sufficient. Technically, Canada is not regarded as an employment-at-will jurisdiction, but in practice is not far from it. In Canada, labour law varies from province to province, but the rule generally is that in Canada, in non-unionized environments, you can generally be fired without reason so long as you are provided with notice and/or severance. This limitation is generally considered sufficiently restrictive for labour lawyers *not* to consider Canada an employment-at-will country. But this definition of "at will" (admittedly the standard one) arguably puts too much emphasis on procedural matters, and too little emphasis on the need for, or rather *lack* of need for, reasons for ending the employment relationship. In Canada, as in the US (but different from most European jurisdictions), you generally don't need a *reason* to fire someone, legally speaking. Canada and the US are alike in this regard. Canada's limits tend to be merely procedural, rather than fundamental. And even in the fully at-will US, there are procedural limits. For example, employees may, after termination, have the right to continue participation in group insurance policies for some period. In some states (but not in others), fired employees have the right to receive their final paycheques immediately. Fired employees are generally also entitled to the benefits implied by any vested retirement plans. So in both Canada and the US, there are *procedural* limits on firing, but employers do not need to provide *reasons* for the decision to fire. The law in both countries is permissive as to reasons when it comes to firing employees – as long as employers avoid certain prohibited reasons, such as race or sex. But even when the *law* itself is permissive as to reasons, the question of *moral* reasons is typically left on the table. The fact that an employer *has* a right to take action does not imply that the employer would *be* right to take action. And nor does it imply that the public would be right to encourage it.

Although a range of examples will be offered here, the primary focus will be on corporate action taken in response to employee behaviour that is not merely offensive to corporate interests or to the sensibilities of corporate executives, but of behaviour that is – by dint of being seriously illegal – as close to uncontroversially *bad* as we can reasonably expect.

14.1.2 The Examples

In March of 2014, the NFL's Baltimore Ravens' running back Ray Rice was indicted for third-degree aggravated assault. Rice had been caught on security video dragging his fiancée, Janay Palmer, out of an elevator after having apparently struck her unconscious (Elliott, 2014). The video was published by the tabloid news website TMZ, after which it went viral. In July of that year, NFL commissioner Roger Goodell banned Rice for two games and fined him $58,000.[2] Two months later, video of the assault itself surfaced – video that showed Rice actually punching Palmer – and the Ravens subsequently cut Rice from the team. The NFL and the Ravens were both subject to substantial criticism (on Twitter and elsewhere) for being slow to take action.

In August of 2014, Desmond Hague, then CEO of sports catering company Centreplate, was caught on video kicking a friend's puppy in an elevator, and yanking the dog's leash so violently that the dog was lifted off its feet ("Des Hague, Former CEO of Centerplate," 2015). The video soon went public, and Centreplate's board put Hague on probation, and required him to donate $100,000 to an animal welfare foundation. But public outrage, expressed via Twitter in particular, was relentless. Centrepoint's board eventually fired Hague. He was subsequently tried and found guilty of animal cruelty, for which he was fined $5000 and ordered not to own any animals for a period of three years.

In fall of 2014, the Canadian Broadcasting Corporation announced that it was "severing ties" with – that is, firing – its marquee radio personality, Jian Ghomeshi (Tucker, 2014). It was subsequently revealed that Ghomeshi had pre-emptively revealed to the CBC accusations by a number of women that he had engaged in what *he* referred to as "rough sex," and what *they* referred to as, effectively, battery. In this case, the Twitter storm followed, rather than presaging, the firing. Sentiment on Twitter might fairly be summarized as implying that firing was the least that Ghomeshi deserved. Ghomeshi was charged by police in 2015, and then tried, and acquitted, in 2016.[3]

In early 2015, a Canadian man named Shawn Simoes was involved in a commotion that involved a group of men hurling obscenities at a female TV reporter, on air. Video of the event went viral, following which Simoes was identified on social media as an employee of Hydro One (the regulated monopoly that provides hydroelectric power within the Canadian province of Ontario). Twitter subsequently lit up with demands that Simoes be fired. The utility soon announced that Simoes had indeed been fired as a result of the incident (Obourn, 2015). However, Simoes was subsequently rehired (Morales, 2015), which resulted in Hydro One being subjected to a hailstorm of Twitter criticism.

In each of these cases, a corporate employee was fired for something that had approximately nothing to do with his talent or his qualifications for the job. And in each case, the public applauded when the corporation took action, but booed when the corporation either hesitated to take such action, was found later to have delayed acting on information it had in hand, or (as in the Simoes case) reversed its decision.[4] And in each of these cases, social media (in particular, Twitter) played a substantial role.

The questions to be dealt with here: Were the corporations in these cases right to take action against their employees? Did leaders at these corporations act rightly? And, more importantly, would other employers be right to take such action against employees in similar circumstances, when urged to do so by a Twitter mob?

14.2 CORPORATE JUSTIFICATION FOR TAKING ACTION

It is important that the bad behaviour in each of these cases happened while the employee in question was off-duty. Organizations more clearly have the relevant jurisdiction when bad behaviour happens *on the job*. An organization is, let us assume, fully within its rights to fire an employee who acts out violently against a fellow employee, or who posts racist messages in the employee lounge, or who sexually harasses a customer or client. Off-duty behaviour poses a harder question.

What moral motives might companies have for firing employees found to have engaged in bad behaviour?[5] That is, why might they think it ethically right to do so? We can imagine at least six distinct kinds of moral reasons, and these are discussed below. I will sketch here only the prima facie case for each of these reasons, in hopes of explaining why each might be a reasonable basis for action, without asserting that the reason in question is, on its own, ever sufficient to justify action against an employee.

First, a corporation might believe it right to fire a misbehaving employee in order to meet its obligation to protect its own employees and customers. An employee (such as Ghomeshi) thought to have engaged in physical and sexual assault against a number of women might well be considered a threat to females in the workplace.[6] An employee taking out his frustrations (as Hague did) on a helpless puppy might well be suspected of having anger management issues that suggest that he is not fit to serve in a position of power.

Second, a corporation might fire an employee accused of off-duty wrongdoing because it suspects that the off-duty misbehaviour in question implies a diminished capacity to carry out assigned tasks in a safe and effective manner. This might apply, for example, to a cargo pilot arrested for possession of cocaine. A clear head is a bona fide job requirement for a commercial pilot. So a pilot found to be taking a strong, addictive stimulant like cocaine in their spare time has not just violated drug laws, but might also reasonably be thought technically unfit for the job.

Third, a corporation might fire an employee in circumstances such as the ones recounted above simply because the relevant behaviour implies a tendency toward very bad judgment. An ethical manager owes it to the corporation to hire and retain only qualified talent. And a necessary requirement for all but the most banal of employments, after all, is the possession of a certain amount of good judgment, and many employees are hired almost exclusively because of their judgment. Being found to have engaged in behaviours of the sorts discussed here might reasonably be thought to betoken a grave lack of judgment, the sort that would radically reduce one's value as an employee. It ought to be acknowledged that this line of reasoning requires an assumption – one that is open to debate – to the effect that that judgement is, in some sense, a global capacity, such that poor judgment in one context (viz. off-duty) with regards to one topic (e.g., how intimate partners ought to be treated) implies poor judgment in other contexts (viz. on-duty) with regards to another topic (e.g., whether to diversify a company's portfolio of products).

Fourth, a corporation might think it right to *punish* the behaviour in question for any of the moral reasons that are normally adduced for the punishment of wrongs. But, in particular, there might be a desire to punish behaviour in order to *denounce* it, morally. That is, the corporation might feel the obligation to proclaim, both to the employee and to the public, that the behaviour in question simply is not the sort of behaviour that can be tolerated. This is akin to the denunciatory role that many see as a central justification for punishment by government officials on behalf of the public under the auspices of criminal law (see Duff and Hoskins, 2018; especially section 5).

Fifth, in some cases an employer might seem to be justified in taking action by the fact that the corporation is *uniquely positioned* to take action of a punitive kind. In the case of Hague (the puppy-kicking CEO), there was a sense that the courts – with only relatively weak animal protection laws at their disposal – would let the CEO off with a slap on the wrist, which is ultimately precisely what they did. The punishment meted out by the corporation in this case, namely, dismissal, was considerably stiffer. In the case of Simoes, whose behaviour was repugnant but not clearly illegal (despite speculation about whether Simoes and his pals may have violated Canadian broadcast standards), the sense was that the bad behaviour in question would go unpunished entirely if Hydro One, the employer, did not take punitive action. So the public urged Hydro One to act, perhaps in part because that was the only way in which Simoes was likely to be punished.

Note the parallel here with cases in which an individual is uniquely able to rescue someone in peril. There may not be a general obligation to rescue, and such obligation as there is might be reduced if there are many individuals similarly situated and capable of effecting rescue; but if ever there is an argument to be made for an obligation to rescue, it would be when you are uniquely situated and capable of taking action (see Singer, 1972). This sort of reasoning may be a big part of why the public seems so enthusiastic about encouraging harsh action by corporations in such situations, despite being typically anxious about the exercise of corporate power.

Finally, corporate managers have a fiduciary obligation to their organizations, and this implies an obligation to minimize negative public reaction and the associated damage to the corporation's reputation. It might be seen as prudent for a corporation to distance itself from a disgraced employee. And if it is prudent for the corporation, then it may be required of duty-bound corporate managers. Firing the employee helps accomplish these goals in two different ways. First, firing distances the company from the wrongdoer in the very straightforward sense of turning a current employee into a *former* employee – someone no longer on payroll, no longer on the website, and no longer entitled to hand out a business card bearing the corporation's logo. Second, firing distances the company from the wrongdoer's behaviour by effectively *repudiating* the behaviour, and thereby clarifying for the public what the company's own values are by asserting that those values are inconsistent with the values embodied by the wrongful behaviour in question.

In the next section we characterize Twitter mobs that demand that corporations fire employees as a form of vigilantism. We will examine the ethics of vigilantism in general, and ask in particular whether this form of vigilantism is justifiable.

14.3 VIGILANTISM

Vigilantism has received surprisingly little attention on the part of ethicists. Most of what has been written about it has been written by criminologists and historians and legal scholars (see, for example, Karmen, 2002; Gerlach, 2001; and Henderson, 2017, respectively). This is surprising because vigilantism is ethically complex, and has been relatively common throughout history and across cultures. It is ripe for ethical analysis. Favourite examples of vigilantism span history and fiction, from the heroic to the despicable, from the angry mob to the lone wolf seeking to right a wrong. Standard examples of vigilantes include Robin Hood, as well as DC Comics' Batman and the Marvel Universe's Punisher. Historical examples range from those who killed Nazi sympathizers in the wake of World War II, to the street patrols carried out by New York's "Guardian Angels" during the 1980s, to the use of "mob justice" in modern India by those frustrated by a sluggish and sometimes corrupt court system. Vigilantes are often – but as the list above makes clear, not always – sympathetic and even romantic characters: they seek to right wrongs, often tapping into our natural sympathy for the aggrieved and the downtrodden.

Below is a short conceptual analysis of vigilantism, followed by a brief ethical analysis.

Vigilantism comes in many forms, in many settings, and is carried out by a wide range of individuals with varying motives. What follows is an attempt to summarize the characteristics of central examples. Vigilantism can be defined as the attempt by those who lack formal authority to impose punishment for wrongs or perceived wrongs. It typically, but not always, involves the use of violence.

1. First, vigilantism occurs against a backdrop of a system of laws but laws imperfectly enforced. It occurs when there is the perception that the formal law-enforcement system cannot or will not do the job of providing justice.[7] This in fact points to two separate requirements for identifying instances of vigilantism. First, there must already be in place some more-or-less formal system for enforcing social rules. To put it in Hobbesian terms, in a war of all against all, nothing can be unjust – there is no *wrong* for the vigilante to *right*. There must, at a minimum, be some form of social cohesion in order for vigilantism to make sense. The notion of vigilantism as "extra-legal" implies that there must be some form of law, however informal, outside of which (but not always in contravention of which) the vigilante *acts*. The second requirement is that, in order for an act to count as an instance of vigilantism, the vigilante must act on the basis of a real or perceived failure of existing, formal systems of justice.
2. A second characteristic of vigilantism is that vigilantism is not self-interested, but rather involves the enforcement of community norms. Neither self-defence nor acts of retribution for past wrongs to oneself ought, strictly, to be counted as acts of vigilantism. The fundamental justification for self-defence is grounded in things like ownership of the self, not in the enforcement of community norms. It is distinctive of vigilantism that vigilantes arrogate to themselves the right to act on behalf of the community, and in its name. This characterization seems descriptively accurate – the central examples of vigilantism share this feature. But it also seems normatively essential, in order to avoid the kinds of self-serving rationalizations that would have individuals taking predatory action as a response to what they then portray as injustices done to them. It is simply not a form of vigilantism to steal from Walmart, even if you think that Walmart is a bad actor and that you therefore are righting a wrong that no one else is going to right.
3. Similarly, we should differentiate vigilantism from the carrying out of vendettas. Vendettas involve seeking what the individual perceives as justice, typically as part of a family feud: an individual's brother is beaten, and justice can only be restored by imposing a similar, or worse, beating on the assailant or the assailant's brother. In archetypical cases of vigilantism, the pursuit of justice is, again, impersonal.

4. Vigilantism should be understood as a morally neutral category. That is, vigilantism per se is neither automatically good nor automatically bad. This way of thinking of vigilantism leaves open the question of whether there are justified instances of vigilantism. In referring to a given action as an instance of vigilantism, we are in no way *endorsing* the social order or system of justice that the vigilante seeks to enforce. Lynchings in rural Mississippi in the 1920s were, at least in some instances (namely, when the victims of those lynchings were themselves thought, rightly or wrongly, to have violated laws), just as much instances of vigilantism as are the shadowy doings of our favourite comic-book heroes. Keeping this category morally neutral is important if we are to avoid begging important questions.
5. Acts of terrorism should not be confused with vigilantism. The distinction may be hard to maintain, and it is tempting to harken back to the old adage that "one man's hero is another man's villain." But terrorism is formally distinguishable from vigilantism (even the most blameworthy vigilantism) in at least two regards. First, where the vigilante seeks justice, the terrorist seeks to instill terror. Second, where the vigilante grounds his actions in the norms of the community, the terrorist seeks to overturn those norms.

Note that while this descriptive analysis is inspired by the archetypical historical examples of vigilantism, it nonetheless captures quite well the phenomenon illustrated in the famous cases described in Section 14.1 of this chapter. The Twitter mob seeking to have a perceived wrongdoer fired typically seems to intend to right a wrong that, collectively, it believes no one else is going to right.[8] It sees extant, formal mechanisms for righting wrongs as inadequate. And members of the mob are almost always at arm's-length from the original wrong. They are distant bystanders, seeking to enforce community standards upon a miscreant who has done no harm to them personally.

It might be argued that a Twitter mob is importantly different from a street mob in that the street mob, but not the Twitter mob, exerts its will by means of *violence*. That difference, while morally important, does not seem conclusive. The use of violence may be common among vigilantes, but I suggest that it is not definitionally necessary. And besides, while Twitter mobs typically act at a distance, and hence are incapable of using force directly, instances in which online anger bleeds over into real-life violence are not unknown. Further, what we should be concerned with is the severity of the punishment, and in many circumstances a successful call for an individual to be fired is arguably a much more serious form of punishment than the imposition of even a moderately severe physical beating.

So, Twitter mobs are vigilante mobs. I will now at this point delve into whether Twitter mobs always, sometimes, or never constitute a *justified* form of vigilantism.

14.4 ETHICAL ANALYSIS

As noted above, philosophical analyses of the ethics of vigilantism are few. The reasons for this are unclear. One possibility is that philosophers simply see vigilantism in general as unjustified, or the circumstances in which it could be justified as too rarefied to warrant attention. One of the only philosophers to look carefully at the ethics of vigilantism, Travis Dumsday (2009), argues (inter alia) that for vigilantism to be justified, the crime in question would have to be "truly grievous" (p. 62) and the law enforcement system would have had to fail "woefully" (p. 61). Such strict requirements presumably mean that justified instances of vigilantism will be few indeed.

The most obvious ethical *criticism* of vigilantism is that the vigilante lacks the formal authority to exact justice. By definition, the vigilante has been neither elected nor appointed to that role. But such a lack of formal authority is a defeasible complaint. Where those who possess formal authority are sufficiently inefficient or negligent in exercising it, the Hobbesian justification[9] for their monopoly on seeking justice is substantially eroded. This then raises questions regarding how the determination is made that those who currently wield formal authority are either inefficient or negligent *enough* to warrant the individual (or mob) taking direct action. Vigilantes will typically argue that formal mechanisms have been found lacking in the present case. But even those who agree here may point out the virtues of a rule utilitarian approach: those who value a formal system for the enforcement of laws overall should respect it, rather than eroding it through demonstrating disrespect, even when that system seems to have failed in particular circumstances.

Two more specific ethical problems related to vigilantism can be pointed to, ones that matter even when formal systems of justice are either inadequate or entirely absent. The first is that vigilantes are typically unlikely to be able to satisfy the epistemic requirements for meting out justice. In a formal system of justice, the epistemic burden is borne by courts through elaborate processes for gathering and weighing evidence. The vigilante will of course claim certainty, but such claims will not always be convincing, not least because they are so often self-serving. A high degree of certainty as to, for example, the identity of the wrongdoer is essential.[10]

Second, vigilantes by all appearances lack the *theory* of punishment that is necessary in order for punishment to be morally justified. This is not to say that they lack some specific theory of punishment, but rather that they lack theory altogether. Because the vigilante has no formal system at all, a fortiori the vigilante has no systematic way of ensuring that punishment is proportional, or that it fits the crime. The vigilante (individual or collective) may well have instincts that are either broadly utilitarian or roughly retributivist. But those instincts will not typically have been well thought through.[11] Admittedly, formal systems of justice sometimes fail in this regard as well, and there continue to be significant disagreements among thoughtful commentators as to whether the "real" purpose of incarceration, for example, is retribution, or deterrence (either general or specific), or incapacitation, or rehabilitation (see Bedau and Kelly, 2017). All systems of laws, and all judicial systems, manifest these failures to some degree or another. Those failings, however, are a matter of degree, and contingent. In the case of vigilantism, the lack of a theory of punishment tends to be complete, and is practically inevitable. Formal justice inevitably has its emotive elements, but vigilantism seldom has anything more.

The final question to be addressed here will be whether corporate leaders are justified in acceding to the demands of such vigilantes. Should corporate leaders be the willing tools of the Twitter mob?

14.5 CORPORATE LEADERSHIP

We saw above that there are several possible ethical justifications for corporations acceding to the wishes of a Twitter mob, and firing an employee who has engaged in wrongdoing off the job. And I'll stipulate here that many (perhaps all) of those reasons are prima facie worthy ones for thinking corporate action justified. But we should be cautious to take such reasons as conclusively suggesting justification for such action – that is, for firing – even in cases in which the employee in question has clearly engaged in substantial wrongdoing.

Cases will, of course, differ. There will be cases in which the mob is, to be blunt, *right* – cases in which the person in question has committed a grievous wrong which will perhaps otherwise go unpunished, and deserves any and all other harms that might befall him. There will also be cases in which the harm is minor, or counts as substantial only from within the worldview of, say, a particular political ideology. But what can we say in general to provide advice to corporate leaders *prior* to the day when they find themselves confronted by this dilemma? Should corporate leaders stand ready to "turn them over" to the Twitter mob,[12] or, like Marshal Seth Bullock, refuse to accede to the mob's demands?

I suggest, perhaps not very controversially, that leaders should be hesitant to take action at the behest of a Twitter mob, against employees who have engaged in wrongdoing. We should be cautious about encouraging what is effectively just another brand of vigilantism. Indeed, by giving in to the demands of the Twitter mob, a corporate leader is not just acceding to, but actively *participating* in, vigilantism. Even though the employer is ethically and legally justified in imposing certain penalties in certain situations – up to and including firing – this does not imply that the employer is justified in imposing firing as a penalty for off-the-job wrongs. In acceding to the wishes of the Twitter mob, the corporation (or its managers) act in a way that is parallel to the actions of the rogue cop. The manager in this case, like the cop, possesses genuine authority. But in firing an employee for off-the-job behaviour, the employer effectively goes rogue, and acts as a vigilante. As noted in the previous section, there are serious ethical worries with regard to vigilantism, even though most of us may be susceptible, in some instance or another, to being affected by its charms.

But three *specific* concerns arise in the sort of vigilantism implied by the kinds of cases we are considering here.

First, punishment by employers raises the spectre of something very close to *double jeopardy* – that is, of being punished for a crime for which one has already been punished, or of which one has indeed already been acquitted. Strictly speaking, from a legal point of view, this is not double jeopardy per se, since it is not an additional prosecution *by the same authority*. But the concern is similar: the wrongdoer is being punished twice, and – importantly – presumably punished twice in the name of the *same set of interests*, namely, the public interest. Vigilantes, like courts of law, act (by definition) in what they take to be the public interest, or in the interest of justice. This is quite different from situations in which the victim of a crime sues the wrongdoer, in civil court, after the wrongdoer has already been tried in a criminal court. In such cases, the two separate legal proceedings serve two different interests, namely, a private and a public one, and hence the concept of double jeopardy does not apply. In the cases under consideration here, two different powers – the courts and an employer – may end up imposing punishment for the same crime, and with the same ends.

Consider also the general lack of *due process* involved in this as in any other case of vigilantism. Part of the justification of any fair system of punishment lies in the fact that that system proceeds according to a set of processes that ensures fairness. When corporations punish for off-the-job wrongs, such due process may be lacking. Of course, large corporations today have HR departments designed in part to ensure that due process *is* followed in all matters related to employees. But not all employers are sophisticated in this way. And public pressures of the kinds exerted in the cases discussed here are very likely to short-circuit such protections as are in place. Lack of due process is a very real concern (and is very likely part of the reason that Shawn Simoes ended up being reinstated by Hydro One).

The final regard in which it is problematic for employers to accede to the demands of Twitter vigilantism – and this is perhaps best regarded as a component of the due process concern – is the risk of a lack of proportionality. That is to say, when punishment (usually firing) is encouraged by the public and carried out by an employer, there is little apparent attention paid to the question of whether the punishment actually fits the crime. In most cases, firing is a very substantial penalty, and so it ought not to be a punishment handed out lightly. Even in cases where the crime is egregious, and clearly merits substantial punishment, it is hard to say that firing is *precisely* the right punishment – neither too severe nor too lenient. Nor is it at all obvious that firing is the right mode of punishment: why is specifically this form of financial punishment the right one?

A recent paper by Vikram Bhargava (2018) identifies what seems to be a version of this worry about proportionality as the core problem with employers acceding to the demands of Twitter mobs. Bhargava examines the issue from the perspective of the philosophy of blame, driving a wedge between the fact that the employee *deserves* blame and the claim that the employer would be justified in *blaming* him. Bhargava (drawing on other scholars) argues that in blaming the employee, the employer engages in an *unjustified* act of blaming, in that such blaming is insufficiently sensitive to the number of other individuals (within the Twitter mob) who have already blamed him (in a tangible, punitive sense). If the individual has already suffered enough blame (and an employer would seldom be able to tell, one way or the other), then it would be unjust – potentially disproportionate – to blame him further.

Courts, for their part, tend to have mechanisms for making it more likely that the punishments they hand out will be proportionate. To begin, lawyers and judges are trained in the *principle* of proportionality. Further, courts generally impose punishments set out in legislation, or in sophisticated sentencing guidelines, and in doing so are also expected to be guided by precedent. They are tasked with balancing the demands of justice with the demands of public safety to determine whether a prison sentence, or a fine, or probation is the right remedy. In cases like the ones discussed here, on the other hand, public outrage tends to focus on a single, one-size-fits all punishment, namely, “fire the bum!”

Finally, it is worth pointing out what outliers the particular cases discussed above really are. All of the cases above involve behaviour that is not just wrongful, but in some sense outrageous. In cases like these, it is all too easy to condemn the behaviour in question, and thus to agree that punishment – *of whatever kind and by whatever means available* – is not just permissible but indeed required. But when the demands of the mob are exactly the same, regardless of the severity of the crime (or in some cases, "crime") caution is warranted.

14.6 CONCLUSION

For all of the reasons above, it seems clear that corporate leaders should be cautious, at the very least, about acceding to social media exhortations that they take action against – in particular, to fire – employees known to have committed wrongs while off duty. And this is in spite of the fact that the egregious behaviours of the men at the centre of the cases with which we began seem so richly deserving of punishment, and the fact that their employers were readily able (and typically willing) to mete out such punishment. Generally, we should be cautious about deriving moral guidance from cases such as the ones offered at the beginning of this chapter. If hard cases make bad law, then surely famous cases offer poor moral guidance.

NOTES

* The author wishes to thank audiences at Rutgers Business School, at the Ted Rogers School of Management, at York University, and at the University of Manitoba for useful feedback on early versions of this chapter. Thanks also to Pnina Alon-Shenker in particular for feedback on the sections on labour law – such errors as remain are the author's, not hers.

1. Twitter is not the only relevant social medium, and is not even the central example in some jurisdictions. In China, for example, Twitter is blocked. The focus on Twitter in this chapter reflects the fact that Twitter is (with notable exceptions) a global technology, and one familiar to most English-language readers.
2. In 2011, Rice had signed a five-year, $40 million contract. So the fine amounted to roughly seven-tenths of 1 percent of his yearly $8 million salary.
3. It is worth noting that few observers regarded Ghomeshi's acquittal as an exoneration. Prosecutors were simply unable to build a sufficiently effective case, in a he-said-she-said context, to satisfy the standard of "guilt beyond a reasonable doubt."
4. It is hard not to notice that of these four cases – chosen not at random, but because they together constitute what seems to be a statistically unusual cluster of high-profile cases all occurring within a period of roughly 12 months – two of them involve violence against women and a third, while not involving violence, nonetheless has disturbing misogynistic overtones. For present purposes, I will ignore this factor, which is no doubt deserving of its own separate treatment. For present purposes, I will treat all four as merely examples of serious wrongful behaviour, and not (as three of them are) as wrongful behaviour aimed at women.
5. In referring here to moral motives, I am taking it for granted that – in some sense at

least – corporations are capable of *having* motives. Little here would need to be changed if the reader chooses to think instead of the moral motives of senior managers. For a discussion of the possibility of determining corporate moral motives, see MacDonald (2019).

6. At least one of Ghomeshi's accusers was a CBC employee, and so some of the wrongful behaviour attributed to Ghomeshi was very directly relevant to the safety of his co-workers. For present purposes, however, we will continue to focus exclusively on his off-duty behaviour.
7. Cannon (2001, Kindle location 229) points out that according to public opinion (or "mountain common law") in the 19th-century American west, seducing another man's wife was grounds for lethal retribution. Thus, vigilantes might be seen as justified in carrying out such a sentence, where "the law offered no remedy (or scapegoat) at the time other than an adultery charge against both parties."
8. Although they act outside of the formal justice system, it is worth noting that in asking for a miscreant to be fired they seek to make use of – perhaps to highjack – a formal system, namely, the HR system of the company in question.
9. Without intending to rely upon Hobbes (1651) too directly, I intend here merely to refer to the rational process by which members of a community lay down their arms and turn over the enforcement of rights to a central authority. Where the central authority has proven ineffectual, and absent some other moral underpinning, the rationale for deference to it vanishes.
10. An editorial in one 19th-century Utah newspaper (the *Salt Lake Daily Tribune*) suggested that "few can be found to rigorously condemn an orderly lynching, which goes no further than slaying the murderer, *after being sure of his identity*." Quoted in Gerlach (2001), Kindle location 2659, emphasis added.
11. Indeed, there is good reason to believe that the mob vigilantism that typifies Twitter vigilantism is anathema to clear reasoning of any kind.
12. The non-trivial difference, of course, is that the Twitter mob wants *someone else* to impose the penalty that they themselves are impotent to impose directly.

REFERENCES

Bedau, Hugo Adam and Kelly, Erin. "Punishment," in Edward N. Zalta (ed.), *The Stanford Encyclopedia of Philosophy*, Winter 2017 Edition, https://plato.stanford.edu/archives/win2017/entries/punishment/ (accessed 6 August 2019).

Bhargava, Vikram. "Firm Responses to Mass Outrage: Technology, Blame, and Employment," *Journal of Business Ethics*, 2018, https://doi.org/10.1007/s10551-018-4043-7.

Cannon, Kenneth L II. "Mountain Common Law: The Extralegal Punishment of Seducers in Early Utah," in Stanford J. Layton (ed.), *Utah's Lawless Fringe: Stories of True Crime*, Signature City Books, Salt Lake City, 2001, pp. 308–27.

"Des Hague, Former CEO of Centerplate, Sentenced for Animal Cruelty." CBC News, 15 April 2015, http://www.cbc.ca/news/canada/british-columbia/des-hague-former-ceo-of-centerplate-sentenced-for-animal-cruelty-1.3034701 (accessed 6 August 2019).

Duff, Antony and Hoskins, Zachary. "Legal Punishment," in Edward N. Zalta (ed.), *The Stanford Encyclopedia of Philosophy*, Fall 2018 Edition, https://plato.stanford.edu/archives/fall2018/entries/legal-punishment/ (accessed 6 August 2019).

Dumsday, Travis. "On Cheering Charles Bronson: The Ethics of Vigilantism," *The Southern Journal of Philosophy*, **47**(1), 2009: 49–67.

Elliott, Rebecca. "Everything You Need to Know About the Ray Rice Case," Time.

com, 11 September 2014, http://time.com/3329351/ray-rice-timeline/ (accessed 6 August 2019).

Gerlach, Larry R. "Ogden's 'Horrible Tragedy': The Lynching of George Segal," in Stanford J. Layton (ed.), *Utah's Lawless Fringe: Stories of True Crime*, Signature City Books, Salt Lake City, 2001, pp. 157–72.

Henderson, Stephen E. "Daredevil: Legal (and Moral) Vigilante," *Ohio State Journal of Criminal Law*, **15**, 2017: 133.

Hobbes. *Leviathan*, 1651.

Karmen, Andrew. "Vigilantism," in Joshua Dressler (ed.), *Encyclopedia of Crime and Justice*, Vol. 4, 2nd edn, Macmillan Reference USA, New York, 2002, pp. 1645–9.

MacDonald, Chris. "Corporate Moral Motivation," *Georgetown Journal of Law & Public Policy*, 2019 (in press).

Morales, Steve. "Why was Hydro One Worker in FHRITP Incident Rehired?" Global News, 3 November 2015, http://globalnews.ca/news/2316399/why-was-hydro-one-worker-in-fhritp-incident-rehired/ (accessed 6 August 2019).

Obourn, Erin. "Firing of Shawn Simoes for Off-Duty 'FHRITP' Video Reflects Employment Trend," CBC News, 2015, http://www.cbc.ca/news/business/firing-of-shawn-simoes-for-off-duty-fhritp-video-reflects-employment-trend-1.3071919 (accessed 6 August 2019).

Singer, Peter. "Famine, Affluence, and Morality," *Philosophy & Public Affairs*, 1972: 229–43.

Tucker, Erika. "Timeline: Jian Ghomeshi Sex Assault Scandal," Global News, 3 December 2014 (updated 11 May 2016), http://globalnews.ca/news/1647091/timeline-sex-assault-allegations-arise-after-cbc-fires-jian-ghomeshi/ (accessed 27 August 2019).

15. There is not enough business ethics in the ethics of digitization

Christoph Lütge

15.1 INTRODUCTION

This is a new age of technology, and we are only beginning to understand its implications, technological and non-technological ones. The current wave of digital technologies has also seen a rise in the ethical discussion of digitization and digital technologies. However, as I shall argue in this chapter, this discussion is lacking – and would benefit from – a distinct voice of *business* ethics. It is important to get the actors from all areas, like civil society, politics and also business, to move forward with regard to the new technologies.

When referring to these technologies, I use the term "Innovation 4.0" as an umbrella concept, since it encompasses others like "Industry 4.0," the "Fourth Industrial Revolution" or simply "The Fourth Revolution" (Floridi, 2016). Among the key issues here are big data, autonomous cars, the Internet of Things, drones and similar military technologies, welfare robots and others like smart grids. These technologies bring lots of benefits with them, in terms of flexibility, adaptability, versatility, speed or comfort. But they can also bring with them benefits which belong to the domain of ethics and sustainability, in terms of saving lives, avoiding accidents, or promoting resource efficiency and thus saving natural resources: For example, the city of Oslo managed to reduce the energy consumption of its streetlights by 62 percent using big data techniques.

On the other hand, these technologies likewise face ethical challenges. To name just some of them:

1. Decision errors by machines which follow inappropriate processes and rules or machines that misinterpret processes. What sounds like a mere technical problem at first can lead to serious cases of injuries, fatalities or unfair treatment. This is the area of Machine Ethics.
2. The second area is Information Ethics. These technologies can be manipulated by hacking. Faulty data might be used. Citizens might

become totally transparent, a dystopian vision as in the current Chinese program we are witnessing (Chin and Wong, 2016). The current European General Data Protection Regulation (GDPR) is set to address some of these issues. We will see how its consequences will develop in the future.

3. The third complex of challenges lies in the domain of Labor Ethics, since human labor is being substituted, on a new level, by machine labor using artificial intelligence (AI) technologies. It is under debate how significant this problem is and how different it is from past technological revolutions. It certainly is a topic that should not be neglected.

15.2 ETHICAL RISKS OF INNOVATION 4.0

Historically, innovation has often been seen in a critical light through the ages. A very common theme was the fear of human beings losing control over their tools due to scientific progress, famously used in Goethe's "Zauberlehrling" ("The Sorcerer's Apprentice," 1797). Similarly, the Luddite Movement in 19th-century England destroyed weaving machinery as a form of protest. However, most of these protests against progress in terms of technology were unsuccessful.

So what risks does Innovation 4.0 create more specifically?

1. *Dependence on accuracy*. Certainly, modern societies have always been dependent on the accuracy of technical systems, of cars, of trains or of elevators. But Innovation 4.0 takes this a level further and to very sensitive areas. Take, for example, the case of telemedicine, where we will probably see machines performing many kinds of surgery on patients in the future – and these need to be very precise indeed. In autonomous driving, even small errors in the programming can lead to grave consequences. And people will most probably see a loss in once autonomous decisions, as for example in the case of autonomous driving, where, in some countries at least, many people have reservations against giving up control over their cars. But they had these with elevators as well.
2. *Cyber-attacks*. Many of these technologies – in theory or in practice – open the door for attacks from the outside. These are legal issues, but of course also ethical ones.
3. *Distribution and concentration of information*. A whole group of ethical risks is concerned with the distribution and concentration of information. These are much talked about in public discussion, even

if they do not necessarily always constitute a new dimension. The age gap in the use of technology, for example, is being contested: we see many senior citizens using these technologies without any problems (Van Wagenen, 2017). It might be similar with the digital divide: recent reports and statistics show that parts of the world like Africa are rapidly closing up here (https://www.theguardian.com/world/series/the-tech-continent-africas-digital-renaissance).

4. *Privacy and danger of data misuse*. This has come much more to the forefront during the last two years, with developments like the GDPR, which became effective 2018 and affected individuals and organizations around the globe. And there are differences in perception of this problem: between (some) European countries and the US, but even more so between these countries and China, for example, which should not be left out of the picture.
5. *Digital literacy*. Digital literacy encompasses a whole complex of issues which, in many countries, will have to be addressed much more seriously in the future. The German school system, for example, is seriously lagging behind (Bulkeley, 2017). And the situation has not really improved much during the last few years.

15.3 ETHICAL BENEFITS OF INNOVATION 4.0

Having cited some of the risks of the new digital technologies, are there also specific (maybe potential) ethical benefits?

1. Starting with telemedicine, it will bring about benefits for people especially in rural areas. It can help establish services which would otherwise not be available, and ultimately help avoid fatalities. It could also help combat depopulation of certain areas.
2. Care robots can help address the problem of ageing societies, which many countries face. Robots specifically designed to do care tasks are not necessarily seen as a dystopia. This is definitely the case in Japan, for example. And these robots are often explicitly *not* designed to look like human beings: studies show that most "users" prefer to look at them as a kind of technology – but one which can be seen as more humane and ethical in performing a specific task.
3. Big data: other than saving cost and gaining time for other tasks, big data analysis seeks to improve or even take over decision making, but will it do so in an overall more negative or positive way? Do human beings really always make better decisions? This is certainly a complex question, and probably too early to answer at the moment. A contro-

versial issue here, for example, is predictive crime mapping, which is already being used in some countries (not in Germany yet). It looks like it helps in improving security, though certainly there are errors to be overcome. In any case, big data technologies can analyse and make use of much more information than human beings ever could.

4. And finally, in terms of energy consumption, smart grids might have a positive effect on the feasibility of renewable power and might help (already do to some extent) meet globally increasing energy demands (Gellings, 2009). This does not just apply to smart grids, but also to many applications in the field of agriculture which are (at least in Germany) seldom discussed or even known to the public. The variety of already existing and possible applications for the digital technologies in agriculture is amazing. Sustainable agriculture can profit greatly from the use of digital technologies, even to a point where it might not be possible without them anymore.

15.4 THE ROLE OF COMPANIES: A BUSINESS ETHICS PERSPECTIVE

From a business ethics perspective, however, many of the ethical benefits of digital technologies can only be gained if the role of companies is taken systematically into account. In most cases, it will be companies who will not only be developing, but implementing those technologies – which is not always sufficiently recognized in the ethical discussions.

Moreover, many of these discussions are quite unaware of the already existing differentiated perspectives on business ethics, or Corporate Social Responsibility (CSR), or Creating Shared Value (CSV). Whether one adopts the CSV concept or whether one prefers to use CSR in some sense, it is fruitful to recognize at least the general point that companies can do something for sustainability, for human rights issues, for the environment and at the same time be profitable. A company can simultaneously advance the social and economic conditions of the community in which it operates while staying competitive. One example here would be Waterhealth International, a profit-oriented enterprise that offers healthy drinking water in underserved areas. This is not an easy task: drinking water is a big issue in many countries and Waterhealth, on the one hand, is aiming to provide five million people in developing countries with drinking water, and, on the other hand, financing themselves as a company through different sources, customers but also private contributions, institutional investors and more.

With regard to Innovation 4.0, I believe there are many applications here. In fact, digitization could be seen as a prerequisite for participating in global markets in many ways, especially in those countries where traditional infrastructure is weak and where new technologies can enable market transactions and open up new markets.

One example is M-Pesa, a mobile phone-based money transfer application which was launched in 2007 by Vodafone. It is very useful for depositing and withdrawing money, paying for goods and services, and more. M-Pesa has seen enormous success in countries (or parts of countries) with a weak banking infrastructure, such as Kenya, Tanzania, Afghanistan, India and Albania. For example, in 2016, seven million accounts had been opened in Tanzania. It has been continuously improved to add functions like term deposits, credit finance and other (Ndung'u, 2018).

Other digital services for underserved markets or areas include digital eLearning, online health services or apps that help bring together entrepreneurs and investors. 3D printing will change production processes vastly when implemented on a large scale, and providing spare parts or entire machinery to developing countries will be enormously easier (going to Mars will probably not be possible without it). Finally, there are farming applications, which might be as simple as reporting weather conditions, but also more complex ones, such as assessing soil quality.

Of course, these are apps and services provided (at least to a large extent) by companies, not by non-profit organizations. So issues of business ethics arise here. What is the public view on these issues?

At least certain parts of the debate on the ethics of digital technologies strike one with their heavily moralizing and accusing tone. It is interesting to see how moralizing concepts like "greed" or similar ones are used frequently in this debate. Here are some examples:

- "Google is a gigantic parasite that makes a fortune from exploiting the creativity and entrepreneurship of others" (*Daily Mail*, 24 March 2013).[1]
- "No Good Can Come Of Microsoft's Greed" (*Daily Press*, 11 February 2008).[2]
- "Google's Greed: How the Search Giant's Lust For Information Is Impacting Your Search Results" (SEO Blog, 22 March 2015).[3]
- "Googles Gier kennt keine Grenzen" (*Berliner Zeitung*, 6 May 2014).[4]
- "I wonder what Steve Jobs is thinking. Doesn't he see, like, he's the guy in that old Apple commercial who's the mean dictator" (Paul Graham on Bloomberg, 10 March 2011).[5]
- "Everybody wants to rule the world" (*The Economist*, 29 November 2014).[6]

- "Googles Gier opfert die Netzneutralität" (netzpolitik.org, 13 August 2010).[7]
- "Why Facebook Is Almost as Greedy as Bernie Madoff" (*Wall Street Journal* Video, 24 May 2012).[8]
- "Google est-il dangereux pour la démocratie?" (lesaffaires.com, 26 February 2013).[9]

This type of moralizing in the digital ethics debate is not limited to certain countries, but widely used all over the world. It is often encountered among those dealing with Internet ethics, data security and related issues. However, when considering the responsibilities of digital tech companies, it should also be taken into account that there are crucial conditions of competition for those companies.

It should be recognized more systematically that digital tech companies, like others, are in competition, sometimes more openly, sometimes less. For example, there is intense competition on the market for mobile devices. Similarly, companies are competing against each other when hunting for user data. With regard to autonomous cars, it is not at all clear right now who will be the leaders in that market. Even if Tesla is comparatively small, they have been quite successful already and definitely stirred up the market, in the US and in Europe, at least. Traditional car companies tend to be quite afraid of them because they wonder now how Tesla will grow in the near future – which could eventually lead to a change in the entire game. And other companies are just beginning to push into the market.

But some would contest whether big digital tech players like Google face competition at all. They see Google rather as a monopolist. This view, however, focuses only on Google as a search engine, though of course the company has in the meantime become much more than that. In fact, in the digital economy, all of the Silicon Valley Big Five (Apple, Google, Amazon, Microsoft, Facebook) are competing against each other in some way, in different areas, different services and especially in the hunt for user data. While many use Google for searching the Internet, there still are other services (like Bing) and there are alternatives to Amazon as Internet retailer. Even in those fields where competition seems less intense, it is often lurking in the background. Companies can never be sure that new companies or services will not turn up within the next few years: just think of AltaVista, which was the most common search engine of the 1990s. So companies need to keep being innovative, to keep being on the forefront of technology – because others might get bigger or better one day.

It is therefore important to keep in mind that digital tech companies are in competition. This competition should be kept fair, and it is a task for business ethics to warn about fairness in competition being endangered.

Fair competition, within adequate rules of the game, yields a number of (classic) ethical benefits in turn, such as promoting innovation, spreading innovations, putting pressure on positions of power (even large digital tech ones) and so on.

To name but one example of how competition affects ethical problems in the world of Innovation 4.0: Uber is certainly seen from many different angles all over the world. But just seeing it in an ethically totally negative light, as is still being done, for example, in many parts of Europe, is too simplistic. In Germany, for example, Uber has been forced to withdraw from a number of cities and is currently only active in Munich and Berlin. Public discussion often uses "ethical" arguments, like working conditions, wage level or tax evasion of drivers. However, in reality, it is mostly taxi drivers' associations who are lobbying against Uber, effectively trying to force new competitors out of the market. And they are not coming up with better digital alternatives, like other apps. There are some, but few are as effective as Uber. And they are usually not available in other countries. But more than that, the entire discussion has often led to a negative public image for ride shares and their digital applications in general – which is not a good result for the users.

15.5 RESPONSIBILITIES OF DIGITAL TECH COMPANIES

Mostly, we can just resort to decades of CSR and CSV discussion, maybe with a digital twist. The economic rationale behind CSR/CSV usually relies on reputational risks and legal risks like fines: the Volkswagen fines add up to roughly 25 billion euros (Parloff, 2018). With cases like these, we have reached a new level. Therefore, doing business ethics becomes simply a kind of risk management for companies, and of course in the digital sector as well. On the basis of this economic rationale of reputation and penalty reduction, by showing a business case, companies can be convinced in principle that they need programs in this area.

The Malampaya project can serve as an example in this regard. This was a pipeline project by Shell in the Philippines in 1998. Basically, there were three ways to build it. First, it could have been built mostly on land, which would have been the cheapest way of doing it. However, it would have endangered the biodiversity of the region. The second option was to build the pipeline in a direct underwater route (and therefore in a more expensive way), but that route went straight through a territory that was considered holy by indigenous people, though they had no legal claim to it. Ultimately, Shell decided to take a third option, the most costly one: to build the pipeline underwater, but on a much longer route around an island far away from the holy territory. There was no legal obligation for Shell to do so, and the additional cost was around US$30 million. Certainly, this is not too much for a company like Shell, but still they would not have spent it if it could have been avoided. The deciding factor at the time probably was the aftermath of the Brent Spar Case from 1995. Shell was probably trying to avoid a similar scandal (Habaradas, 2013). The interesting turn, however, came in 2007, when the World Resources Institute, using more sophisticated ways of calculation, found that the most expensive option actually turned out to have been the more economical one: they took into account other costs, for example, costs of delayed completion. The indigenous people could not have stopped the project entirely, but, by going to court, could have delayed it massively. The delays would have resulted in penalties and other costs, and calculating all these showed that the option chosen indeed made economic sense.

Not all cases will be nice stories like this one. Still, there might be more of them than companies think at first. Stories like these can help companies in calculating in better ways, and in investing money in CSR initiatives. And I believe the same holds in the area of digitization: digital tech companies should improve their calculations, calculate rather in the long(er) run, and consider systematically the interests of others who may be relevant for their future success, for example, in terms of reputation. This will be beneficial especially for those companies active in social media (and to some extent already is the case).

From a more general point of view, taking ethical responsibilities (without waiting for changes in the legal framework) has become both a necessity as well as an advantage in competition for companies. Studies show that it helps in raising profits (Wang et al., 2016), securing the capability for innovation (Martinez-Cornesa et al., 2017), improving risk management (Shiu and Yang, 2017), improving market position (Martinez-Conesa et al., 2017) and customer satisfaction (Lins et al., 2017) and also motivating employees and recruiting new talents (Saeidi, 2015).

A word of caution: in the case of digital technologies, there might be a twist, as mentioned. Companies can do a lot of things on their own, but can they do everything? In some sectors of the industry, it will be more difficult to take responsibilities on your own than in others. Take the example of the banking sector. Broadly speaking, there is not as much room for direct action by banks as in other branches, simply because the banking sector is very tightly regulated. The situation in the digital tech sector might be similar. Arguing with a programming language will be extremely difficult, just as appealing to the conscience of an algorithm. Therefore, I believe we will often need rather more formal than informal rules here. By this, I do not just mean detailed regulation (which we will also witness), but sector-specific ethical guidelines on a more abstract level. Such guidelines need to be subject to societal discussion, they need to address problems that people worry about – even if they might not be able to solve each of these problems. But I believe openly addressing them is better than not mentioning them at all.

Asimov's laws of robotics serve as a famous example. Of course, robotics today uses rules which are much more complicated. But maybe we need rules as simple as the original ones, for autonomous cars, for the use of AI, for health data and others. These technologies will actually need ethical rules to a much greater extent than previous technologies – simply because they will have to rely on societal acceptance in order to be effective. Without societal acceptance, autonomous cars or AI applications will not be used. And surveys reveal that skepticism is quite high throughout Europe. For example, a recent study by the Bertelsmann Foundation found that Germans are particularly mistrusting when it comes to autonomous cars. Skepticism rises with age but the extent to which it does is a bit surprising. The chief reasons given by the subjects in this study are fears of being injured by those cars, fears of losing control over their own cars and also fears of personal data getting stolen. There will be a lot of work to do for the car industry.

The second word of caution concerns the question of whether we will see machines like those in *Terminator* or *Matrix* or *I Robot* in the near future. While those machines often seem the chief concern in public discussions on ethics of AI – even fueled by statements from celebrities like Steven Hawking or Elon Musk – these problems are not the most urgent ones on the agenda, in particular from a business ethics point of view. For the moment, and at least in the medium run, totally different questions will be much more pressing, such as

- questions of liability and accountability
- data protection issues
- data security
- and others.

I will turn to some of these next.

15.6 RESPONSIBILITIES IN THE CASE OF AUTONOMOUS DRIVING

Digital tech companies face serious issues that are undermining their reputation, for example, a number of accidents involving autonomous cars have already happened. In March 2017, an Uber Volvo crashed while driving autonomously. The police said that the technology was not responsible, and no one was injured. In March 2018, however, another Uber Volvo fatally hit a woman crossing the road in Tempe, Arizona, an accident which probably no human driver could have avoided. The car's sensor technology was, however, deactivated on purpose to avoid false positives, and the driver was not acting appropriately.

What do these (and similar) cases tell us? I believe they show that we need clear rules about how the technology is to be used by customers. If the driver sitting behind the wheel is being distracted, this means there is a lack of clear and simple rules. And companies should be required to communicate these rules in adequate ways.

A third (fatal) accident, this time with a Tesla, happened in March 2018 in Mountain View, California, and a fourth (non-fatal) one in Laguna Beach, California, in May 2018. In both cases, it turned out that the respective driver ignored several warnings by the "autopilot" system. This shows that it may be ethically questionable to call a certain mode "autopilot" (which Tesla did), suggesting false connotations, since the driver of a Tesla car is required to keep their hands on the wheel at all times. Just stating that this is a matter of your own responsibility will not be sufficient – as with many other cases from different industries (like the already classic Nestlé baby milk case; see Smith, 1990). Especially when, in a perhaps not-so-distant future, these cars may be introduced on a massive scale, companies' responsibilities will have to be laid out much more clearly.

On the other hand, this technology will most probably bring about a number of ethical benefits, especially in terms of avoiding accidents and fatal crashes. More than 90–95 percent of all car accidents are chiefly caused by human mistakes.[10] In Germany, this would mean ultimately saving around 3000 lives each year – which clearly is an ethical goal in itself. Therefore, the introduction of these autonomous vehicles may actually be socially and ethically mandated, not just ethically neutral. But we will need ethical rules for autonomous cars to gain the societal acceptance necessary for unlocking this ethical potential (for a general discussion on ethics of autonomous cars, see Lin, 2015). I will turn to such a case now.

15.7 THE GERMAN ETHICS CODE FOR AUTONOMOUS DRIVING

In several instances, internationally, regulations have been passed,[11] based, mostly, on legal considerations of road safety. However, to date there have been few, if any, cases of a broader ethics code for autonomous or automated driving preceding actual regulation and being based on a broadly composed ethics committee of independent experts.

In July 2016, the German Federal Minister of Transport and Digital Infrastructure appointed a national ethics committee for automated and connected driving. The committee was composed of 14 members, three of which were professors of law, three were professors of ethics and two professors of technical disciplines. Among the others were two representatives of automotive companies, the president of the association of consumer protection groups, the president of the German automobile club ADAC, a Catholic bishop and a former Public Prosecutor General. The chairman was Udo di Fabio, a former judge of the German Federal Constitutional Court. In addition, hearings with additional experts from technical, legal and ethical disciplines were conducted, as well as a driving test with several (semi-) autonomous cars. In June 2017, the committee presented a code of ethics which was published in German (with annotations, BMVI, 2017a) and in English (BMVI, 2017b; see also my comments in Lütge, 2017). It consists of 20 ethical guidelines. In this section of the chapter, I shall now present some of the most important of these guidelines. Many of these will have significant direct or indirect bearing on the car industry – and their ethics policies.

1. The ethics code relies on the principle of *personal autonomy* as a central principle for ethics of technology. It is indeed a key question for autonomous cars how personal autonomy and technological imperatives and constraints can be brought into a healthy relation.
2. The code explicitly states that "the protection of individuals takes precedence over all other utilitarian considerations . . . The licensing of automated systems is not justifiable unless it promises to produce at least a diminution in harm compared with human driving, in other words a positive balance of risks." The interesting point about this guideline is that it agrees with balancing risks against one another rather than with ruling out any calculation at all (as a pure deontological perspective might). The ethics code here sides with the view of ethics as reducing harm, and achieving a net advantage over relevant alternatives. The committee agreed that autonomous cars carry ethical benefits with them, which is an important argument for their introduction (see guideline 6, though). These benefits also include the possibility of substantially improving mobility for handicapped people.
3. One guideline makes the public sector responsible for guaranteeing the safety of autonomous cars. It stresses that an *official license* is needed for automated driving and that the licensing cannot be left to the responsibility of car manufacturers alone. Acceptance among

the population might be jeopardized if automated driving was not subjected to appropriate rules.

4. The code explicitly stresses that highly automated driving is *ethically desirable* and might even be mandatory: "The introduction of more highly automated driving systems, especially with the option of automated collision prevention, may be socially and ethically mandated if it can unlock existing potential for damage limitation."
5. In the case of *unavoidable accidents*, human beings again take priority over damage to property and also to animals. But more than that, according to the code, "any distinction based on personal features (age, gender, physical or mental constitution) is strictly prohibited. It is also prohibited to offset victims against one another. General programming to reduce the number of personal injuries may be justifiable. Those parties involved in the generation of mobility risks must not sacrifice non-involved parties."

   The difficult issue is to avoid a machine or code selecting targets according to personal characteristics (this is ruled out), however, still allowing for a programmer to program a code which reduces the overall number of personal injuries – in whatever way. This is a complex problem, which is usually not as simple as selecting pedestrian A or B. First, damage to property might be very substantial, as in the case of a power blackout for an entire city or an exploding fuel truck. But even if one decides, as the committee did, to opt for personal injuries always taking priority, there might be different probabilities for injuries or casualties of different targets. This could result in complicated situations in which it would not be ethical to forego the opportunity to reduce the overall "damage" to persons.

   However, what the code explicitly does *not* say is that individual victims in different scenarios are allowed to be offset against each other. To some extent, this is the lesson of the German Luftsicherheitsgesetz (Aviation Security Act) being ruled unconstitutional by the German Federal Constitutional Court in 2006. The Aviation Security Act would have allowed the shooting down of hijacked aircraft which were thought to be used as weapons. In that case, individually known subjects would have been sacrificed for the sake of others. In the case of anonymous programming, however, no victims are known individually in advance. Rather, it is an abstract guideline, the exact consequences of which cannot be foreseen, and which reduces the overall risk for all people affected by it (it could be regarded as similar to the risk that comes with vaccination). Such a guideline clarifies, to the extent possible, the situation for programmers by giving them a general ethical guideline.

Not allowing non-involved parties to be sacrificed implies that it cannot be a general rule for a software code to unconditionally save the driver. However, the driver's well-being cannot be put last either.

6. Two guidelines shift the *accountability*, which at the moment, according to the Vienna Convention on Road Traffic (1968), still lies with the driver (or the car owner), to the "manufacturers or operators" of the car and its technological systems. It is clear that if the driver (or the car owner) cannot control the car fully in each single situation and is not required to do so (on higher levels of automation), he or she cannot be accountable for the car's behavior anymore, but only the companies who built it or who are operating its relevant systems. This guideline will certainly have enormous impact, not only on the car industry but, for example, on insurance companies as well.
7. The committee was convinced that *public information* about issues of automated cars is necessary, and that one or several suitable independent bodies will be required to conduct this task. It does not have to be state-run, but could be a non-governmental organization (such as, for example, a consumer organization) which would take over the task of critically monitoring companies' actions.
8. The issue of *security* against cyber-attacks was high on the committee's agenda, and it is an issue much discussed in public whether and how autonomous cars might be hacked and turned into weapons. While the general guideline is quite clear, there will be much work left to the details of programming.
9. Already way before the European General Data Protection Regulation (GDPR) became effective in 2018 (with consequences observed worldwide), *data protection and data sovereignty* were probably one of the most discussed issues in big data ethics and ethics of digitization in general, and with the committee no less. The baseline here is that data belong to the users and keepers of a car. They can voluntarily allow their data to be used by companies, however, what the code stresses is that there should be a systematic search for alternatives among search engines, social networks or similar, in order to generate appropriate competition. Privacy by design was used as a guideline here for connected driving: in the German annotations to the code it is noted that benefits in terms of comforts are not sufficient to justify lack of privacy or neglect of data sovereignty.
10. Finally, one guideline is concerned with *machine learning*, an issue highly important for autonomous driving, since self-learning systems may lead to increased safety in a number of ways. A learning car might learn to avoid certain situations or congested routes. However, it is also a sensitive issue, since a self-learning system might evolve in

> ways that programmers have not thought of beforehand, as in the case of Microsoft's bot Tay.[12] Therefore, first, the code only allows for self-learning in non-safety-critical matters. And second, the code calls for a neutral body to develop standards for such self-learning, its scenarios and acceptability.

It will be seen in the years to come how much and what sort of impact these guidelines will have on the policies of companies.

15.8 CONCLUSION

Digital technologies will need ethical guidelines in order to work. And they will need more than just detailed regulation in order to gain societal acceptance. One example is the recent German Ethics Code for Autonomous Vehicles.[13] Such guidelines should also take into account that there might be differences in attitudes between Europe, North America and other regions, in terms of attitudes toward digitization, attitudes toward innovation and more. This might even lead to different needs in the respective ethics too: Europe might need more explicitly pro-innovation ideas, but the situation might be different in the US.

Business ethics, as of now, is not sufficiently represented in many of the ethical discussions. These discussions sometimes lack an understanding of corporate processes, even a basic understanding that companies are in competition (in one way or another) and need to make profits (Lütge, 2019). And because of that, simple moralizing solutions which aim at changing intentions will be futile. The tone might profit from a bit of "demoralizing."

What the business ethics point of view can offer, on the other hand, is an already existing and substantial ethical toolbox for companies. But when applying them, we should stay being pro-innovation in general. Yes, business ethics will always be a critical enterprise. But as business ethicists, we should also be careful not to overdo it. Digital technologies need good ethical rules and guidelines. And it is the companies who will make them – hopefully with the help of business ethics as an academic discipline.

NOTES

1. http://www.dailymail.co.uk/debate/article-2314375/A-gigantic-parasite-Forget-touchy-feely-posturing-Googles-tiny-tax-shows-greedy-ruthless-really-is.html (accessed 7 August 2019).

2. http://articles.dailypress.com/2008-02-11/features/0802110006_1_windows-media-digital-production-yahoo (accessed 7 August 2019).
3. http://firstpagesage.com/seo-blog/thought-leadership/googles-greed-search-giants-lust-information-impacting-search-results/#sthash.tEiEE1Yy.dpuf (accessed 7 August 2019).
4. http://www.berliner-zeitung.de/digital/-suchmaschine-googles-gier-kennt-keine-grenzen,10808718,27043470.html (accessed 7 August 2019).
5. http://www.zdnet.com/article/steve-jobs-the-mean-dictator-paul-graham/ (accessed 7 August 2019).
6. http://www.economist.com/news/briefing/21635077-online-businesses-can-grow-very-large-very-fastit-what-makes-them-exciting-does-it-also-make (accessed 7 August 2019).
7. https://netzpolitik.org/2010/googles-gier-opfert-die-netzneutralitat/ (accessed 7 August 2019).
8. http://www.wsj.com/video/why-facebook-is-almost-as-greedy-as-bernie-madoff/5945C59A-102F-4027-8AFE-4F127EDC6589.html (accessed 7 August 2019).
9. https://www.lesaffaires.com/blogues/julien-brault/google-est-il-dangereux-pour-la-democratie/554735 (accessed 7 August 2019).
10. See, for example, https://www.sciencealert.com/driverless-cars-could-reduce-traffic-fatalities-by-up-to-90-says-report (accessed 7 August 2019).
11. For an overview of passed US bills, see http://cyberlaw.stanford.edu/wiki/index.php/Automated_Driving:_Legislative_and_Regulatory_Action (accessed 7 August 2019).
12. http://www.telegraph.co.uk/technology/2016/03/24/microsofts-teen-girl-ai-turns-into-a-hitler-loving-sex-robot-wit/ (accessed 7 August 2019).
13. Another case is the European AI4People ethical guidelines for AI, published in November 2018 (Floridi et al., 2018).

REFERENCES

BMVI (2017a). https://www.bmvi.de/SharedDocs/DE/Publikationen/DG/bericht-der-ethik-kommission.pdf?__blob=publicationFile (accessed 7 August 2019).

BMVI (2017b). https://www.bmvi.de/SharedDocs/EN/publications/report-ethics-commission.pdf?__blob=publicationFile (accessed 7 August 2019).

Bulkeley, Andrew (2017). German schools slowly going digital. *Handelsblatt Today*, 11 October 2017, https://www.handelsblatt.com/today/politics/education-german-schools-slowly-going-digital/23572964.html (accessed 7 August 2019).

Chin, Josh and Gillian Wong (2016). China's new tool for social control: a credit rating for everything. *Wall Street Journal*, 28 November.

EU General Data Protection Regulation (2016). http://ec.europa.eu/justice/data-protection/reform/index_en.htm (accessed 25 March 2016).

Floridi, Luciano (2016). *The Fourth Revolution: How the Infosphere is Reshaping Human Reality*. Oxford: Oxford University Press.

Floridi, L., J. Cowls, M. Beltrametti et al. (2018). AI4People – an ethical framework for a good AI society: opportunities, risks, principles, and recommendations. *Minds and Machines*, **28**(4), 689–707.

Gellings, Clark W. (2009). *The Smart Grid: Enabling Energy Efficiency and Demand Response*. New York: Fairmont Press.

Habaradas, Raymund B. (2013). Preserving paradise: Shell's sustainable development programs in the Philippines. In Prem Ramburuth, Christina Stringer and Manuel Serapio (eds), *Dynamics of International Business: Asia-Pacific Business Cases*. Cambridge: Cambridge University Press, pp. 47–60.

Lin, Patrick (2015). Why ethics matter for autonomous cars. In M. Maurer,

Christian Gerdes, Barbara Lenz and Hermann Winner (eds), *Autonomes Fahren, Technische, Rechtliche und Gesellschaftliche Aspekte*. Heidelberg: Springer, pp. 70–85.

Lins, K.V., H. Servaes and A. Tamayo (2017). Social capital, trust, and firm performance: the value of corporate social responsibility during the financial crisis. *The Journal of Finance*, **72**(4), 1785–824.

Lütge, Christoph (2017). The German Ethics Code for Automated and Connected Driving. *Philosophy & Technology*, **30**(4), 547–58.

Lütge, Christoph (2019). *The Ethics of Competition: How a Competitive Society is Good for All*. Cheltenham, UK and Northampton, MA, USA: Edward Elgar.

Martinez-Conesa, I., P. Soto-Acosta and M. Palacios-Manzano (2017). Corporate social responsibility and its effect on innovation and firm performance: an empirical research in SMEs. *Journal of Cleaner Production*, **142**(4), 2374–83.

Ndung'u, Njuguna (2018). The M-Pesa technological revolution for financial services in Kenya: a platform for financial inclusion. In David Lee Kuo Chuen and Robert Deng (eds), *Handbook of Blockchain, Digital Finance, and Inclusion*, Vol. 1. Cambridge, MA: Academic Press, pp. 37–56.

Parloff, Roger (2018). How VW paid $25 billion for Dieselgate – and got off easy. ProPublica, 6 February, https://www.propublica.org/article/how-vw-paid-25-billion-for-dieselgate-and-got-off-easy (accessed 7 August 2019).

Saeidi, S.P., S. Sofian, P. Saeidi, S.P. Sayyedeh and A. Seyyed (2015). How does corporate social responsibility contribute to firm financial performance? The mediating role of competitive advantage, reputation, and customer satisfaction. *Journal of Business Research*, **68**(2), 341–50.

Shiu, Y.-M. and S.-L. Yang (2017). Does engagement in corporate social responsibility provide strategic insurance-like effects? *Strategic Management Journal*, **38**(2), 455–70.

Smith, N.C. (1990). *Morality and the Market: Consumer Pressure for Corporate Accountability*. London: Routledge.

Van Wagenen, Juliet (2017). Seniors and technology: understanding golden-agers in the digital age, *Health Tech Magazine*, 20 June, https://healthtechmagazine.net/article/2017/06/seniors-begin-embrace-digital-age (accessed 7 August 2019).

Vienna Convention on Road Traffic (1968, updated 2014, effective since 2016), https://treaties.un.org/Pages/ViewDetailsIII.aspx?src=TREATY&mtdsg_no=XI-B-19&chapter=11&Temp=mtdsg3&lang=en (accessed 7 August 2019).

Wang, Q., J. Dou and S. Jia (2016). A meta-analytic review of corporate social responsibility and corporate financial performance: the moderating effect of contextual factors. *Business & Society*, **55**(8), 1083–121.

16. Future Earth leadership*

Eleanor O'Higgins and Laszlo Zsolnai

As consumption and human numbers have risen, humankind has ushered in a new era called the "Anthropocene" (Crutzen, 2002; Steffen et al., 2011) in which we are altering the biogeochemistry of the planet itself, destabilizing climate and influencing co-evolution at the planetary level. The Anthropocene appears to be a regrettable exit from the relatively placid past ten thousand years – the Holocene – a period of climate stability in which "civilization" arose (Brown, 2015).

Important indicators show that the state of the Earth (the sum of our planet's interacting physical, chemical, biological, and human processes) has drastically deteriorated over the last 50 to 60 years. A set of global indicators studied by the Stockholm Resilience Center shows accelerating socio-economic trends, such as population, real GDP, foreign direct investment, the urban population, primary energy use, fertilizer consumption, water use, paper production, transportation, telecommunications, and international tourism. These phenomena have, in turn, caused deteriorating ecological trends (such as carbon dioxide, nitrous oxide, methane, surface temperature, ocean acidification, marine fish capture, tropical forest loss, domesticated land, and degradation of terrestrial biosphere) since the 1950s (IGBP, 2015).

Recent climate research discovered self-reinforcing feedback mechanisms of the Earth System that can generate a "Hothouse Earth" pathway characterized by "much higher global average temperature than any interglacial in the past 1.2 million years" and "sea levels significantly higher than at any time in the Holocene" (Steffen et al., 2018, p. 8252). Stabilizing the Earth System requires actions including the "stewardship of the entire Earth System (biosphere, climate, and societies)," "decarbonization of the global economy, enhancement of biosphere carbon sinks," and "behavioral changes, technological innovations, new governance arrangements, and transformed social values" (Steffen et al., 2018, p. 8252).

In October 2018, the Intergovernmental Panel on Climate Change (IPCC) issued a report on the implications of global warming. The report was prepared in response to an invitation from the United Nations

Framework Convention on Climate Change (UNFCCC) when it adopted the Paris Agreement in 2015. It involved 91 authors and review editors from 40 countries, with more than 6000 scientific references cited and the dedicated contribution of thousands of expert and government reviewers worldwide. In no uncertain terms, it rejects the previous global warming goal to a maximum of 2°C as being too high, and recommends a high of no more than 1.5°C, having seen damage wreaked by the 1°C rise in global temperature since pre-industrial times (defined as 1850–1900) already, in the form of floods, droughts, forest fires, and heatwaves (IPCC, 2018). A 2°C rise would destroy 99 percent of coral reefs, damage crops, damage or kill certain habitats and ecosystems, causing poverty and mass migration. The 12-year survival plan put forward by the IPCC would mean unprecedented changes to the way we live, affecting land, energy, industry, buildings, transport, and cities. The benefits of limiting temperature rise to 1.5°C would constrain further damage to coral reefs, habitats, and displacement somewhat. To meet this stricter target, by 2030, our global CO_2 emissions must fall to 45 percent of 2010 levels.

16.1 MAINSTREAM BUSINESS PRACTICE

Mainstream business organizations consider the natural environment and human persons as mere tools for accomplishing their purposes and goals. Their dominating self-centered orientation leads to decisions that produce large-scale ecological and social destruction. The perverse nature of the decisions made by mainstream business organizations is visible in phenomena such as decision-making under risk and discounting in space and time. Prospect theory and the general theory of discounting can help us to describe and analyse these phenomena (Zsolnai, 2018).

Prospect theory states that the majority of decision-makers prefer sure but smaller gains over greater but uncertain gains (i.e., decision-makers are usually risk averse in choices involving sure gains). Moreover, a majority of decision-makers prefer to suffer greater but uncertain losses than smaller but certain losses. This is because decision-makers are more sensitive to losses than to gains (Kahneman and Tversky, 1979).

Thus, prospect theory predicts that risky decisions made by mainstream business organizations often endanger the long-term safety and integrity of the natural environment and human populations. This is because the probability of the occurrence of a catastrophe caused by modern, large-scale technologies is usually low, but it is never zero. Yet the potentially negative consequences (losses) can be horrifying, including the destruction of ecosystems and enormous losses to society. Recent examples of these kinds of ecological and human tragedies include the Fukushima Nuclear Plant accident, the Bhopal disaster, and the BP oil spill in the Gulf of Mexico.

This is consistent with how decision-makers usually over-value things that are in the here and now compared to things that are further away and/or later in time, which are "discounted," that is, decision-makers discount gains that are distant in space and time. If the distance of a thing in space and/or in time is great enough, then its present value becomes extremely small. Also, the present value depends on the discount rate that is applied; the greater the discount rate, the smaller the present value. The present value of a thing is thus determined by the discount rate and its distance in space and time. If the present generation wished to take into account the needs of two generations in the future and to protect the ecosystem health and the cultural heritage of mankind for three generations – say, 120 years hence – then an extremely low or even a negative discount rate would be needed.

Decision-makers who strongly discount things in space and time are neither interested in solving long-term (or distant) ecological and human problems, nor considering the global impacts of their activities on the natural environment and human communities. The international trade in hazardous wastes is an illustrative case in point. Developed countries transport and dump hazardous wastes in distant and less-developed countries, and do not display much interest in the ecological human health impacts of these materials, paralleling the ultra-low wages often paid to laborers in developing countries.

By combining the main lessons of prospect theory and the general theory of discounting we can obtain insight into the disembedding of mainstream business organizations from society and nature.

Let us consider the following decision-related problem. There are two alternatives available to a modern business organization. The first is to make a sure gain ("G") here and now and a loss of yL at some point further away/later in time with a probability of 1/y, where y > 1. The second alternative is to make a sure loss ("L") here and now, and a gain of xG at some point further away/later in time with a probability of 1/x, where x > 1.

Mainstream business organizations typically prefer the first alternative to the second one (Table 16.1). This means that mainstream business organizations are likely to be engaged in fostering activity which supports here and now options: they may be studying them, devoting power to them, building relationships with them, and advocating or lobbying for them. Similarly, mainstream business organizations are liable to be disengaged with outcomes that are further away and later in time: the tendency

Table 16.1 Self-centered and myopic choices of mainstream business organizations

	Certain, here and now	Uncertain, further and later
Gains	*Favor*	Avoid
Losses	Avoid	*Favor*

Source: Zsolnai (2018), p. 35.

is to deny their existence, lobby against them, or maintain a position of silence about them.

The self-centered and myopic orientation of mainstream businesses leads to practices that are socially and environmentally disembedded, and largely contribute to the Hothouse Earth trajectory.

16.2 HANS JONAS'S IMPERATIVE OF RESPONSIBILITY

In his magnum opus *The Imperative of Responsibility*, Hans Jonas (1984) argues for a new kind of ethics appropriate in our age.

Jonas states that the nature of human action has changed so dramatically in our times that it calls for a radical change in ethics as well. He emphasizes that in previous ethics, all dealing with the non-human world was ethically neutral. "Ethical significance belonged to the direct dealing of man with man, including man dealing with himself: all traditional ethics is anthropocentric . . . The effective range of action was small, the time span of foresight, goal-setting, and accountability was short, control of circumstances limited" (Jonas, 1984, pp. 4–5).

New dimensions of responsibility emerged because *nature* became a subject of human responsibility. This is underlined by the fact of the irreversibility and cumulative character of man's impact on the living world. Man should seek "not only the human good but also the good of things extra human, that is, to extend the recognition of 'ends in themselves' beyond the sphere of man and make the human good include the care of them" (Jonas, 1984, pp. 7–8).

Jonas summarizes the imperative of responsibility like this, "Act so that the effects of your action are compatible with the permanence of genuine human life." Or, expressed negatively, "Act so that the effects of your action are not destructive of the future possibility of such life" (Jonas, 1984, p. 11). This extends the usual conception of ethics beyond the heart of human relationships (Ciulla, 2014) and broadens ethical leadership to encompass considerations of the whole Earth.

Based on Jonas's imperative of responsibility and considering the present state of the Earth, we suggest a formulation of a prime duty of today's business leadership as follows:

Cease to contribute to Hothouse Earth and strive to stabilize the climate system of the Earth.

This duty requires more than shallow, cosmetic changes in mainstream business thinking and practices. Rather, it requires deep and radical rethinking of the basic underlying business and leadership models of mainstream business and invention of new ones which can fit in the reality of the Anthropocene.

16.3 LEADERSHIP OF NEW PROGRESSIVE BUSINESS MODELS

The introduction of the fundamentally new kind of ethics in business requires a rethink of conventional business methods to meet the criteria of ecological sustainability, respect for future generations, and of prosocialness, as should be reflected in corporate values, purposes, and criteria of success. This entails doing business in a new and different way, in short, the creation and adoption of a new paradigm – progressive business models. The formation and implementation of progressive business models is central to responsible leadership today. This necessitates choices about markets, value propositions and particular organizational structures, processes, and cultures (Smith et al., 2010). There are many ways to construct progressive business models. While progressive business models may differ in their construction, they have many features in common which define their progressivity.

We now detail the interrelated characteristics of progressive business models. The top of the list is committed leadership, without which the other characteristics could not be enacted.

16.3.1 Committed Leadership

As we have shown, choices made by mainstream business do not necessarily lend themselves to progressive business models, so leaders of progressive business must be able and willing to go against the tide of conventional business wisdom. Bauman (2018) recognizes Warren

Buffett as a courageous leader who is not afraid to disagree with popular opinion.

Typically, the image of an "effective" business leader today is someone who is hard-charging, quick acting, compelling, and charismatic, people who must be followed. Mainstream thinking today may have a tendency to become "seduced by 'leadership bling, by who's on the red carpet, who got rich quick, by who seems sexy and full of charisma and decisiveness'" (Koehn, 2017a). Such leaders focus on short-term results and winning (Bauman, 2018).

In contrast, Koehn has written a book delineating five extraordinary historic leaders, among them, Abraham Lincoln, who faced and overcame crises by finding inner strength, rooted deeply in the need to fight for the greater good (Koehn, 2017b). Koehn believes that what really matters in elected leaders, as in business leaders, is strong and decent character, wanting to serve others and advance the collective good. Leaders should be people who can find and personify a worthy purpose, inspiring the people around them to accomplish that purpose. Progressive business leaders must have a clear vision and direction, galvanize necessary change, and ensure implementation of the progressive measures (Szekely and Strebel, 2013). This is especially the case since the pursuit of progressive business often involves difficult navigation (Smith et al., 2010) among various goals such as value creation for multiple stakeholders, some of whose interests may conflict. Committed leaders must be at the forefront of connecting with internal and external stakeholders.

Koehn (2017a, 2017b) calls for reflection, and sometimes waiting and doing nothing before taking action on a difficult issue, as opposed to the popular conception of effective leaders as quickly and aggressively decisive. This may have the perverse effect of actually sabotaging the mission of the enterprise. In parallel, complex problems cannot be solved in one or two swift strokes. Such problems do not have a single definitive answer, and solutions usually involve many possible approaches and actions simultaneously and/or sequentially, another instance of the need for leaders to be capable of difficult navigation (Koehn, 2018).

Therefore, progressive companies must be led from the top by visionary, determined leaders and teams. This is essential in creating the enterprise in the first place or in sustaining progressivity in an existing company.

The other characteristics of progressive business models call for and depend on this special leadership:

- *Exponential.* New progressive business models entail radical change from incumbent models, that is, the ambition should be exponential, rather than simple gradual improvement (Volans, 2016). The contrast to what exists should be transformative (Haslam, 2016), involving a reframing and even disruption of fundamental beliefs, challenging conventional thinking (de Jong and van Dijk, 2015). This is double-loop learning that forces a transformation in fundamental assumptions to institute change, instead of single-loop learning which confines itself to change within an existing framework (Yunus et al., 2010). It is important to leave the comfort zone, as exemplified by the way the French Football Federation, led by its head coach Didier Deschamps, rebuilt the national team that eventually won the World Cup in 2018, by ensuring that up-and-coming young players would have played their club football abroad, gaining broad experience and a worldview (Lyttleton and Eastham, 2018). Exponential thinking can prompt various quintessential business model conversions in areas such as ownership, value chain composition, and processes. Even after a progressive business model has been established, companies should not become complacent, as it still requires constant experimentation on a smaller scale to keep the model relevant to changing circumstances and mitigate risk, for example, embracing technology or finding new relevant stakeholders, and so on.

- *Sustainable/Circular/Frugal.* Sustainability in progressive companies is two-fold. On the one hand is the sustainability of the enterprise itself, as it thinks long term. Complementing this is that progressive companies integrate the sustainability of the planet into their business models. Seven in ten shares of US companies are owned by longer-term investors – individuals, index funds, and more sophisticated long-term investors, so companies which discard the traditional quarterly earnings merry-go-round are more likely to be given the breathing space to flourish sustainably (Koller and Darr, 2017) and it has been shown that a long-term approach can lead to superior performance for revenue and earnings, investment, market capitalization, and job creation (Barton et al., 2017). The concentration in progressive companies is on an enduring timeline which appears to provide business advantages.

  The corresponding side of sustainability is the ecological one, whereby progressive companies are future respecting through attempts to reduce pollution and preserve depletable resources. This is where frugality is important, so that resources are not wasted. Progressive companies studied in our book have made serious efforts to tackle environmental issues, reducing waste and pollution simultaneously, being restorative and regenerative by design. Progressive companies are in the forefront of reporting on their environmental efforts, documenting activities and impacts, making themselves publicly accountable to multiple stakeholders, including the increasing number of impact investment funds.

- *Embracing paradox*. By its very nature, progressive business embraces paradox as it tries to pursue different goals simultaneously, some of which may appear to clash with each other. Often, corporate responsibility is seen to be costly to the bottom line, which may antagonize shareholders or even threaten the survival of the enterprise. However, progressive businesses frequently differentiate themselves and achieve competitive advantage by means of their progressivity itself. Embracing paradox means that instead of asking themselves whether to implement A *or* B, managers should be seeking ways to implement both A *and* B (Smith et al., 2010). Embracing paradox in a practical way can offer win-win solutions. Neilsen (2008, p. 334) describes Aristotelian praxis that should depict the leader of a progressive business who pursues several simultaneous ends – "wealth creation, making myself a better person, making the world a better place."
- *Integration*. It is quite a feat to embrace paradox, and yet be integrated, as the two concepts appear, at first glance, to be inconsistent with each other. However, the ability to adopt paradox successfully depends on effective integration. Integration means that activities are coordinated harmoniously and efficiently across the system, through systemic thinking. In this sense, the system is not only the internal company system, but incorporating its external system in which it is enmeshed. Szekely and Strebel (2013) emphasize that an integrated approach to achieve sustainability entails balance between three dimensions of environmental, social, and economic emphases, avoiding directional risk. One manifestation of integration is integrated reporting, which covers not only financial statements, but reporting on progressive business criteria in an interrelated way. A strongly committed leader can implant and cultivate a unifying culture and set of ethical values which then acts as an integrating mechanism.
- *Socially oriented*. Progressive companies are different to others in putting social impact at the forefront, specifying social profit objectives, alongside financial ones, and seeking pro-social owners where possible (Yunus et al., 2010). Hence, the self-evaluation of a progressive company would assess its achievements on behalf of society, and more broadly how it meets the criteria of ecological sustainability and respect for future generations, along with pro-socialness.
- *Stakeholder oriented*. The business model innovation literature specifies the need for cooperation and collaboration with partners. Yunus

et al. (2010) suggest that social businesses are not involved in a competitive contest, but can learn from one another instead, so creating something bigger. Also, rather than protecting intellectual property, it is shared in the hope that best practices will become widespread. This is especially important in the achievement of social ends, where stakeholder networks extend well beyond the business value chain. Thus, the case companies portray the features of the "engaged" configuration in the stakeholder model (O'Higgins, 2010). Firstly, the firm is integrated into social networks with a variety of stakeholders, where stakeholder management is based on fairness, interdependency, relationships, dialogue, and trust. Decisions are grounded on discourse with stakeholders, balancing interests of the firm and legitimate stakeholders. In parallel, implementation of decisions take place in a context of long-term ongoing developmental partnership. The impact on the firm itself is positive, offering potential for substantial learning and internal development. Genuine relational trust must be at the core of stakeholder relationships that produce value for all parties, that is, a partnership rather than a transactional model, founded on mutual interest, long-term horizon, and collaboration, centered on shared purpose (Isaacs and Neale, 2018).

16.3.2 New Financing Models

Socially responsible investing (SRI) which was a sideshow in investing is becoming increasingly mainstream. For example, in the UK, assets held in ethical funds have more than trebled over the past decade as investors pour money into green and socially responsible funds. The embrace of corporate purpose, Environmental, Social and Governance (ESG) Criteria, and long-term investment strategy by even hard mainstream fund managers like BlackRock, State Street, and Vanguard, and the adoption and promotion by the World Economic Forum of "The New Paradigm: A Roadmap for an Implicit Corporate Governance Partnership Between Corporations and Investors to Achieve Sustainable Long-Term Investment and Growth" are further evidence of this new trend in financing. The UN Principles for Responsible Investment capture the essentials of this movement:

- Principle 1: We will incorporate ESG issues into investment analysis and decision-making processes.
- Principle 2: We will be active owners and incorporate ESG issues into our ownership policies and practices.
- Principle 3: We will seek appropriate disclosure on ESG issues by the entities in which we invest.

- Principle 4: We will promote acceptance and implementation of the Principles within the investment industry.
- Principle 5: We will work together to enhance our effectiveness in implementing the Principles.
- Principle 6: We will each report on our activities and progress towards implementing the Principles.

In fact, evidence suggests that sustainable investing can result in long-term returns, or at least match the returns of ordinary investors. In a meta-analysis of 2200 studies over 40 years, 90-plus percent found that ESG factors are positive with regard to returns (Friede et al., 2015). Since 1990, the MSCI KLD 400 Social Index, comprising companies with strong sustainability profiles, has outperformed the S&P 500 with annualized returns of 11.2 versus 10.7 percent (Haefele, 2018).

These new financing models are themselves progressive, exponentially different to traditional investing, embracing apparent paradox, integrative of many forward-looking ESG practices.

16.4 PROGRESSIVE LEADERSHIP EXEMPLARS

There are numerous cases of innovative companies and progressive business leaders, which base their activities on an extended ecological worldview and address the challenges of the Anthropocene. We present two instructive cases. One is Unilever, a progressive multinational promoting sustainable living and its Chief Executive Officer (CEO), Paul Polman, while the other is Patagonia, a pioneer in ecological clothing and its founder, Yvon Chouinard.

16.4.1 Unilever and Paul Polman

> Unilever has been around for 100-plus years. We want to be around for several hundred more. So if you buy into this long-term value-creation model, which is equitable, which is shared, which is sustainable, then come and invest with us. If you don't buy into this, I respect you as a human being, but don't put your money in our company.

Thus spoke Paul Polman on his first day as chief executive of Unilever in 2009 when he announced that he was scrapping the company's FTSE 100 quarterly earnings reports. At the time, it was a bold move, totally out of keeping with accepted wisdom. Thus, from the outset of his tenure, Polman showed his courage and willingness to defy tradition and lead exponential change. He was also putting down a marker for corporate sustainability. He later told the *Harvard Business Review* he felt able to make such a move because "I figured I couldn't be fired on my first day." It is significant that nearly a decade on, investors generally expect longer-term thinking and action and sustainability credentials (Walker, 2018).

Unilever is a global British-Dutch consumer goods company whose Sustainable Living Plan includes three main goals: improving health and well-being, reducing environmental impact, and enhancing livelihoods. Its website states that 2.5 billion people use Unilever products on any given day to "look good, feel good and get more out of life." Turnover in 2017 was €53.7 billion, with 58 percent of business in emerging markets. Employees number 161,000 people and 47 percent of managers are women.

The Unilever Foundation improves quality of life through the provision of hygiene, sanitation, access to clean drinking water, basic nutrition, and improving self-esteem. Unilever promotes this through their partnerships with Oxfam, Population Services International (PSI, a global non-profit organization focused on the encouragement of healthy behavior and affordability of health products), Save the Children, UNICEF, and the World Food Program.

Unilever creates value for customers by supplying them with responsibly sourced products. It earns enough profit to be sustainable and supply the products that their consumers demand. It works every day to attain the goals that it has set for itself, in a Sustainable Living Plan to grow as a company, while protecting the environment. In 2017, the company maintained zero non-hazardous waste to landfill.

CEO Paul Polman joined Unilever in 2009. He eliminated earnings guidance and quarterly reporting and rejected hedge funds as investors, thus changing the way business is done by Unilever. Polman redefined the role of CEO as statesman – someone who runs his or her business responsibly and successfully, with integrity. The vision of Paul Polman of Unilever is integrated and multi-faceted, encompassing the complexity inherent in running a giant multinational company with its diversified array of businesses and stakeholder engagements into the everyday modus operandi of the organization. The wholehearted adoption and pursuit of the Unilever Sustainable Living Plan has provided a focus from the top for all. Unilever is also an example of the pro-social orientation, where shareholders are being educated that the company should strive for more than financial profit. Indeed, it should expand its ambition to make a profound social impact on people's lives, in both developed and developing countries and communities.

At the prestigious Responsible Business Awards in London in October 2018, for companies demonstrating true leadership through impact, scalability, and innovation, with over 400 entries, Unilever was the outright winner in two of 14 categories: human rights and supply chain management.

On human rights the commendation reads:

> Unilever's work across a number of fronts is highly admirable from palm oil to land rights to modern slavery. Its commitment to meaningful transparency is especially impressive. Few companies put names and numbers on salient human rights issues within their company – especially when it comes to hard-to-fix issues. Secondly, Unilever's willingness to effect change through partnership-based dialogue and progressive political engagement is noteworthy as well. A real model for an increasingly critical topic in global corporations today.

On supply chain management the commendation reads:

> Unilever's approach to updating its responsible sourcing policy and extending it to include another 27,000 suppliers, many of which had never before been asked to consider responsible sourcing, environmental concerns or human rights issues, is truly innovative and impressive. Judges were particularly impressed by how in 2017 Unilever took a significant step in supply chain transparency by publishing a list of 1400 of the palm oil mills in its supply chain. It is the first consumer goods company to do so and a model to follow.

In September 2018, Unilever was recognized by the UN Global Compact as one of 34 LEAD companies from every region of the world and 19 sectors for demonstrating ongoing commitment to the UN Global Compact and its Ten Principles for responsible business. These companies were identified as being among the most engaged participants of the world's largest corporate sustainability initiative.

However, Unilever is not without challenges to sustaining it progressive stance. It was expected that Paul Polman would be departing his post in 2019 after ten years in office, given that he has always declared the natural tenure for a CEO is five to ten years. However, the confirmation of his retirement in January 2019 came about in a rather precipitate way after he had lost a battle with shareholders to end the company's joint UK-Netherlands listings and move headquarters entirely to Rotterdam. The question always arises as to whether the departure of an inspirational leader will spell the end of progressivity. Polman's appointed successor was Unilever veteran, Alan Jope, a Scot who had experience in important emerging markets such as China and Russia, and latterly had been running Unilever's personal care business, its biggest division. Mr Jope faced slowing growth and changes in consumer habits, alongside watchful shareholders, following Paul Polman's tenure when Unilever's shares had far outperformed the FTSE 100 Index, rising by 150 percent, while the FTSE was up by only 70 percent. Would these pressures on Mr Jope cause him to deviate from his predecessor's progressive positions? After six months in office, Mr Jope declared that he was continuing to pursue growth, but not at the expense of Unilever's long-term stakeholder model. Moreover, he asserted that this model was supported by shareholders (Abboud, 2019).

With respect to implementation, because no company has ever made such sustainable commitments before, Unilever does not know for certain that it will meet its goals and succeed. The company has had to query how realistic some of its goals are, especially with respect to the environment, as enunciated in its Unilever Sustainable Living Plan. Thus, the time frame for halving its environmental footprint while doubling sales has been pushed back from 2020 to 2030.

Unilever, as a global company with a huge diverse product portfolio, has to please its customers in developing markets simultaneously with those in developed markets, creating different value propositions for the different demands. This may be a difficult juggling act, as it has to compete with more focused competitors in its diverse markets. These may be progressive or traditional rivals.

A critical challenge to Unilever is its very existence. As a listed company, the performance of the company is under constant scrutiny; there is constant pressure to realize value by making money for shareholders in the relatively short term, even if short-termism has proved disadvantageous to the very shareholders seeking fast returns. It takes moral courage and determination not to buckle.

An allied existential threat is from a potential takeover by a non-progressive business. In 2017, Kraft Heinz initiated a $143 billion hostile takeover attempt of Unilever. Unilever quickly spurned the offer stating the company was firmly against the merger under any terms. Kraft Heinz is controlled by 3G Capital, a Brazilian private equity firm, which partnered with Warren Buffet on the proposed deal. The contrast between Unilever and Kraft Heinz could not be greater, as it was observed that Kraft Heinz is focused on cost cutting and is among companies least committed to sustainability (Gelles, 2017). The firm withdrew its offer two days later. Paul Polman had vowed to fight the takeover, declaring it represented a clear clash between a long-term, sustainable business model for multiple stakeholders and a model entirely focused on shareholder primacy (Daneshkhu and Barber, 2017). This was a moment that called for courageous and committed leadership, as Koehn (2018) points out is necessary in a crisis. Paul Polman was not found wanting.

Nonetheless, in the aftermath, although Unilever remains an exemplary company, the reality of meeting shareholder demands is an ever increasing one. Although the takeover bid was quickly abandoned, it has imposed pressure on Unilever to accelerate a three-year profitability and growth plan "to capture value more quickly," which could compromise its progressive business model. This is by way of warding off further unwanted approaches – despite Unilever's considerable outperformance in returns to investors over the FTSE 100 Index, sustained over ten years, as it balances its economic returns with its broader social purposes.

16.4.2 Patagonia and Yvon Chouinard

Yvon Chouinard is a self-made entrepreneur who created Patagonia in 1973 with the idea of manufacturing, repairing, reselling, and recycling products. The company provides a lifetime guarantee for all of its sports wares. If a product can no longer be repaired, Patagonia will recycle it and reimburse the customer (Hoang, 2017). The business idea is that the products should last for a lifetime. In a famous advertisement, Patagonia proclaimed an anti-growth strategy, exemplified with full-page advertisement on Black Friday, 2011. The advertisement reads, "Don't Buy This Jacket." The text in the ad reported the environmental costs of the company's top-selling sweater and recommended that buyers should think twice before buying it or some other products.

Patagonia's philosophy of doing business is as follows: "Build the best product. Cause no unnecessary harm. Use business to inspire and implement solutions to the environmental crisis." The company is committed to sustainable "natural growth" and to sell its products to people that need them (Hanh, 2007, p. 217).

The company acknowledges that Patagonia is part of the problem.

> [We in Patagonia] make products using fossil fuels, build factories that use water and other resources, create waste and emit carbon into the air. We ship our products around the world in boxes and plastic bags. We consume electricity – using renewable and non-renewable resources. We drive cars and ride on airplanes. As individuals, we consume products . . . probably more than we need. (Patagonia, 2016)

The challenge then is to focus on what Patagonia can do to reduce, neutralize or even reverse the root causes of climate change. The horizon of responsibility includes:

1. reducing the environmental impact of Patagonia and its supply chain
2. supporting grassroots activists by paying an Earth tax
3. using Patagonia's voice to advocate for systemic change
4. empowering customers by making quality products that can be repaired
5. supporting regenerative practices in ranching and agriculture
6. envisioning a new approach to business.

Number 1 involves measuring Patagonia's carbon footprint. In 2015, the estimated emissions of Patagonia's global operations were 3617 metric tons of CO_2. When opening new stores Patagonia prefers to improve existing buildings. Green building projects is part of its strategy. Patagonia has developed an employee transportation "Drive – Less" program, which provides monetary incentives to employees to ride a bike, use carpool or take public transportation. The result of this program was that 900 employees collectively drive 690,000 fewer miles, reducing CO_2 emissions by 500,000 pounds.

The Chemical and Environmental Impacts Program is a supply chain initiative of Patagonia to manage chemicals in a more careful way. The program covers all areas of environmental systems including waste, water use, and energy use. Another supply chain initiative was to become a founding member of the "Fair Labor Association" (FLA) in 1996. In 2007, the program "The Footprint Chronicles" began to trace the social and environmental impact of Patagonia's products. In 2011, Patagonia implemented a human-trafficking detection tool. The audits of suppliers revealed that labor brokers charged migrant workers from Asian countries up to $7000 to get a job in Taiwanese factory mills that supply Patagonia.

Numbers 2 and 3 involve supporting grassroots activists by paying an Earth tax. This funding started in 1985. Patagonia gave 1 percent of its sales revenue for the preservation and restoration of the natural environment. In 2015, the amount given to grassroots environmental groups was $70 million. Patagonia's employees can work up to 320 hours for environmental groups while receiving full payment from Patagonia. Another program aims to oppose the construction of new dams and support a transition towards lower-impact energy and water sources that cause no harm.

Number 4 involves making products that are durable, and using raw materials that "cause less environmental harm than their counterparts." One motto is "Repair is a radical act." In one of Patagonia's advertisements, the text reads: "To make one of our bestselling jackets it requires 135 liters of water, so by repairing it you will save many natural resources, CO_2 emissions and waste." "Don't buy what you don't need. Think twice before you buy anything". In 2015, an internal scorecard was implemented to rate the quality of Patagonia products on a scale from 1–10 (1 being the worst, 10 the best). Quality is defined and measured by a product's durability, reparability, multi-functionality, non-obsolescence, and lack of environmental harm.

Number 5 involves the environmental program "worn wear." The message is "invest in quality and repair when things break, and celebrate the clothing that travels with us through life." Patagonia has the largest garment repair center in the USA.

Number 6 involves the start-up of an internal investment fund to help "like-minded responsible start-up companies bring about positive benefit to the environment." The purpose is to inspire and use business to help solve the environmental crisis. Another initiative is to be guided by the Stockholm Resilience Center concept of "planetary boundaries."

In 2016, Patagonia achieved more than $710 million in sales. Each year, 1 percent of the sales revenue is donated to hundreds of environmental organizations. Making a profit is not the primary goal of the company. Patagonia is inspired by a Zen master that says profit happens "when you do everything else right" (Chouinard, 2016, p. 151). Naomi Klein, who never endorses any multinational company, writes "Yvon Chouinard's experiment . . . is like nothing that has come before, and therefore deserves our closest attention," in a Foreword to Chouinard's book (Chouinard, 2016, pp. viii–ix).

Chouinard's general view of business people is not positive, but at the same time he acknowledges that business can contribute to the common good. He writes:

> I've been a business man for almost sixty years . . . I've never respected the profession. It's business that has to take the majority of the blame for being the enemy of nature, for destroying native cultures, for taking from the poor and giving to the rich, and for poisoning the Earth with the effluent from its factories. Yet business can produce food, cure disease, control population, employ people, and generally enrich our lives. And it can do these good things and make a profit without losing its soul . . . (Chouinard, 2016, p. 1)

According to Chouinard, mainstream business is a ruthless enterprise. But business has the potential to do good, and good deeds including pro-social and pro-environmental activities. Chouinard acknowledges that practicing Buddhism is a fruitful way to do business. Through his entire life he has shown that his business is not based on greed. His personal life is very frugal. Sometimes he speaks about himself as a "dirt bag" because he lives in the same jacket for decades. Chouinard's high ecological sensitivity is remarkable, as well as his extraordinary generosity towards pro-environmental and pro-social groups and organizations.

Led with conviction by Chouinard, his creation, Patagonia encompasses the hallmarks of progressivity – exponentially different to other clothing businesses at its foundation in 1973 and continuously since; sustainable/circular/frugal; consciously embracing the paradox of consumption of Earth's resources, but reducing them at the same time; integrative and systematic in its approach to its many sustainable activities, working with multiple stakeholders including customers, environmental groups, value chain participants – with the aim of a better society that is consistent with ecological sustainability.

16.5 CONCLUSION

The continuation of the existence of humanity and other life forms is at stake. In fact, we are on track for more than 4°C of warming of the climate. That is the temperature difference between the last Ice Age and the world now (Prairie Climate Centre, 2016). This kind of change might render the planet uninhabitable to human beings and to many other species.

"Business as usual" or mere shallow reform policies like tangential CSR initiatives by mainstream business just further fuel the climate of the Earth and contribute to destroying its ecological systems. However, exemplar progressive business model companies offer hope that business can offer solutions to our ecological crisis. Paraphrasing Thomas Berry, we can say that from here on, the primary judgment of business institutions, the whole business profession, and all programs and activities of business organizations will be determined by the extent to which they inhabit, ignore or foster a Stable Earth-Human system (Brown, 2015). This places a major responsibility on the leadership of business organizations. It is also an opportunity to express moral leadership in the Hans Jonas tradition.

Without radical reform and reorientation of their mainstream practices, business leaders may experience what Robert Oppenheimer recalled after the test explosion of the first nuclear bomb in New Mexico on 16 July 1945: 'Now I am become Death, the destroyer of the worlds' (Bhagavad-Gita, Chapter XI, Verse 32). In this chapter, we hope we have offered viable alternatives to this doomsday scenario.

NOTE

* This chapter is built on and develops the main findings of the paper "Business ethics for the Anthropocene" by Laszlo Zsolnai, Knut J. Ims, and Antonio Tencati (2016) presented at the TABEC in St. Gallen in 2016, and the book, *Progressive Business Models: Creating Sustainable and Pro-social Enterprise* edited by Eleanor O'Higgins and Laszlo Zsolnai (London: Palgrave Macmillan, 2017).

REFERENCES

Abboud, L. (2019). "Unilever chief signals shift from food to beauty," *Financial Times*, 12 June, p. 16.

Barton, D., Manyika, J., Koller, T., Palter, R., Godsall, J., and Zoffer, J. (2017). "Where companies with a long-term view outperform their peers," McKinsey & Company, McKinsey Global Institute, February. http://www.mckinsey.com/global-themes/long-term-capitalism/where-companies-with-a-longterm-view-outperform-their-peers (accessed 9 September 2018).

Bauman, D.C. (2018). "Plato on virtuous leadership: an ancient model for modern business," *Business Ethics Quarterly*, **28**(3), 251–74.
Brown, P.G. (2015). "Ethics for economics in the Anthropocene," in Peter G. Brown and Peter Timmerman (eds), *Ecological Economics for the Anthropocene. An Emerging Paradigm*. New York: Columbia University Press, pp. 66–88.
Chouinard, Y. (2016). *Let My People Go Surfing. The Education of a Reluctant Businessman*, 2nd edn. Foreword by Naomi Klein. New York: Penguin Books.
Ciulla, J.B. (2014). *Ethics, the Heart of Leadership*. Santa Barbara, CA: Praeger.
Crutzen, P.J. (2002). "Geology of mankind," *Nature*, **415**(3), January, 23.
Daneshku, S. and Barber, L. (2017). "Paul Polman: how I fended off a hostile takeover bid," *Financial Times*, 3 December.
de Jong, M. and van Dijk, M. (2015). Disrupting beliefs: a new approach to business model innovation, *McKinsey Quarterly*, July. https://www.mckinsey.com/~/media/McKinsey/Business%20Functions/Strategy%20and%20Corporate%20Finance/Our%20Insights/Disrupting%20beliefs%20A%20new%20approach%20to%20business%20model%20innovation/Disrupting%20beliefs%20A%20new%20approach%20to%20business%20model%20innovation.ashx (accessed 15 October 2016).
Friede, G., Busch, T., and Bassen, A. (2015). "ESG and financial performance: aggregated evidence from more than 2000 empirical studies," *Journal of Sustainable Finance & Investment*, **5**(4), 210–33. doi: 10.1080/20430795.2015.1118917.
Gelles, D. (2017). "Why the Kraft Heinz bid for Unilever could make an odd match," *New York Times*, 17 February. https://www.nytimes.com/2017/02/17/business/dealbook/why-the-kraft-heinz-bid-for-unilever-could-make-an-odd-match.html (accessed 9 September 2018).
Haefele, M. (2018). "Sustainable investing can help to propel long-term returns," *Financial Times*, 24 September, 9.
Hanh, T.N. (2007). *The Art of Power*. New York: HarperOne.
Haslam, P. (2016). "The acceptable face of capitalism: high morals for the high street," *Faith in Business Quarterly*, **18**(1), 1–5.
Hoang, L. (2017). "Patagonia's circular economy strategy," *News & Analysis*, 16 January. https://www.businessoffashion.com/articles/news-analysis/how-patagonia-transformed-the-circular-economy (accessed 9 September 2018).
IGBP (2015). "The great acceleration." https://www.stockholmresilience.org/research/research-news/2015-01-15-new-planetary-dashboard-shows-increasing-human-impact.html (accessed 30 August 2018).
IPCC (2018). "Global warming of 1.5°C." https://www.ipcc.ch/pdf/session48/pr_181008_P48_spm_en.pdf (accessed 10 October 2018).
Isaacs, K. and Neale, A. (2018). "The flywheel philosophy," *strategy+business*, 20 September. https://www.strategy-business.com/article/The-Flywheel-Philosophy?gko=2a0c6 (accessed 11 October 2018).
Jonas, H. (1984). *The Imperative of Responsibility: In Search of an Ethics for the Technological Age*. Chicago, IL and London: University of Chicago Press.
Kahneman, D. and Tversky, A. (1979). "Prospect theory: an analysis of decision under risk," *Econometrica*, March, 263–91.
Koehn, N. (2017a). "Five leaders forged in crisis, and what we can learn from them," *Harvard Business School Working Knowledge*, 4 October. https://hbswk.hbs.edu/item/5-leaders-forged-in-crisis-and-what-we-can-learn-from-them (accessed 9 September 2018).
Koehn, N. (2017b). *Forged in Crisis: The Power of Courageous Leadership in Turbulent Times*. New York: Scribner.

Koehn, N. (2018). "The leadership journey of Abraham Lincoln," *McKinsey Quarterly*, May. https://www.mckinsey.com/featured-insights/leadership/the-leadership-journey-of-abraham-lincoln (accessed 9 September 2018).
Koller, T. and Darr, R. (2017). "Earnings calls are a waste of time – and 3 other ways to fight the fast money," MarketWatch, 30 January. http://www.marketwatch.com/story/4-ways-companies-can-fight-back-against-short-term-investors-2017-01-30 (accessed 9 September 2018).
Lyttleton, B. and Eastham, J. (2018). "Five smart behaviors that helped France win the 2018 World Cup can help business too," *strategy+business*, 12 September. https://www.strategy-business.com/article/Five-Smart-Behaviors-That-Helped-France-Win-the-2018-World-Cup-Can-Help-Businesses-Too?gko=5bc50 (accessed 5 October 2018).
Neilsen, R.P. (2008). "Varieties of win-win solutions to problems with ethical dimensions," *Journal of Business Ethics*, **88**, 333–49.
O'Higgins, E.R.E. (2010). "Corporations, civil society, and stakeholders: an organizational conceptualization," *Journal of Business Ethics*, **94**, 157–76.
O'Higgins, E. and Zsolnai, L. (eds) (2017). *Progressive Business Models: Creating Sustainable and Pro-social Enterprise*. London: Palgrave Macmillan.
Patagonia (2016). http://www.patagonia.com/international (accessed 15 May 2016).
Prairie Climate Centre (2016). "Four degrees of separation: lessons from the last ice age." http://prairieclimatecentre.ca/2016/10/four-degrees-of-separation-lessons-from-the-last-ice-age/ (accessed 4 September 2018).
Smith, W.K., Binns, A., and Tushman, M.L. (2010). "Complex business models: managing strategic paradoxes simultaneously," *Long Range Planning*, **43**, 448–61.
Steffen, W., Persson, A., Deutsch, L. et al. (2011). "The Anthropocene: from global change to planetary stewardship," *AMBIO*, **40**, 739–61.
Steffen, W., Rockström, J., Richardson, K. et al. (2018). "Trajectories of the Earth System in the Anthropocene," *Proceedings of the National Academy of Sciences USA*, **115**(33), 14 August, 8252–9. doi: 10.1073/pnas.1810141115.
Szekely, F. and Strebel, H. (2013). "Incremental, radical and game-changing: strategic innovation for sustainability," *Corporate Governance*, **13**(5), 467–81.
Volans (2016). *Breakthrough Business Models: Exponentially More Social, Lean, Integrated and Circular*. London: Business and Sustainable Development Commission.
Walker, O. (2018). "If you plant seeds, you have to let them grow," *Financial Times*, 2 July, 10.
Yunus, M., Moingeon, B., and Lehmann-Ortega, L. (2010). "Building social business models: lessons from the Grameen experience," *Long Range Planning*, **43**, 308–25.
Zsolnai, L. (2018). *Ethics, Meaning, and Market Society*. New York: Routledge.
Zsolnai, L., Ims, K.J., and Tencati, A. (2016). "Business ethics for the Anthropocene," Paper presented at the Transatlantic Business Ethics Conference, University of St. Gallen, 28 September–1 October 2016.

Index